WORLD UNSEEN

Through the mind of
Anthony Borgia

A Compilation of Three Volumes:

Life in the World Unseen (1954)
More About Life in the World Unseen (1956)
Here and Hereafter (1959)

Compiled by Saskia Praamsma

SQUARE CIRCLES
PUBLISHING

THE WORLD UNSEEN—A COMPILATION
Includes
Life in the World Unseen (1954)
More About Life in the World Unseen (1956)
Here and Hereafter (1959)
Robert Hugh Benson *through the mind of* Anthony Borgia

ISBN: 978-0-9856176-9-1

SQUARE CIRCLES PUBLISHING
P. O. Box 9682 / Pahrump, NV 89060
www.squarecirclespublishing.com
www.lifeonotherworlds.com

* * *

Profits from the sale of this work are donated to
FreeSchools World Literacy
www.freeschools.org
www.servicetohumanity.org

CONTENTS

Book Two—MORE ABOUT LIFE IN THE WORLD UNSEEN

Book Three—HERE AND HEREAFTER

INTRODUCTION

FROM THE COMPILER

I S THERE really such a thing as heaven, where God has "prepared a place for us"? Or does life for us begin and end on planet Earth? Are all those orbs in the seemingly infinite universe just there for us to admire as we gaze up into the night sky? Or is there life on those other worlds?

When we die our body remains behind on this planet, but where does the *real* us—soul, spirit, consciousness—go? Can something so vital one minute disappear into nothingness the next? Some say that we cannot know, that nobody has ever come back to tell us. But is this true? Many believe that angelic beings as well as "the dead" can transmit information to us telepathically via gifted human receivers, and many accounts brought through from "the other side" indicate that the universe is teeming with life. This compilation of three popular books channeled though Anthony Borgia—*Life in the World Unseen, More About Life in the World Unseen,* and *Here and Hereafter*—will give you a glimpse of the places we are destined to inhabit when our lives on Earth are over.

Note: Book One, *Life in the World Unseen,* has been slightly reformatted, combining the two original sections, as explained in the Preface, into one: "*Beyond This Life*" (Chapters 1-10) and "*The World Unseen*" (Chapters 1-15) are now Chapters 1-25.

SASKIA PRAAMSMA
March 2013

BOOK ONE

(1954)

LIFE
IN THE WORLD
UNSEEN

ANTHONY BORGIA

FOREWORD

BY SIR JOHN ANDERSON, BART.

I AM VERY pleased to have the opportunity of writing the foreword for this volume, which gives a vivid and picturesque picture of life in the spiritual spheres, experienced by those who have lived their earth life in accordance with the divine law. This also confirms what I have found to be true, during my investigations with regard to the philosophy of thought.

This will reassure those who are now living a life of good purpose, and encourage others to change their wavelength of thought, and so avoid their entry into the dark spheres of the spirit world, as a consequence of their acceptance of the evil vibrations on earth, which have brought so much tribulation to this world.

Thought is the creative force of the universe, as our every action is the result of thought, for good or evil. As we pass through this earth life, we build our inheritance in the world of spirit, which will be no more and no less than the reflection of the quality of our thought desire here.

Cause and effect is an immutable universal law. Man is a free agent to act in accordance with his freewill of thought. What happens to the soul when it enters the world of spirit, is the result of the selective choice of the ego on earth. The punishment for evil is the remorse of the immortal soul, inflicted entirely by the personal reaction of the individual conscience.

In the past, the responsibilities of life and the consequences of individual action have been obscure to the mass mind of humanity. For this reason, the orthodox religions have failed to establish the peace of the world as envisaged by the Great Master.

Civilization is at the parting of the ways, and it is to be hoped that more informative literature, such as this, will be forthcoming, to enable the spiritual regeneration of the world to proceed, so that peace and harmony may reign supreme!

JOHN ANDERSON
[1954]

PREFACE

KNOWLEDGE IS the best antidote for fear, especially if that fear should be of the possible or probable state of existence after we have made the change from this life to the next.

To discover what kind of place is the next world, we must inquire of someone who lives there, and record what is said. That is what has been done in the present volume.

The communicator, whom I first came to know in 1909—five years before his passing into the spirit world—was known on earth as Monsignor Robert Hugh Benson, a son of Edward White Benson, former Archbishop of Canterbury.

Until the present scripts were written he had never communicated with me directly, but I was once told (by another spirit friend) that there were certain matters he wished to set right. The difficulties of communication were explained to him by spirit friends and advisers, but he held to his purpose. And so when a suitable time was reached, he was told that he could communicate through a friend of his earthly days, and it has been my privilege to act as his recorder.

The first script was composed under the title of *Beyond This Life;* the second under that of *The World Unseen.*

In the former, the communicator gives, in a general survey, an account of his passing and his subsequent travels through various parts of spirit lands. In the latter script he deals at much greater length with a number of important and interesting facts and facets of spirit life, upon which previously he had touched only lightly or in passing.

For example, in *Beyond This Life* he mentions the highest realms and the lowest. In *The World Unseen* he actually visits them and describes what he saw and what took place in both regions. Although each of the two scripts is complete in itself, the second greatly extends and amplifies the first, and together they form a composite whole.

We are old friends, and his passing hence has not severed an early friendship; on the contrary, it has increased it, and provided many more opportunities of meeting than would have been possible had he remained on earth. He constantly expresses his delight upon his ability to return to earth in a natural, normal, healthy, and pleasant manner, and to give some account of his adventures and experiences in the spirit world, as one who "being dead (as many would regard him), yet speaketh."

ANTHONY BORGIA

CHAPTER ONE

MY EARTH LIFE

WHO I AM really matters not. Who I was matters still less. We do not carry our earthly positions with us into the spirit world. My earthly importance I left behind me. My spiritual worth is what counts now, and that, my good friend, is far below what it should be and what it *can* be. Thus much as to who I am. As to who I was, I should like to give some details concerning my mental attitude prior to my passing here into the world of spirit.

My earth life was not a hard one in the sense that I never underwent physical privations, but it was certainly a life of hard mental work. In my early years I was drawn towards the Church because the mysticism of the Church attracted my own mystical sense. The mysteries of religion, through their outward expression of lights and vestments and ceremonies, seemed to satisfy my spiritual appetite in a way that nothing else could. There was much, of course, that I did not understand, and since coming into spirit I have found that those things do not matter. They were religious problems raised by the minds of men, and they have no significance whatever in the great scheme of life. But at the time, like so many others, I believed in a wholesale fashion, without a glimmering of understanding, or very little. I taught and preached according to the orthodox text-books, and so I established a reputation for myself. When I contemplated a future state of existence I thought—and that vaguely—of what the Church had taught me on the subject, which was infinitesimally small and most incorrect. I did not realize the closeness of the two worlds—ours and yours—although I had ample demonstration of it. What occult experiences I had were brought about, so I thought, by some extension of natural laws, and they were rather to be considered as incidental than of regular occurrence, given to the few rather than to the many.

The fact that I was a priest did not preclude me from visitations of what the Church preferred to look upon as devils, although I never once, I must confess, saw anything remotely resembling what I could consider as such. I did not grasp the fact that I was what is called, on the earth-plane, a sensitive, a psychic—one gifted with the power of "seeing," though in a limited degree.

This incursion of a psychic faculty into my priestly life I found to be considerably disturbing since it conflicted with my orthodoxy. I sought advice in the matter from my colleagues, but they knew less than I knew, and they could only think of praying for me that these "devils" might be removed from me. Their prayers availed me nothing—that was to be expected as I now see. Had my experiences been upon a high spiritual plane there is the chance that I should have been regarded in the light of a very holy man. But they were not so; they were just such experiences as occur to the ordinary earthly sensitive. As happening to a priest of the Holy Church they were looked upon as *temptations* of "the devil." As happenings to one of the laity they would have been regarded as *dealings* with "the devil," or as some form of mental aberration. What my colleagues did not understand was that this power was a *gift*—a precious gift, as I understand now—and that it was personal to myself, as it is to all those who possess it, and to pray to have it removed is as senseless as to pray that one's ability to play the piano or paint a picture might be removed. It was not only senseless, it was unquestionably wrong, since such a gift of being able to see beyond the veil was given to be exercised for the good of mankind. I can at least rejoice that *I* never prayed for release from these powers. Pray I did, but for more light on the matter.

The great barrier to any further investigation of these faculties was the Church's attitude towards them, which was—and is—unrelenting, unequivocal, narrow, and ignorant. However long were any investigations or in whatever direction, the Church's final judgment was always the same, and its pronouncements unvarying—"such things have their origin in the devil." And I was bound by the laws of that Church, administering its sacraments and delivering its teachings, while the spirit world was knocking upon the door of my very existence, and trying to show me, *for myself to see,* what I had so often contemplated—our future life.

Many of my experiences of psychic happenings I incorporated into my books, giving the narratives such a twist as would impart to them an orthodox religious flavor. The truth was there, but the meaning and purpose were distorted. In a larger work I felt that I had to uphold the Church against the assaults of those who believed in the spiritual survival of bodily death, and that it was possible for the spirit world to communicate with the earth world.

And in that larger work I ascribed to "the devil" against my better judgment, what I really knew to be nothing other than the working of natural laws, beyond and entirely independent of any orthodox religion, and certainly of no evil origin.

To have followed my own inclinations would have entailed a complete upheaval in my life, a renunciation of orthodoxy, and most probably a great material sacrifice, since I had established a second reputation as a writer. What I had already written would then have become worthless in the eyes of my readers, and I should have been regarded as a heretic or a madman. The greatest opportunity of my earthly life I thus let pass. How great was that opportunity, and how great were my loss and regret, I knew when I had passed into this world whose inhabitants I had already seen so many times and on so many different occasions. The truth was within my grasp, and I let it fall. I adhered to the Church. Its teachings had obtained too great a hold upon me. I saw thousands believing as I did, and I took courage from that, as I could not think that they could all be wrong. I tried to separate my religious life from my psychic experiences, and to treat them as having no connection with one another. It was difficult, but I managed to steer a course that gave me the least mental disturbance, and so I continued to the end, when at last I stood upon the threshold of that world of which I had already had a glimpse. Of what befell me when I ceased to be an inhabitant of the earth and passed into the great spirit world, I hope now to give you some details.

CHAPTER TWO

PASSING
TO SPIRIT LIFE

THE ACTUAL process of dissolution is not necessarily a painful one. I had during my earth life witnessed many souls passing over the border into spirit. I had had the chance of observing with the physical eyes the struggles that take place as the spirit seeks to free itself forever from the flesh. With my psychic vision I had also seen the spirit leave, but nowhere was I able to find out—that is, from orthodox sources—what exactly takes place at the moment of separation, nor was I able to gather any information upon the sensations experienced by the passing soul. The writers of religious textbooks tell us nothing of such things for one very simple reason—*they do not know*.

The physical body many times appeared to be suffering acutely, either from actual pain or through labored or restricted breathing. To this extent such passings had all the appearance of being extremely painful. "Was this really so?" was a question I had often asked myself. Whatever was the true answer I could never really believe that the actual physical process of dying was a painful one, notwithstanding that it appeared so. The answer to my question I knew I would have one day, and I always hoped that at least my passing would not be violent, whatever else it might be. My hopes were fulfilled. My end was not violent, but it was labored, as were so many that I had witnessed.

I had a presentiment that my days on earth were drawing to a close only a short while before my passing. There was a heaviness of the mind, something akin to drowsiness, as I lay in my bed. Many times I had a feeling of floating away and of gently returning. Doubtless during such periods those who were concerned with my physical welfare were under the impression that, if I had not actually passed, I was sinking rapidly. During such lucid intervals that I had I endured no feelings of physical discomfort. I could see and hear what was going on around me, and I could "sense" the mental distress that my condition was occasioning. And yet I had the sensation of the most extraordinary exhilaration of the mind. I knew for certain that my time had come to pass on, and I was full of eagerness to be gone. I had no fear, no misgivings, no doubts, no regrets—so far—at thus leaving the earth world. (My regrets were to come later, but of these I shall speak in due course.) All that I wanted was to be away.

I suddenly felt a great urge to rise up. I had no *physical* feeling whatever, very much in the same way that physical feeling is absent during a dream, but I was mentally alert, however much my body seemed to contradict such a condition. Immediately I had this distinct prompting to rise, I found that I was actually doing so. I then discovered that those around my bed did not seem to perceive what I was doing, since they made no effort to come to my assistance, nor did they try in any way to hinder me. Turning, I then beheld what had taken place. I saw my physical body lying lifeless upon its bed, but here was I, the *real* I, alive and well. For a minute or two I remained gazing, and the thought of what to do next entered my head, but help was close at hand. I could still see the room quite clearly around me, but there was a certain mistiness about it as though it were filled with smoke very evenly distributed. I looked down at myself wondering what I was wearing in the way of clothes, for I had obviously risen from a bed of sickness and was therefore in no condition to move very far from my surroundings. I was extremely surprised to find that I had on my usual attire, such as I wore when moving freely and in good health about my own house. My surprise was only momentary since, I thought to myself, what other clothes should I expect to be wearing? Surely not some sort of diaphanous robe? Such costume is usually associated with the conventional idea of an angel, and I had no need to assure myself that I was not that!

Such knowledge of the spirit world as I had been able to glean from my own experiences instantly came to my aid. I knew at once of the alteration that had taken place in my condition; I knew, in other words, that I had "died." I knew, too, that I was alive, that I had shaken off my last illness sufficiently to be able to stand upright and look about me. At no time was I in any mental distress, but I was full of wonder at what was to happen next, for here I was, in full possession of all my faculties, and, indeed, feeling "physically" as I had never felt before.

Although this has taken some time in the telling, in order that I might give you as much detail as possible, the whole process must have taken but a few minutes of earth time.

As soon as I had had this brief space in which to look about me and to appreciate my new estate, I found myself joined by a former colleague—a priest—who had passed to this life some years before. We greeted each other warmly, and I noticed that he was attired like myself. Again this in no way seemed strange to me, because had he been dressed in any other way I should have felt that something was wrong somewhere, as I had only known him in clerical attire. He expressed his great pleasure at seeing me again, and for my part I foresaw the gathering up of the many threads that had been broken by his "death."

For the first moment or so I allowed him to do all the talking; I had yet to accustom myself to the newness of things. For you must remember that I had just relinquished a bed of final sickness, and that in casting off the physical body I had also cast off the sickness with it, and the new sensation of comfort and freedom from bodily ills was one so glorious that the realization of it took a little while to comprehend fully. My old friend seemed to know at once the extent of my knowledge, that I was aware that I had passed on, and that all was well.

And here let me say that all idea of a "judgment seat" or a "day of judgment" was entirely swept from my mind in the actual procedure of transition. It was all too normal and natural to suggest the frightful ordeal that orthodox religion teaches that we must go through after "death." The very conception of "judgment" and "hell" and "heaven" seemed utterly impossible. Indeed, they were wholly fantastic, now that I found myself alive and well, "clothed in my right mind," and, in fact, clothed in my own familiar habiliments, and standing in the presence of an old friend, who was shaking me cordially by the hand, and giving me greeting and good wishes, and showing all the outward—and in this case genuine manifestations of being pleased to see me, as I was pleased to see him. He, himself, was in the best of spirits as he stood there giving me such a welcome as, upon the earth-plane, two old friends accord each other after long separation. That, in itself, was sufficient to show that all thoughts of being marched off to my judgment were entirely preposterous. We both were too jolly, too happy, too carefree, and too natural, and I, myself, was waiting with excitement for all manner of pleasant revelations of this new world, and I knew that there could be none better than my old friend to give them to me. He told me to prepare myself for an immeasurable number of the pleasantest of surprises, and that he had been sent to meet me on my arrival. As he already knew the limits of my knowledge, so his task was that much the easier.

As soon as I managed to find my tongue, after our first breaking the silence, I noticed that we spoke just as we had always done upon the earth—that is, we simply used our vocal cords and spoke, quite as a matter of course. It required no thinking about, and indeed I did not think about it. I merely noted that it was so. My friend then proposed that as we had no further need or call to stay in the surroundings of my passing, we might move away, and that he would take me to a very nice "place" that had been made ready for me. He made this reference to a "place," but he hastened to explain that in reality I was going to my own house, where I should find myself immediately "at home." Not knowing, as yet, how one proceeded, or, in other words, how I was to get there, I placed myself entirely in his hands, and that, he told me, was precisely what he was there for!

I could not resist the impulse to turn and take a last look at the room of my transition. It still presented its misty appearance. Those who were formerly standing round the bed had now withdrawn, and I was able to approach the bed and gaze at "myself." I was not the least impressed by what I saw, but the last remnant of my physical self seemed to be placid enough. My friend then suggested that we should now go, and we accordingly moved away.

As we departed, the room gradually became more misty until it faded farther from my vision, and finally disappeared. So far, I had had the use, as usual, of my legs as in ordinary walking, but in view of my last illness and the fact that, consequent upon it, I should need some period of rest before I exerted myself too much, my friend said that it would be better if we did not use the customary means of locomotion—our legs. He then told me to take hold of his arm firmly, and to have no fear whatever. I could, if I wished, close my eyes. It would, he said, perhaps be better if I did so. I took his arm, and left the rest to him as he told me to do. I at once experienced a sensation of floating such as one has in physical dreams, though this was very real and quite unattended by any doubts of personal security. The motion seemed to become more rapid as time went on, and I still kept my eyes firmly closed. It is strange with what determination one can do such things here. On the earth-plane, if similar circumstances were possible, how many of us would have closed our eyes in complete confidence? Here there was no shadow of doubt that all was well, that there was nothing to fear, that nothing untoward could possibly take place, and that, moreover, my friend had complete control of the situation.

After a short while our progress seemed to slacken somewhat, and I could feel that there was something very solid under my feet. I was told to open my eyes. I did so. What I saw was my old home that I had lived in on the earth-plane, my old home—but with a difference. It was improved in a way that I had not been able to do to its earthly counterpart. The house itself was rejuvenated, as it seemed to me from a first glance, rather than restored, but it was the gardens round it that attracted my attention more fully.

They appeared to be quite extensive, and they were in a state of the most perfect order and arrangement. By this I do not mean the regular orderliness that one is accustomed to see in public gardens on the earth-plane, but that they were beautifully kept and tended. There were no wild growths or masses of tangled foliage and weeds, but the most glorious profusion of beautiful flowers so arranged as to show themselves to absolute perfection. Of the flowers themselves, when I was able to examine them more closely, I must say that I never saw either their like or their counterpart, upon the earth, of many that were there in full bloom. Numbers were to be found, of course, of the old familiar blossoms, but by far the greater number seemed to be something entirely new to my rather small knowledge of flowers. It was not merely the flowers themselves and their unbelievable range of superb colorings that caught my attention, but the vital atmosphere of eternal life that they threw out, as it were, in every direction. And as one approached any particular group of flowers, or even a single bloom, there seemed to pour out great streams of energizing power which uplifted the soul spiritually and gave it strength, while the heavenly perfumes they exhaled were such as no soul clothed in its mantle of flesh has ever experienced. All these flowers were living and breathing, and they were, so my friend informed me, incorruptible.

There was another astonishing feature I noticed when I drew near to them, and that was the sound of music that enveloped them, making such soft harmonies as corresponded exactly and perfectly with the gorgeous colors of the flowers themselves. I am not, I am afraid, sufficiently learned, musically, to be able to give you a sound technical explanation of this beautiful phenomenon, but I shall hope to bring to you one with knowledge of the subject, who will be able to go into this more fully. Suffice it for the moment, then, to say that these musical sounds were in precise consonance with all that I had so far seen—which was very little—and that everywhere there was perfect harmony.

Already I was conscious of the revitalizing effect of this heavenly garden to such an extent that I was anxious to see more of it. And so, in company with my old friend, upon whom I was here relying for information and guidance, I walked the garden paths, trod upon the exquisite grass, whose resilience and softness were almost comparable to "walking on air," and tried to make myself realize that all this superlative beauty was part of my own home.

There were many splendid trees to be seen, none of which was malformed, such as one is accustomed to see on earth, yet there was no suggestion of strict uniformity of pattern. It was simply that each tree was growing under perfect conditions, free from the storms or wind that bend and twist the young branches, and free from the inroads of insect life and many other causes of the misshapenness of earthly trees. As with the flowers, so with the trees. They live for ever incorruptible, clothed always in their full array of leaves of every shade of green, and for ever pouring out life to all those who approach near them.

I had observed that there did not appear to be what we should commonly call shade beneath the trees, and yet there did not appear to be any glaring sun. It seemed to be that there was a radiance of light that penetrated into every corner, and yet there was no hint of flatness. My friend told me that all light proceeded directly from the Giver of all light, and that this light was divine life itself, and that it bathed and illumined the whole of the spirit world where lived those who had eyes spiritually to see.

I noticed, too, that a comfortable warmth pervaded every inch of space, a warmth perfectly even and as perfectly sustained. The air had a stillness, yet there were gentle perfume-laden breezes—the truest zephyrs—that in no way altered the delightful balminess of the temperature.

And here let me say to those who do not care much for perfumes of any sort: Do not be disappointed when you read these words, and feel that it could never be heaven to you if there were something there you do not like. Wait, I say, until you witness these things, and I know that then you will feel very differently about them.

I have gone into all these things in a rather detailed fashion because I am sure there are so many people who have wondered about them.

I was struck by the fact that there were no signs of walls or hedges or fences; indeed, nothing, so far as I could see, to mark off where my garden began or ended. I was told that such things as boundaries were not needed, because each person knew instinctively, but beyond doubt, just where his own garden ended. There was therefore no encroaching upon another's grounds, although all were open to any who wished to traverse them or linger within them. I was wholeheartedly welcome to go wherever I wished without fear of intruding upon another's privacy. I was told I should find that that was the rule here, and that I would have no different feelings with respect to others walking in my own garden. It exactly described my sentiments at that moment, for I wished, then and there, that all who cared would come into the garden and enjoy its beauties. I had no notions whatever of ownership personally, although I knew that it was my own "to have and to hold." And that is precisely the attitude of all here—ownership and partnership at one and the same time.

Seeing the beautiful state of preservation and care in which all the garden was kept, I inquired of my friend as to the genius who looked after it so assiduously and with such splendid results. Before answering my question he suggested that as I had but so very recently arrived in the spirit land, he considered it advisable that I should rest, or that at least I should not overdo my sightseeing. He proposed, therefore, that we should find a pleasant spot—he used the words in a comparative sense, because all was more than *pleasant* everywhere—that we should seat ourselves, and then he would expound one or two of the many problems that had presented themselves to me in the brief time since I had passed to spirit.

Accordingly, we walked along until we found such a pleasant place beneath the branches of a magnificent tree, whence we over-looked a great tract of the countryside, whose rich verdure undulated before us and stretched far away into the distance. The whole prospect was bathed in glorious celestial sunshine, and I could perceive many houses of varying descriptions picturesquely situated, like my own, among trees and gardens. We threw ourselves down upon the soft turf, and I stretched myself out luxuriously, feeling as though I were lying upon a bed of the finest down. My friend asked me if I was tired. I had no ordinary sensation of earthly fatigue, but yet I felt somewhat the necessity for a bodily relaxation. He told me that my last illness was the cause of such a desire, and that if I wished I could pass into a state of complete sleep. At the moment, however, I did not feel the absolute need for that, and I told him that for the present I would much prefer to hear him talk. And so he began.

" 'Whatsoever a man soweth,' he said, 'that shall he reap.' Those few words describe exactly the great eternal process by which all that you see, actually here before you, is brought about. All the trees, the flowers, the woods, the houses that are also the happy homes of happy people—everything is the visible result of 'whatsoever a man soweth.' This land, wherein you and I are now living, is the land of the great harvest, the seeds of which were planted upon the earth-plane. All who live here have won for themselves the precise abode they have passed to by their deeds upon the earth."

I was already beginning to perceive many things, the principal one of which, and that which touched me most closely, being the totally wrong attitude adopted by religion in relation to the world of spirit. The very fact that I was lying there where I was, constituted a complete refutation of so much that I taught and upheld during my priestly life upon earth. I could see volumes of orthodox teachings, creeds, and doctrines melting away because they are of no account, because they are not true, and because they have no application whatever to the eternal world of spirit and to the great Creator and Upholder of it. I could see clearly now what I had seen but hazily before, that orthodoxy is manmade, but that the universe is God-given.

My friend went on to tell me that I should find living within the homes, that we could see from where we were lying, all sorts and conditions of people—people whose religious views when they were on the earth were equally varied. But one of the great facts of spirit life is that souls are exactly the same the instant after passing into spirit life as they were the instant before. Deathbed repentances are of no avail, since the majority of them are but cowardice born of fear of what is about to happen—a fear of the theologically-built eternal hell that is such a useful weapon in the ecclesiastical armory, and one that perhaps has caused more suffering in its time than many other erroneous doctrines. Creeds, therefore, do not form any part of the world of spirit, but because people take with them all their characteristics into the spirit world, the fervid adherents to any particular religious body will continue to practice their religion in the spirit world until such times as their minds become spiritually enlightened. We have here, so my friend informed me—I have since seen them for myself—whole communities still exercising their old earthly religion. The bigotry and prejudices are all there, religiously speaking. They do no harm, except to themselves, since such matters are confined to themselves. There is no such thing as making converts here!

Such being the case, then, I supposed that our own religion was fully represented here. Indeed, it was! The same ceremonies, the same ritual, the same old beliefs, all are being carried on with the same misplaced zeal—in churches erected for the purpose. The members of these communities know that they have passed on, and they think that part of their heavenly reward is to continue with their manmade forms of worship. So they will continue until such time as a spiritual awakening takes place. Pressure is never brought to bear upon these souls; their mental resurrection must come from within themselves. When it does come they will taste for the first time the real meaning of freedom.

My friend promised that if I wished we could visit some of these religious bodies later, but, he suggested, that as there was plenty of time it would be better if first of all I became quite accustomed to the new life. He had, so far, left unanswered my question as to who was the kindly soul who tended my garden so well, but he read my unspoken thought, and reverted to the matter himself.

Both the house and the garden, he told me, were the harvest I had reaped for myself during my earth life. Having earned the right to possess them, I had built them with the aid of generous souls who spend their life in the spirit world performing such deeds of kindness and service to others. Not only was it their work, but it was their pleasure at the same time. Frequently this work is undertaken and carried out by those who, on earth, were expert in such things, and who also had a love for it. Here they can continue with their occupation under conditions that only the world of spirit can supply. Such tasks bring their own spiritual rewards, although the thought of reward is never in the minds of those who perform them. The desire of being of service to others is always uppermost.

The man who had helped to bring this beautiful garden into being was a lover of gardens upon the earth-plane, and, as I could see for myself, he was also an expert. But once the garden was created there was not the incessant toil that is necessary for its upkeep, as with large gardens upon earth. It is the constant decay, the stresses of storm and wind, and the several other causes that demand the labor on earth. Here there is no decay, and all that grows does so under the same conditions as we exist. I was told that the garden would need practically no attention, as we usually understand the term, and that our friend the gardener would still keep it under his care if I so wished it. Far from merely wishing it, I expressed the hope that he certainly would do so. I voiced my deep gratitude for his wonderful work, and I hoped that I might be able to meet him and convey to him my sincere appreciation and thanks. My friend explained that that was quite a simple matter, and that the reason why I had not already met him was the fact of my very recent arrival, and that he would not intrude until I had made myself quite at home.

My mind again turned to my occupation while on earth, the conducting of daily service and all the other duties of a minister of the Church. Since such an occupation, as far as I was concerned, was now needless, I was puzzled to know what the immediate future had in store for me. I was again reminded that there was plenty of time in which to ponder the subject, and my friend suggested that I should rest myself and then accompany him upon some tours of inspection—there was so much to see and so much that I should find more than astonishing. There were also numbers of friends who were waiting to meet me again after our long separation. He curbed my eagerness to begin by saying that I must rest first, and for which purpose, what better place than my own home?

I followed his advice, therefore, and we made our way towards the house.

CHAPTER THREE

FIRST EXPERIENCES

I HAVE ALREADY mentioned that when I was first introduced to my spirit home I observed that it was the same as my earth home, but with a difference. As I entered the doorway I saw at once the several changes that had been brought about. These changes were mostly of a structural nature and were exactly of the description of those that I had always wished I could have carried out to my earthly house, but which for architectural and other reasons I had never been able to have done. Here, earthly needs had no place, so that I found my spirit home, in general disposition, exactly as I had ever wished it to be. The essential requisites indispensably associated with an earthly homestead were, of course, completely superfluous here—for example, the severely mundane matter of providing the body with food. That is one instance of the difference. And so with others it is easy enough to call to mind.

As we traversed the various rooms together, I could see many instances of the thoughtfulness and kindness of those who had labored so energetically to help me reconstruct my old home in its new surroundings. While standing within its walls I was fully aware of its permanence as compared with what I had left behind me. But it was a permanence that I knew I could end; permanent only so long as I wished it to be so. It was more than a mere house; it was a spiritual haven, an abode of peace, where the usual domestic cares and responsibilities were wholly absent.

The furniture that it contained consisted largely of that which I had provided for its earthly original, not because it was particularly beautiful, but because I had found it useful and comfortable, and adequately suited my few requirements. Most of the small articles of adornment were to be seen displayed in their customary places, and altogether the whole house presented the unmistakable appearance of occupancy. I had truly "come home."

In the room that had formerly been my study I noticed some well-filled bookshelves. At first I was rather surprised to see such things, but upon further thought I could see no reason, if such as this house could exist at all with all its various adjuncts, why books should not also have their place within the scheme. I was interested to learn what was the nature of the books, and so I made a closer examination. I found that conspicuous among them were my own works. As I stood in front of them I had a clear perception of the reason, the real reason, for their being there. Many of these books contained those narratives that I spoke of earlier, in which I had told of my own psychic experiences after giving them the necessary religious turn. One book in particular seemed to stand out in my mind more than the others, and I came to the full realization that I now wished that I had never written it. It was a distorted narrative, where the facts, as I had really known them, were given unfair treatment, and where the truth was suppressed. I felt very remorseful, and for the first time since coming into this land I had regret. Not regret that I had, at last, arrived in the spirit world, but sorrow that, with the truth before me, I had deliberately cast it aside to place in its stead falsehood and misrepresentation. For I knew that so long as my name lived—that is, so long as it had any commercial value—that book would continue to be reproduced and circulated and read—and regarded as the absolute truth. I had the unpleasant knowledge that I could never *destroy* what I had thus done.

There was, at no time, any sense of condemnation over this. On the contrary, I could feel a distinct atmosphere of intense sympathy. Whence it came, I knew not, but it was real and concrete nevertheless. I turned to my friend, who, during my inspection and discovery, had been standing discreetly and understandingly at a little distance apart, and I asked for his help. It was instantly forthcoming. He then explained to me that he knew exactly what had lain before me concerning this book, but that he was debarred from making any reference to it before I made the discovery for myself. Upon my doing so, and upon my subsequent appeal for his help, he was at once enabled to come to my aid.

My first question was to ask him how I could put this matter right. He told me that there were several ways in which I could do so, some more difficult—but more efficacious—than others. I suggested that perhaps I could go back to the earth-plane and tell others of this new life and the truth of communication between the two worlds. Many, many people, he said, had tried, and were still trying, to do so, and how many were believed? Did I think that I should have any better fortune? Certainly none of those who read my books would ever come within miles of receiving or crediting any communication from me. And did I realize, also, that if I were to present myself to such people they would at once call me a "devil," if not the very Prince of Darkness himself!

"Let me," he continued, "place a few considerations before you concerning this subject of communication with the earth world. You know full well that such is possible, but have you any conception of the difficulties surrounding it?

"Let us assume that you have found the means to communicate. The first thing you will be called upon to do will be to furnish clear and definite identification of yourself. Quite probably, upon your first declaring who you are, there will be some hesitation at accepting your name simply because it carried weight when you were incarnate. However important or famous we happen to be when upon the earth-plane, as soon as we are gone to the spirit plane, we are referred to in the past tense! Whatever works of a literary nature we may leave behind us are then of far greater importance than their authors, since to the earth world we are 'dead.' To the earth, the living voice is gone. And although we are still very much alive—to ourselves as well as to others here—to the earth people we have become memories, sometimes permanent, more often than not memories that rapidly fade, leaving mere names behind them. We know, moreover, that we are very much more alive than we have ever been before; the majority of earth people will consider that we could never be more 'dead'!

"You will be *commanded*, then, to provide a deal of identification. That is quite proper in such circumstances, provided it is not carried to extremes, as so often it is. After fulfilling this condition, what next? You will wish to intimate that you are alive and well. If the people with whom you are communicating are no mere dabblers, no doubt will be placed upon your statement. But if you wish to send such news to the world in general through the customary channels, those who believe it is really you who have spoken will be those who already know of, and practice communication with, the spirit world. For the rest, who will believe it is you? None—certainly none of your former readers. They will say that it cannot be *you*, but that it is a 'devil' impersonating you. Others will quite probably take no notice whatever. There would, of course, be a number who would imagine that, because you have passed into the world of spirit, then you will at once have become endowed with the profoundest wisdom, and that all you say will be infallible utterances. You can see some of the difficulties that will confront you in this simple matter of telling the truth to those who still sit in the darkness of the earth world."

My friend's forecast grieved me considerably, but I appreciated the extreme difficulties, and I was persuaded to leave the project for the time being. We would consult others wiser than ourselves, and perhaps some course would be outlined whereby I could achieve my desires. I might find that with the passage of time—speaking in a mundane sense—my wishes might change. There was no need to distress myself. There was much that I could see and do, and much experience to be gained that would be invaluable to me if, in the end, I resolved to try and carry out my intentions. His best advice was that I should have a thorough rest, during which time he would leave me. If, when I was quite refreshed, I would send out my thought to him, he would receive it and return to me at once. So, making myself "comfortable" upon a couch, I sank into a delightful state of semi-sleep, in which I was fully conscious of my surroundings, yet at the same time I could feel a downpouring of new energy, which coursed through my whole being. I could feel myself becoming, as it were, lighter, with the last traces of the old earth conditions being driven away for ever.

How long I remained in this pleasant state, I have no knowledge, but eventually I fell into a gentle slumber from which I awoke in that state of health which in the spirit world is *perfect*. I at once remembered my friend's proposal, and I sent out my thoughts to him. Within the space of a few seconds of earth time he was walking in through the door. His response was so bewilderingly rapid that my surprise sent him into merry laughter. He explained that in reality it was quite simple. The spirit world is a world of thought; to think is to act, and thought is instantaneous. If we think ourselves into a certain place we shall travel with the rapidity of that thought, and that is as near instantaneous as it is possible to imagine. I should find that it was the usual mode of locomotion, and that I should soon be able to employ it.

My friend at once noticed a change in me, and he congratulated me upon my regaining my full vigor. It is impossible to convey, even in a small measure, this exquisite feeling of supreme vitality and well-being. When we are living upon the earth-plane we are constantly being reminded of our physical bodies in a variety of ways—by cold or heat, by discomfort, by fatigue, by minor illnesses, and by countless other means. Here we labor under no such disabilities. By that I do not mean that we are just unfeeling logs, insensible to all external influences, but that our perceptions are of the mind, and that the spirit body is impervious to anything that is destructive. We feel through our minds, not through any physical organs of sense, and our minds are directly responsive to thought. If we should feel coldness in some particular and definite circumstances, we undergo that sensation with our minds, and our spirit bodies in no way suffer. We are never continuously reminded of them. In the realm of which I am now speaking, all is exactly attuned to its inhabitants—its temperature, its landscape, its many dwellings, the waters of the rivers and streams, and, most important of all, the inhabitants one with another. There is therefore nothing that can possibly create any unhappiness, unpleasantness, or discomfort. We can completely forget our bodies and allow our minds to have free play, and through our minds we can enjoy the thousands of delights that the same minds have helped to build up.

At times we may feel saddened—and at times we are amused—by those who, still upon the earth, ridicule and pour scorn and contempt upon our descriptions of the spirit lands. What do these poor minds know? Nothing! And what would these same minds substitute for the realities of the spirit world? They do not know. They would take away from us our beautiful countryside, our flowers and trees, our rivers and lakes, our houses, our friends, our work, and our pleasures and recreations. For what? What conception can these dull minds have of a world of spirit? By their own stupid admissions, no conception whatever. They would turn us into wraiths, without substance, without intelligence, and merely surviving in some dim, shadowy, vaporous state, dissevered from everything that is human. In my perfect health and abounding vitality, and living among all the beauties of this world of strict reality—a mere *hint* of which I have only so far given you—I am forcibly impressed by the magnitude of ignorance shown by particular minds upon earth.

The time had come, I felt, when I would like to see something of this wonderful land, and so, in company with my friend, we set forth on what was, for me, a voyage of discovery. Those of you who have traveled the earth for the sake of seeing new lands will understand how I felt at the outset.

To obtain a wider view, we walked to some higher ground, whence a clear panorama unfolded before the eyes. Before us the countryside reached out in a seemingly unending prospect. In another direction I could clearly perceive what had all the appearance of a city of stately buildings, for it must be remembered that all people here do not possess a uniformity of tastes, and that even as on earth, many prefer the city to the country, and vice versa, while again some like both. I was very keenly interested to see what a spirit city could be like. It seemed easy enough to visualize the country here, but cities seemed so essentially the work of man in a material world. On the other hand, I could advance no logical reason why the spirit world should not also build cities. My companion was greatly amused by my enthusiasm, which, he declared, was equal to a schoolboy's. It was not his first acquaintance with it, however; most people when they first arrive are taken in the same way! And it affords our friends a never-ending pleasure to show us round.

I could see a church in the distance built on the usual lines externally, and it was proposed that we might go in that direction, and include other things on the way. And so we set off.

We followed a path that led for part of the way beside a brook, whose clear water sparkled in the light of the heavenly sun. As the water pursued its course it gave forth many musical notes that constantly changed and weaved themselves into a medley of the most dulcet sounds. We drew to the edge that I might look at it closer. It seemed to be almost like liquid crystal, and as the light caught it, it scintillated with all the colors of the rainbow. I let some of the water run over my hand, expecting it, by its very look, to be icy cold. What was my astonishment to find that it was delightfully warm. But still more it had an electrifying effect which extended from my hand right up the arm. It was a most exhilarating sensation, and I wondered what would it be like to bathe fully within it. My friend said that I should feel myself being charged with energy, but there was not a sufficient depth of water to immerse myself in it properly. I should have the opportunity, as soon as we came to a larger body of water, to indulge in a bathe. When I withdrew my hand from the brook, I found that the water flowed off in flashing drops, leaving it quite dry!

We resumed our walk, and my friend said he would like to take me to visit a man who lived in a house which we were now approaching. We walked through some artistically laid out gardens, crossed a well-turfed lawn, and came upon a man seated at the outskirts of a large orchard. As we drew near he rose to meet us. My friend and he greeted one another in the most cordial fashion, and I was introduced as a new arrival. It was explained to me that this gentleman prided himself upon the fruit in his orchard, and I was invited to sample some of it. The owner of this pleasant retreat seemed to be a man of middle years, as far as I could judge, though he could have been much older than he appeared to be at first sight. I have since learned that to try to guess the ages of people here is a difficult and almost dangerous task! For you must know—to digress a little—that it is the law that, as we progress spiritually, so do we shake off the semblance of age as it is known on earth. We lose the wrinkles that age and worldly cares have marked upon our countenances, together with other indications of the passage of years, and we become younger in appearance, while we grow older in knowledge and wisdom and spirituality. I am not suggesting that we assume an exterior of extreme juvenility, nor do we lose those external indications of personality. To do that would make us all of a deadly uniformity, but we do, in truth, return—or advance, according to our age when we pass into spirit—towards what we have always known as "the prime of life."

To resume: Our host led us into the orchard where I beheld many trees in a high state of cultivation, and in full fruit. He looked at me for a moment, and then he took us to a splendid tree that looked strongly like a plum tree. The fruit was perfect in shape, with a deep rich coloring, and it hung in great clusters. Our host picked some of it, and handed it to us, telling us that it would do us both good. The fruit was quite cool to the touch, and it was remarkably heavy for its size. Its taste was exquisite, the flesh was soft without being difficult or unpleasant to handle, and a quantity of nectar-like juice poured out. My two friends watched me closely as I ate the plums, each bearing upon his face an expression of mirthful anticipation. As the juice of the fruit streamed out, I fully expected to spill an abundance of it upon my clothes. To my amazement, although the juice *descended* upon me I could find, upon examination, no traces of it! My friends laughed uproariously at my astonishment, and I thoroughly enjoyed the joke, but I was much mystified. They hastened to explain to me that as I am now in an incorruptible world anything that is "unwanted" immediately returns to its own element. The fruit juice that I thought I had spilled upon myself had returned to the tree from which the fruit was plucked.

Our host informed me that the particular type of plum which I had just eaten was one that he always recommends to people who have but newly arrived in spirit. It helps to restore the spirit, especially if the passing has been caused by illness. He observed, however, that I did not present the appearance of having had a long illness, and he gathered that my passing had been fairly sudden—which was quite true. I had had only a very short illness. The various fruits that were growing were not only for those who needed some form of treatment after their physical death, but all enjoyed eating thereof for its stimulating effect. He hoped that, if I had no fruit trees of my own—or even if I had!—I should come as often as I liked and help myself. "The fruit is always in season," he added, in great amusement, "and you will never find any of the trees without plenty of fruit upon them." In response to my question as to how they grow, he replied that like so many other questions in this land, the answer was only possible from those of the higher realms, and even if we were told that answer, there is more than a strong probability that we should not understand until such time as we, ourselves, went to dwell in those realms. We are quite content, he said in effect, to take so many things just as they are, without inquiring into how they come about, and we know that those things provide a never-failing supply because they come from a never-failing Source. There is no real need to delve into such matters, and most of us are quite content to enjoy them with heartfelt thanks. As to the actual supply of fruit, our host said that all he knew was that as he picked his fruit other fruit came and took its place. It never over-ripened because it was perfect fruit, and, like ourselves, imperishable. He invited us to walk through the orchard where I saw every kind of fruit known to man, and many that were known only in spirit. I sampled some of the latter, but it is impossible to give any indication of the delicious flavor of them because there is no earthly fruit that I know of with which comparison can be made. We can only, at any time, give such an indication to the senses by comparison with that which we have already experienced. If we have not had that experience then we are at a complete and absolute loss to convey any new sensation, and nowhere is this more appreciable than in the sense of taste.

My friend explained to our genial host that he was escorting me round to show me the land of my new life, and the latter gave us many good wishes to speed us upon our way. He repeated his invitation to visit him whenever I wished, and even if he were not about at the time of any call I might make, I was to help myself to the fruit to my heart's content. He said I should find that the fruit trees would perform the duties of a host as well as—even better than—he could! And so with further expressions of thanks and goodwill, we again set forth.

We returned to our former path beside the brook, and continued our walk in the direction of the church. After we had proceeded for a little way, I noticed that the brook began to broaden out until it expanded into the dimensions of a fair-sized lake. We could see many groups of happy people gathered at the side of the water, some of whom were bathing. The lake was bounded by an encirclement of trees, and there were flowers in abundance arranged in such a way that although a certain orderliness was observable, yet there was no hint of distinct ownership. They belonged to all in equal right, and I observed most particularly that no attempt was made by anyone to pick, or root up, or otherwise disturb them. One or two people were to be seen with both their hands placed round some of the blooms in almost a caressing manner, an action which seemed to me so unusual that I asked my friend for enlightenment on the matter. He replied by taking me over to a young girl who was thus curiously occupied. I was rather diffident of so intruding, but I was told to "wait and see." My friend bent down beside her, and she turned her head and gave him a friendly word and smile of welcome. I concluded that they were old friends, but such was not the case. In fact, he told me afterwards that he had never seen her before, and he explained that here in spirit we need no formal introductions; we constitute one large united gathering in the matter of ordinary "social" intercourse. After we have been here a little while, and become accustomed to our new environment and mode of living, we find that we never intrude since we can read at once the mind of a person who wishes for a period of seclusion. And when we see people out in the open—in garden or countryside—we are always welcome to approach and hold friendly converse with them.

This young lady was, like myself, a newcomer, and she told us how some friends had shown her the method of gathering from the flowers all that the flowers had so lavishly to give. I bent down beside her, and she gave me a practical demonstration of what to do. By placing the hands, she said, round the flower so as to hold it in a sort of cup, I should feel the magnetism running up my arms. As I moved my hands towards a beautiful bloom, I found that the flower upon its stem moved towards *me!* I did as I was instructed, and I instantly felt a stream of life rushing up my arms, the while a most delicate aroma was exhaled by the flower. She told me not to pick the flowers because they were for ever growing; they were part of this life, even as we are ourselves. I was very grateful for her timely admonition, since it was the most natural thing in the world to pick flowers that were already in such profusion. It was not quite the same in the case of the fruit, I learned, because the fruit was meant to be consumed. But the flowers were themselves decorative, and to cut down the flower by picking it was equivalent to cutting down the fruit trees. There were flowers, however, that were growing expressly for the purpose of being picked, but these under immediate consideration had as their principal function that of health-giving. I inquired of our young friend if she had tried some of the good fruit we had just sampled, and she replied that she had.

My friend suggested that I might like to go closer to the water's edge, and that if the young lady were alone, perhaps she would care to join us in our excursions. She responded that nothing would give her greater pleasure, and so we all three moved towards the lake. I explained to her that my friend was a seasoned inhabitant of these lands, and that he was acting as my guide and adviser. She seemed to be glad of our company, not that she was lonely, for such a thing does not exist in this realm, but she had had few friends while on earth and had always lived something of a solitary life, although she had never, on that account, been indifferent to, or unmindful of, the cares and sorrows of others. Since coming into spirit she had found so many kindly souls of a similar disposition to herself, and she supposed that perhaps we had been in like case. I told her briefly a few things about myself, and as I was still wearing my earthly attire—that is to say, its counterpart!—she knew me, more or less, for what I had been professionally. My friend being similarly clothed, she laughingly said that she felt she was in safe hands!

It was recalled to my mind what had been said about bathing, but I was rather at a loss how to broach the matter of the necessary equipment for the purpose. However, my friend saved the situation by referring to it himself.

All we needed for the purpose of enjoying a bathe was the necessary water in which to bathe! Nothing could be simpler. We were just to go into the water precisely as we were. Whether we could swim or not, was of no consequence. And I must say I was astonished at this strange departure from the usual procedure, and I naturally hesitated a little. However, my friend quite calmly walked into the lake until he was thoroughly immersed, and the two of us followed his example.

What I was expecting to result from this I cannot say. At least I anticipated the customary effect of water upon one in similar circumstances on earth. Great, then, was my surprise—and my relief—when I discovered that the water felt more like a warm cloak thrown round me than the penetration of liquid. The magnetic effect of the water was of like nature to the brook into which I had thrust my hand, but here the revivifying force enveloped the whole body, pouring new life into it. It was delightfully warm and completely buoyant. It was possible to stand upright in it, to float upon it, and of course, to sink completely beneath the surface of it without the least discomfort or danger. Had I paused to think I might have known that the latter was inevitably bound to be the case. The spirit is indestructible. But beyond this magnetic influence there was an added assurance that came from the water, and that was its essential *friendliness*, if I may so call it. It is not easy to convey any idea of this fundamentally spiritual experience. That the water was living one could have no doubt. It breathed its very goodness by its contact, and extended its heavenly influence individually to all who came within it. For myself, I experienced a spiritual exaltation, as well as a vital regeneration, to such an extent that I quite forgot my initial hesitancy and the fact that I was fully clothed. The latter now presented a perfectly natural situation, and this was further enhanced by my observing my two companions. My old friend, of course, was perfectly used to the water, and our new friend seemed to have accommodated herself rapidly to new usages.

My mind was saved further perturbation when I recalled that as I withdrew my hand from the brook the water ran off it, leaving it quite dry. I was already prepared, then, for what ensued as we came out of the lake. As I emerged the water merely ran away, leaving my clothes just as they were before. It had penetrated the material just as air or atmosphere on earth will do, but it had left no visible or palpable effect whatever. We and our clothes were perfectly dry!

And now another word about the water. It was as clear as crystal, and the light was reflected back in every ripple and tiny wave in almost dazzlingly bright colors. It was unbelievably soft to the touch, and its buoyancy was of the same nature as the atmosphere, that is to say, it supported whatever was on it, or in it. As it is impossible to fall here by accident, as one does on earth, so it is impossible to sink in the water. All our movements are in direct response to our minds, and we cannot come to harm or suffer accident. It is, I am afraid, rather difficult to give a description of some of these things without going beyond the range of earthly minds and experience. So much has to be witnessed at first hand to gain any adequate idea of the wonders of these lands.

A short walk brought us to the church that I had seen in the distance, and which I had expressed a keenness to visit.

It was a medium-sized building in the Gothic style, and it resembled the "parish church" familiar on earth. It was situated in pleasant surroundings, which seemed the more spacious by the absence of any railings or walls to define its ecclesiastical limits. The surface of the stone of which it was constructed had the newness and freshness of recent building, but in point of fact, it had been in existence many years of earth time. Its exterior cleanliness was merely consonant with all things here—there is no decay. Nor is there any smoky atmosphere to cause blackening and discoloration! There was, of course, no churchyard attached. Even though some people cling so tenaciously to their old earthly religious predilections and practices here, it is hardly to be supposed that in erecting a church in which to carry them on, they would also include an entirely useless burial ground!

Close beside the main door there was the customary notice board, but this gave only the nature of the services, which were those of the Established Church. No mention was made at all of the times of the services, and I wondered how any congregation of this kind could possibly assemble where time, as it is known on earth, has no existence. For here there is no night and day by the alteration of which time can be measured. It is perpetual day. The great celestial sun forever shines, as I have already told you. Neither do we have the many other indications of time that force themselves upon the earthly consciousness—such, for example, as hunger and fatigue. Nor in the more lengthy passage of time such as the aging of the physical body and the dulling of the mental faculties. Here we have no recurrent seasons of spring, autumn and winter. Instead we enjoy the glory of perpetual summer—and we never tire of it!

As usual, I turned to my friend for information on this point of congregational assemblage. To gather the people to the church was perfectly simple, he said. Whoever is in charge has only to send out his thoughts to his congregation, and those that wish to come forthwith assemble! There was no need for bell-ringing. The emission of thought is far more thorough and exact! That is simple so far as the congregation is concerned. They have merely to wait until the thought reaches them, either in a direct call to attend, or by the urge to attend. But where does the ministering clergyman obtain *his* indication of the approach of service-time? That question, I was told, raised a much greater problem.

With the absence of earth-time in the spirit world, our lives are ordered by events; *events,* that is, that are *part* of our life. I do not refer now to incidental occurrences, but to what, on earth, would be regarded as recurrent happenings. We have many such events here, as I hope to show you as we proceed, and in doing so you will see how we *know* that the performance of certain acts, individually or collectively, are clearly brought to our minds. The establishment of this church we were now inspecting saw also the gradual building up of a regular order of services, such as those who belong to its particular denomination on earth are familiar with. The clergyman who is acting as pastor to this strange flock would feel, by his duties on earth, the approach of the usual "day" and "time" when the services were held. It would be, in this respect, instinctive. It would, moreover, grow stronger with practice, until this mental perception would assume absolute regularity, as it is considered on the earth-plane. With this firmly established, the congregation have but to await the call from their minister.

The notice board gave a list of the usual services commonly seen outside an earthly church of the same denomination. One or two items were noticeably absent, however; such as the provision for marriages and baptisms. The former omission I could understand; the latter could only imply that baptism was unnecessary, since only the baptized would be in "heaven"—where presumably they deemed this church to be situated!

We went within, and found ourselves in a very lovely building, conventional in design, and containing little that is not to be seen in any such church upon the earth-plane. There were some beautiful stained-glass windows portraying scenes in the lives of the "saints," through which the light poured evenly from all sides of the church at the same time, producing a strange effect in the air from the colors of the window-glass. Provision for heating the building was, of course, quite superfluous. There was a fine organ at one end, and the main altar, built of stone, was richly carved. Beyond this, there was a certain plainness which in no way detracted from its general beauty as a piece of architecture. Everywhere was there evidence of a lavish care being expended upon it, which, considering where this church was existing, is not surprising, when it is remembered under what dispensation such a building can exist at all!

We sat down for a little while, finding a calm and peaceful air about the whole place, and then we decided that we had seen all there was to be seen, and we made our way out into the open.

CHAPTER FOUR

HOME OF REST

AS WE walked along, at least two of us pondered upon what we had seen—and its implications. Our young friend, who told us her name was Ruth, put a number of questions to us, but I withheld any attempt to answer, since I was but a newcomer myself, in favor of my friend—whose name, Edwin, I have omitted to give so far.

Ruth, it appeared, had never been an active churchgoer whilst on earth, but she was a kindly soul, as it was plain to see; and it was plain to see, also, that her abstention from churchgoing had made no difference to her ultimate destination as viewed by the earth. Her service to others had done more for her spiritual welfare than all the outward display of congregational religion, which so often *is* but outward display. Like myself, she was very surprised to find, here in spirit, the complete paraphernalia of orthodox religion. Edwin told her that she had only seen one example of it so far, and there were plenty of others. Having seen this, however, one had seen them all, more or less. Each denomination, of course, holds to its own particular creed and formularies, such as it had on earth, with a few minor differences, as we had just seen.

Such spiritual somnolence is no novelty in spirit. The earth world is to blame. Religious contentions and controversies are at the bottom of all the ignorance and lack of knowledge that so many people bring with them into the spirit world, and if the minds of such people are stubborn and they are unable really to think for themselves, then do they remain shackled to their narrow religious views, thinking it to be all the truth, until a day of spiritual awakening dawns for them. Then they will see that their slavish adherence to their creeds is holding them back. It is to be so much lamented that for every one who leaves, forever, these misguided congregations, another will come to fill his place—until the time comes when the whole earth knows the truth of the world of spirit. Of course they do no harm as they are, here, beyond retarding their own spiritual progression. Once they realize what they are doing to themselves, and take the first step forward, their joy knows no bounds. They will realize the "time" they have apparently wasted.

Now it may be asked, if, with the acquisition of knowledge and truth, these extensions of earthly religions into the spirit world are better done away with, what will you put in their place? It sounds like a condemnation of communal worship.

By no means. We have our communal worship here, but it is purged of every trace of meaningless creeds, of doctrines and dogmas. We worship the Great and Eternal Father in truth, absolute truth. We are of one mind, and one mind only. And no one is called upon to believe blindly—or to profess to do so something which is utterly incomprehensible to *any* mind. There are many, many things here which we do not understand—and it will take eons of time before we even have a faint gleam of understanding them. But we are not asked to understand them; we are asked to take them as they are. It makes no difference whatever to our soul's progression. We shall be able to progress far—and far beyond that—before we shall ever need to *think* about understanding such things. And so we have one mind in our worship of the All-highest.

Such are the matters we discussed—it was Edwin who expounded—as we walked along in the beautiful air of God's heaven.

Ruth espied a rather stately building set among some well-wooded grounds, which also aroused my curiosity. On appealing to our guide, Edwin told us that it was a home of rest for those who had come into spirit after long illness, or who had had a violent passing, and who were, in consequence, suffering from shock. We wondered if it would be possible to peep inside, without appearing to be curiosity seekers. He assured us that it would be quite in order to do so, as he had given his services there, and was therefore *persona grata*. Added to which was the fact that he knew we had that necessary sympathy which would banish any thought of inquisitiveness. As we drew near I could see that the building was in no sense a hospital in outward semblance, whatever its functions might be. It was built in the classical style, two or three stories high, and it was entirely open upon all sides. That is to say, it contained no windows as we know them on earth. It was white in color as far as the materials of its composition were concerned, but immediately above it there was to be seen a great shaft of blue light descending upon, and enveloping, the whole building with its radiance, the effect of which was to give a striking blue tinge to the whole edifice. This great ray was the downpouring of life—a healing ray—sent to those who had already passed here, but who were not yet awake. When they were fully restored to spiritual health, there would be a splendid awakening, and they would be introduced into their new land.

I noticed that there was quite a number of people seated upon the grass in the grounds, or walking about. They were relatives and friends of those who were undergoing treatment within the hall of rest, and whose awakening was imminent. Although, doubtless, they could have been summoned upon the instant when necessary, yet, following their old earthly instinct, they preferred to wait close at hand for the happy moment. They were all supremely joyful, and very excited, as could be seen by the expressions on their faces, and many were the friendly smiles we received as we walked among them. Many of them, too, came forward to welcome us among them, thinking that we had come for the same reason as themselves. We told them of our true purpose, however, and they sped us on our way.

I observed that most of the people waiting in the gardens were not habited in their earth clothes, and I assumed that most of them had been in spirit for some considerable time. Such was not necessarily the case, Edwin told us. They had the right to wear their spirit robes by virtue of the fact that they were inhabitants of this realm we were now in. And the robes they wore were eminently suited to both the place and the situation. It is difficult to describe this costume because so much rests in being able to give some comparison with a particular earthly fabric. Here we have no such materials, and all outward appearances are produced, not by the texture of the material, but by the kind and degree of light that is the essence of a spirit robe. Those that we now saw were in "flowing" form and of full length, and the colors—blue and pink in varying degrees of intensity—seemed to interweave themselves throughout the whole substance of the robes. They looked very comfortable to wear, and like everything here, they require no attention to keep them in a state of perfect preservation, the spirituality of the wearer alone accounting for that.

The three of us were still wearing our earthly style of raiment, and Edwin suggested that, for our present purposes, we might change to our natural element in the matter of clothes. I was quite willing, of course, to fall in with any suggestion that he might like to make, as I turned to him for everything in my lack of knowledge. Ruth also seemed very keen to try this change, but the question that puzzled us both was how it was to be accomplished.

Possibly there are people on the earth-plane who are willing to believe that such a situation as this would involve the ceremony of being formally presented with a spirit robe in the presence of a goodly gathering of celestial beings, who had come to witness the bestowing of our heavenly reward, and to be officially invited to take our "eternal rest"!

Let me hasten to say that *such was most emphatically not the case.*

What *did* take place was very simply this: immediately I had expressed the wish to follow Edwin's suggestion of discarding my earthly style of clothes, those very clothes faded away—dissolved—and I was attired in my own particular spirit robe, of the same description as those I could see about me. Edwin's had changed likewise, and I noticed that his seemed to send out a greater strength of color than mine. Ruth's was the same as mine, and needless to say, she was full of joyful delight with this new manifestation of the spirit. My old friend had experienced the change before, so his costume was not new to him. But speaking for myself—and I am sure for Ruth—I never at any moment felt the slightest embarrassment or strangeness or self-consciousness in this revolutionary—as it might seem to be—alteration in our external appearance. On the contrary, it seemed quite natural and perfectly in order, and unquestionably it was in proper keeping with our present surroundings, the more so, as I soon discovered when we walked into the home of rest. Nothing would have been more incongruous than earthly apparel in such a building, which in its interior disposition and accommodations was totally unlike anything to be seen upon the earth-plane.

As we entered, Edwin was greeted as an old friend by one who came forward to meet us. He briefly explained his mission and our presence there, and we were made welcome to see all that we wished.

An outer vestibule led into a lofty hall of considerable dimensions. The space that would ordinarily be devoted to windows was occupied by tall pillars set some distance apart, and this arrangement was carried out through all four walls. There was very little in the way of interior decoration, but it must not be supposed from this that the apartment had a cold, barrack-like appearance. It was anything but that. The floor was carpeted with some very soft covering in a sober design, and here and there a handsomely wrought tapestry was hanging upon the walls, occupying the whole of the floor space were extremely comfortable-looking couches, each of which bore a recumbent form, quite still, and obviously sleeping profoundly. Moving quietly about were a number of men and women intent upon watching the different couches and their burdens.

I noticed as soon as we entered this hall that we came under the influence of the blue ray, and its effect was one of pronounced energizing as well as tranquility. Another noticeable quality was the entire absence of any idea of an officialdom. There was no question of patronage, nor did I feel the least shade of being among strangers. Those in attendance upon the sleepers did so, not in the attitude of a certain task to be done willy-nilly, but as though they were performing a labor of love in the sheer joy of doing it. Such, indeed, was precisely the case. The glad awakening of these sleeping souls was an ever recurrent joy to them, no less than to the people who had come to witness it.

I learned that all the "patients" in this particular hall had gone through lingering illnesses before passing over. Immediately after their dissolution they are sent gently into a deep sleep. In some cases the sleep follows instantly—or practically without break—upon the physical death. Long illness prior to passing into the spirit world has a debilitating effect upon the mind, which in turn has its influence upon the spirit body. The latter is not serious, but the mind requires absolute rest of varying duration. Each case is treated individually, and eventually responds perfectly to its treatment. During this sleep-state the mind is completely resting. There are no unpleasant dreams, or fevers of delirium.

While gazing upon this perfect manifestation of Divine Providence, the thought came to me of those absurd earthly notions of "eternal rest," "everlasting sleep," and the many other equally foolish earthly conceptions, and I wondered if, by some chance or other, this sleep I was now beholding had been distorted by earthly minds into a state of eternal slumber, whither all souls pass at dissolution, there to await, in countless years' time, the awful "last day"—the dread "Day of Judgment." Here was the visible refutation of such a senseless belief.

Neither of my two friends had awakened in this—or other—hall of rest, so they told me. Like myself, they had suffered no lengthy illness, and the end of their earth lives had come quite quickly and quite pleasantly.

The patients resting upon their couches looked very peaceful. Constant watch is kept upon them, and at the first flutterings of returning consciousness, others are summoned, and all is ready for the full awakening. Some will wake up partially, and then sink back again into slumber. Others will shake off their sleep at once, and it is then that those experienced souls in attendance will have, perhaps, their most difficult task. Until that moment, in fact, it has been mostly a matter of watching and waiting. In so many cases it has to be explained to the newly awakened soul that he has "died" and is alive. They will remember usually their long illness, but some are quite unaware that they have passed over into spirit, and when the true state of affairs has been gently and quietly explained to them, they often have an urgent desire to go back to the earth, perhaps to those who are sorrowing, perhaps to those for whose care and welfare they were responsible. They are told that nothing can be done by their going back, and that others of experience will take care of those circumstances that are so distressing them. Such awakenings are not happy ones by comparison with those who wake up with the full realization of what has taken place. Were the earth more enlightened, this would be the more often the case, and there would be a great deal less distress to the newly awakened soul.

The earth world thinks itself very advanced, very "civilized." Such estimation is begotten of blind ignorance. The earth world, with all things appertaining thereto, is looked upon as of the very first importance, and the spirit world is regarded as something dim and distant. When a soul finally arrives there, it is quite time enough to begin thinking about it. Until that time comes there is no need even to bother about it. That is the attitude of mind of thousands upon thousands of incarnate souls, and here, in this hall of rest, we witnessed people awakening from their spirit sleep. We saw kind and patient spirits trying so hard to convince these same people that they had really "died." And this hall of rest is but one place out of many where the same service is being carried on unceasingly, and all because the earth world is so very superior in knowledge!

We were shown another large hall similarly appointed, where those whose passing had been sudden and violent were also in their temporary sleep. These cases were usually more difficult to manage than those we had just seen. The suddenness of their departure added far greater confusion to the mind. Instead of a steady transition, the spirit body had in many cases been forcibly ejected from the physical body, and precipitated into the spirit world. The passing over had been so sudden that there seemed to them to be no break in their lives. Such people are taken in hand quickly by bands of souls who devote all their time and the whole of their energies to such work. And in the hall of rest we could now see the results of their labors. Had so many of these souls had but a small knowledge of spirit matters, these awakenings would have been so much the happier.

I do assure you it is not a pleasant sight to see these gentle, patient helpers wrestling mentally—and sometimes almost physically—with people who are wholly ignorant of the fact that they are "dead." It is a most saddening sight, which I can vouch for from firsthand evidence, for have I not seen it? And who is to blame for this state of affairs? Most of these souls blame themselves when they have been here long enough to appreciate their new condition, or alternatively, they blame the world they have but recently left for tolerating such blindness and stupidity.

Edwin hinted that perhaps we had seen all that we wished, and truth to tell, both Ruth and I were not sorry to leave. For it must be recalled that we were both comparatively new arrivals, and we had not yet sufficient experience to be able to withstand sights that were in themselves distressing. So we passed out into the open again, and we took a path that skirted a large orchard of fruit trees, similar to, though much more extensive than that wherein I had had my first taste of celestial fruit. It was close at hand for the use of the newly awakened—and, of course, for anyone else who wished to partake of the stimulating fruit.

It occurred to me that Edwin was expending a good deal of his time upon us, perhaps at the expense of his own work. But he told us that what he was now doing, was, in many respects, his usual work—not only to help people to become accustomed to their new surroundings, but to help those who were just beginning to shake off their old religious ideas, and break away from the stifling of their minds as members of orthodox communities here. I was glad to know this, because it meant that he would continue to be our *cicerone*.

Now that we were again in the open, the question arose: should we continue to wear our spirit dress, or should we go back to our old attire? As far as Ruth was concerned, she would not hear of any changing back. She declared her perfect satisfaction with what she was wearing, and demanded of us to know what possible earthly costume could ever improve upon it. In the face of such a powerful argument, we were bound to submit. But what of Edwin and me? My friend had only reverted to his earthly cassock to keep me company and to help me feel at home. And so I decided that I would stay as I now was—in my spirit apparel.

As we walked along we fell to chatting about the various earthly notions touching the personal appearance of spirit people. Ruth mentioned "wings" in connection with "angelic beings," and we were all at once agreed that such an idea was nothing less than preposterous. Could any means of locomotion be more clumsy or ponderous, or thoroughly unpracticable? We supposed that artists of ancient days must have been largely responsible for this wide departure from actuality. One presumes they thought that some means of personal locomotion was essential for spirit people, and that the ordinary mundane method of using one's legs was far too earthly to be admitted, even as a remote possibility, into the heavenly realms. Having no knowledge whatever of the power of thought here, and its direct application in the literal movement of ourselves through these realms, they were thrown back upon the only means of movement through space known to them—the use of wings. One wonders if there are still earth people who really believe that we are only partly removed from some form of large bird! Among the thinking, modern science has managed to dispel some of the absurd conceptions so long prevalent.

We had not gone very far when Edwin bethought him that we might like to make our way to the city which we could see plainly not too far away. I say "not too far away", but that should not be misunderstood into meaning that distance here is of any account. It certainly is not! I mean that the city lay sufficiently close for us to visit it without making any deviation from our general direction. Ruth and I agreed at once that we should like to proceed there forthwith, as a city of the spirit world must be something of a new revelation to us in itself.

Then the question came to our minds: should we walk, or should we employ a faster method? We both felt that we should like to try exactly what the power of thought can do, but as before, in other circumstances, we were both devoid of any knowledge of how to put these forces into action. Edwin told us that once we had performed this very simple process of thinking, we should have no difficulty whatever in the future. In the first place, it was necessary to have confidence; and in the second, our concentration of thought must not be a half-hearted affair. To borrow an earthly allusion, we "wish ourselves" there, wherever it may be, and *there* we shall find ourselves! For the first few occasions it may be required to make something of a conscious effort; afterwards we can move ourselves whithersoever we wish—one might almost say, without thinking! To recall earthly methods, when you wish to sit down, or walk, or perform any one of the many earthly actions that are so familiar, you are not conscious of making any very definite effort of thought in order to bring about your desires. The thought very rapidly passes through your mind that you wish to sit down, and you sit down. But you have given no heed to the many muscular movements, and so on, involved in the simple action. They have become as second nature. And so it is precisely the same with us here. We just think that we wish to be in a certain place, and we are there. I must, of course, qualify that statement by saying that all places are not open to us here. There are many realms where we are not able to enter except in very special circumstances, or only if our state of progression permits. That, however, does not affect the method of locomotion here; it merely restricts us in certain well-defined directions.

Being severely practical, I mentioned to Edwin that as we wished, all three of us, to be together, then must we not all wish to be at the same place, and must we not have some very definite locality in mind upon which to fasten our thoughts? He replied that there were several factors to be borne in mind in this particular instance. One factor was that it was our initial essay in thought locomotion, and that he would, more or less, "take charge" of us. We should automatically remain in close contact with each other, since we had voiced the wish and intention of doing so. These two facts together were sufficient to afford us a safe and sure arrival in company at our desired destination! When we became quite proficient in these methods we should have no difficulty in this connection.

It must be remembered that thought is as instantaneous as it is possible to imagine, and there is no possibility of our losing ourselves in illimitable space! I had had my first example of traveling through space in this way immediately after my passing, but then I had moved comparatively slowly with my eyes firmly closed. Edwin then suggested that it would give us some pleasant amusement if we were to try an experiment for ourselves. He assured us that we could not, in any circumstances, come to any harm whatever. He proposed that Ruth and I should project ourselves to a small clump of trees lying about a quarter of a mile away—as measured by the earth. We all three sat on the grass and we gazed at our objective. He suggested that if we felt at all nervous that we might hold each other's hands! Ruth and I were to go alone, while he would remain on the grass. We were just to think that we wished to be beside yonder trees. We looked at one another with a great deal of merriment, both of us wondering what would happen next, and neither of us taking the initiative. We were pondering thus, when Edwin said: "Off you go!" His remark must have supplied the requisite stimulus, for I took Ruth's hand, and the next thing we knew we found ourselves standing beneath the trees!

We looked at one another, if not in amazement, then in something that was very much like it. Casting our eyes whence we had just come, we saw Edwin waving his hand to us. Then a strange thing happened. We both beheld immediately before our faces what seemed to be a flash of light. It was not blinding, nor did it startle us in any way. It simply caught our attention just as the earthly sun would do when coming from behind a cloud. It illumined the small space before our eyes as we stood there. We remained quite still, full of expectancy for what might transpire. Then clearly, beyond any vestige of doubt, we heard—whether with the ear or with the mind, I could not then say—the voice of Edwin asking us if we had enjoyed our brief journey, and to go along back to him in exactly the same way as we had left him. We both made some remark upon what we had heard, trying to decide if it were really Edwin we had heard speaking. Scarcely had we mentioned our perplexity at this latest demonstration of the spirit, when Edwin's voice spoke again, assuring us that *he* had heard *us* as we cogitated upon the matter! So surprised and altogether delighted were we with this fresh manifestation of the power of thought, following so swiftly upon the other, that we determined to return to Edwin upon the instant, and demand a full explanation. We repeated the procedure, and there we were, once more, seated one each side of my old friend, who was laughing joyously at our wonderment.

He was prepared for the onslaught that came—for we bombarded him with questions—and he told us that he had purposely kept this surprise for us. Here, he said, was another instance of the concreteness of thought. If we can move ourselves by the power of thought, then it follows that we should also be able to send our thoughts by themselves, unhindered by all ideas of distance. When we focus our thoughts upon some person in the spirit world, whether they be in the form of a definite message, or whether they are solely of an affectionate nature, those thoughts will reach their destination without fail, and they will be taken up by the percipient. That is what happens in the spirit world. *How* it happens, I am not prepared to say. That is another of the many things we take as we find, and rejoice therein. We had, so far, used our "organs of speech" in conversing with each other. It was quite natural, and we hardly gave the matter any thought. It had not occurred either to Ruth or myself that some means of communication at a distance must be available here. We were no longer limited by earthly conditions, yet so far we had not observed anything that would take the place of the usual mode of intercommunication upon the earth. This very absence should, perhaps, have told us to expect the unexpected.

Although we can thus send our thoughts, it must not be assumed that our minds are as an open book for all to read. By no means. We can, if we so will, deliberately keep our thoughts to ourselves; but if we should think idly, as it were, if we should just let our thoughts ramble along under a loose control, then they can be seen and read by others. One of the first things to be done upon arrival here is to realize that thought is concrete, that it can create and build, and then our next effort is to place our own thoughts under proper and adequate control. But like so much else in the spirit world, we can soon learn to adjust ourselves to the new conditions if we have a mind to do so, and we shall never lack the most willing helpers in any or all of our difficulties. The latter, Ruth and I had already found out with relief and gratitude.

Ruth was by now very impatient to be off to visit the city, and she insisted that Edwin should take us there immediately. And so, without further delay, we rose up from the grass, and with a word from our guide, we set forth.

CHAPTER FIVE

HALLS OF LEARNING

AS WE approached the city, it was possible for us to gather some idea of its extensive proportions. It was, I hardly need say, totally unlike anything I had yet seen. It consisted of a large number of stately buildings each of which was surrounded with magnificent gardens and trees, with here and there pools of glittering water, clear as crystal, yet reflecting every shade of color known to earth, with many other tints to be seen nowhere but in the realms of spirit.

It must not be imagined that these beautiful gardens bore the slightest resemblance to anything to be seen upon the earth-plane. Earthly gardens at their best and finest are of the very poorest by comparison with these that we now beheld, with their wealth of perfect colorings and their exhalations of heavenly perfumes. To walk upon the lawns with such a profusion of nature about us held us spellbound. I had imagined that the beauty of the countryside, wherein I had had all my experience of spirit lands so far, could hardly be excelled anywhere.

My mind had reverted to the narrow streets and crowded pavements of the earth; the buildings huddled together because space is so valuable and costly; the heavy, tainted air, made worse by streams of traffic; I had thought of hurry and turmoil, and all the restlessness of commercial life and the excitement of passing pleasure. I had no conception of a city of eternal beauty, as far removed from an earthly city as the light of day is from black night. Here were fine broad thoroughfares of emerald green lawns in perfect cultivation, radiating, like the spokes of a wheel, from a central building which, as we could see, was the hub of the whole city. There was a great shaft of pure light descending upon the dome of this building, and we felt instinctively—

without Edwin having to tell us—that in this temple we could together send up our thanks to the Great Source of all, and that there we should find none other than the Glory of God in Truth.

The buildings were not of any great height as we should measure and compare with earthly structures, but they were for the most part extremely broad. It is impossible to tell of what materials they were composed because they were essentially spirit fabrics. The surface of each smooth as of marble, yet it had the delicate texture and translucence of alabaster, while each building sent forth, as it were into the adjacent air, a stream of light of the palest shade of coloring. Some of the buildings were carved with designs of foliage and flowers, and others were left almost unadorned, as far as any smaller devices were concerned, relying upon their semi-classic nature for relief. And over all was the light of heaven shining evenly and uninterruptedly, so that nowhere were there dark places.

This city was devoted to the pursuit of learning, to the study and practice of the arts, and to the pleasures of all in this realm. It was exclusive to none, but free for all to enjoy with equal right. Here it was possible to carry on so many of those pleasant and fruitful occupations that had been commenced on the earth-plane. Here, too, many souls could indulge in some agreeable diversion which had been denied them, for a variety of reasons, whilst they were incarnate.

The first hall that Edwin took us into was concerned with the art of painting. This hall was of very great size and contained a long gallery, on the walls of which were hanging every great masterpiece known to man. They were arranged in such a way that every step of earthly progress could be followed in proper order, beginning with the earliest times and so continuing down to the present day. Every style of painting was represented, gathered from all points of the earth. It must not be thought that such a collection, as we were now viewing, is only of interest and service to people who have a full appreciation and understanding of the painter's art. Such could not be farther from the case.

There was a goodly number of people in the gallery when we entered, some of whom were moving about wherever their fancy took them. But there were many groups listening to the words of able teachers, who were demonstrating the various phases in the history of art as exemplified upon the walls, and they were, at the same time giving such a clear and interesting exposition that none could fail to understand.

A number of these pictures I recognized as I had seen their "originals" in the earth's galleries. Ruth and I were astonished when Edwin told us that what we had seen in those galleries were not the originals at all! *We were now seeing the originals for the first time.* What we had seen was an earthly counterpart, which was perishable from the usual causes—for example, from fire or the general disintegration through the passage of time. But here we were, viewing the direct results of the thoughts of the painter, created in the etheric *before* he actually transferred those thoughts to his earthly canvas. It could be plainly observed, in many cases, where the earthly picture fell short of that which the painter had in his mind. He had endeavored to reproduce his exact conception, but through physical limitations this exact conception had eluded him. In some instances it had been the pigments that had been at fault when, in the early times, the artist had been unable to procure or evolve the particular shade of color he wanted. But though he lacked physically, his mind had known precisely what he wished to do. He had built it up in the spirit—the results of which we were now able to see—while he had failed to do so on the material canvas.

That was one major difference that I noticed in the pictures, by comparison with what I had seen on the earth-plane. Another great point of dissimilarity—and the most important—was the fact that here all these pictures were *alive*. It is impossible to convey any idea of this paramount difference. These spirit pictures *must* be seen here to understand it. I can only just suggest an idea. These pictures, then, whether landscape or portrait, were never flat; that is, they did not seem to have been painted upon a flat canvas. They possessed, on the other hand, all the completeness of relief. The subject stood forth almost as though it were a modela model whereof one could take hold of all the elements that went to the making up of the subject of the picture. One felt that the shadows were real shadows cast by real objects. The colors glowed with life, even among the very early works before much progress had been made.

A problem came into my mind, for a solution of which I naturally turned to Edwin. It was this: as it would be undesirable, perhaps, as well as impracticable, to hang in these galleries *every* painting that emanated from the earth-plane, any idea of preferential treatment based upon the judgment of others did not seem quite consonant with spirit law, in so far as I was acquainted with it. What system is used for the selection of paintings to hang upon these walls? I was told that it was a question that is frequently asked by visitors to this gallery. The answer is that by the time an artist, whether he be good, bad, or just commonplace, has adjusted himself to his new life, he has no further illusions—if he ever harbored any—of his own work. Usually an extreme diffidence sets in, fostered by the immensity and the superlative beauty of this realm. So that in the end the problem becomes one of scarcity rather than superabundance!

When we gazed at the portraits of so many men and women whose names had worldwide fame, whether they lived in distant times or in the present day, it gave Ruth and me a strange feeling to think that we were now inhabitants of the same world as they, and that they, like ourselves, were very much alive, and not mere historic figures in the chronicles of the earth world.

In other parts of this same building were rooms wherein students of art could learn all that there is to be learnt. The joy of these students is great in their freedom from their earthly restrictions and bodily limitations. Here instruction is easy, and the acquisition and application of knowledge equally facile to those who wish to learn. Gone are all the struggles of the student in the surmounting of earthly difficulties both of the mind and of the hands, and progress towards proficiency is consequently smooth and rapid. The happiness of all the students whom we saw, itself spread happiness to all who beheld it, for there is no limit to their endeavors when that bugbear of earthly life—fleeting time—and all the petty vexations of the mundane existence have been abandoned for ever. Is there any wonder that artists within this hall, and, indeed, in every other hall in the city, were enjoying the golden hours of their spiritual reward?

To have made a really exhaustive study of all the pictures in the gallery would have taken us too long for our present purposes, which were to acquire as comprehensive an idea of this realm as we could, so that later we could find our way about the more easily, and return to such places as had the most attraction for us. This was Edwin's idea, and Ruth and I were heartily in agreement with it. And so we tarried no longer in the hall of painting, and we passed on to another immense building.

This was the hall of literature, and it contained every work worthy of the name. Its interior was divided into smaller rooms than in the hall of painting. Edwin led us into one spacious apartment which contained the histories of all the nations upon the earth-plane. To anyone who has a knowledge of earthly history, the volumes with which the shelves of this section of the great library were filled, would prove illuminating. The reader would be able to gain, for the first time, the *truth* about the history of his country. Every word contained in these books was the literal truth. Concealment is impossible, because nothing but the truth can enter these realms.

I have since returned to this library and spent much profitable time among its countless books. In particular I have dipped into history, and I was amazed when I started to read. I naturally expected to find that history would be treated in the manner with which we are all familiar, but with the essential difference that now I should be presented with the truth of all historical acts and events. The latter I soon discovered to be the case, but I made another discovery that for the first moment left me astounded. I found that side by side with the statements of pure fact of every act by persons of historical note, by statesmen in whose hands was the government of their countries, by kings who were at the head of those same countries, side by side with such statements was the blunt naked truth of each and every motive governing or underlying their numerous acts—the truth beyond disputation. Many of such motives were elevated, many, many of them were utterly base; many were misconstrued, many distorted. Written indelibly upon these spirit annals were the true narratives of thousands upon thousands of human beings, who, whilst upon their early journey, had been active participants in the affairs of their country. Some were victims to others' treachery and baseness; some were the cause or origin of that treachery and baseness. None was spared, none omitted. It was all there for all to see—the *truth*, with nothing extenuated, nothing suppressed. These records had no respect for persons, whether it be king or commoner, churchman or layman. The writers had just set down the veridical story as it was. It required no adornment, no commentary. It spoke for itself. And I was profoundly thankful for one thing—that this truth had been kept from us until such time as we stood where we were now standing, when our minds would, in some measure, be prepared for revelations such as were here at hand.

So far I have mentioned only political history, but I also delved into church history, and the revelations I received in that direction were no better than those in the political sphere. They were, in fact, worse, considering in whose name so many diabolical deeds were committed by men who, outwardly professing to serve God, were but instruments of men as base as themselves.

Edwin had forewarned me of what to expect in consulting these histories, but I had never anticipated the degree of fullness I should find in the narration of the true facts. The supposed motives given in our earthly history books were wide of the mark of the real motives on so many numberless occasions!

Although these books bore witness against the perpetrators of so many dark deeds in the earth world's history, they also bore witness to many deeds both great and noble. They were not there specifically for the purpose of providing evidence for and against, but because literature has become part of the fabric of human life. People take pleasure in reading. Is it not quite in accord with this life that there should be books for us to read? They may not be exactly the same as the earth books, but they are in precise keeping with all else here. And it is found that the pursuit of knowledge is far greater here than upon the earth-plane, since the necessity of turning our minds to the pressing needs and exigencies of incarnate life no longer exists here.

We passed through many other rooms where volumes upon every subject imaginable were at the disposal of all who wished to study them. And perhaps one of the most important subjects is that which has been called by some truly enlightened soul "psychic science"—for science it is. I was astonished by the wealth of literature under this heading. Upon the shelves were books denying the existence of a spirit world, and denying the reality of spirit return. Many of the authors of them have since had the opportunity of looking again at their own works—but with very different feelings! They had become, *in themselves*, living witnesses against the contents of their own books.

We were very much struck by the beautiful bindings in which the books were encased, the material upon which they were inscribed, and the style of inscription. I turned to Edwin for information upon these points. He told me that the reproduction of books in the world of spirit was not the same process as in the case of paintings. I had seen for myself how the truth had been suppressed in the earthly volumes either through deliberate intent or through ignorance of the real facts. In the case of the paintings the artist had desired to depict in truth, so to speak, but through no real fault of his own he had been unable to do so. He had not perpetuated untruth, therefore; on the contrary, his mind had recorded what was entirely true. An author of a book would hardly write it with intentions diametrically opposed to those expressed within it. Who, then, writes the book of truth in spirit? *The author of the earthly volume writes it—when he comes into the spirit world.* And he is glad to do it. It becomes his work, and by such work he can gain the progress of his soul. He will have no difficulty with the facts, for they are here for him to record, and he records them—but the truth this time! There is no need to dissemble—in fact, it would be useless.

As to inscribing the books, are there not printing machines upon the earth? Of course there are! Then surely the spirit world is not to be the worse provided for in this respect? We have our methods of printing, but they are totally unlike those of the earth. We have our experts, who are also artists at their work, and it is work they love doing, or else they would not be doing it. The method of reproduction here is wholly a process of the mind, as with all else, and author and printer work together in complete harmony. The books that result from this close co-operation are works of art; they are beautiful creations which, apart altogether from their literary contents, are lovely to look upon. The binding of the book is another expert process, carried out by more artists, in wonderful materials never seen upon the earth, since they are of spirit only. But the books thus produced are not dead things that require a concentration of the whole mind upon them. They live just as much as the paintings we saw were living. To pick up a book and begin reading from it meant also to perceive with the mind, in a way not possible on earth, the whole story as it was being told, whether it be history or science, or the arts. The book, once taken in the hand by the reader, instantly responds, in very much the same way as the flowers respond when one approaches close to them. The purpose is different, of course.

All the vast numbers of books we saw were there for all to use at their leisure and to their heart's delight. There were no restrictions, no tiresome rules and regulations. Standing with all this enormous wealth of knowledge about us, I was staggered at my own ignorance, and Ruth felt the same. However, Edwin reassured me by telling us that we must not let the sight of so much knowledge frighten us, as we have the whole of eternity before us! It was a comforting reminder, and strange to say, a fact that one is inclined to overlook. It takes time to shake off finally that feeling of impermanence, of transience, that is so closely associated with the earth life. And in consequence we feel that we must see everything as quickly as we can, in spite of the fact that time, as a factor in our lives, has ceased to function.

By now Edwin thought it due to Ruth to show her something that would have an especial appeal to her, and so he took us into the hall of fabrics. This was equally spacious, but the rooms were of greater dimensions than those of the two halls we had just viewed. Here were contained the scores upon scores of beautiful materials and cloths woven throughout the centuries, and of which practically nothing remains upon the earth-plane. It was possible to see here specimens of the materials that we read about in histories and chronicles in the descriptions of state ceremonies and festive occasions. And whatever may be said for the change of style and taste that has taken place throughout the ages, the earth world has lost a vast deal of its color in exchange for a dull drabness.

The colorings in many of the old materials were simply superb, while the magnificently-wrought designs revealed to us the art that has been lost to earth. Though perishable to the earth, they are imperishable to the spirit world. After making due allowance for the etherealization of these fabrics by their being in the spirit world, there remained in our minds a sufficiently vivid conception of what these rich fabrics must have looked like in their earthly element. Here again, it was possible to observe the gradual progress made in the designing and making of earthly materials, and it must be admitted, as far as I was able to judge, that progress proceeded up to a point when a retrograde movement was noticeable. I am, of course, speaking in a general sense.

A room of tapestries contained some superb examples of the artists' genius, the earthly counterparts of which have long since gone out of existence. Annexed to this apartment were smaller rooms where many happy, industrious souls were studying and practicing the art of tapestry weaving, with other equally happy souls ever at their side to help and instruct. This was not a tedious work of pupil and teacher, but the enjoyment of pure pleasure, which both could terminate for other things at any time they so wished. Ruth said that she would dearly love to join one of the groups engaged upon a large tapestry, and she was told that she could do so whenever she wished, and that she would be welcomed with all the joy in the world into this community of friends. However, she would, for the present, remain with us upon our expeditions.

It may be thought that what we had seen as yet were nothing more than celestial museums, containing, it is true, magnificent specimens not to be seen upon earth, but museums, nevertheless. Now earthly museums are rather cheerless places. They have an aroma of mustiness and chemical preservatives, since their exhibits have to be protected from deterioration and decay. And they have to be protected from man, too, by uninspiring glass cases. But here there are no restrictions. All things within these halls are free and open for all to see and hold in the two hands. There is no mustiness, but the beauty of the objects themselves sends out many subtle perfumes, while the light of heaven streams in from all quarters to enhance the glories of man's handicrafts. No, these are no museums; very far from it. They are temples, rather, in which we spirit people are conscious of the eternal thanks that we owe to the great Father for giving us such unbounded happiness in a land of which so many upon earth deny the reality. They would sweep all this away for what? They know not. There are many, many, beauties upon the earth-plane, but we in spirit must have none! Perhaps that is another reason why such deep sympathy is felt for us when we pass into spirit—because we have left behind us for ever all that is beautiful, to pass into a state of emptiness—a celestial vacuum. All that is beautiful, then, becomes exclusive to the earth world. Man's intelligence is of no further use when once he has passed to here, because here there is nothing upon which to exercise it! Just emptiness! No wonder that the realities and the immense fullness of the spirit world come as such a shock of revelation to those who were anticipating an eternity of celestial nothingness!

It is essential to understand that every occupation and every task performed by the inhabitants of this and higher realms is done willingly, for the pure wish of doing so, and never from the attitude of having to do it "whether they like it or not." There is no such thing as being compelled to undertake a task. Never is unwillingness felt or expressed. That is not to say that the impossible is attempted. We may be able to see the outcome of some action or another—or if we cannot, there are others of greater wisdom and knowledge who can—and we shall know whether to commence our task or withhold for the time being. We never want here for help and advice. You may recall my own suggestion earlier of trying to communicate with the earth to set right some matters in my own life, and that Edwin advised that I should seek advice later on upon the practicability of that course. So that it is the truth to say that the wish to do and to serve is the keynote here. I mention these matters so that a better understanding may be obtained of a particular hall that Edwin took us into after we left the hall of fabrics.

This was, to all intents and purposes, a school where souls, who had had the misfortune to miss the benefits of some earthly knowledge and learning, could here equip themselves intellectually.

Knowledge and learning, education or erudition do not connote spiritual worth, and the inability to read and write do not imply the absence of it. But when a soul has passed into this life, when he sees the great, broad spiritual thoroughfare opening before him with its opportunities both manifold and multiform, he sees also that knowledge can help him on his spiritual way. He may not be able to read. Are all those splendid books to remain for ever closed to him now that he has the opportunity to read, while lacking the ability? Perhaps it will be asked: surely it is not necessary to be able to read in the spirit world? Things being what they are, there must be some form of mental perception to be gathered from books without the material aid of printed words? The same question might be asked of pictures and of all else here. Why the need for anything tangible? If we pursue this line of thought it will take us to that state of vacuity I have just mentioned.

The man who is unable to read will *feel* with his mind that something is contained within the book that he takes into his hands, but he will not know instinctively, or in any other way, the contents of it. But one who can read will, immediately upon his commencing to do so, find himself *en rapport* with the author's thoughts as set down, and the book will thus respond to him who reads.

To be able to write is not necessary, and many who have been unable to do so before passing here, have not bothered to supply the omission after their arrival.

We found in this school many souls busy with their studies, and thoroughly enjoying themselves. To acquire knowledge here is not tedious, because the memory works perfectly—that is, unfailingly—and the powers of mental perception are no longer hampered and confined by a physical brain. Our faculties for understanding are sharpened, and intellectual expansion is sure and steady. The school was the home of realized ambitions to most of the students within it. I chatted with a number of them, and each told me that what he was studying now, he had longed to study on earth, but had been denied the opportunity for reasons that are all too familiar. Some had found that commercial activities had left no time, or that the struggle for a living had absorbed all the means to do so.

The school was very comfortably arranged; there was, of course, no hint of regimentation. Each student followed his own course of study independently of anyone else. He seated himself comfortably, or he went into the lovely gardens without. He began when he wanted, and he finished when he wanted, and the more he dipped into his studies the more interested and fascinated he became. I can speak from personal experience of the latter, since there is much that I have studied in the great library since my first introduction to it.

As we left the school, Edwin suggested that we might like to sit on the grass beneath some fine trees and rest ourselves. That was simply his way—a perfectly natural one—of expressing it. We do not suffer bodily fatigue, but at the same time we do not continue endlessly at the same occupation; that would mean monotony, and there is no monotony here such as we used to endure on earth. But Edwin knew from experience the different emotions that take place in the minds of newly arrived souls into spirit lands, and so he halted for the time being our further explorations.

CHAPTER SIX

SOME QUESTIONS
ANSWERED

EDWIN TOLD us that a very large majority of people are no sooner arrived in spirit than a burning enthusiasm overtakes them as the spirit world reveals itself to them in the new life, and they immediately want to rush back to the earth and tell the world all about it. He had already explained to me some of the difficulties in my own suggestion of returning.

Another very natural tendency was to ask numberless questions upon this life in general, and he remarked that in this both Ruth and I had exercised quite an unusual restraint! Certainly I had refrained from asking too many questions, but then, Edwin had explained as much as we should be able to understand as we proceeded. I confessed, though, now that he broached the matter, that there were many things about which I should very much like to know. Ruth said she had the same feelings, and that doubtless many of our queries coincided. The difficulty was where to begin.

We had allowed our journeyings to bring forth their own problems for Edwin's solution, but there were other considerations of a general nature which arose from the contemplation of spirit lands as a whole. One of the first that arose to my mind as we sat on the grass, with heavenly flowers round about us, was the extent of this realm in which we were now living. It reached as far as the eye could see—and that was a great deal farther than we could ever see upon the earth-plane on the finest and clearest day in the summer. This in itself was too wonderful for words, but it also gave an indication of the immensity of this particular realm. And we had only seen the tiniest fraction of it so far! We still thought in terms of earthly distances. Was there any boundary to this realm? Did it stretch still farther beyond the range of our vision? If there were any termination, what was beyond? Could we go and see for ourselves?

Certainly there was a boundary to this realm, Edwin explained to us. And we could go and see it for ourselves whenever we wished. Beyond this were other and still more realms. Each soul as it passed into spirit passed into that realm for which it had fitted itself when upon the earth—into that realm and no other. Edwin had in the beginning described this land as the land of the great harvest—a harvest that was sown on earth. We could judge for ourselves, then, whether we considered that harvest a good one or a poor one. We should find that there were others infinitely better—and others infinitely worse. In plain words, there are other realms immeasurably more beautiful than that in which we were now happily living; realms of surpassing beauty into which we cannot penetrate until such time as we have earned the right to enter, either as visitors or as inhabitants. But though we may not pass into them, the glorious souls who dwell in them can come into realms of less celestial rarity, and can visit us here. Edwin himself had seen some of them, and we hoped to do so as well. Indeed, they constantly make visitations to consult and converse with the dwellers here, to give advice and help, to give rewards and commendations, and there was no doubt but that my own matter could be placed before one of these master souls for his guidance upon it.

At certain times, too, these transcendent beings make special visitations when the whole realm is celebrating a great occasion, such, for example, as the two major earth festivals of Christmas and Easter. Ruth and I were very astonished at the latter, because we thought them both to be so essentially of the earth. But it was the manner of celebrating them, and not the festivals themselves, which was particular to the earth. In the spirit lands both Christmas and Easter are looked upon as birthdays: the first, a birth into the earth world; the second, a birth into the spirit world. In this realm the two celebrations synchronize with those upon the earth, since there is then a greater spiritual link between the two worlds than would be the case if the festivals were held independently of season. It is not so, however, in the higher realms, where laws of a different nature are in operation.

On the earth-plane the anniversary of Christmas has remained fixed for many centuries on a certain date. The exact day of the first Christmas has been lost, and it is impossible now to ascertain with any precision, by earthly means, when it occurred. Even were it possible, it is too late to make any alteration, since the present fixture has been established by long tradition and practice. The feast of Easter is movable—a stupid custom, since oft-times the chosen date bears no relation to the first and original date. There is some hope that a change will be made, and the feast stabilized. In no sense are we subservient to the earth in these matters, but at the same time a foolish obstinacy would lead us nowhere. Therefore it is that we *cooperate* with the earth-plane in our united rejoicings.

The higher realms have their own very good reasons for what may seem to be a departure from a recognized order. Such reasons do not concern us—until we ourselves pass to those higher states.

Beyond those two great festivals we do not have much else in common with the earth world in the matter of feasts. The most of the latter are merely ecclesiastical feasts which have no spiritual significance in the broadest sense, since so many are the outcome of religious doctrines which have no application in the spirit world. The feast of Epiphany, for example, is founded upon a very colorful story, and was in ancient times celebrated by the people in a secular fashion as well as a religious. It is now solely religious, and of very little moment here. The feast of Pentecost is another instance of the Church's blindness. The Holy Spirit—to use the Church's phrase—has been, is, and always will be descending upon all those who are worthy to receive it! Not upon one specific occasion, but always.

Both Ruth and I were very interested to learn how Christmas was celebrated in these realms, since, on the earth, beyond a few church services, the feast of the Nativity has developed into a secular affair, the main feature being that of prodigious eating and drinking. Edwin told us that in spirit we can experience the same degree of happiness as is the case on earth where that happiness is the outcome or expression of kindness; where our merrymaking is blended with the knowledge or the remembrance of whose great day we are celebrating. Those of us who wish—and there are many such—can decorate our houses and dwelling-places with evergreens, as we were accustomed to do on earth. By evergreens I mean those particular trees and shrubs that are so-called on earth. Here everything is eternally "evergreen"! We join together in merry company, and if it is felt that the time would not be right without our having something to eat, then, is there not a superabundance of that most perfect fruit, that I have told you about, to delight the hearts of the most fastidious?

But I have only told of the more personal side of this feast. It is at this time that we have visitants of the higher realms to see us, perfect beings, among whom is he whose earthly birth we are celebrating. And these beauteous souls have but to pass upon their way to fill us with such an ecstasy of spiritual exaltation as to remain with us for long after their return to their high estate.

At Easter time we have similar visitations, but there is a far greater degree of rejoicing, because to us the birth into the spirit world must, by the very nature of things, be of far greater significance. Indeed, when once we have left the earth-plane we are inclined to forget our earthly birthday, since the greater contains the lesser. It is only our earthly connections, if we have any, that will serve to remind us.

I have enlarged upon this subject somewhat to try to show you that we are not living in a state of fervid religious emotion for all eternity. We are human, though so many people still on the earth-plane would have us to be otherwise! Such people will inevitably be in the same relative position as ourselves one day, and nothing is so calculated to instill humility as the realization of what one once held as firm and decided opinions.

I have digressed a little from our first topic as we threw ourselves on the grass, but in our conversation one thing led to another until we seemed to have wandered some way from our course.

Mention has only been made of the higher realms. What of the lower sphere that Edwin spoke about when I referred to the boundaries of this particular realm? We could visit them whenever we desired. We can always proceed to a realm lower than our own, while we cannot always mount higher. But it was by no means advisable to wander into the lower spheres except under expert guidance or before proper tuition had been given. Before informing us more fully upon this subject, Edwin advised us to see more of our own pleasant land first.

And now as to what constitutes the precise boundaries of this realm. We are accustomed to a knowledge of the rotundity of the earth and to seeing with our eyes the distant horizon. In contemplating this world of spirit we must abandon in many respects that idea of distance which we measure with the eye, since distance becomes annihilated by our immensely rapid means of transit. Any suggestion of terrestrial flatness is soon dispelled by the view of hills and rolling downs.

Again, the atmosphere is crystal clear and our sight is not limited by the instrument of a physical body. We are not confined to keeping our feet on the ground. If we can move ourselves laterally over these lands by the power of our thought, we can also move ourselves vertically—Edwin told us. And I must say that this had never occurred to Ruth and me as yet. We were still in some ways limited by our earthly notions and habits of thought. If we could sink beneath the waters without harm, but rather with enjoyment, then, of course, we must be able to mount into the "air" with the same safety and enjoyment! Ruth did not express any very keen desire to do so—just yet! She preferred to wait, she said, until she had become more thoroughly acclimatized. I wholeheartedly shared her sentiments in the matter, which caused our good friend the greatest amusement.

In alluding to these few features I have done so because the earth world has always looked upon the spirit world as being relatively up or down. These are really considerations of a highly scientific nature, and I am not competent to enlarge upon them; moreover, as an inhabitant of these lands my whole outlook, both mental and spiritual, has had to undergo sweeping and fundamental changes, in spite of the fact that I had some small knowledge before I passed over. It is really of little moment to know the precise location of the spirit world with its many realms or spheres.

Where is the boundary between the earth world and the spirit world? Upon the instant of my passing, of which, you will remember, I was fully conscious, when I arose from my bed in response to a very definite urge, *at that moment I was in the spirit world.* The two worlds, then, must interpenetrate one another. But as I moved away under the support and able guidance of Edwin, I was conscious of moving in no definite direction. I might have been traveling up, or down, or along. Movement, there certainly was. Edwin later informed me that I had passed through the lower spheres—and unpleasant ones—but that through the authority of his mission of coming to help me into my realm, we were both fully protected from any and every description of unpleasant influence. We were, in effect, completely invisible to all but those of our own realm and higher.

The transition from one realm to another is gradual as far as outward appearance is concerned, as well as in other respects, so that it would be difficult to assign to any particular locality the designation of boundary. That is exactly how the boundaries of our own realm are situated. They seem to melt almost imperceptibly into one another.

Edwin now proposed that by way of practical illustration we should go and see one of these boundaries that had perplexed us so much. We again placed ourselves under Edwin's expert guidance, and we moved off.

At once we found ourselves upon a very wide expanse of grassland, but we both noticed that the turf felt less soft beneath our feet; it was, in fact, becoming hard as we walked along. The beautiful emerald green was fast vanishing, and the grass was taking on a dull yellow appearance, very similar to earthly grass that has been scorched by the sun and has lacked water. We saw no flowers, no trees, no dwellings, and everywhere seemed bleak and barren. There was no sign of human life, and life seemed to be rapidly disappearing from beneath our feet, as by now the grass had ceased altogether, and we were upon hard ground. We noticed, too, that the temperature had fallen considerably. Gone was all that beautiful, genial warmth. There was a coldness and dampness in the air which seemed to cling to our beings, and cast a chill over our very souls. Poor Ruth clung to Edwin's arm, and I am not ashamed to say that I did the same, and was very glad to do so. Ruth then visibly shivered, and stopped abruptly, imploring us not to go any farther. Edwin threw his arms around both our shoulders, and told us that we had no need to be the least afraid, as he had the power to protect us fully. However, he could see the state of deep depression, as well as oppression, that had fallen upon us, and so he turned us gently round, placed his arms about our waists, and we once more found ourselves sitting beneath our own lovely trees, with the glorious flowers close beside us, and our own warm air once more closing upon us with its heavenly balm.

It is perhaps superfluous to add that Ruth and I were both glad to be back again in the city. We had been only on the *threshold* of the lower spheres, but we had gone far enough to gather more than an inkling of what lay beyond. I knew that it would be some time yet before I would penetrate there, and I could now clearly perceive the wisdom of Edwin's admonitions.

As we were on the subject of these spiritual boundaries, and in spite of the fact that we had temporarily ceased our explorations, I could not refrain from asking Edwin about the frontiers of the higher realms. I knew that there could not possibly be anything unpleasant about these, and so I hinted that, by way of contrast and to offset our recent chilling experience in the other direction, we might perhaps visit the border through which our celestial visitants pass. Edwin said that there was no objection whatever, and so once again we started off.

Again we found ourselves upon grassland, but with a striking difference. The turf upon which we were walking was infinitely softer than that of the interior of the realm. The green of the verdure was even brighter than we had thought possible. The flowers were growing in still greater profusion, and the intensity of color, of perfume, and of health-giving power transcended anything we had encountered. The very air seemed to be imbued with rainbow tints. There were few dwellings at the spot where we were immediately standing, but behind us were to be seen some of the most stately and beautiful houses I have ever seen. In these houses, so our friend told us, lived wondrous souls who, though nominally belonging to our own realm, were by virtue of their spiritual progression and particular gifts and work, in close contact with the higher realms, into which they had full authority and the requisite power to pass upon their various occasions. Edwin promised that we should return to this place after we had seen as much of the city as we wished, and there we could discuss—in one of the houses—my future work, as well as Ruth's. He had taken Ruth under his wing, and for her part she expressed her gratitude for his kindness in doing so. It had several times crossed my mind what form of spiritual work I could engage myself upon, as soon as I had become sufficiently familiar with the new life and the new land.

Just as we had been heavy with chill and oppression at the borderline of the dark spheres, so were we now warmed and filled with such an elation that we were almost silent in wonderment. As we moved along, bathed in radiance, we felt such a spiritual exhilaration that Edwin's description of the visitations of personages from the higher realms at once came to my mind, and I almost knew what to expect when I should be fortunate enough to witness such a visitation. Standing here, one had the overwhelming desire to strive for that progression that would entitle one to inhabit one of the lovely houses, and to qualify for the honor of serving one of the dwellers in this higher sphere at whose gateway we were standing.

We walked a little way forward, but we could proceed no farther. There were no visible barriers, but we felt that we could not breathe if we went onward. The whole atmosphere was becoming so much the more rarefied the farther we penetrated, that in the end we were bound to retrace our steps on to our own ground.

I could see many souls dressed in the most tenuous of garments, the soft colors of which seemed hardly to belong to them but to float about the fabric of their robes—if fabric one can call it. Those of them who came sufficiently near smiled to us with such a friendly greeting that we knew we were not in any way intruding, and some waved their hands to us. My friend told us that they were aware of our purpose there, and for that reason they would not approach us. They would allow us to enjoy our experience by ourselves, and quietly to absorb the beauties and splendors of this wonderful borderland.

And so, rather reluctantly, we turned; and we quickly found ourselves back in the city in our former spot under the trees. We both felt more buoyant than ever after this brief visit, and I am sure Edwin did too, notwithstanding his having been in spirit so much longer than we had.

We did not speak for a little while after our return, each of us engaged upon our own thoughts, and when we finally broke our silence, it was to ply our good Edwin with questions. To enumerate all these questions would be tedious, so I will give, in a consecutive form, Edwin's answers as a whole.

First, with regard to the lower spheres, whose threshold had so depressed us. I have since visited them in company with Ruth and Edwin, and I have made expeditions through them, just as we are now making through our own realm. I therefore do not want to anticipate what I wish to say later as to our experiences there. For the present, then, I will only say that when we paid our visit to the boundary, we made our way there directly and rapidly, and we had no consciousness of the intermediate states through which we passed. It was for this reason that our sudden change of environment was so noticeable. Had we made our progress slowly we should have perceived the gradual decline of all those pleasant and enjoyable features that constitute the heaven of this realm. And those who dwelt within this area of decline are in the same relative position to ourselves in respect of movement: they would be inhibited from passing higher just as we were on the borders of that higher realm.

The same conditions obtained in our journey to the borders of the higher realm. We traversed the distance so quickly that we were unable to observe the gradual alteration in our surroundings. Otherwise we should have seen the country taking on a higher degree of etherealization, a greater intensification of color and brightness, observable not only in the physical features of the realm, but also in the spirit raiment of those whose homes approximated the more closely to the border.

To visit the lower realms it is necessary to have—for one's own protection—certain powers and symbols, of which Edwin told us he was in full possession. Such places are not for curiosity seekers, and no one would be foolish enough to go there for any purpose other than a legitimate one. Those who wander in that direction alone, without authority, are soon turned back by kindly souls whose work it is to save others from the perils that lie beyond. Many souls are continuously passing backwards and forwards across that sad border in the performance of their work. It is true that we saw no signs of anyone near us when we were there, but like ourselves, when we made our journey there, they move quickly to their destination.

At the border to the higher realms there is no need for such sentinels to keep others from crossing, because the natural law prevents it. When those of a lower realm travel to a higher, it is always by authority, either vested in the traveler, or in some other person of a higher sphere, who will act as escort. In the former case, such authority takes the form of symbols or signs that are given to the holder, who will always and upon every occasion receive—even unasked—every assistance he may need. Many of these symbols have the power in themselves of preserving the traveler from the overwhelming effects of the higher spiritual atmosphere. This latter would not damage the soul, of course, but a soul thus unprepared would find itself in much the same situation as upon earth when one emerges into brilliant sunlight after a *prolonged* stay in *complete* darkness. But as in the case of the earthly sunshine one can, after a suitable lapse of time, become again perfectly at ease in the normal bright light, it is not so in the case of the higher realms. There is no such adaptability there. The "blinding" effect will be continuous to one of a lower state. But with a perfect dispensation, means are provided so that the visiting soul shall undergo no spiritual discomfort or unhappiness. And that is just what one would expect, since such visits are made for happy reasons, and not as tests of spiritual stamina and endurance. When it is necessary to make a journey to even higher spheres, it then becomes imperative, in many cases, that an inhabitant of those realms should, as it were, throw a cloak over his charge, in just the same way as Edwin, upon a lower scale, threw his protecting arms about us when we journeyed to the lower sphere.

Such, in substance, was what Edwin told us in reply to our many queries.

We now felt that we were sufficiently "rested," and upon Edwin proposing that we might care to resume our inspection of the city, we accordingly did so.

CHAPTER SEVEN

MUSIC

M USIC BEING such a vital element in the world of spirit, it is not surprising that a grand building should be devoted to the practice, teaching, and the fostering of every description of music. The next hall that our friend took us into was entirely dedicated to this important subject.

When I was on earth I never considered myself a musician, in an active sense, but I appreciated the art without very much understanding it. I had heard some splendid vocal music during my brief sojourns at different times in one of our metropolitan cathedrals, and I had had some very scanty experience of listening to orchestral music. Most of what I saw in this hall of music was new to me, and a great deal of it very technical. I have since added appreciably to my small knowledge, because I found that the greater the knowledge of music the more it helped one to understand so many things of the life here, where music plays so important a part. I do not suggest that all spirit people should become musicians in order to comprehend their own existence! The imposing of such a condition upon us would never be consonant with the natural laws here. But most individuals have some latent, innate musical sense, and by encouraging it here, so much the greater can be their joy. The latter, in effect, is exactly what I did. Ruth already possessed some extensive musical training, and so she felt very much at home in this great college.

The hall of music followed the same broad system as the other halls of the arts. The library contained books dealing with music as well as the scores of vast quantities of music that had been written on earth by composers who had now passed into spirit, or by those who were still upon the earth. What are called upon earth "master-works," were fully represented among the musical scores upon the shelves, and I was interested to learn that there was hardly a work that had not since been altered by the composer himself since coming into spirit. The reasons for such "improvements" I shall make plain later on. As before, the library provided a complete history of music from the very earliest times, and those who were able to read music—not necessarily instrumentally, but with a familiarity of what the printed notes indicated—were enabled to see before them the great strides that the art had made during the ages. Progression, it seems, has been slow, as in other arts, and freakish forms of expression have obtruded themselves. Needless to say the latter are not entertained here for reasons connected with those that inspire composers to alter their works after passing here.

Also contained in the library were so many of those books and musical works that have long since disappeared from earthly sight, or else are very scarce and so beyond the reach of so many folk. The musical antiquary will find all those things that he has sighed for on earth, but which have been denied him, and here he can consult, freely, works that, because of their preciousness, would never be allowed into his hands on earth. Many apartments were set aside for students who can learn of music in every branch, from theory to practice, under teachers whose names are known the earth world over. Some there are, perhaps, who would think that such famous people would not give their time to the teaching of simple forms of music to simple lovers of music. But it must be remembered, as with the painters, composers have a different appraisement of the fruits of their brains after passing into spirit. In common with us all here, they see things exactly as they are—including their compositions. They find, too, that the music of the spirit world is very different in outward results from music performed on earth. Hence they discover that their musical knowledge must undergo sweeping changes in many cases before they can begin to express themselves musically. In music, it can be said that the spirit world starts where the earth world leaves off. There are laws of music here which have no application to the earth whatever, because the earth is neither sufficiently progressed on the one hand, and on the other because the spirit world is of spirit, while the earth world is of matter. It is doubtful if the earth-plane will ever become ethereal enough to hear many of the forms of spirit music in the higher realms. Innovations have been tried, so I have been told, on the earth-plane, but the result is not only barbaric, but childish as well. Earthly ears are not attuned to music that is essentially of the spirit realms. By some strange chance earth people have essayed to produce such music on the earth-plane. It will never do—until the ears of those still incarnate have undergone a fundamental alteration.

The many types of musical instrument so familiar on earth were to be seen in the college of music, where students could be taught to play upon them. And here again, where dexterity of the hands is so essential the task of gaining proficiency is never arduous or wearisome, and it is, moreover, so much more rapid than upon the earth. As students acquire a mastery over their instrument they can join one of the many orchestras that exist here, or they can limit their performance to their many friends. It is not by any means surprising that many prefer the former because they can help to produce, in concert with their fellow musicians, the tangible effects of music upon a larger scale when so many more can enjoy such effects. We were extremely interested in the many instruments that have no counterpart upon the earth-plane. They are, for the most part, specially adapted to the forms of music that are exclusive to the spirit world, and they are for that reason very much more elaborate. Such instruments are only played with others of their kind for their distinctive music. For that which is common to the earth, the customary instrument is sufficient.

It is natural that this building should be possessed of a concert hall. This was a very large hall capable of seating comfortably many thousands. It was circular in shape, with seats rising in an unbroken tier from the floor. There is, of course, no real necessity for such a hall to be under cover, but the practice merely follows others in this realm—our own dwelling-houses, for example. We do not really need those but we like them, we have grown used to them while upon earth, they are perfectly natural to life, and so we have them.

We had observed that the hall of music stood in grounds far more extensive than those we had already seen, and the reason was soon made clear to us. At the rear of the hall was the great center of concert performances. It consisted of a vast amphitheatre like a great bowl sunk beneath the level of the ground, but it was so large that its real depth was not readily apparent. The seats that were farthest away from the performers were exactly upon ground level. Immediately surrounding these seats were masses of the most beautiful flowers of every possible hue, with a grassy space beyond, while the whole area of this outdoor temple of music was encompassed by a magnificent plantation of tall and graceful trees. Although the seating arrangements were upon such an expansive scale, much more so than would be at all practicable upon earth, yet there was no sense of being too far from the performers, even in the farthest seats. It will be recalled that our vision is not so restricted in spirit as upon earth.

Edwin suggested to us that we might like to hear a concert of the spirit world, and then he made a strange proposal. It was that we should not take our places in the seats of the theatre, but that we should take up a position at some distance. The reason, he said, would be manifest as soon as the music began. As a concert was due to start very shortly, we followed his mysterious suggestion, and seated ourselves on the grass at some considerable distance from the actual amphitheatre. I wondered whether we should be able to hear very much so far away, but our friend assured us that we should. And, indeed, we were joined by numbers of other people, at that very moment, who, doubtless, had come for the same purpose as ourselves. The whole place, which was empty when Edwin had first brought us in, now contained many people, some strolling about, and others, like us, seated contentedly on the grass. We were in a delightful spot, with the trees and flowers and pleasant people all about us, and never have I experienced such a feeling of real, genuine enjoyment as came upon me at this moment. I was in perfect health and perfect happiness, seated with two of the most delightful companions, Edwin and Ruth; unrestricted by time or weather, or even the bare thought of them; unhampered by every limitation that is common to our old incarnate life.

Edwin told us to walk over to the theatre and look down over the seats once again. We did so, and to our astonishment we found that the whole vast hall was packed with people, where there was not a soul to be seen but a *short time* before. The musicians were in their places awaiting the entrance of their conductor, and this great audience had arrived as if by magic—or so it seemed. As it was apparent that the concert was about to begin, we returned to Edwin at once. In answer to our question as to how the audience had arrived so suddenly and unperceived, he reminded me of the method of bringing together the congregation of the church that we had visited in the first days of our travels. In the case of this concert, the organizers had merely to send out their thoughts to people at large who were particularly interested in such performances, and they forthwith assembled. As soon as Ruth and I had shown our interest and desires in these concerts, we should establish a link, and we should find these thoughts reaching us whenever they were emitted.

We could, of course, see nothing of the performers from where we were situated, and so when a hush came upon all around us, we were thus sufficiently informed that the concert was to begin. The orchestra was composed of some two hundred musicians, who were playing upon instruments that are well-known to earth, so that I was able to appreciate what I heard. As soon as the music began I could hear a remarkable difference from what I had been accustomed to hear on the earth-plane. The actual sounds made by the various instruments were easily recognizable as of old, but the quality of tone was immeasurably purer, and the balance and blend were perfect. The work to be played was of some length, I was informed, and would be continued without any break.

The opening movement was of a subdued nature as regards its volume of sound, and we noticed that the instant the music commenced a bright light seemed to rise up from the direction of the orchestra until it floated, in a flat surface, level with the topmost seats, where it remained as an iridescent cover to the whole amphitheatre. As the music proceeded this broad sheet of light grew in strength and density, forming, as it were, a firm foundation for what was to follow. So intent was I upon watching this extraordinary formation that I could scarcely tell what the music was about. I was conscious of its sound, but that was really all. Presently, at equal spaces round the circumference of the theatre, four towers of light shot up into the sky in long tapering pinnacles of luminosity. They remained poised for a moment, and then slowly descended, becoming broader in girth as they did so, until they assumed the outward appearance of four circular towers, each surmounted with a dome, perfectly proportioned. In the meanwhile, the central area of light had thickened still more, and was beginning to rise slowly in the shape of an immense dome covering the whole theatre. This continued to ascend steadily until it seemed to reach a very much greater height than the four towers, while the most delicate colors were diffused throughout the whole of the etheric structure. I could understand now why Edwin had suggested that we should sit outside the theatre proper, and I could follow, also, why composers should feel impelled to alter their earthly works after they have arrived in spirit. The musical sounds sent up by the orchestra were creating, up above their heads, this immense musical thought-form, and the shape and perfection of this form rested entirely upon the purity of the musical sounds, the purity of the harmonies, and a freedom from any pronounced dissonance. The form of the music must be pure to produce a pure form.

It must not be assumed that every description of discord was absent. To lack discord would be to produce monotony, but the discords were legitimately used and properly resolved.

By now the great musical thought-form had assumed what appeared to be its limit of height, and it remained stationary and steady. The music was still being played, and in response to it the whole coloring of the dome changed, first to one shade, then to another, and many times to a delicate blend of a number of shades according to the variation in theme or movement of the music.

It is difficult to give any adequate idea of the beauty of this wonderful musical structure. The amphitheatre being built below the surface of the ground, nothing was visible of audience, of performers, or of the building itself, and the dome of light and color had all the appearance of resting on the same firm ground as were we ourselves.

This has taken but a brief while in the telling, but the musical thought-form occupied such time in formation as would be taken by a full-length concert on the earth-plane. We had, during this period, watched the gradual building of the outward and visible effect of music. Unlike the earth where music can only be heard, there we had both heard and *seen* it. And not only were we inspired by the sounds of the orchestral playing, but the beauty of the immense form it created had its spiritual influence upon all who beheld it, or came within its sphere. We could feel this although we were seated without the theatre. The audience within were basking in its splendor and enjoying still greater benefit from the effulgence of its elevating rays. On the next occasion we should take our places in the huge auditorium.

The music at last came to a grand finale, and so ended. The rainbow colors continued to interweave themselves. We wondered how long this musical structure would survive, and we were told that it would fade away in roughly the same time as would be taken by an earthly rainbow—comparatively a few minutes. We had listened to a major work, but if a series of shorter pieces were played, the effect and lasting power would be the same, but the shapes would vary in form and size. Were the form of greater duration, a new form would conflict with the last, and the result to the eye would be the same as two different and unconnected pieces of music, when played together, would be to the ear.

The expert musician can plan his compositions by his knowledge of what forms the various harmonic and melodic sounds will produce. He can, in effect, build magnificent edifices upon his manuscript of music, knowing full well exactly what the result will be when the music is played or sung. By careful adjustment of his themes and his harmonies, the length of the work, and its various marks of expression, he can build a majestic form as grand as a Gothic cathedral. This is, in itself, a delightful part of the musical art in spirit, and it is regarded as musical architecture. The student will not only study music acoustically, but he will learn to build it architecturally, and the latter is one of the most absorbing and fascinating studies.

What we had witnessed had been produced upon a scale of some magnitude; the individual instrumentalist or singer can evolve on a greatly reduced scale his own musical thought-forms. In fact, it would be impossible to emit any form of musical sound deliberately without the formation of such a form. It may not take a definite shape such as we saw; that comes from more experience, but it would induce the interplay of numerous colors and blending of colors. In the spirit world all music is color, and all color is music. The one is never existent without the other. That is why the flowers give forth such pleasant tones when they are approached, as it will be remembered of my early experience with flowers. The water that sparkles and flashes colors is also creating musical sounds of purity and beauty. But it must not be imagined that with all this galaxy of color in the spirit world there is also a pandemonium of music going on unremittingly. The eye is not wearied by the fullness of color here. Why should our ears be wearied by the sweet sound the colors send forth? The answer is that they are not, because the sounds are in perfect accord with the colors, as the colors are with the sounds. And the perfect combination of both sight and sound is *perfect harmony*.

Harmony is a fundamental law here. There can be no confliction. I do not suggest that we are in a state of perfection. We should be an immensely higher realm if we were, but we are in perfection in so far as this realm is concerned. If we, as individuals, become more perfect than the realm in which we live, we, *ipso facto*, become worthy of advancing to a higher state, and we do so. But while we are where we are, in this realm or higher, we are living in a state of perfection according to the limits of that realm.

I have dwelt rather at length upon our musical experiences because of the great position of music in our lives and in the realm in which we are living. The whole attitude to music held by so many people of the earth undergoes a great change when they eventually come to spirit. Music is looked upon by many on the earth-plane as merely a pleasant diversion, a pleasant adjunct to the earthly life, but by no means a necessity. Here it is part of our life, not because we make it so, but because it is part of natural existence, as are flowers and trees, grass and water, and hills and dales. It is an element of spiritual nature. Without it a vast deal of the joy would depart out of our lives. We do not need to become master-musicians to appreciate the wealth of music that surrounds us in color and sound, but as in so many other features of this life, we accept and enjoy to the full, and in the enjoyment of our heritage we can afford to smile at those who persist in believing that we live in a world of emptiness.

A world of emptiness! What a shock so many people have upon their coming into the spirit world, and how immensely glad and relieved they are to find that it turns out quite pleasant after all; that it is not a terrifying place; that it is not one stupendous temple of hymn-singing religion; and that they are able to feel *at home* in the land of their new life. When this joyful realization has come to them, some of them are reminded that they looked upon the various descriptions of this life, that have come from us from time to time, as "rather material"! And how pleased they are to discover that it is so. What is it, if it is not "material"? The musicians that we heard playing were playing upon very real, solid instruments from very real music. The conductor was a very real person, conducting his orchestra with a very material baton! But the beautiful musical thought-form was *not* so very material as were its surroundings or the means to create it, in just the same relative way as an earthly rainbow, and the sun and moisture that cause it.

At the risk of making myself very tedious I have reverted more than once to this strange fallacy that the world I am living in, here in spirit, is vague and shadowy. It is strange that some minds strive always to banish from the world of spirit every tree and flower, and the other thousand and one delights. There is something of conceit in this—that makes such things exclusive to the earth world. At the same time, if any soul thinks that such things have no business to exist in the spirit world, he is at liberty to abstain from both the sight and enjoyment of them by betaking himself to some barren spot where his susceptibilities will not be offended by such earthly objects as trees and flowers and water (and even human beings), and there he can give himself up to a state of beatific contemplation, surrounded by the heavenly nothingness that he thinks should be heaven proper. No soul is forced into an unwilling task here, nor into surroundings that he considers uncongenial. I venture to assert that it will not be long before such a soul emerges from his retreat and joins his fellows in the enjoyment of all the delights of God's heaven. There is just one fault—among one or two others—that the earth world possesses: the overwhelming superiority, in its own mind, over every other world, but principally over the spirit world. We can afford to be amused, though our amusement turns to sadness when we see the distress of souls upon their arrival here, when they realize that they are, at last, faced with eternal truth beyond all question or doubt. It is then that humility so often sets in! But we never reproach. The reproaching comes from within each soul itself.

And what, perhaps, it will be asked, has all this to do with our musical experiences? Just this: that after every new experience I have thought the same thoughts, and very nearly spoken the same words to both Ruth and Edwin. Ruth has always echoed my words; Edwin has always been in agreement with me, though, of course, what we were seeing was not new to him by any means. But he still marveled at all things here, as indeed do we all, whether we have but just arrived, or whether we have been over here many years of earth time.

As we walked along after the concert, Edwin pointed out to us the dwelling places of many of the teachers in the various halls of learning, who preferred to live close to the seats of their work. They were, for the most part, unpretentious houses, and it would have been comparatively easy to guess the occupation of the owner, so we were told, from the various evidences within of their work. Edwin said that we should always be welcome should we ever wish to call upon any of the teachers. The exclusiveness which must necessarily surround such people when they are incarnate vanishes when they come into spirit. All values become drastically altered in such matters. The teachers themselves do not cease their own studies because they are teaching. They are ever investigating and learning, and passing on to their pupils what they have thus gained. Some have progressed to a higher realm, but they still retain their interest in their former sphere, and continuously visit it—and their many friends—to pursue their teaching.

But we have already spent some time on this subject, and Edwin is waiting to take us on to other places of importance in the city.

CHAPTER EIGHT

PLANS FOR FUTURE WORK

A SHORT WALK brought us to a large rectangular building which, our friend informed us, was the hall of science, and my fair companion and I were at a loss to know how science, as we always understood the word on earth, could have any place in the spirit world. However, we were soon to learn many things, the chief of which was that the earth world has the spirit world to thank for all the major scientific discoveries that have been made throughout the centuries.

The laboratories of the world of spirit are many decades in advance of those of the earth-plane. And it will be years before many revolutionary discoveries are allowed to be sent through to the earth world, because the earth has not yet sufficiently progressed.

Neither Ruth nor I had any very great leaning towards science and engineering, and Edwin, knowing our taste in this direction, proposed that we should give but a moment or two to this particular hall.

In the hall of science every field of scientific and engineering investigation, study, and discovery was covered, and here were to be seen so many of those men whose names have become household words, and who, since passing into spirit, have continued their life's work with their fellow scientists with the full and immense resources of the spirit world at their command. Here they can solve those mysteries that baffled them when they were on earth. There is no longer any such thing as personal rivalry. Reputations have no more to be made, and the many material handicaps are abandoned forever. It follows that where such a gathering of savants can exist, together with their unlimited resources, the results must be correspondingly great. In the past ages all the epoch-making discoveries have come from the spirit world. Of himself, incarnate man can do very little. Most people are content to consider the earth-world as sufficient unto itself. Indeed it is not! The scientist is fundamentally a man of vision; it may be limited, but it is there nevertheless. And our own spirit scientists can—and do—impress their earthly colleagues with the fruits of their investigation. In many cases where two men are working upon the same problem, the one who is in spirit will be far ahead of his confrere who is still on earth. A hint from the former is very often enough to set the latter upon the right track, and the result is a discovery for the benefit of humanity. In so many cases humanity has so benefited, but, alas, in so many cases humanity has suffered sorrow and tribulation through the devilish perversion of those discoveries. Every one of them that is sent from the spirit world is for the advantage and spiritual progression of man. If perverted minds use those same things for the destruction of man, then man has only himself to blame. That is why I affirmed that the earth world has not spiritually progressed enough to have many more splendid inventions that have already been perfected here. They are ready and waiting, but if they were sent through to the earth-plane in its present state of spiritual mind, they would be misused by unscrupulous people.

The people of the earth have it in their power to see that modern inventions are employed solely for their spiritual and material good. When the time comes that real spiritual progress is made, then the earth-plane can expect a flood of new inventions and discoveries to come through from the scientists and engineers of the spirit world. But the earth-plane has a long and sorrowful way to go before that time comes. And in the meantime the work of the spirit scientist continues.

We in spirit do not require the many inventions of the earth-plane. I think I have sufficiently indicated that our laws are totally different from those of the earth-plane. We have no use for inventions that will increase our speed of travel as with you. Our own method of transit is as rapid as thought, because thought is the motive power. We have no need for methods of saving life, because we are indestructible. We have no need for the hundreds of inventions to make life easier, safer, more comfortable and enjoyable, because our life is all that, and more than that already. But in this hall of science many, many devoted men were working for the betterment of the earth-plane through the medium of their researches, and lamenting that so much could not be given to the earth because it would not be safe as yet to do so.

We were permitted to see the progress that had been made in locomotion, and we were amazed at the advance that had been made since the days when we were on the earth-plane. But that is as nothing to that which is to come. When man exercises his will in the right direction, there will be no end to the enormous rewards that he will gain in material progress, but material progress must go hand in hand with spiritual progress. And until they do the earth world will not be permitted to have the many inventions that are ready and waiting to be sent through.

The generality of people of the earth world are very stubborn. They resent any encroachment on their preserves, or upon what they have presumptuously claimed as their preserves. It was never intended that when the results of our scientists' researches are communicated to the earth they were to be seized upon by the few to the exclusion of all others. Those that have done so find that they have to pay a very heavy price for their brief span of earthly prosperity. Neither was it intended that the two worlds, ours and yours, should be as they are now—so far apart in thought and contact. The day will assuredly come when our two worlds will be closely interrelated, when communication between the two will be a commonplace of life, and then the great wealth of resources of the spirit world will be open to the earth world, to draw upon for the benefit of the whole human race.

The sight of so much activity on the part of my fellow inhabitants of this realm had set my mind to thinking about my own future work and what form it could take. I had no very definite ideas upon the matter, and so I mentioned my difficulty to Edwin. Ruth, it seems, was troubled similarly, so there were the two of us, having, for the first time since our arrival, some small feelings of restlessness. Our old friend was not the least surprised; he would have been more surprised, he said, if we had felt otherwise. It was a sensation common to all, sooner or later—the urge to be doing something useful for the good of others. It was not that we were tired of seeing our own land, but that we had rather a self-conscious feeling. Edwin assured us that we could continue to go upon our explorations indefinitely if we so wished, and that none would criticize or comment upon our actions. It would thus be treated as a matter of our own concern. However, we both felt that we should like to settle the question of our future work, and we appealed accordingly for the guidance of our good friend. Edwin suggested at once that we repair to the borders of the higher realms, where, it will be recalled, he said earlier we should be able to go into this matter. And so we left the hall of science, and once more we found ourselves on the outskirts of our realm.

We were taken to a very beautiful house, which from its appearance and situation was clearly of a higher degree than those farther inland. The atmosphere was more rarefied, and as far as I could observe we were approximately upon the same spot as on our first visit to the boundary. Edwin led us into the house with all the freedom in the world, and bade us welcome. As soon as we entered I knew instinctively that he was giving us welcome to *his own home.* Strange to say, we had never inquired about his home or where it was situated. He said he had purposely kept our minds off the subject, but that was only his natural diffidence. Ruth was enchanted with everything she saw, and scolded him for not telling us all about it much sooner. The house was built of stone throughout, and although to the eye it might have appeared somewhat bare, yet friendliness emanated from every corner. The rooms were not large, but of medium size, and suitable for all Edwin's purposes. There were plenty of comfortable chairs, and many well-lined bookshelves. But it was the general feeling of calm and peace that pervaded the whole dwelling that struck us most forcibly.

Edwin bade us be seated and make ourselves at home. There was no need for us to hurry, and we could discuss our problem *in extenso.* At the outset I frankly admitted that I had no particular ideas upon what I could do. While on earth I had been fortunate enough to be able to follow my own inclinations, and I had had, consequently, a busy life. But my work was finished—at least in one respect—when my earthly life ended. Edwin then proposed that perhaps I would like to join him in his work, which was principally concerned with taking in hand newly-arrived souls whose religious beliefs were the same as we had held upon earth, but who, unlike ourselves, were unable as yet to realize the truth of the change they had made, and of the unreality of so much of their religion.

Much as I liked my friend's proposal, I did not feel competent enough to undertake such work, but Edwin waved aside my objection. I should, he said, work with him—at first at any rate. When I had become used to the task I could continue independently if I so wished. Speaking from experience, Edwin said that two or more people—and here he glanced at Ruth—could very often give far greater help to an individual soul than could one working entirely alone. The weight of numbers seemed to have a greater power of conviction upon one who was particularly stubborn in holding on to his old earthly religious ideas. Since Edwin felt that I would be of real service to him, I was very pleased to accept his offer to join forces with him. And here Ruth brought herself forward as another candidate for service under him, subject, of course, to his approval. Not only was the latter instantly forthcoming, but her offer was gratefully accepted. There was much, said he, that a young woman could do, and the three of us, working in such complete harmony and amity, should be able to do some useful work together. I was more than glad that Ruth was to join us, since it meant that our happy party would not be broken up.

There was, however, another matter that was in my mind, and it concerned that one particular book that I wished I had not written when I was on earth. I was not rendered unhappy by the thought of this still persisting, but I wanted to be free of it, and although, no doubt, my new work would eventually bring me that complete peace of mind, I felt that I would like to deal with the matter in a more direct way. Edwin knew what I was hinting at, and he recalled to me what he had already said about the difficulties of communication with the earth world. But he had also mentioned that we might seek guidance from higher up. If I still wished to try my hand at communication then we might appeal for that guidance and advice now, and thus we could settle the whole question of my future work.

Edwin then left us and retired into another room. I had hardly been chatting with Ruth for a moment about our new occupation when our old friend returned bringing with him a very striking looking man who, I knew at once, had come from a higher sphere in answer to Edwin's call. He did not appear to be one of our own countrymen, and my observation was correct, since he was an Egyptian, as Edwin told us later on. He spoke our own tongue perfectly. Edwin introduced us, and explained my wishes and the possible difficulties of their fulfillment.

Our visitor was possessed of a very strong personality, and he gave one the strong impression of calmness and placidity. He would, one imagined, always remain perfectly unruffled.

We all seated ourselves comfortably, and Edwin acquainted him with the extent of my knowledge concerning communication with the earth world.

The Egyptian placed some considerations before me. If, said our visitor, I was fully determined that by returning to the earth-plane to speak I should retrieve the situation that was giving me cause to regret, then he would do everything to assist me to achieve my purpose. It would not be possible to do what I wanted, though, for some years to come. But in the meantime I was to accept his definite assurance that I should eventually be able to communicate, and he made me a promise to that effect. If I would have patience, all should be as I wished. I was to leave the whole matter in the hands of those who had the ordering of these things, and all would be well. The time—to use an earthly term—would soon pass, and the occurrence of certain events, meanwhile, would make the path clear and would provide the requisite opportunity.

It must be remembered that what I was asking was not merely to return to the earth-plane to endeavor to record the fact that I still lived! What I wanted was to try to undo something that I wished I had never done. And it was a task, I could see, that could not be accomplished in a moment. What I had written I could never unwrite, but I could ease my mind by telling the truth, as I now know it, to those who were still on the earth-plane.

The kindly Egyptian then rose and we shook hands. He congratulated us on the way we had accustomed ourselves to our new conditions of life, wished us joy of our new work whenever we should start, and finally gave me a repeated promise that my own particular wishes should have their certain fulfillment. I tried to express my gratitude for all his help, but he would not hear of it, and with a wave of the hand he was gone. We remained for a while discussing our plans—I was looking forward keenly to starting our work.

It must not be thought that we were part of a campaign to convert people, in the religious sense in which that word is used on earth. Far from it. We do not interfere with people's beliefs nor their viewpoints; we only give our services when they are asked for in such matters, or when we see that by giving them we can effect some useful purpose. Neither do we spend our time walking about evangelizing people, but when the call comes for help then we answer it instantly. But there comes a time when spiritual unrest will make itself felt, and that is the turning point in the life of many a soul who has been confined and restricted by wrong views, whether religious or otherwise. Religion is not responsible for all mistaken ideas!

There is a surprising number of people who do not realize that they have passed from the earth in the death of the physical body. Resolutely they will not believe that they are what the earth world calls "dead." They are dimly aware that some sort of change has taken place, but what that change is they are not prepared to say. Some, after a little explanation—and even demonstration—can grasp what has actually happened; others are stubborn, and will be convinced only after prolonged reasoning. In the latter case we are ofttimes obliged to leave such a soul for a while to allow a little quiet contemplation to work its way. We know we shall be sought out the instant that soul feels the power of our reasoning. In many respects it is tiring work, though I use the word "tiring" in its strictly limited sense of the spirit world.

Ruth and I were both more than grateful to Edwin for his generous help in our affairs, and I was particularly so, both to him and the Egyptian, for the excellent prospect of communicating with the earth world. In view of our decisions to cooperate with Edwin in his work he made the suggestion that as we had seen a little—but only a very little—of our own realm, we might now profitably make a visit to the dark realms. Ruth and I both concurred, adding that we had by now sufficient self-confidence to withstand anything of an unpleasant nature that might be before us. We should, of course, be under the immediate protection and guidance of our old friend. Needless to say that without this we should not have attempted to go, even had we been permitted.

We left Edwin's beautiful house, quickly traversed our own realm, and again we were on the borders of the lower realms. Edwin warned us that we should feel that sense of chilling which we experienced before, but that by an effort of will we could throw it off. He placed himself in the middle of us, Ruth and I each taking one of his arms. He turned and looked at us, and was apparently satisfied with what he saw. I glanced at Ruth and I noticed that her robe—as had Edwin's—had taken on a dull color, approaching almost grey. Looking at myself I discovered that my own dress had undergone a similar change. This was certainly perplexing, but our friend explained that this toning down of our natural colors was but the operation of a natural law, and did not mean that we had lost what we had already gained. The practical application of such a law meant that we should not be conspicuous in uncongenial surroundings, nor should we carry the light of our realm into those dark places to blind the vision of those who dwelt there.

We were walking along a great tract of barren country. The ground was hard under foot; the green of trees and grass was gone. The sky was dull and leaden, and the temperature had dropped very considerably, but we could feel an internal warmth that counteracted it. Before us we could see nothing but a great bank of mist that gathered in density as we advanced, until finally we were within it. It swirled round in heavy, damp clouds, and it seemed almost like a dead weight as it pressed upon us. Suddenly a figure loomed out of the mist and came towards us. He was the first person we had met as yet, and recognizing Edwin, he gave him a friendly greeting. Edwin introduced us and told him of our intentions. He said he would like to join us, as perhaps he could be of some help to us, and we readily accepted his kind offer. We resumed our journey, and after a further passage through the mist, we found that it began to clear a little until it vanished altogether. We could now see our surroundings clearly. The landscape was bleak in the extreme with, here and there, a dwelling house of the meanest order. We came closer to one of the latter, and we were able to examine it better.

It was a small, squat house, squarely built, devoid of ornament, and looking altogether thoroughly uninviting. It even had a sinister look in spite of its plainness, and it seemed to repel us from it the nearer we approached it. There was no sign of life to be seen at any of the windows or round about it. There was no garden attached to it; it just stood out by itself, solitary and forlorn. Edwin and our new friend evidently knew both the house and its inmate quite well, for upon going up to the front door, Edwin gave a knock upon it and without waiting for an answer opened it and walked in, beckoning us to follow. We did so and found ourselves in the poorest sort of apology for a house. There was little furniture, and that of the meanest, and at first sight to earthly eyes one would have said that poverty reigned here, and one would have felt the natural sympathy and urge to offer what help one could. But to our spirit eyes the poverty was of the soul, the meanness was of the spirit, and although it roused our sympathy it was sympathy of another kind, of which material help is of no avail. The coldness seemed almost greater within than without, and we were told that it came from the owner of the house himself.

We passed into a back room and met the sole occupant seated in a chair. He made no attempt to rise or give any sign of welcome. Ruth and I remained in the background while the other two went forward to speak to our unwilling "host." He was a man just past middle years. He had something of an air of faded prosperity and the clothes he wore had been obviously neglected, whether through indifference or other causes—in the light of my earthly recollections!—I was unable to say. He rather scowled at the two of us as Edwin brought us forward as new visitors. It was a moment or two before he spoke, and then he railed at us rather incoherently, but we were able to gather that he deemed himself to be suffering under an injustice. Edwin told him in plain terms that he was talking nonsense, because injustice does not exist in the spirit world. A heated argument followed, heated, that is to say, on the part of our host, for Edwin was calm and collected, and in truth, wonderfully kind. Many times did the former glance at Ruth, whose gentle face seemed to brighten the whole dingy place. I, too, looked at Ruth, who held my arm, to see how this strange man was affecting her, but she was unperturbed.

At length he quietened down and seemed much more tractable, and then he and Edwin had some private conversation together. At the end of it he told Edwin that he would think about it, and that he could call again if he wished and bring his friends with him. Upon this he arose from his chair, escorted us to the door, and showed us out. And I observed that he was *almost* becoming affable—though not quite. It was as if he was reluctant to submit to being pleasant. He stood at his front door watching us as we walked away, until we must have been nearly out of sight.

Edwin seemed very pleased with our visit, and then he gave us some particulars of the strange man.

He had, he said, been in spirit some years now, but in his earth life he had been a successful business man—successful, that is, as far as the earth-plane judges such things. He had not thought of much else than his business, and he always considered that any means were justified in gaining his own ends, provided they were legal. He was ruthless in his dealings with all others, and he elevated efficiency to the level of a god. In his home all things—and people—were subservient to him. He gave generously to charity where there was likely to accrue the greatest advantage and credit. He supported his own religion and church with vigor, regularity, and fervor. He felt that he was an ornament to the church, and he was much esteemed by all those connected with it. He added some new portions to the edifice at his own expense, and a chapel was named after him as the donor. But from what Edwin had been able to glean from his story, he had scarcely committed one decent, unselfish action in the whole of his life. His motive was always self-aggrandizement, and he had achieved his purpose on earth at the absolute expense of his life in the spirit world.

And now his grievance was that after having lived such an exemplary life—in his own estimation—he should be condemned to live in such comparative squalor. He refused to see that he had *condemned himself* to it, and that there was none other to blame but himself. He complained that the church had misled him all along, since his munificence had been received in such fashion that he believed his gifts to the church would weigh heavily in his favor in the "hereafter." Again he could not see that it is motive that counts, and that a happy state in the spirit world cannot be bought for hard cash. A small service willingly and generously performed for a fellow mortal builds a greater edifice in spirit to the glory of God than do large sums of money expended upon ecclesiastical bricks and mortar erected to the glory of man—with full emphasis upon the donor.

This man's present mood was anger, which was all the greater because he had never been denied anything whilst upon the earth. He had never been accustomed to such degrading circumstances as those at present. His difficulties were increased by the fact that he did not know quite whom to blame. Expecting a high reward, he had been cast into the depths. He had made no real friends. There seemed to be no one—of his own social position, he said—who could advise him in the matter. Edwin had tried to reason with him, but he was in an unreasoning frame of mind, and had been so for some long time. He had had few visitors because he repelled them, and although Edwin had made many visits to him, the result was always the same—a stolid adherence to his sense of injustice.

Upon Edwin's latest call, in company with Ruth and myself, and with the friend whom we had met on the way, there were distinct symptoms of a coming change. They were not manifest at first, but as our visit drew to a close he had shown signs of relenting from his stubborn attitude. And Edwin was sure that it was due as much to Ruth's softening presence as to his own powers of reasoning with him. He felt sure, too, that were we to return to him on our way back, we should find him in a different frame of mind altogether. He would be unwilling to admit too soon that the fault was his entirely, but perseverance will work wonders.

Ruth was naturally pleased that she had been able to be of service so quickly, though she disavowed any claim to have done anything but merely stand there as an observer! Edwin, however, at once pointed out to her that while she disclaimed any action of an external order, she had shown a real sympathy and sorrow for this unhappy man. That explained his frequent glances at her. He had felt that commiseration, and it had done him good, although he was unaware of the cause of it. And here Ruth begs me to add that her very small share would have been of little use in this man's recovery had it not been for Edwin's long and unceasing work on his behalf.

This was our first encounter with unfortunates of the lower spheres, and I have been somewhat protracted in giving details of it. It was, in many respects, straightforward by comparison with what we met later, and in recounting it I have done so because it was an introduction to our future work. For the present, however, it was not intended that we should do anything but make our observations of the dark realms.

The four of us resumed our journey. There were no paths to follow, and the ground was becoming decidedly rocky in formation. The light was rapidly diminishing from a sky that was heavy and black. There was not a soul, not a house, nor any sign of life to be seen. The whole district seemed colorless and empty, and we might have been wandering in another world. We could see dimly ahead of us, after the passage of some time, something which had the appearance of dwellings, and we moved in their direction.

The terrain was now rocks and nothing else, and here and there we could see people seated with their heads down, seemingly almost lifeless, but in reality in the depths of gloom and despair. They took no notice of us whatever as we passed them, and very soon we drew level with the dwellings we had viewed distantly.

CHAPTER NINE

THE DARK REALMS

A T CLOSE view it became clear that these dwellings were nothing more than mere hovels. They were distressing to gaze upon, but it was infinitely more distressing to contemplate that these were the fruits of men's lives upon earth. We did not enter any of the shacks—it was repulsive enough outside, and we could have served no useful purpose at present by going in. Edwin therefore gave us a few details instead.

Some of the inhabitants, he said, had lived here, or hereabouts, year after year—as time is reckoned upon earth. They themselves had no sense of time, and their existence had been one interminable continuity of darkness through no one's fault but their own. Many had been the good souls who had penetrated into these Stygian realms to try to effect a rescue out of the darkness. Some had been successful; others had not. Success depends not so much upon the rescuer as upon the rescued. If the latter shows no glimmer of light in his mind, no desire to take a step forward on the spiritual road, then nothing, literally nothing, can be done. The urge *must* come from within the fallen soul himself. And how low some of them had fallen! Never must it be supposed that those who, in the earth's judgment, had failed spiritually, are fallen low. Many such have not failed at all, but are, in point of fact, worthy souls whose fine reward awaits them here. But on the other hand, there are those whose earthly lives have been spiritually hideous though outwardly sublime; whose religious profession designated by a Roman collar, has been taken for granted as being synonymous with spirituality of soul. Such people have been mocking God throughout their sanctimonious lives on earth where they lived with an empty show of holiness and goodness. Here they stand revealed for what they are. But the God they have mocked for so long does not punish. *They punish themselves.*

The people living within these hovels that we were passing were not necessarily those who upon earth had committed some crime in the eyes of the earth people. There were many people who, without doing any harm, *had never, never done any good to a single mortal upon earth.* People who had lived entirely unto themselves, without a thought for others. Such souls constantly harped upon the theme that they had done no harm to anyone. But they had harmed themselves.

As the higher spheres had created all the beauties of those realms, so had the denizens of these lower spheres built up the appalling conditions of their spirit life. There was no light in the lowest realms; no warmth, no vegetation, no beauty. But there is hope—hope that every soul there will progress. It is in the power of each soul to do so, and nothing stands in his way but himself. It may take him countless thousands of years to raise himself one inch spiritually, but it is an inch in the right direction.

The thought inevitably came into my mind of the doctrine of eternal damnation, so beloved by orthodox religion, and of the everlasting fires of so-called hell. If this place we were now in could be called hell—and no doubt it would be by theologians—then there was certainly no evidence of fire or heat of any kind. On the contrary, there was nothing but a cold, dank atmosphere. Spirituality means warmth in the spirit world; lack of spirituality means coldness. The whole fantastic doctrine of hellfire—a fire which burns but never consumes—is one of the most outrageously stupid and ignorant doctrines that has ever been invented by equally stupid and ignorant churchmen. Who actually invented it no one knows, but it is still rigorously upheld as a doctrine by the church. Even the smallest acquaintance with spirit life instantly reveals the utter impossibility of it, because it is against the very laws of spirit existence. This concerns its literal side. What of the shocking blasphemy that it involves?

When Edwin, Ruth, and I were on earth we were asked to believe that God, the Father of the Universe, punishes—*actually punishes*—people by condemning them to burn in the flames of hell for all eternity. Could there ever be any grosser travesty of the God that orthodoxy professes to worship? The churches—of whatever denomination—have built up a monstrous conception of the Eternal Father of Heaven. They have made of Him, on the one hand, a mountain of corruption by shallow lip service, by spending large sums of money to erect churches and chapels to His "glory," by pretending a groveling contrition for having "offended Him," by professing to fear Him—*fear* Him

Who is all love! And on the other hand, we have the picture of a God Who, without the slightest compunction, casts poor human souls into an eternity of the worst of all sufferings—burning by fires that are unquenchable.

We are taught glibly to beg for God's mercy. The church's God is a Being of extraordinary moods. He must be continually placated. It is by no means certain that, having begged for mercy, we shall get it. He must be feared—because He can bring down His vengeance upon us at any moment; we do not know when He will strike. He is vengeful and unforgiving. He has commanded such trivialities as are embodied in church doctrines and dogmas that at once expose not a great mind, but a small one. He has made the doorway to "salvation" so narrow that few, very few souls will ever be able to pass through it. He has built up on the earth-plane a vast organization known as "the Church," which shall be the sole depository of spiritual truth—an organization that knows practically *nothing* of the state of life in the world of spirit, yet *dares* to lay down the law to incarnate souls, and *dares* to say what is in the mind of the Great Father of the Universe, and *dares* to discredit His name by assigning to Him attributes that *He could not possibly possess*. What do such silly, petty minds know of the Great and Almighty Father of Love? Mark that!—of *Love*. Then think again of all the horrors I have enumerated. And think once more. Contemplate this: a heaven of all that is beautiful, a heaven of more beauty than the mind of man incarnate can comprehend; a heaven, of which one tiny fragment I have tried to describe to you, where all is peace and goodwill and love among fellow mortals. All these things are built up by the inhabitants of these realms, and are upheld by the Father of Heaven in His love for all mankind.

What of the lower realms—the dark places we are now visiting? It is the very fact that we are visiting them that has led me to speak in this fashion, because standing in this darkness I am fully conscious of one great reality of eternal life, and that is that the high spheres of heaven are within the reach of every mortal soul that is, or is yet to be, born upon earth. The potentialities of progression are unlimited, and they are the right of every soul. God condemns no one. Man condemns himself, but he does not condemn himself eternally; it rests with himself as to when he shall move forward spiritually. Every spirit hates the lower realms for the unhappiness that is there, and for no other reason. And for that reason great organizations exist to help every single soul who is living in them to rise out of them into the light. And that work will continue through countless ages until every soul is brought out from these hideous places, and at last all is as the Father of the Universe intended it to be.

This, I am afraid, has been a long digression, so let us return to our travels. You will recall my mention of the many heavenly perfumes and scents that come from the flowers and that float upon the air. Here in these dark places the very opposite was the case. Our nostrils were at first assailed by the most foul odors; odors that reminded us of the corruption of flesh in the earth world. They were nauseating, and I feared that it would prove more than Ruth—and indeed I, myself—could stand, but Edwin told us to treat them in the same way as we had mastered the coldness of the temperature—by simply closing our minds to them—and that we should be quite unaware of their existence. We hastened to do so, and we were perfectly successful. It is not only "sanctity" that has its odor!

In our travels through our own realm we can enjoy all the countless delights and beauties of it, together with the happy converse of its inhabitants. Here in these dark lands all is bleak and desolate. The very low degree of light itself casts a blight upon the whole region. Occasionally we were able to catch a glimpse of the faces of some unfortunates as we passed along. Some were unmistakably evil, showing the life of vice they had led upon the earth; some revealed the miser, the avaricious, the "brute beast." There were people here from almost every walk of earthly life, from the present earthly time to far back in the centuries. And here was a connecting link with names that could be read in those truthful histories of nations in the library we visited in our own realm. Both Edwin and his friend told us that we should be appalled at the catalogue of names, well known in history, of people who were living deep down in these noxious regions—men who had perpetrated vile and wicked deeds in the name of holy religion, or for the furtherance of their own despicable, material ends. Many of these wretches were unapproachable, and they would remain so—perhaps for numberless more centuries—until, of their own wish and endeavor, they moved however feebly in the direction of the light of spiritual progression.

We could see, as we walked along, whole bands of seemingly demented souls passing on their way upon some prospective evil intent—if they could find their way to it. Their bodies presented the outward appearance of the most hideous and repulsive malformations and distortions, the absolute reflection of their evil minds. Many of them seemed old in years, but I was told that although such souls had been there perhaps for many centuries, it was not the passage of time that had so dealt with their faces, but their wicked minds.

In the higher spheres the beauty of mind rejuvenates the features, sweeps away the signs of earthly cares and troubles and sorrows, and presents to the eye that state of physical development which is at that period of our earthly lives which we used to call "the prime of life."

The multitudinous sounds that we heard were in keeping with the awful surroundings, from mad raucous laughter to the shriek of some soul in torment—torment inflicted by others as bad as himself. Once or twice we were spoken to by some courageous souls who were down there upon their task of helping these afflicted mortals. They were glad to see us and to talk to us. In the darkness we could see them and they could see us, but we were all of us invisible to the rest, since we were provided with the same protection for the dark lands. In our case Edwin was taking care of us collectively as newcomers, but those whose work lies in rescue had each his own means of protection.

If any priest—or theologian—could have but one glimpse of the things that Edwin, Ruth, and I saw here, he would never say again, as long as he lived, that God, the Father of Love, could ever condemn any mortal to such horrors. The same priest, seeing these places, would not himself condemn anyone to them. Is he more kind and merciful than the Father of Love Himself? No! It is man alone who qualifies himself for the state of his existence after he passes into spirit.

The more we saw of the dark lands the more I realized how fantastic is the teaching of the orthodox church to which I belonged when on earth, that the place which is referred to as eternal hell is ruled over by a Prince of Darkness, whose sole aim is to get every soul into his clutches, and from whom there is no escape once a soul has entered his kingdom. Is there such an entity as the Prince of Darkness? There might conceivably be one soul infinitely worse than all the others, perhaps it will be said, and such as he could be considered as the very King of Evil. Edwin told us that there was no evidence whatever of such a personage. There were those from the upper spheres who had traversed every inch of the lower realms, and they had discovered no such being. There were also those whose knowledge was prodigious, and who positively affirmed that the existence of such a person had no foundation in fact. Doubtless there are many who, collectively, are a great deal more evil than their fellows in darkness. The idea that a King of Evil exists, whose direct function is to oppose the King of Heaven, is stupid; it is primitive and even barbaric. The Devil as a solitary individual does not exist, but an evil soul might be called a devil, and in that case there are many, many devils. It is this fraternity, according to the teachings of one orthodox church, that constitutes the sole element of spirit return. We can afford to laugh at the absurdities of such teachings. It is no novelty for some wondrous and illustrious spirit to be called a devil! We still retain our sense of humor, and it causes us very great amusement, sometimes, to hear some stupid priest, spiritually blind, professing to know about things of the spirit of which, in reality, he is totally and completely ignorant. The spirit people have broad backs, and they can support the weight of such fallacious rubbish without experiencing anything but pity for such poor blind souls.

It is not my intention to go into further details of these dark spheres. At least, not at present. The Church's method of frightening people is not the method of the spirit world. Rather would we dwell upon the beauties of the spirit world, and try to show something of the glories that await every soul when his earthly life is ended. It remains with every single soul individually whether this beautiful land shall be his lot sooner, or whether it shall be later.

We held a short consultation together, and decided that we should now like to return to our own realm. And so we made our way back to the land of mist, passed quickly through, and once again we were in our own heavenly country with the warm, balmy air enveloping us. Our new friend of the dark realms then left us after we had expressed our thanks for his kindly services. I then bethought me that it was high time I went to have a peep at my house, and so I asked Ruth and Edwin to join me, as I had no wish to be alone or separated from their pleasant company. Ruth had not yet seen my home, but she had often wondered—so she said—what it would be like. And I thought that a little of the fruit from the garden would be most acceptable after our visit—short though it was—to the lower realms.

Everything in the house was in perfect order—as I left it to go upon our travels—as though there were someone permanently looking after it. Ruth expressed her complete approval of all she saw, and congratulated me upon my choice of a home.

In reply to my query as to the invisible agency that was responsible for the good order of the house during my absence, Edwin answered me by himself asking the question: what is there to disturb the order of the house? There can be no dust, because there is no decay of any sort whatsoever. There can be no dirt, because here in spirit there is nothing to cause it. The household duties that are so very familiar and so very irksome on the earth-plane, are here non-existent. The necessity for providing the body with food was abandoned when we abandoned our physical body. The adornments of the home, such as the hangings and upholstery, do not ever need renewal, because they do not perish. They endure until we wish to dispense with them for something else. And so what remains that might require attention? We have, then, but to walk out of our houses, leaving all doors and windows open—our houses have no locks upon them! And we can return when we wish—to find that everything is as we left it. We might find some difference, some improvement. We might discover, for instance, that some friend had called while we were away, and had left some gift for us, some beautiful flowers, perhaps, or some other token of kindness. Otherwise we shall find that our house bids us welcome itself, and renews our feeling of "being at home."

Ruth had wandered all over the house by herself—we have no stupid formalities here—and I had asked her to make the whole house her own whenever she wished, and to do whatever she liked. The antique style of the architecture appealed to her artistic nature, and she reveled in the old wooden paneling and carvings—the latter being my own embellishments—of the past ages. She eventually came to my small library, and was interested to see my own works among the others upon the shelves. One book, in particular, she was attracted to, and was actually perusing it when I entered. The title alone revealed much to her, she said, and then I could feel her sweet sympathy pouring out upon me, as she knew what was my great ambition, and she offered me all the help which she could give me in the future towards the realization of this ambition.

As soon as she had completed her inspection of the house, we foregathered in the sitting-room, and Ruth asked Edwin a question which I had been meaning to ask him myself for some time: Was there a sea somewhere? If there were lakes and streams, then, perhaps there was an ocean? Edwin's answer filled her with joy: Of course, there was a seaside—and a very beautiful one, too; Ruth insisted upon being conducted there at once, and, under Edwin's guidance, we set forth.

We were soon walking along a beautiful stretch of open country with the grass like a green velvet carpet beneath our feet. There were no trees, but there were many fine clumps of healthy-looking shrubs, and, of course, plenty of flowers growing everywhere. At length we arrived at some rising ground, and we felt that the sea must be beyond it. A short walk brought us to the edge of the grassland, and then the most glorious panorama of ocean spread out before us.

The view was simply magnificent. Never had I expected to behold such sea. Its coloring was the most perfect reflection of the blue of the sky above, but in addition it reflected a myriad rainbow tints in every little wavelet. The surface of the water was calm, but this calmness by no means implies that the water was lifeless. There is no such thing as lifeless or stagnant water here. From where we were, I could see islands of some considerable size in the distance—islands that looked most attractive and must certainly be visited!

Beneath us was a fine stretch of beach upon which we could see people seated at the water's edge—but there was no suggestion of overcrowding! And floating upon this superb sea, some close at hand—others standing a little way out, were the most beautiful boats—though I think I am not doing them full justice by calling them mere boats. Ships would be more apposite. I wondered who could own these fine vessels, and Edwin told us that we could own one ourselves if we so wished. Many of the owners lived upon them, having no other home but their boat. It made no difference. There they could live always, for here it is perpetual summer.

A short walk down a pleasant winding path brought us to a sandy seashore. Edwin informed us that it was a tideless ocean, and that at no place was it very deep by comparison with terrestrial seas. Storms of wind being impossible here, the water was always smooth, and in common with all water in these realms, it was of a pleasantly warm temperature that could occasion no feelings of cold—or even chilliness—to bathers. It was, of course, perfectly buoyant, possessed no single harmful element or characteristic, but it was, on the contrary, life-sustaining. To bathe in its waters was to experience a perfect manifestation of spiritual force. The sand upon which we were walking had none of the unpleasant features associated with the seashore of the earth-plane. It was never tiring to walk on. Although it had every appearance of sand as we had always known it, yet to the tread it was firm in consistency although soft to the touch of the hand. In fact, this peculiar quality rendered it more like well-kept lawns to walk on, so closely did the grains hold together. We took some handfuls of the sand, and allowed it to run through our fingers, and great was our surprise to find that it lacked every trace of grittiness, but seemed to the touch more akin to some smooth, soft powder. Yet examined closely it was undeniably solid. It was one of the strangest phenomena we had met so far. Edwin said that that was because we had, in this particular instance, carried out a more minute examination of what we were beholding than we had done hitherto in other things. He added that if we chose to make a close scrutiny of all that we saw, whether it be the ground we walked on, the substance of which our houses were made, or the thousand and one other objects that go to make up the world of spirit, we should be living in a state of continual surprise, and there would be revealed to us some small idea—but only a very small idea—of the magnitude of the Great Mind—the Greatest Mind in the Universe—that upholds this and every other world. Indeed, the great scientists of the earth-plane find, when they come to live in the spirit world, that they have a completely new world upon which to commence a fresh course of investigations. They begin *de novo* as it were, but with all their great earthly experience behind them. And what joy it brings them, in company with their scientific colleagues, to probe the mysteries of the spirit world, to collect their data, to compare their new knowledge with the old, to record for the benefit of others the results of their investigations and discoveries. And all through they have the unlimited resources of the spirit world upon which to draw. And joy is in their hearts.

Our little experiment with the sand led us to place our hands in the sea. Ruth fully expected it to taste of salt, but it did not, much to her surprise. As far as I could observe, it had no taste at all! It was sea more by virtue of its great area and the characteristics of the adjacent land than anything else. In all other respects it resembled the water of the brooks and lakes. In general appearance the whole effect was totally unlike the earthly ocean, due, among other things, to the fact that there was no sun to give its light from one quarter only and to cause that change of aspect when the direction of the sunlight changes. The overspreading of light from the great central source of light in the spirit world, constant and unmoving, gives us perpetual day, but it must never be assumed that this constancy and immobility of light means a monotonous and unchanging land- or seascape. There are changes going on the whole time; changes of color such as man never dreamt of—until he comes to the spirit world. The eyes of the spirit person can see so many beautiful things in the world of spirit that the eyes of incarnate man cannot see unless he be gifted with the psychic eye.

We wanted very much to visit one of the islands that we could see in the distance, but Ruth felt that it would be a nice experience to travel over the sea in one of the fine vessels that were close to the shore. But the difficulty arose—that is, it seemed as though it might arise!—as to the boat. If, as I understood, these were "privately" owned, we should first have to become acquainted with one of the owners. Edwin, however, could see how Ruth was so longing to go upon the water that he soon explained the exact position— to her unbounded joy.

It seemed that one of these elegant boats belonged to a friend of his, but had it been otherwise we should have found that we would be welcome to go aboard any one of them, introducing ourselves—if we wished to observe that formality, though it was unnecessary—to whomsoever we found on board. Had we not already received, wherever we went, that friendly reception and assurance that we were welcome? Then why should there be any departure, in the case of the boats of the sea, from the fundamental rule of hospitality that operates in the spirit world? Edwin drew our attention to a very beautiful yacht that was riding "at anchor" close to the shore. From where we were she had all the appearance of having had much attention devoted to her—our opinion was afterwards confirmed. She was built on the most graceful lines, and the grand upward sweep of her bows held the promise of power and speed. She looked much the same as an earthly yacht, that is, *externally*.

Edwin sent a message across to the owner, and in reply received an instantaneous invitation to us all. We therefore wasted no time, and we found ourselves upon the deck of this most handsome vessel, being greeted with great good cheer by our host, who immediately took us off to present us to his wife. She was very charming, and it was obvious to see that the two made a perfect couple. Our host could see that Ruth and I were both very keen to see over the boat, and knowing from Edwin that we had not been long in spirit, he was so much the more pleased to do so.

Our first observations at close hand showed us that many devices and fittings that are essential to earthly ships were here absent. That indispensable adjunct, an anchor, for instance. There being no winds, tides, or currents in spirit waters, an anchor becomes superfluous, though we were told that some boat-owners have them merely as an ornament and because they did not feel their vessels would be complete without them. There was unlimited space on deck, with a copious provision of very comfortable looking chairs. Below deck were well-appointed saloons and lounges. Ruth, I could see, was disappointed because she could see no evidence whatever of any motive power to drive the vessel, and she naturally concluded that the yacht was incapable of independent movement. I shared her disappointment, but Edwin had a merry twinkle in his eye which ought to have told me that things are not always what they seem to be in the spirit world. Our host had received our thoughts, and he immediately took us up into the wheelhouse. What was our astonishment when we saw that we were slowly and gently moving away from the shore! The others laughed merrily at our bewilderment, and we ran to the side to watch our progress through the water. There was no mistake about it, we were really on the move, and gathering speed as we went. We returned at once to the wheelhouse, and demanded an instant explanation of this apparent wizardry.

CHAPTER TEN

A VISITATION

O
UR HOST told us that the power of thought is almost unlimited in the spirit world, and that the greater the power of any particular effort or concentration of thought the greater the results. Our means of personal locomotion here is by thought, and we can apply that same means to what the earth world would call "inanimate objects." Of course, in the spirit world nothing is inanimate, and because of this, then our thoughts can have a direct influence upon all the countless things of which the world of spirit is composed. Ships are meant to float and move upon the waters; they are animated by the living force that animates all things here, and if we wish to move them over the water we have but to focus our thoughts in that direction and with that intention, and our thoughts produce the desired result of movement. We could, if we wished, call upon our scientific friends to provide us with splendid machinery to supply the motive power, and they would be only too pleased to oblige us. But we should have to focus our thoughts upon the machinery to make it generate the necessary driving force. Why, then, go this long way round to produce the same result, when we can do so directly and just as efficiently?

But it must not be concluded that anyone can move a boat through the water merely by thinking that it shall do so. It requires, like so many other things, the requisite knowledge, its application upon well-ordered lines, and practice in the art. A natural aptitude greatly helps in these matters, and our host told us that he mastered the subject in a very short time. Once the ability has been gained, it gives one, so he said, a most satisfying feeling of power rightly applied, and not only of power, but the power of thought, in a way that is not perhaps possible in some other ways. Perfect as the movement of ourselves can be through the realms, yet the movement of such a large object as a boat, simply and easily, magnifies the wonder of the whole of spirit life. Our host explained that this was only his own point of view, and was not to be taken as an axiom. His enthusiasm was increased by his enthusiasm for the water and a love of ships.

We noticed that he guided the boat in the usual manner, with a rudder operated by the wheel in the deck-house. That, he said, was because he found it sufficient work to provide the movement of the boat. In time, if he wished, he could combine the two actions in one. But he much preferred to use the old method of steering by hand as it gave him physical work to do, which was, in itself, such a pleasure. Once having given motion to the ship, he could forget about it until he wished to stop. And the mere wishing to stop, however suddenly or gradually, brought the vessel to a standstill. There was no fear of accidents! They do not—cannot—exist in these realms.

All the while our host was explaining these matters to Ruth and me— Edwin was busily engaged in conversation with our host's wife—our speed had increased to a steady rate, and we were moving in the direction of one of the islands. The yacht was traveling through the sea with the most perfect, steady motion. There was no vibration, naturally, from any machinery, but the very movement through the water could be perceptibly felt, while the sounds from the gentle waves as the boat cut along made the loveliest musical notes and harmonies as the many colors of the disturbed water changed their tints and blends. We observed that in our wake the water quickly settled into its former state, leaving no appearance of our having passed through it. Our host handled his craft skillfully, and by increasing or diminishing its speed he could create, by the different degree of movement of the water, the most striking alternations of color and musical sound, the brilliant scintillations of the sea showing how alive it was. It responded to the boat's every movement as though they were in complete unison—as indeed they were.

Ruth was simply ecstatic in her enjoyment, and ran to our host's wife in the full ardor of her new experience. The latter, who fully appreciated her young friend's feelings, was just as enthusiastic. Although it was no novelty, in the sense of a first experience, she said she could never cease to marvel, however familiar she should become with her ship-home, at the glorious dispensation that provided such beauties and pleasures for the dwellers in spirit lands.

We had by now approached sufficiently near to the island to be able to view it quite well, and the boat turned in her course and followed the coastline. After continuing along in this fashion for a little while, we sailed into a small bay which formed a picturesque natural harbor.

The island certainly came up to our expectations in its scenic beauty. There were not many dwellings upon it; those that were to be seen were more summer-houses than anything else. But the great feature of the place was the number of trees, none of them very tall, but all were of particularly vigorous growth. And in the branches we could see scores of the most wonderful birds, whose plumage presented a riot of color. Some of the birds were flying about, others—the larger variety—were walking majestically along the ground. But all of them were unafraid of us. They walked with us as we strolled along, and when we held up our hands, some small bird would be sure to perch upon our fingers. They seemed to know us, to know that any harm coming to them was an utter impossibility. They did not require to make a constant search for food nor exercise a perpetual vigilance against what on earth would be their natural enemies. They were, like ourselves, part of the eternal world of spirit, enjoying in their way, as we do in ours, their eternal life. Their very existence there was just another of those thousands of things that are given to us for our delight.

The birds which had the most gorgeous plumage were evidently of the kind that live in the tropical parts of the earth-plane, and which are never seen by the eye of man until he comes to the spirit world. By the perfect adjustment of temperature they were able to live in comfort with those of less spectacular appearance. And all the while they were singing and twittering in a symphony of sound. It was never wearying, in spite of the quantity of sound that was going on, because in some extraordinary fashion the musical sounds blended with each other. Neither were they piercing in quality despite the fact that many of the small birds' songs were themselves high-pitched. But it was their trusting friendliness that was so delightful by comparison with the earthly birds, whose life there takes them into another world almost. Here we were part of the same free world, and the understanding between the birds and ourselves was reciprocal. When we spoke to them we felt that they knew just what we were saying, and in some subtle way we seemed to know just what *their* thoughts were. To call to any particular bird meant that that bird understood, and it came to us.

Our friends, of course, had encountered all this before, but to Ruth and me it was a new and very wonderful experience. And the thought came to me that had I really considered the matter, and perhaps used my mind a little more, I might have known that we should eventually see something of this sort. For why, I asked myself, should the Great Father of Heaven create all the beautiful birds solely for the earth-plane?—and make them to live in places that are frequently quite inaccessible to man, where he can never see them and enjoy them? And even those that he *can* see and enjoy—are they to perish for ever? Would the far greater world of spirit be denied the beautiful things that are given to the earth world? Here was the answer before and around us. It is in the conceit and self-importance of man that he should think that beauty is expressly created for *his* pleasure while on earth. Incarnate man thinks he has the monopoly of beauty. When he becomes discarnate he eventually wakes up to the fact that he has never really seen *how great* beauty can be, and he becomes silent and humble, perhaps for the first time in his life! It is a salutary lesson, the awakening in spirit, believe me, my dear friend—with many a shock to accompany it.

The perfect blaze of color from all the birds we could see about us was almost too much for us to take in at one visit. They were beyond description, and I shall not even attempt it. We strolled on through delightful groves, past the musical murmuring of the many brooks, through glades of velvet grass, as in an absolute fairyland of nature. We met people on the way, who called a greeting to us, or waved their hands. They were all happy among the birds. We were told that this part of the island was exclusive to the birds, and that no other form of animal life intruded upon them. Not that there was any fear or danger that they would come to harm, because that would be impossible, but because the birds were happier with their own kind.

We eventually returned to the boat, and put to sea again. We were interested to discover whence our host had acquired his floating home. Such an intricate piece of building would require experts, most surely, to plan it, and others to build it. He told us that a boat was evolved under precisely the same conditions as our spirit houses, or any other buildings. A prerequisite is that we must earn the right to possess it. That we understood. What, then, of the many people in spirit who on earth designed and built boats of every description, either as a means of livelihood or as a form of recreation? Would the latter, particularly, abandon such pleasure when they could continue in their handicraft? Here they have the means and the motive to carry on with their task, whether it be for work or for pleasure. And it can be said that though many build their boats for the pleasure of doing so, yet they give great pleasure to many others who have a fondness for the sea and ships. Their pleasure becomes their work, and their work is pleasure.

The task of actually constructing a craft is highly technical, and the methods of the spirit world, so entirely different from those of the earth-plane, have to be mastered. Although we must earn the right to possess in the spirit world, we have the aid of our friends in the actual building. We can form in our minds, when on earth, the shape of something we long to have—

a garden, a home, or whatever it may be. It will then be a thought-form, and will be converted from that into actual spirit substance by the help of experts.

Our return was as delightful as our outward journey. When we drew into the land again, our host extended a permanent invitation to us to visit them on board whenever we wished, and enjoy with them all the recreation of sailing on the sea.

As we walked along the sandy beach Edwin recalled to our minds the great building in the center of the city, by telling us that very shortly there would be a visitation from a being of the higher realms, and for which many would be foregathering in the domed temple. Would we care to join him? It was not in any sense to be considered a specific act of worship for which this personage was visiting the realm. Such things as worship do not require conscious effort (they come spontaneously from the heart), but our visitant would bring with him not only his own radiance, but the radiance of the heavenly sphere which he graced. We at once expressed our eagerness to go with him, as we both felt that we would not have ventured there alone, since we had all along been under Edwin's guidance.

As we walked down the broad avenue of trees and gardens, we formed part of a great concourse of people who were all proceeding in the same direction, and obviously for the same purpose. Strange to say, that although we were among so many people, yet we never experienced the feeling, so common on earth, of being amongst a large crowd. It was an extraordinary feeling, which Ruth shared with me. We supposed that we had expected our old earthly sensations would have overcome us; the fear that in such an immense assembly of people there would be something of the confusion that one is accustomed to on the earth-plane; the jostling and the noise, and above all the sense of time passing, when our enjoyment would be over and passed. To have such ideas as these was quite ridiculous, and Ruth and I laughed at ourselves—as did Edwin—for expressing such notions, or entertaining them for an instant. We felt—because we knew—that everything was in perfect order; that everyone knew what to do or where to go; that there was no question of another's superiority over ourselves for reasons of privilege. We felt that we were expected for the support we should give, and that a personal welcome was waiting for us. Was not this sufficient to banish all feelings of discomfort or uneasiness?

There was, moreover, a unity of mind among us that is not possible on the earth-plane even with those of the same religious beliefs. What earthly religion is there where all its adherents are entirely of one mind? There is none. It has been thought essential on earth that to offer up thanks and worship to the Supreme Being there must be a complexity of ritual and formularies and ceremonies, with creeds and dogmas and strange beliefs, over which there is as much diversity of views as there are numbers of different religions.

It may be said that I have already told of the establishment of communities of those same religions here in the spirit world, so that the spirit world is in no better case than the earth world. When the earth world becomes really enlightened these communities here will disappear. It is the blindness and stupidity of the earth world that causes them to be here at all. They are given tolerance, and they must exercise tolerance themselves, otherwise they would be swept away. They must never attempt to influence or coerce any soul into believing any of their erroneous doctrines. They must confine themselves strictly to themselves but they are perfectly and absolutely free to practice their own false religion among themselves. The truth awaits them on the threshold of their churches as they leave their places of worship, not when they have entered. When a soul at length perceives the futility of his particular and peculiar religious beliefs he quickly dissociates himself from them, and in full freedom and complete truth—which has no creeds or ecclesiastical commandments—he offers up his thoughts to his Heavenly Father just as they flow from his mind, free and unaffected, stripped of all jargon, simple and heartfelt.

But we have our temples where we can receive the great messengers from the highest realms, fitting places to receive the Father's representatives, and where such messengers can send our united thanks and our petitions to the Great Source of all. We do not worship blindly as on earth.

As we drew close to the temple we could already feel ourselves being, as it were, charged with spiritual force. Edwin told us that this was always the case because of the immense power, brought by the higher visitants, which remained undiminished within a wide circle of the temple. It was for this reason that the temple stood completely isolated, with no other buildings near it. Gardens alone surrounded it—a great sea of flowers, extending, it almost seemed, as far as the eye could see, and presenting such a galaxy of brilliant color, in great banks and masses, as the earth could never contemplate. And arising from all this were the most heavenly sounds of music and the most delicate perfumes, the effect upon us being that pure exaltation of the spirit. We felt that we were lifted up above ourselves right out into another realm.

The building itself was magnificent. It was stately, it was grand, it was an inspiration in itself. It appeared to be made of the finest crystal, but it was not transparent. Massive pillars were polished until they shone like the sun, while every carving flashed its brilliant colors until the whole edifice was a temple of light. Never did I think such scintillations possible, for not only did the surfaces reflect the light in the ordinary way, they gave out a light of their own that could be felt spiritually.

Edwin took us to some seats which we knew to be our own—we had that feeling of familiarity with them as one does with a favorite chair at home.

Above us was the great dome of exquisitely wrought gold, which reflected the hundreds of colors that shone from the rest of the building. But the focus of all attention was upon the marble sanctuary—which word I must use for want of a better—at the end of the temple. It had a shallow balustrade with a central opening at the head of a flight of steps leading down on to the floor. We could hear the sounds of music, but whence it came I knew not, because there was no sign of any musicians. The music was evidently provided by a large orchestra—of strings only, for there were no sounds of the other instruments of the orchestra.

The sanctuary, which was of spacious dimensions, was filled with many beings from higher realms, with the exception of a space in the center, which I guessed was reserved for our visitant. We were all of us seated, and we conversed quietly amongst ourselves. Presently we were aware of the presence of a stately figure of a man with jet-black hair, who was closely followed—very much to my surprise—by the kindly Egyptian whom we had met in Edwin's house on the boundary of our realm. To those who had already witnessed such visitations, their arrival was at once the indication of the coming of the high personage, and we all accordingly rose to our feet. Then, before our eyes, there appeared first a light, which might almost be described as dazzling, but as we concentrated our gaze upon it we immediately became attuned to it, and we felt no sensation of spiritual discomfort. In point of fact—as I discovered later—the light really became attuned to *us*; that is to say, it was toned down to accord with ourselves and our realm. It grew in shade to a golden hue upon the extremities, gradually brightening towards the center. And in the center there slowly took shape the form of our visitant. As it gained in density we could see that he was a man whose appearance was that of youth—spiritual youth—but we knew that he carried with him to an unimaginable degree the three comprehensive and all-sufficing attributes of Wisdom, Knowledge, and Purity. His countenance shone with transcendental beauty; his hair was of gold, while round his head was a lustrous diadem. His raiment was of the most gossamer-like quality, and it consisted of a pure white robe bordered with a deep band of gold, while from his shoulders there depended a mantle of the richest cerulean blue, which was fastened upon his breast with a great pink pearl. His movements were majestic as he raised his arms and sent forth a blessing upon us all. We remained standing and silent while our thoughts ascended to Him Who sent us such a glorious being. We sent our thanks and we sent our petitions. For myself, I had one boon to ask, and I asked for it.

It is not possible for me to convey to you one fraction of the exaltation of the spirit that I felt while in the presence, though distant, of this heavenly guest. But I do know that not for long could I have remained in that temple while he was there without undergoing the almost crushing consciousness that I was low, very, very low upon the scale of spiritual evolution and progression. And yet I knew that he was sending out to me, as to us all, thoughts of encouragement, of good hope, of kindness in the very highest degree, that made me feel that I must never, never despair of attaining to the highest spiritual realm, and that there was good and useful work ready for me to do in the service of man, and that in the doing thereof I would have the whole of the spiritual realms behind me—as they are behind every single soul who works in the service of man.

With a final benediction upon us, this resplendent and truly regal being was gone from our sight.

We remained seated for a while, and gradually the temple began to empty. I had no inclination to move, and Edwin told us we could stay as long as we wished. The building was, therefore, practically empty when I saw the figure of the Egyptian approaching us. He greeted us warmly, and asked me if I would be good enough to go with him, as he wished to introduce me to his "master." I thanked him for his continued interest in me, and what was my astonishment when he led me into the presence of the man with whom he had entered the sanctuary. I had only been able to see him from my seat, but close to I could see that a pair of dark sparkling eyes matched his raven hair, which was made the more pronounced by the slight paleness of his complexion. The colors of his attire were blue, white, and gold, and although these were of a very high order, they were not of such intensity as were those of the principal visitor. I had the impression that I was in the presence of a wise man—which indeed he was—and of a man with a great sense of fun and humor. (It must be ever remembered that fun and humor are not, and never will be, the sole prerogative of inhabitants of the earth-plane, however much they may like to claim a monopoly of them, and however much they may like to deny us our lighthearted merriment. We shall continue to laugh in spite of their possible disapproval!)

The kind Egyptian presented me to his master, and the latter took me by the hand and smiled upon me in such a manner as to take away, completely, any feelings of diffidence that I had. In fact, he simply diffused assurance in one's self, and he placed one perfectly at ease. One would, without disrespect, call him the perfect host. When he spoke to me his voice was beautifully modulated, soft in tone, and so very kindly. His words to me filled me with joy even as they left me filled with wonder: "My beloved master," he said, "whom you have just seen, bids me tell you that your prayer is answered, and that you shall have your desire. Fear not, for promises that are made here are always fulfilled." Then he told me that I should be asked to wait for a period before the fulfillment, because it was necessary that a chain of events should take place before the right circumstances were brought about in which my desires should find fruition. The time would soon pass, he said, and I could, meanwhile, carry on with my intended work with my friends. If at any time I wished for advice my good Edwin would always be able to call upon our Egyptian friend, whose guidance was ever at my service. Then he gave me his blessing, and I found myself alone. Alone with my thoughts, and with the abiding memory and the celestial fragrance of our transplendent visitants.

I rejoined Edwin and Ruth, and told them of my happiness. They were both overjoyed at my great good news which had come from so exalted a source. I felt now that I would like to return to my house, and I asked Edwin and Ruth if they would accompany me. Thither we repaired, and we walked straight into my library. Upon one of the shelves was a particular book written by myself when upon the earth-plane, and which I wished that I had never written. I removed the book that was immediately next to it, leaving the space unoccupied. According to my answered prayer I should fill that space with another book, written after I had come to spirit, the product of my mind when I had seen the truth.

And linking arms together, we all three walked out into the garden—and into the heavenly sunshine of eternity.

CHAPTER ELEVEN

THE FLOWERS

AFTER I had passed into the spirit world, one of my earliest experiences was the consciousness of a feeling of sadness, not of my own sadness, for I was supremely happy, but of the sadness of others, and I was greatly puzzled to know whence it came.

Edwin told me that this sadness was rising from the earth world, and was caused by the sorrow felt at my passing. It soon ceased, however, and Edwin informed me that forgetfulness of me by the earth people had already set in. That experience alone, my good friend, is one that can be relied upon to induce feelings of humility, if no humility before existed!

I had, I assure you, set small store by popularity. The discovery, therefore, that my memory was fast fading from the minds of earth people occasioned me no distress whatever. I had written and preached for the good they might do, and that, as I now learnt, was microscopically small. I was told that many people, whose public favor was considerable when they were incarnate, discovered, when they had shed their earthly bodies, that their fame and high favor had not preceded them into the world of spirit. Gone was the admiration which had been their common everyday experience. It naturally saddened such souls to leave behind them their earthly prominence, and it gave them something of a sense of loneliness, the more so when, in addition, the earth world quickly forgot all about them.

My own earthly reputation had been of no very great magnitude, but I had managed to carve a niche for myself among my co-religionists.

My transition had been calm and peaceful, and unattended by any unpleasant circumstances. It was no wrench for me to leave the earth world. I had no ties but my work. I was, therefore, greatly blessed. Edwin told me of others whose passing was extremely unhappy, and whose spiritual state upon their arrival here was still more unhappy. Many who were great upon earth found themselves very small in spirit. And many who were unknown upon earth found themselves here so spiritually well known as to be almost overcome by it. It is not all, by any means, who are destined for the beautiful realms of eternal sunshine and summer.

I have already given you a glimpse of those realms of darkness and semi-darkness, where all is cold and bleak and barren, and wherein souls have their abode, souls who can rise up out of the darkness if they so wish it and will work for that end. There are many who spend their heaven visiting these dim regions to try to draw out of their misery some of these unfortunates, and to set them upon the path of light and spiritual progression.

It has been my privilege to go with Edwin and Ruth to visit the dark places beyond the belt of mist that separates them from the light. It is not my purpose to take you into those realms of misery and unhappiness just yet. Later on I shall hope to give you some account of our experiences. For the moment there are other—and pleasanter—matters upon which I should like to speak.

There are many souls upon the earth-plane who seek to probe the manifold mysteries of life. They propound theories of diverse kinds purporting to explain this or that, theories which, in the course of time, come to be looked upon as great truths. Some of these hypotheses are as remote from the truth as it is possible to imagine; others are merely nonsensical. But there are also people who refuse even to think for themselves, and who stolidly uphold the belief that while they are incarnate they are not meant to know anything of the life of spirit that lies before them all. They affirm that it is not God's purpose that they should be told of such matters, and that when they come to spirit they will know all things.

These are two extremes of thought—the theorists and the partisans of the "closed door." Both schools receive some severe shocks when they enter spirit lands to live for all time. Individuals with strange theories find those theories demolished by the simple fact of finding themselves faced with the absolute truth. They discover that life in the spirit world is not nearly so complex as they would have it to be. In so many instances it is vastly simpler than life upon earth, because we do not have the problems that constantly harass and worry earth people, problems, for example, of religion and politics, which throughout the ages have caused social upheavals that are still having their repercussions in the earth world at the present time. The student of occult matters is apt to fall into the same error as the student of religious matters. He makes assertions every bit as dogmatic as those that emanate from orthodox religion, assertions that are mostly as far from the truth.

The period of time in which I have lived in the spirit world is as nothing—nothing!—by comparison with some of the great souls with whom it has been my privilege to speak. But they have shown me something of their vast store of knowledge, things, that is, that my mind was capable of understanding. For the rest, I—in company with millions of others—am perfectly contented to wait for the day when my intelligence is sufficiently advanced to grasp the greater truths.

A matter that gives rise to some perplexity concerns the flowers that we have in the spirit world. Some would ask: why flowers? What is their purpose or significance? Have they any symbolical meaning?

Let us put the same questions to earth people concerning the flowers that grow upon the earth-plane. Have the earthly flowers any special significance? Have *they* some symbolical meaning? The answer to both questions is *No!* Flowers are given to the earth world to help to beautify it, and for the delight and enjoyment of those who behold them. The fact that they serve other useful purposes is an added reason for their existence. Flowers are essentially beautiful, evolved from the Supreme Creative Mind, given to us as a precious gift, showing us in their colorings, in their formations, and in their perfumes an infinitesimally small expression of that Great Mind. You have this glory upon the earth-plane. Are we to be deprived of it in the spirit world because it is considered that flowers are rather earthy, or because no deep, abstruse meaning can be assigned to their existence?

We have the most glorious flowers here, some of them like the old familiar cherished blooms of the earth-plane, others known only to the spirit world, but all alike are superb, the perpetual joy of all of us who are surrounded with them. They are divine creations, each single flower breathing the pure air of spirit, and upheld by their Creator and by all of us here in the love that we shower upon them. Had we no wish for them—an impossible supposition!—they would be swept away. And what should we have in their stead? Where, otherwise, would the great wealth of color come from which the flowers provide?

And it is not only the smaller growing flowers that we have here. There is no single flowering tree or shrub that the mind can recall that we do not possess, flourishing in superabundance and perfection, as well as those trees and shrubs that are to be seen nowhere else but in the spirit world. They are always in bloom, they never fade or die, their perfumes are diffused into the air where they act like a spiritual tonic upon us all. They are at one with us, as we are with them.

When we are first introduced to the flowers and trees and all the luxuriance of spirit nature, we instantly perceive something that earthly nature never seemed to possess, and that is an inherent intelligence within all growing things. Earthly flowers, although living, make no immediate personal response when one comes into close touch with them. But here it is vastly different. Spirit flowers are imperishable, and that should at once suggest more than mere life within them, and spirit flowers, as well as all other forms of nature, are created by the Great Father of the Universe through his agents in the realms of spirit. They are part of the immense stream of life that flows directly from Him, and that flows through every species of botanic growth. That stream never ceases, never falters, and it is, moreover, continuously fed by the admiration and love which we, in this world of spirit, gratefully shed upon such choice gifts of the Father. Is it, then, to be wondered at, when we take the tiniest blossom within our hands, that we should feel such an influx of magnetic power, such a revivifying force, such an upliftment of one's very being, when we know, in truth, that those forces for our betterment are coming directly from the Source of all good. No, there is no other meaning behind our spirit flowers than the expressed beauty of the Father of the Universe, and, surely, that is enough. He has attached no strange symbolism to His faultless creations. Why should we?

A large majority of the flowers are not meant to be picked. To pick them is not to destroy them—it is to cut off that which is in direct contact with the Father. It is possible to gather them, of course; no disastrous calamity would follow if one did. But whosoever picked them would certainly regret it very deeply. Think of some small article that you possess and treasure above all your other earthly possessions, and then consider deliberately destroying it. It would cause you extreme sadness to do so, although the loss incurred might be intrinsically trifling. Such would be your emotions when you heedlessly culled those spirit flowers that are not intended for gathering.

But there are blooms, and plenty of them, that are expressly there to be picked, and many of us do so, taking them into our houses just as we used to do on earth, and for the same reason.

These severed flowers will survive their removal for just so long as we wish to retain them. When our interest in them begins to wane they will quickly disintegrate. There will be no unsightly withered remnants, for there can be no death in a land of eternal life. We simply perceive that our flowers have gone, and we can then replace them if we so wish.

CHAPTER TWELVE

THE SOIL

To OBTAIN an adequate idea of the ground upon which we walk and on which our houses and buildings are erected, you must clear your mind of all mundane conceptions. First of all, we have no roads as they are known on earth. We have broad, extensive thoroughfares in our cities and elsewhere, but they are not paved with a composite substance to give them hardness and durability for the passage of a constant stream of traffic. We have no traffic, and our roads are covered with the thickest and greenest of grass, as soft to the feet as a bed of fresh moss. It is on these that we walk. The grass never grows beyond the condition of being well-trimmed and yet it is living grass. It is always retained at the same serviceable level, perfect to walk upon and perfect in appearance.

In such places where smaller paths are desirable, and where grass would seem unsuitable, we have such pavements as are customary in the earth world. But they are constructed of very different materials. The paving is, for the most part, a description of stone, but it is without the usual dull drabness of color. It closely resembles the alabaster-like material of which so many of the buildings are constructed. The colors vary, but they are all of delicate pastel shades.

This stone, like the grass, is very pleasant to walk upon, though, naturally, it is not as soft. But there is a certain quality about it, a certain springiness, if one may so term it, something like the resilience of certain earthly timber that is utilized in the making of floors. That is the only way in which I can convey any idea of the difference between earthly stone and spirit stone.

There is never, of course, any unsightly discoloration to be observed upon the surface of these stone walks. They always preserve their initial freshness. Often the pavements reveal a network of delightful designs formed by the use of different colored materials, and blending harmoniously with their immediate surroundings.

As one approaches the boundaries to the higher realms, the pavements become noticeably more translucent in character, and they seem to lose some of their appearance of solidity, though, indeed, they are solid enough!

When one draws near the boundaries of the lower realms, the pavements become heavy in appearance, they begin to lose their color until they look leaden and opaque, and they have the semblance of extreme solidity—almost like the granite of the earth-plane.

Round about our own individual homes we have lawns and trees and flower-beds, with trim garden paths of stone similar to that which I have just described to you. But of bare "earth" you would see little or none. Indeed, I cannot call to mind ever having seen any such bare plots, for here there is no neglect through indifference or indolence, or from other causes that are all too familiar to specify. Where we have earned the right to possess our spirit home we have also within us the constant desire to maintain and improve upon its beauty. And that is not very difficult to accomplish, since beauty responds to, and thrives upon, the appreciation of it. The greater attention and recognition we give to it, so much the greater will be its response, and it assumes to itself still greater beauty. Spirit beauty is no abstract thing, but a real living force.

The view from my own home here is one of green fields, of houses of charm pleasantly situated amid woods and gardens, and with a distant view of the city. But nowhere are there to be seen any ugly tracts of bare or barren ground. Every inch that presents itself to the eye is cared for, so that the whole landscape is a riot of color, from the brilliant emerald green of the grass to the multi-colored flowers in the gardens, coronated by the blue of the heavenly sky above.

It may be wondered of what is the actual ground composed in which the flowers and trees are growing—is it earth of some sort?

There is soil, certainly, but it has not the same mineral constituents as that of the earth-plane, for it must be understood that life here is derived *directly* from the Great Source. The soil varies in color and density in different localities in just the same way as upon the earth-plane. I have not investigated it closely, any more than I took particular heed of earthly soil. I can, however, give you some small idea of its appearance and characteristics.

Firstly, then, it is perfectly dry—I could detect no trace of moisture. I found that it ran off the hand in much the same way that dry sand will do.

Its colors vary in a wide range of tones, but never does it approach the dark heavy look of earthly soil. In some places it is of fine granular formation, while in others it is composed of much coarser particles—that is, relatively coarser.

One of the unexpected properties of this soil is the fact that, while it can be taken into the hand and allowed to run from it smoothly and freely, yet when it is undisturbed it remains fully cohesive, supporting as firmly as the earthly soil all that is growing within it.

The color of the "earth" is governed by the color of whatever botanic life it supports. And here again there is no special significance, no deep symbolical reason for this particular order of things. It is simply that the color of the soil is complementary to the color of the flowers and trees, and the result, which could not be otherwise, is that of inspiring harmony—harmony to the eye, harmony to the mind, and the most soothing musical harmony to the ear. What better reason could there be? And what simpler?

Assuredly, this world of spirit is not made up of a bewildering series of profound and complex mysteries, explicable only to the few. There are mysteries, certainly, just as there are upon the earth-plane. And just as there are great brains upon the earth-plane who can solve those mysteries, so here there are greater brains still—immeasurably greater—who can provide an explanation when our intellects are ready to receive it and understand it.

But there are many people in the earth world who earnestly believe that we in spirit live in a continual state of perfervid religious emotion, that every concomitant of spirit life, every form and degree of personal activity, every atom of which the great world of spirit is composed, must have some pious, devotional signification. Such a stupid notion is wide, very wide of the mark. Search through the earth world, and do you find any such unnatural ideas attached to the multiplicity of life that lies within it? There is no religious import in a beautiful earthly sunset. Why should our spirit flowers—to take one instance among many—have any other reason for their existence than that which I have already given you, namely, a magnificent gift to us all from the Father of us all for our greater happiness and enjoyment?

There are still many, many souls on earth who solemnly uphold it as an article of "faith" that paradise, as they call it, will be one long interminable round of singing "psalms and hymns and spiritual canticles." Nothing could be more fantastic. The spirit world is a world of activity, not indolence; a world of usefulness, not uselessness. Nothing in the spirit world is useless; there is a sound reason and purpose for everything. Neither the reason nor the purpose may be plain to everyone at first, but that does not alter the truth of the matter.

Boredom can find no place here as a general state of affairs. People *have* been known to become bored, but that very boredom begets their first step— or their next step—in spiritual progression through their engaging in some useful work. There are myriads of tasks to be performed, and myriads of souls to perform them, but there is always room for one more, and it will ever be so. Am I not living in a world that is both unlimited and illimitable?

We do not inhabit a land that bears all the outward marks of an Eternal Sunday! Indeed, Sunday has no place, no existence even, in the great scheme of the spirit world. We have no need to be forcibly reminded of the Great Father of the Universe, by setting aside one day to Him, and forgetting Him for the rest of the week. We have no week. With us it is eternal day, and our minds are fully and perpetually conscious of Him, so that we can see His hand and His mind in everything that surrounds us.

I have deviated a little from what I set out to tell you, but it is expedient to emphasize certain features of my narrative, because so many souls of the earth world are almost shocked to be told that the spirit world is a solid world, a substantial world, with real, live people in it! They think that that is far too material, far too like the earth world; hardly, in fact, one step removed from it, with its spirit landscape and sunshine, its houses and buildings, its rivers and lakes, inhabited by sentient, intelligent beings!

This is no land of "eternal rest." There is rest in abundance for those who need it. But when the rest has restored them to full vigor and health the urge to perform some sensible, useful task rises up within them, and opportunities abound.

To return to the particular characteristics of spirit soil.

As we approach the dark regions the soil, such as I have described to you, loses its granular quality and its color. It becomes thick, heavy, and moist, until it finally gives place entirely to stones, and then rock. Whatever grass there is looks yellow and seared.

As we draw closer to the higher realms the particles of the soil become finer, the colors more delicate, with a hint of translucency. A greater degree of resilience is at once observable underfoot when walking upon the thresholds of these higher realms, but the resilience comes as well from the nature of the realm as from the distinct change in the ground.

On close examination the fine soil reveals almost jewel-like qualities both of color and form. The particles are never misshapen, but conform to a definite geometric plan.

Ruth and I plunged our hands into some of the soil and allowed it to trickle through our fingers in a gentle stream. As it descended there issued from it the sweetest musical tones, as though it were falling upon some tiny musical instrument and causing the keys to produce a ripple of sound.

A keen ear will hear many musical sounds upon the earthly seashore as the water sweeps back and forth over the beach, but no keen ear is necessary to hear the rich harmonics when the ground of the spirit world is made to speak and sing.

The sounds emitted in this way vary as much as the colors and elements themselves vary. They are there for all to hear, and they can be produced at will by the very simple action I have described.

How is this brought about, you will ask?

Color and sound—that is, musical sound—are interchangeable terms in the spirit world. To perform some act that will produce color is also to produce a musical sound. To play upon a musical instrument, or to sing, is to create color, and each creation is governed and limited by the skill and proficiency of the instrumentalist or singer. A master musician, as he plays upon his instrument, will build above himself a most beautiful musical thought-form, varying in its colors and blends of shades in strict accordance with the music he plays. A singer can create a similar effect in relation to the purity of the voice and the quality of the music. The thought-form thus erected will not be very large. It is a form in miniature. But a large orchestra or body of singers will construct an immense form, governed, of course, by the same law.

The musical thought-form produces no sound itself. It is the result of sound, and is, as it were, a self-contained unit. Although music will bring forth color, and color will yield music, each is restricted to the one resultant form. They will not go on reproducing each other in a constant, unending, or gradually diminishing, alternation of color and sound.

It must not be thought that with all the vast galaxy of colors from the hundreds of sources in the spirit world, our ears are being constantly assailed with the sounds of music; that we are living, in fact, in an eternity of music that is sounding and resounding without remission. There are few minds—if any—that could possibly endure such a continuous plethora of sound, however beautiful it may be. We should sigh for peace and quietness: our heaven would cease to be heaven. No, the music is there, but we please ourselves entirely whether we wish to hear it or listen to it. We can completely isolate ourselves from all sound, or we can throw ourselves open to all sound, or just hear that which pleases us most.

There are times upon the earth-plane when you can hear the strains of distant music without being in any way disturbed by it; on the contrary, you may find it very pleasant and soothing. So it is with us here in spirit. But there is this great difference between our two worlds—our potentialities for music of the highest order are immeasurably greater than are yours upon the earth-plane. The mind of a spirit person who has a deep love of music will naturally hear more, because he so wishes, than one who cares little for it.

To revert to the experiment that Ruth and I carried out when we let the soil run through our fingers: We both of us derive great enjoyment from listening to music, Ruth much more so than myself, since she has been trained in the musical art and therefore has a higher appreciation and grasp of musical technicalities. I have told you how, the instant the soil left our hands, we could hear the delightful sounds issuing from it. Another person performing the same action, but who possessed no particular musical susceptibilities, would scarcely be conscious of any sound at all.

The flowers and all growing things respond immediately to those who love them and appreciate them. The music that they send out operates under precisely the same law. An attunement upon the part of the percipient, with that with which he comes into contact or relationship, is a prerequisite condition. Without that attunement it would be impossible to be conscious of the musical strains that issue forth from the whole of spirit nature. By spirit nature I mean, of course, all the growing things, the sea and lakes—indeed, all water—the soil, and the rest.

The greater the power of the individual of appreciating and understanding beauty in all its multifarious forms, the greater will be the outflowing of magnetic force. In the spirit world nothing is wasted nor expended uselessly. We never have forced upon us something that we do not want, whether it be music or art, entertainment or learning. We are free agents, in every sense of the term, within the confines of our own realm.

It would be a most terrifying thought to imagine that the spirit world is one immense pandemonium of music, continuing ceaselessly, totally unavoidable, presenting itself on every conceivable occasion and in every possible place and situation! No!—the spirit world is conducted on much better lines than that! The musical sounds are most certainly there, but it rests solely with ourselves whether we shall hear them or not. And the secret is personal attunement.

There are people upon the earth-plane who possess the ability of mentally isolating themselves from their surroundings to such a degree that they can become oblivious to all sounds, however intense, that might be going on around them. This state of complete mental detachment will serve as an analogy—though a rather elementary one—of the effect that we can produce upon ourselves in spirit, to the exclusion of such sounds as we have no wish to hear. Unlike the earth world, we do not need to bring to bear any great force of concentration. It is but another process of thought, just as we use our minds to effect personal locomotion, and after a brief sojourn in spirit we are soon able to perform these various mental functions without any conscious effort. They are part of our very nature, and we are merely applying, in an extended form, without earthly limitations and restrictions, mental methods that are perfectly simple to apply. On the earth-plane our physical bodies, in a heavy physical world, prevented similar mental processes from producing any physical result. In the spirit world we are free and unfettered, and those actions of the mind show an instant and direct result, whether it be to move us with the quickness of our thought, or whether it be to shut out any sight or sound that we do not wish to experience.

On the other hand, we can—and do—open our minds and attune ourselves to absorb the many glorious sounds that come rising up all round us. We can open our minds—or close them—to the many delectable perfumes that spirit nature casts abroad for our happiness, and contentment. They act like a tonic upon the mind, but they are not forced upon us—we merely help ourselves to them as we wish. It must ever be borne in mind that the spirit lands are founded upon law and order. But the law is never oppressive nor the order irksome, because the same law and order have helped to provide all the countless beauties and wonders of this heavenly realm.

CHAPTER THIRTEEN

BUILDING METHODS

NOT THE least important, among the many "physical" features of the realm in which I live, are the numerous buildings devoted to the pursuit of learning and the fostering of the arts familiar to the earth-plane. These magnificent edifices present to the eye all the signs one would expect of the permanence of eternity. The materials of which they are constructed are imperishable. The surfaces of the stone are as clean and fresh as on the day when they were raised up. There is nothing to soil them, no heavy smoke-laden atmosphere to eat into them, no winds and rains to wear down the works of exterior decoration. The materials of which they are built are of the spirit world, and therefore they have a beauty that is not earthly.

Although these fine halls of learning have every suggestion of permanency, they could be demolished if it were considered expedient or desirable to do so. In some cases it has been so considered. Such buildings have been removed, and others have taken their place.

The spirit world is not static. It is ever vibrant with life and movement. Contemplate, for a moment, the normal conditions of the earth world, with the many changes that are taking place continuously—the gradual reconstruction of towns and cities, the alterations in the countryside. Some of these changes have not always been deemed improvements. However that may be, changes are made, and the procedure is looked upon as one of progression. What, then, of the spirit world? Are no changes to take place in the world in which I live? Most certainly they are!

We do not exactly "move with the times"—to use a familiar earthly phrase, because we are always very much *ahead* of the times! And we have every need to be—*to meet the heavy demands placed upon us by the earth world.*

Let us take one specific instance—just one.

As the earth world progresses in civilization—in its own estimation—the means and methods of waging war become more devastating and whole-sale. In place of hundreds killed in battles in ancient times, the slain are now counted in hundreds of thousands. Every one of those souls has finished with his earthly life—though not with the consequences of it—and, in so many cases, the earth world has finished with him too. The individual may survive as a memory to those whom he has left behind him; his physical presence is gone. But his spirit presence is unalterably with us. The earth world has passed him on to us, oftentimes not really caring what has befallen him. He will leave behind him those whom he loved, and who loved him, but the earth world—so it thinks—can do nothing for him, nor for those who mourn his passing. It is we, in the spirit world, who will care for that soul. With us there is no shifting the responsibility on to other shoulders, and so passing upon our way. We are faced with strict realities here.

The earth world, in its blind ignorance, hurls hundreds of thousands of souls into this, our land, but those who dwell in the high realms are fully aware, long before it happens, of what is to take place upon the earth-plane, and a fiat goes forth to the realms nearer the earth to prepare for what is to come.

These dire calamities of the earth-plane necessitate the building of more and ever more halls of rest in the spirit world. That is one occasion—and perhaps the greatest—for the changes that are always taking place here. But there are others and more pleasant.

Sometimes the wish is expressed by a great number of souls for an extension to be made to one of the halls of learning. There is seldom any difficulty about such a desire, since it is in no sense a selfish one, because it will be there for all to use and enjoy.

It was in reply to a question which I put to Edwin that he told me that a new wing was to be added to the great library, where I have spent so many profitable and enjoyable moments since I came to spirit. It was suggested that perhaps Ruth and I would like to witness a spirit building in actual course of being erected. Accordingly, we made our way to the city and to the library.

There was a large number of people already gathered there with the same intent as ourselves, and while we were waiting for operations to begin, Edwin told us something of the preliminary details that are necessary before work actually begins.

As soon as some new building is desired, the ruler of the realm is consulted. Of this great soul, and of others similar to him in spiritual character and capacity, I will tell you later. Knowing, as he does, so intimately, the needs and wishes of all in his realm, there never arises a case where some building is required for the use and service of all but that the wish is granted. The ruler then transmits the request to those in authority above him, who in turn refer it to those still higher. We then foregather in the central temple in the city, where we are received by one whose word is law, the great soul who, many years ago of earthly time, made it possible for me to communicate thus with the earth world.

Now, this seemingly involved procedure of passing on our request from one to another, may suggest to the mind the tortuous methods of officialdom with its delays and protractedness. The method may be somewhat similar, but the time taken in performance is a very different matter. It is no exaggeration to say that within the space of a few earthly minutes our request has been stated, and the permission—with a gracious blessing accompanying it—has been granted. On such occasions as these we have cause for rejoicings, and we seize the opportunity to the full.

The next step is to consult the architects, and it may be readily imagined that we have a host of masters upon whom we can draw without limitation. They work for the sheer joy it brings them in the creation of some grand edifice to be used in the service of their fellows. These good men collaborate in a way that would be almost impossible upon the earth-plane. Here they are not circumscribed by professional etiquette, or limited by the narrowness of petty jealousies. Each is more than happy and proud to serve with the other, and never is there discord or disagreement through endeavoring to introduce, or force, the individual ideas of the one at the expense of another's. Perhaps you will say that such complete unanimity is far and away beyond the bounds of human nature and that such people would not be human if they did not disagree, or otherwise show their individuality.

Before you dismiss my statement as highly improbable, or as the painting of a picture of perfection impossible to attain except within the very highest realms of all, let me state the simple fact that discord and disagreement, upon such a matter as we are now considering, could not possibly exist in this realm wherein is my home. And if you still insist that this is impossible, I say *No*—it is perfectly natural. Whatever gifts we may possess in spirit, it is part of the essence of this realm that we have no inflated ideas of the power or excellence of those gifts. We acknowledge them in humility alone, without self-importance, unobtrusively, selflessly, and we are grateful for the opportunity of working, *con amore*, with our colleagues in the service of the Great Inspirer.

This, in substance, is what one of these great architects himself told me with reference to his own work.

After the plans for the new buildings have been drawn up in consultation with the ruler of the realm, there is a meeting of the master-masons. The latter were mostly masons when they were upon the earth-plane, and they continue to exercise their skill in spirit lands. They do so, of course, because the work appeals to them, even as it did when they were incarnate, and here they have faultless conditions under which they can carry on their work. They do so with a grand freedom and liberty of action that was denied them upon earth, but which is their heritage here in the spirit world. Others, who were not masons by trade, have since learned the spirit methods of building—for the sheer joy of doing so, and they give valuable aid to their more skilled confrères.

The masons, and one another, are the only people concerned in the actual construction, since spirit buildings do not require much that has to be included within the disposition of earthly buildings. Such, for example, as the necessary provision for lighting by artificial means, and for heating. Our light comes from the great central source of all light, and the warmth is one of the *spiritual* features of the realm.

The addition which was being made to the library consisted of an annex, and it was not of any very great dimensions. Our spirit library has at least one feature in common with earthly libraries. A time comes when the quantity of books exceeds the space in which to house them, and in our case the excess is inclined to be greater, because not only do we have copies of earthly books upon the shelves, but there are also volumes that have their source solely in spirit. By this, I mean that such books have no counterpart on earth. Included among them are works concerning spirit life alone, the facts of life here, and spiritual teachings, written by authorities who have an infallible knowledge of their subject, and who reside in the higher spheres. There are also the histories of nations and events, with the facts set down *in strict accordance with the absolute truth,* written by men who now find that equivocation is impossible.

The building of this annex was not, therefore, what one would denominate a major effort, and it required the help of but a comparative few. It was simple in design, consisting of two or three medium-sized rooms.

We were standing fairly close to the group of architects and masons, headed by the ruler of the realm. I noticed particularly that they had all the appearance of being extremely happy and jovial, and many were the jokes that circulated round this cheerful band.

It was strange to Ruth and me—Edwin had witnessed this sort of thing before—to think that a building was shortly to go up, because since my arrival in the spirit world I had seen no signs of any building operations going on anywhere. Every hall and house was already erected, and it never occurred to me that anything further would be required in this direction. A little thought, of course, would have revealed that spirit houses are always in course of being built, while others are being demolished if they are no longer wanted. The halls of learning all looked so very permanent to my unaccustomed eyes, so very complete, that I could not think it would ever be necessary to make any additions to them.

At length there were signs that a beginning was to be made.

It must be remembered that the act of building in the spirit world is essentially an operation of thought. It will not be surprising, therefore, when I tell you that nowhere were there to be seen the usual materials and paraphernalia associated with earthly builders, the scaffolding and bricks and cement, and the various other familiar objects. We were to witness, in fact, an act of creation—of creation by thought—and as such no "physical" equipment is necessary.

The ruler of the realm stepped forward a few paces, and, with his back towards us, but facing the site upon which the new wing was to arise, he spoke a brief but appropriate prayer. In simple language he asked the Great Creator for His help in the work they were about to undertake.

His prayer brought an instantaneous response, which was in the form of a bright beam of light that descended upon him and upon those gathered immediately behind him. As soon as this happened the architects and masons moved up close beside him.

All eyes were now turned upon that vacant spot beside the main building, to which we noticed that a second beam of light was passing directly from the ruler and the masons. As the second beam reached the site of the annex it formed itself into a carpet of coruscation upon the ground. This gradually grew in depth, width, and height, but it seemed, as yet, to lack any suggestion of substance. It matched the main building in color, but that was all so far.

Slowly the form gained in size until it reached the required height. We could now see plainly that it matched the original structure in general outline, while the carved devices similarly corresponded.

While it was in this state the architects approached and examined it closely. We could observe them moving within it, until at length they passed from view. They were gone but a moment when they returned to the ruler with the report that all was in order.

Edwin explained to us that this rather ghostly edifice was in reality an adumbration of the finished structure, shaped in exact facsimile before an intensification of thought was applied to produce a solid and completed building. Any mistake or fault would be detected when the building was in this tenuous state, and corrected at once.

No rectification, however, being necessary in this particular instance, the work was proceeded with immediately.

The downstream of light now became very much more intense, while the horizontal stream from the ruler and his collaborators assumed, after the lapse of a minute or two, a similar degree of intensity. We could now perceive the nebulous form acquiring an unmistakable appearance of solidity as the concentration of united thought laid layer upon layer of increased density upon the simulacrum.

From what I observed it seemed to devolve upon the ruler to supply to each of the masons just that quantity and description of force that each required upon his separate task. He acted, in fact, as a distributive agent for the magnetic power that was descending directly upon him. This split up into a number of individual shafts of light of different color and strength, which corresponded with his direct appeals to the Great Architect. There was no faltering or diminution of the application of thought substance to be perceived anywhere. The masons themselves seemed to work with a complete unanimity of concentration, since the building attained full solidity with a remarkable degree of evenness.

After what appeared to Ruth and me a very short period, the building ceased to acquire any further density, the vertical and horizontal rays were cut off, and there stood before us the finished wing, perfect in every detail, an exact match and extension to the main edifice, beautiful alike in color and form, and worthy of the high purpose to which it was to be devoted.

We moved forward to examine more closely the results of the feat that had just been accomplished. We ran our hands over the smooth surface, as though to convince ourselves that it was really solid! Ruth and I were not the only people to do this, as there were others who were witnessing for the first time—and with equal wonderment—the immense power of directed thought.

The procedure which governs the building of our personal houses and cottages differs a little from that which I have just described to you. An indispensable prerequisite to the ownership of a spirit home is the right to own it, a right which is gained solely by the kind of life we live when incarnate, or by our spiritual progression after our transition to the spirit world. Once we have earned that right there is nothing to prevent our having such a residence if we should wish for one.

It has often been said that we build our spirit homes during our earthly lives—or after. That is so only in a broad sense. What we have built is the right to build, for it requires an expert to erect a house that would justify the name. My own home was built for me during my earthly life by builders just as proficient as those who helped to erect the annex to the library. My friends, headed by Edwin, had looked after all the details entailed in such work. They had sought out the men to undertake the task, and the latter had carried into effect a fine piece of craftsmanship.

When that day shall dawn upon which my spiritual progression will carry me onwards, I shall leave my house. But it will rest entirely with myself whether I leave my old home as it stands for others to occupy and enjoy, or whether I demolish it.

It is customary, I am told, to make a gift of it to the ruler of the realm for his disposal to others at his discretion.

CHAPTER FOURTEEN

TIME AND SPACE

I T IS commonly thought by people of the earth-plane that in the spirit world time and space do not exist. That is wrong. We have both, but our conception of them differs from that of the earth world.

We sometimes use the phrase, "before the dawn of time," to convey an idea of the passage of eons of time, but we have no notion of what is really embodied in that phrase.

On the earth-plane the measurement of time had its source in the revolution of the earth upon its axis, giving a division of time known to us as night and day. The recurrence of the four seasons gave that larger measure, during which the earth revolved round the sun. The invention of clocks and calendars brought a convenient means of measuring time within the reach of all of us.

In the spirit world we have no clocks or other mechanical contrivances to indicate the passage of time. It would be the simplest thing in the world for our scientists to provide us with such if we felt the need for them. But we have no such need. We have no recurrent seasons, no alternations of light and darkness as external indications of time, and, in addition, we have no personal reminders, common to all the incarnate, of hunger and thirst and fatigue, together with the aging of the physical body. How, then, can we have any possible heed of the flight of time? How, in fact, does time exist at all?

We have two conceptions of time, one of which, as upon the earth-plane, is purely relative. Five minutes, let us say, of acute pain suffered by the physical body will so affect the mind that the passing moments will seem an age. But five minutes of intense joy and happiness will seem to have flown with the rapidity of the same number of seconds.

Those of us in the spirit world who live in the realms of happiness and perpetual summer will have no cause to find "time hang heavily." In this sense we are simply not conscious of the flight of time.

In the dark realms the reverse is the case. The period of darkness will seem interminable to those who live there. However much such souls may yearn for a coming of the light, yet it never comes to them. They themselves must perforce take the first step *towards* the light that awaits them without their low realm. A period of existence within these dark regions, amounting to nothing more than a year or two of earthly time, will seem like an eternity to the sufferers.

If, normally, we have none of the customary means of measuring time because we have no need to do so, we can—and we do—return to make contact with the earth-plane, where we can ascertain the exact time of day, the day of the year, and the year itself.

Some people, who would not otherwise have done so, have returned to the earth world for the very purpose of satisfying their curiosity as to the number of years they have been in the spirit world. I have spoken to some who have made this journey, and they were all amazed to discover the unsuspected scores of years that had passed by since their transition.

Speaking for myself, I have found the time pass rapidly since I came into spirit, but I have always known, throughout the whole of that period, what was the year of the Christian Era. The reason in my own case was simply that I had been promised that I should one day be able to communicate with the earth world. I had, therefore, been keenly interested in watching, in company with the great souls who were closely concerned, the concatenation of events that were to lead, among other things, to the achievement of my wish.

Edwin, who met me upon the threshold of the spirit world and conducted me to my new home, was similarly acquainted with the passage of time, for he, in turn, had been watching me!

It may be thought that time, in the sense of being a measured succession of existence, has little or no influence beyond the earth-plane. But it most certainly does have an influence upon the spirit-plane.

All earthly events, whether concerning nations or individuals, are subject to, or governed by, time. And insofar as those events have their application to, or extension into, the spirit world, so do we in the spirit world come under the influence of time, or its operation. We might take the festival of Christmas as the simplest and readiest example. We celebrate this festival in the spirit world at the same *time* as do you. Whether December 25th is the correct date, historically, for the event which it commemorates, is a question we are not concerned with for our present purposes. What matters is that the two celebrations, yours and ours, are synchronized and recurrent year by year. We are not subservient to the earth world in this; our purpose is solely one of cooperation.

In normal times upon the earth-plane at that period of the year, there rises throughout the earth world a great force of goodwill and kindliness. Many people, who at other seasons are inclined to be forgetful, will frequently remember those of their family and friends who have passed into spirit lands, and they will send them thoughts of affection which we in spirit are always so happy to receive and to reciprocate. The celebration of Christmas is always preceded by thoughts of pleasant anticipation. If there were nothing else to guide us, these alone would be sufficient to tell us that the time of the feast was drawing near. In the spirit world, at that time, it is common enough to hear one person say to another: "Christmas on the earth-plane is drawing near." But the person so addressed might have been completely unaware of the fact.

In the particular example of Christmas we are not dependent entirely upon the earth-plane for our knowledge of the approaching anniversary. On this special occasion we are always visited by great souls from the higher realms, and were all other means to fail us, this would be an infallible indication of the passing of another year in earthly time.

Those of us who are in close and constant connection with the earth will know, of course, as well as do you, the year, the month, and the day. We shall know, too, the exact hour of earth time. There is no difficulty about this, nor is there any mystery. When we come into your conditions we can make use of the very means that you yourselves employ—and what could be simpler? As a rule it is not necessary for us to be continually aware of the precise day and hour, or otherwise to keep account of them. When we actively cooperate with you your thoughts to us are sufficient indication that a certain moment has recurred when we meet to work or converse together. Such thoughts are all that we need. It is in the ordinary nature of things in spirit that, generally speaking, we should lose all sense of the continuity of time in measured succession as you know it. We allow things to remain so, unless we have cause to do otherwise. When we look forward to the arrival of relative or friend into the spirit world it is towards the *event* that we cast our minds, not the year in which the event is to take place.

Thus far I have given you a few facts of my own knowledge derived from my own experience, and therefore what I have told you applies to the specific realm wherein I live.

Of the higher realms I have no knowledge at first hand, and the amount of information that I have gleaned from conversations with inhabitants of those realms has been governed and restricted by my ability to understand. All that I can say, therefore, concerning time in the upper spheres is that in such elevated states we come into realms where knowledge, among many other spiritual attributes, is of a very high order. Personages from those realms have more than astonished me with the accuracy of their foreknowledge of events that were to take place upon the earth-plane. Their means of acquiring this information is far beyond the comprehension of us in this realm. It is sufficient for the moment to record that it is so, and that time, therefore, is not confined to realms of a less exalted state of spiritual progression.

When we come to the subject of space we find that, broadly speaking, we are governed *up to a point* by the same law as upon the earth-plane. We have eternity of time, but we have also infinity of space.

Space *must* exist in the spirit world. Take my own realm alone, as an example. Standing at the window of one of the upper rooms of my house I can see across huge distances whereon are many houses and grand buildings. In the *distance* I can see the city with many more great buildings. Dispersed throughout the whole wide prospect are woods and meadows, rivers and streams, gardens and orchards, and they are all occupying space, just as all these occupy space in the earth world. They do not interpenetrate any more than they interpenetrate upon the earth-plane. Each fills its own reserved portion of space. And I know, as I gaze out of my window, that far beyond the range of my vision, and far beyond and beyond that again, there are more realms and still more realms that constitute the designation *infinity of space*. I know that I can travel uninterruptedly through enormous areas of space, areas far greater than the whole of the earth world trebled in size, or greater. I have not yet traversed anything like one fraction of the full extent of my own realm, but I am free to do so whenever I wish. I have been told by good friends from the higher realms that I could penetrate even those rarefied states if occasion demanded. I should be given the facilities and the protective cloak that are necessary in such cases to make the journey, so that, potentially, my field of movement is gigantic.

Viewed with earthly eyes only, this immense region would obviously be beyond the reach of most people, since movement through such spaces on earth would be restricted by the means of transportation at their command, as well as by other considerations. One thousand miles of earthly space is a great distance, and to cover it takes some considerable time if the slower means of transport are employed. Even with the fastest method a certain time must elapse before the end of the thousand miles journey is reached. But in the spirit world thought alters the whole situation. We have space, and we have a certain cognizance of time in its relation to space. Thought can annihilate time in its relation to space, but it cannot annihilate space.

I can stand before my house and I can bethink myself that I would like to visit the library in the city which I can see some "miles" away in the distance. No sooner has the thought passed with precision through my mind than I find myself—if I so desire it—standing before the very shelves that I wish to consult. I have made my spirit body—and that is the only body I have!—travel through space with the rapidity of thought, and that is so rapid that it is equivalent to being instantaneous. And what have I done? I have covered the intervening space instantaneously, but the space still remains there with everything it contains, although I had no cognizance of time or the passage of time.

When I have completed my visit to the library I meet some friends upon the steps, and they suggest that we adjourn to the home of one of them. With this pleasant prospect in view we decide to walk through the gardens and woods. The house is some "distance" away, but that does not matter, because we never suffer from "physical" fatigue, and we are not otherwise engaged. We walk along together, talking happily, and after a certain lapse of "time" we arrive at the house of our friend, and we have covered the intervening space on foot. On the journey from my house to the library I overcame the distance in between, and I dispensed with time for the occasion. On the way back I experienced an intuitive apprehension of time by walking slowly, and I restored a perception of distance to my mind by moving upon the solid ground and the grassy fields of this realm.

Time—in its spirit sense—and space are relative in the spirit world, just as they are upon the earth-plane. But our conceptions of them differ widely, yours being restricted by the earthly considerations of sunrise and sunset, and the various modes of transit. We have everlasting day, and we can move ourselves slowly by walking, or we can transport ourselves instantaneously whithersoever we wish to be. In the spirit world time can thus be made to stand still! And we can restore our sense of it by quietly resting, or by walking. It is only our general sense of time that we restore, not the passage of time. But when we receive your thoughts from the earth world, telling us that you are ready for us to come to you, then, once again, we are fully aware of the passage of earthly time.

And you must admit that we are invariably punctual in keeping our appointments with you!

CHAPTER FIFTEEN

GEOGRAPHICAL
POSITION

WHAT IS the geographical position of the spirit world in relation to the earth world? Many people have wondered this at different times—and I include myself among the many!

And that leads to a further question concerning the disposition of other realms than those of which I have given you some details.

I have told you how, when I had reached a critical moment as I lay upon my final bed of earthly sickness, I at length felt an irresistible urge to rise up, and that I yielded to that urge easily and successfully. In this particular case the line of demarcation was very fine between the end of my earthly life and the beginning of my spirit life, because I was in full possession of my senses, fully conscious. The actual transition from one world to the other was in this respect imperceptible.

But I can narrow things down still further by recalling that there came a moment when the physical sensations attendant upon my last illness left me abruptly, and in place of them a delightful feeling of bodily ease and peace of mind completely enveloped me. I felt that I wanted to breathe deeply, and I did so. The impulse to rise from my bed, and the passing of all physical sensations, mark the instant of my physical "death" and my birth into the world of spirit.

But when this took place I was still in my own earthly bedroom, and therefore a part, at least, of the spirit world must interpenetrate the earth world. This particular experience will give us something of a point of departure for our geographical explorations.

The next event in my transition was the arrival of my good friend Edwin, and our meeting after the lapse of years. The meeting took place seemingly in the bedroom. Then, after we had greeted each other and chatted for a brief space, Edwin proposed that we should depart from our present surroundings, which, in the circumstances, were rather doleful. He took me by the arm, told me to close my eyes, and I felt myself gently moving through space. I had no clear perception of direction. I only knew that I was traveling, but whether up or down or horizontally, it was impossible for me to say. Our rate of progress increased until at last I was told to open my eyes, and then I found myself standing before my spirit home.

Since that day I have learnt many things, and one of my first lessons was in the art of personal locomotion by other means than walking. There are immense distances here to cover, and sometimes we need to cover them instantly. We do so by the power of thought as I have already outlined to you. But the strangest thing to me, at first, was the fact that when I moved myself through space at any greater speed than ordinary walking, I found that I had no sense of absolute direction, but one of movement only. If I chose to shut my eyes whilst traveling with moderate speed I merely shut out the scenery, or whatever else were my surroundings. It must not be thought that it is possible to lose one's way. That would be out of the question!

This absence of a sense of direction in no way interferes with our initial thought function in personal locomotion. Once we have determined to journey to a certain place, we set our thoughts in motion and they, in turn—instantaneously—set our spirit bodies in motion. One might almost say "it requires no thinking about!" I have spoken to other people on these matters, and compared notes generally—it is a thing we all do when we are newly-arrived in the spirit world; and we never lack willing friends to help us in our early difficulties. I have found that it is common to all here in spirit, this absence of any directional perception when moving rapidly. Of course, when we travel instantaneously there is no "time" to observe any object whatsoever. There is no observable interval of time between the moment we leave for, and the moment we arrive at, our destination.

It will be appreciated from this factor of directional unawareness, if I may so term it, that to assign a precise location to the spirit world, relative to the earth world, is a difficult matter. Indeed, I doubt if anyone fairly new to spirit life could possibly hazard a guess as to his relative geographical position! Of course, there are scores upon scores of people who never bother their heads about such things. They have severed all connection with the earth world, and they have done with it for all time. They know positively that they are alive and in the spirit world, but as to the exact position of that world in the universe, they have no intention of troubling themselves. But our own case is different. I am in very active communion with the earth world, and I think it would be of interest if I were to try to give some idea just where the spirit lands are situated.

The spirit world is divided into spheres or realms. These two words of designation have passed into current acceptation among most of those on the earth-plane who have a knowledge of, and practice, communication, with our world. In speaking to you thus, I have used the words interchangeably. They suffice for our purpose—one can think of none better.

These spheres have been given numbers by some students, ranging from the first, which is the lowest, up to the seventh, the highest. It is customary among most of us here to follow this system of numbering. The idea originated, I am told, from our side, and it is a very useful and convenient method of conveying the information of one's position upon the ladder of spiritual evolution.

The spheres of the spirit world are ranged in a series of bands forming a number of concentric circles around the earth. These circles reach out into the infinity of space, and they are invisibly linked with the earth world in its lesser revolution upon its axis, and, of course, in its greater revolution round the sun. The sun has no influence whatever upon the spirit world. We have no consciousness of it at all since it is purely material.

An exemplification of the concentric circles is afforded us when we are told that a visitant from a higher sphere is coming *down* to us. He is relatively *above* us, both spiritually and spatially.

The low realms of darkness are situated close to the earth-plane, and interpenetrate it at their lowest. It was through these that I passed with Edwin when he came to take me to my spirit home, and it was for that reason that he recommended that I keep my eyes firmly closed until he should tell me to open them again. I was sufficiently alert—too much so, because I was fully conscious—otherwise to see some of the hideousness that the earth world has cast into these dark places.

With the spirit world made up of a series of concentric circles, having the earth world approximately at the center, we find that the spheres are subdivided laterally to correspond broadly with the various nations of the earth, each subdivision being situated immediately over its kindred nation. When you consider the enormous variety of national temperament and characteristics distributed throughout the earth-plane, it is not surprising that the people of each nation should wish to gravitate to those of their own kind in the spirit world, just as much as they wish to do when upon the earth-plane. Individual choice, of course, is free and open to every soul; he may live in whatsoever part of his own realm that he pleases. There are no fixed territorial frontiers here to separate the nations. They make their own invisible frontiers of temperament and customs, but the members of all the nations of the earth are at liberty to intermingle in the spirit world, and to enjoy unrestricted and happy social intercourse. The language question presents no difficulty, because we are not obliged to speak aloud. We can transmit our thoughts to each other with the full assurance that they will be received by the person whom we are mentally addressing. Thus language constitutes no barrier.

Each of the national subdivisions of the spirit world bears the characteristics of its earthly counterpart. That is but natural. My own home is situated in surroundings that are familiar to me and that are a counterpart of my earthly home in general appearance. These surroundings are not an exact replica of the earthly surroundings. By which, I mean that my spirit home is located in the type of countryside with which I and my friends are very familiar.

This dividing of the nations extends only to a certain number of realms. Beyond that, nationality, as such, ceases to be. There we retain only our outward and visible distinctions, such as the color of our skin, whether it be yellow, white or black. We shall cease to be nationally conscious such as we are when upon the earth-plane and during our sojourn in the realms of less degree. Our homes will no longer have a definite national appearance, and will partake more of pure spirit.

You will recall how, in building the annex to the library, I introduced you to the ruler of the realm. Each realm has such a personage, though the term ruler is not a really good one, because it is apt to convey something of a wrong impression. It would be much happier and far more exact to say that he *presides* over the realm.

Although each realm has its own resident ruler, all the rulers belong to a higher sphere than that over which they preside.

The position is such that it calls for high attributes on the part of its holder, and the office is held only by those who have had long residence in the spirit world. Many of them have been here thousands of years. Great spirituality is not alone sufficient; if it were, there are many wonderful souls who could hold such office with distinction. But a ruler must possess a great deal of knowledge and experience of humanity, and in addition he must always be able to exercise wise discretion in dealing with the various matters that come before him. And all the ruler's experience and knowledge, all his sympathy and understanding, are ever at the disposal of the inhabitants of his realm, while his kindness and infinite patience are always in evidence. This great soul is ever accessible to any who wish to consult him, or who bring him their problems for solution.

We have our problems, just as do you upon the earth-plane, although *our* problems are very different from yours. Ours are never of the nature of those harassing worries and cares of the earth world. Speaking for myself, *my* first problem, soon after my transition, was how to set right what I considered to be a wrong I had done when I was incarnate. I had written a book in which I had treated the truth of communication with the earth world with great unfairness. When I spoke to Edwin upon the subject he—all unknown to me—had sought the advice of the ruler of the realm, and the result was that another great soul had come to discuss the matter with me, and to offer help and advice in my difficulty. It was the ruler's knowledge of my affairs in the first instance that eventually brought about a happy ending to my trouble.

It will be seen from this that a ruler's knowledge of the people over whom he presides is vast. Lest it should be thought that it is humanly impossible for one mind to carry so much knowledge of the affairs of so many people as there must be in one realm, it must be understood that the mind of the incarnate is limited in its range of action by the physical brain. In the spirit world we have no physical brain to hamper us, and our minds are fully and completely retentive of all knowledge that comes to us. We do not forget those things we have learnt in the spirit world, whether they be spiritual lessons or plain facts. But it takes time, as you would say, to learn, and that is why the rulers of realms have spent many thousands of earthly years in the spirit world before they are placed in charge of so many people. For the rulers have to guide and direct them, help them in their work, and unite with them in their recreation; to be an inspiration to them, and to act towards them, in every sense of the word, as a devoted father. There is no such thing as unhappiness in this realm—if for no other reason than that it would be impossible with such a grand soul to smooth away the troubles.

Each sphere is completely invisible to the inhabitants of the spheres below it, and in this respect, at least, it provides its own boundary.

In journeying to a lower realm one sees the terrain gradually degenerating.

As we draw towards a higher realm, just the opposite takes place: we see the land around us becoming more ethereal, more refined, and this forms a natural barrier to those of us who have not yet progressed sufficiently to become inhabitants of that realm.

Now, I have already told you how the realms are one above the other. How, then, does one proceed from one to the next, either above or below? There must be some point or points in each realm where there is a distinct upward inclination to the one and a distinct declivity to the other. Simple though it sounds, that is precisely the case.

It is not difficult to imagine, perhaps, a gradual descent to regions that are less salubrious. We can call to our aid our earthly experiences, and recollect some rocky places that we could visit and descend, treacherous to the feet, leading us down into dark caverns, cold and damp and uninviting, where we could imagine all manner of noisome things lurking in readiness for us. We can then remember that *above* us, though out of sight, there shines the sun, spreading warmth and light upon the earth, while yet we seem to be in another world altogether. We might wander about through underground caves until we become lost and are shut off completely from the land *above* us. But we know that there is one way up at least, if we can but find it, and if we persevere in our attempts to scale the dangerous rocky pathway.

If we commence our world of spirit in the lowest recess of this earthly picture of the subterranean caves, we can see how each of the realms is connected with the realm immediately above it. The earthly analogy is, of course, an elementary one, but the process and the principle are the same. The transition in the spirit world from one realm to another is literal—as literal as passing from the dark cavern to the sunlight above, as literal as walking from one room in your house to another, whether upstairs or down.

To pass from this realm where I live to the next higher, I shall find myself walking along gently rising ground. As I proceed I shall see all the unmistakable signs—and feel them—of a realm of greater spiritual refinement. There will eventually come a point in my walking when I can go no further because I shall feel most uncomfortable spiritually. If I should be foolish enough to try to defy these feelings, I should, at length, find that I was completely unable to venture a foot forward without undergoing sensations which I could not possibly bear. I should not be able to see anything before me, only that which lay behind me. But whether we are standing at one of the boundaries, or whether we are well within the confines of our own realm, there comes a certain line in the bridge between the realms where the higher realm becomes invisible to less spiritual eyes. Just as certain light rays are invisible to earthly eyes, and certain sounds and musical notes are inaudible to earthly ears, so are the higher realms invisible to the inhabitants of the lower realms.

And the reason is that each realm possesses a higher vibrational rate than that below it, and is therefore invisible and inaudible to those who live below it.

Thus we can see that another natural law operates for our own good.

CHAPTER SIXTEEN

THE LOWEST REALMS

THERE IS a very bright and beautiful sphere of the spirit world which has been given the picturesque and most apposite title of the "Summerland."

The dark regions might almost be called the "Winterland," but for the fact that the earthly winter possesses a grandeur all its own, while there is nothing but abomination about the lower realms of the spirit world.

So far I have only touched briefly upon the dark realms, taking you just within the threshold, but in company with Edwin and Ruth, I have actually penetrated deeply into those regions.

It is not a pleasant subject, but I have been advised that the facts should be given, not with the intention of frightening people—that is not the spirit world's methods or aims—but to show that such places exist solely by virtue of an inexorable law, the law of cause and effect, the spiritual reaping that succeeds the earthly sowing; to show that to escape moral justice upon the earth-plane is to find strict and unrelenting justice in the spirit world.

As we proceed slowly from our own realm towards these dark lands, we shall find a gradual deterioration taking place in the countryside. The flowers become scanty and ill-nourished, giving the appearance of a struggle for existence. The grass is parched and yellow, until, with the last remnants of sickly flowers, it finally disappears altogether, to be superseded by barren rocks. The light steadily diminishes until we are in a gray land, and then comes the darkness—deep, black, impenetrable darkness; impenetrable, that is, to those who are spiritually blind. Visitors from a higher realm can see in this darkness without themselves being seen by the inhabitants, unless it becomes vitally necessary so to indicate their presence.

Our visits have carried us to what we verily believe to be the lowest plane of human existence.

We began the descent by passing through a belt of mist which we encountered as the ground became hard and barren. The light rapidly dwindled, dwellings were fewer and fewer, and there was not a soul to be seen anywhere. Great tracts of granite-like rocks stretched out before us, cold and forbidding, and the "road" we followed was rough and precipitous. By now, darkness had enshrouded us, but we could still see all our surroundings perfectly clearly. It is rather a strange experience this, of being able to see in the dark, and when one first undergoes it there seems to be an air of unreality about it. But, indeed, it is real enough.

As we climbed down through one of the numerous fissures in the rocks, I could see and feel the loathsome slime that covered the whole surface of them, a dirty green in color and evil smelling. There was, of course, no danger of our falling. That would be impossible for any dwellers in these realms.

After we had journeyed downwards for what seemed to be a great distance—I should imagine it to have been of one mile of earthly measurement, at least—we found ourselves in a gigantic crater, many miles in circumference, whose sides, treacherous and menacing, towered above us.

The whole of this area was interspersed with huge masses of rock, as though some enormous landslide or cataclysm had disrupted them from the upper rim of the crater and sent them hurtling down into the depths below, there to scatter themselves in every direction, forming natural caverns and tunnels.

In our present position we were well above this sea of rocks, and we observed a dull cloud of poisonous vapor rising from it, as though a volcano were below and upon the point of erupting. Had we not been amply protected we should have found these fumes suffocating and deadly. As it was, they left us completely unharmed, although we could perceive with our intuitive faculties the degree of malignity of the whole place. Dimly, we could see through this miasma what might have been human beings, crawling like some foul beasts over the surface of the upper rocks. We could not think, Ruth and I, that they *were* human, but Edwin assured us that once they had walked upon the earth-plane as men, that they had eaten and slept, and breathed the earthly air, had mixed with other men on earth. But they lived a life of spiritual foulness. And in their death of the physical body they had gone to their true abode and their true estate in the spirit world.

The rising vapor seemed to shroud them somewhat from our vision, and we descended until we were level with the tops of the rocks.

As I had expressed my willingness to be taken by Edwin whithersoever he thought would best befit my purpose, and as I knew I should be able to withstand whatever sights I saw, we moved nearer to some of these creatures of hideousness. Ruth was accompanying us, and, needless to say, she would never have been permitted to enter these noxious realms had it not been known, without any shadow of doubt, that she was fully capable of the highest degree of self-possession and fortitude. Indeed, I not only marveled at her composure, but I was profoundly thankful to have her by my side.

We walked closer to one of the sub-human forms that lay sprawled upon the rocks. What remnant of clothing it wore might easily have been dispensed with, since it consisted of nothing but the filthiest rags, which hung together in some inconceivable way, leaving visible great gaps of lifeless-looking flesh. The limbs were so thinly covered with skin that one fully expected to see bare bones showing forth. The hands were shaped like the talons of some bird of prey, with the fingernails so grown as to have become veritable claws. The face upon this monster was barely human, so distorted was it, and malformed. The eyes were small and penetrating, but the mouth was huge and repulsive, with thick protruding lips set upon a prognathic jaw, and scarcely concealing the veriest fangs of teeth.

We gazed earnestly and long at this sorry wreck of what was once a human form, and I wondered what earthly misdeeds had reduced it to this awful state of degeneration.

Edwin, who was experienced in these sights, told us that in time we should gain certain knowledge in our work, which would enable us to read from the faces and forms of these creatures what it was that had reduced them to their present state. There would be no need to accost them to find out at least some of their life's story, for there it was written for the experienced to read. Their very appearance, too, would be a safe guide as to whether they needed help, or whether they were still content to abide in their sunken state.

The object that was now before us, said Edwin, would warrant little sympathy as he was, because he was still steeped in his iniquity and was obviously showing not the least sign of regret for his loathsome earthly life. He was dazed at his loss of physical energy, and puzzled in his mind to know what had befallen him. His face showed that, given the opportunity, he would continue his base practices with every ounce of power that remained to him.

That he had been several hundred years in the spirit world could be seen by the few tattered remnants of his garb, which bespoke a former age, and he had spent the greater part of his earth life inflicting mental and physical tortures upon those who had the misfortune to come into his evil clutches.

Every crime that he had committed against other people had, at last, reverted to, and descended upon, himself. He now had before him—he had done so for hundreds of years—the memory, the indelible memory of every act of evil he had perpetrated against his fellows.

When he was upon earth, he had acted under a false pretence of administering justice. In very truth, his justice had been nothing but a travesty, and now he was seeing exactly what true justice really meant. Not only was his own life of wickedness continually before him, but the features of his many victims were ever passing before his mind, created out of that same memory which is registered unfailingly and ineradicably upon the subconscious mind. *He cannot ever forget, he must always remember.* And his condition was aggravated by the anger of feeling like a trapped animal.

We stood together, a little group of three, but we could not feel one tiny vestige of sympathy for this inhuman monster. He aroused none within us. He was receiving his just merits—no more, no less. *He had judged himself and condemned himself, and now he was suffering the punishment he had, solely and entirely, inflicted upon himself.* Here was no case of an avenging God inflicting condign punishment upon a sinner. The sinner was there, truly, but he was the visible manifestation of the unalterable law of cause and effect. The cause was in his earthly life; the effect was in his spirit life.

Had we been able to detect one tiny glimmer of that light—it is a real light that we see—which is an unmistakable sign of spiritual stirrings within, we might have done something for this soul. As it was, we could do nothing but hope that one day this dreadful being would call for help in true earnestness and sincerity. His call would be answered—unfailingly.

We turned away, and Edwin led us down through an opening in the rocks on to more or less level ground. We could see at once that this part of the crater was more thickly peopled—if one can use the term "people" of such as we saw there.

The inhabitants were variously occupied: some were seated upon small boulders, and gave every appearance of conspiring together, but upon what devilish schemes it was impossible to say. Others were in small groups perpetrating unspeakable tortures upon the weaker of their kind who must, in some fashion, have fallen foul of their tormentors. Their shrieks were unbearable to listen to, and so we closed our ears to them, firmly and effectively. Their limbs were indescribably distorted and malformed, and in some cases their faces and heads had retrograded to the merest mockery of a human countenance. Others again we observed to be lying prone upon the ground as though exhausted from undergoing torture, or because of expending their last remaining energy upon inflicting it, before they could gather renewed strength to recommence their barbarities.

Interspersed throughout the great area of this dreadful region were pools of some sort of liquid. It looked thick and viscid, and inexpressibly filthy, as, indeed, it was. Edwin told us that the stench that came from these pools was in keeping with all else that we had seen here, and he advised us earnestly not to dream of testing the matter for ourselves. We followed his advice implicitly.

We were horrified to see signs of movement in some of the pools, and we guessed, without Edwin having to tell us, that frequently the inhabitants slip and fall into them. They cannot drown because they are as indestructible as we are ourselves.

We witnessed all manner of bestialities and grossness, and such barbarities and cruelties as the mind can scarcely contemplate. It is not my purpose nor my wish to give you a detailed account of what we beheld. We had, by no means, reached the very bottom of this foul pit, but I have given you quite sufficient details of what is to be found in the realms of darkness.

And now you will ask: how does this all come about? How or why are such places allowed to exist?

Perhaps the matter will become clearer when I tell you that every soul who lives in those awful places once lived upon the earth-plane. The thought is dreadful, but the truth cannot be altered. Do not think for one moment that I have exaggerated in my brief description of these regions. I assure you that I have not done so. *I have, in fact, given you an understatement.* The whole of these revolting regions exist by virtue of the same laws that govern the states of beauty and happiness.

The beauty of the spirit world is the outward and visible expression of the spiritual progression of its inhabitants. When we have earned the right to possess things of beauty, they are given to us through the power of creation. In this sense we can be said to have created them ourselves. Beauty of mind and deed can produce nothing but beauty, and hence we have flowers of heavenly beauty, trees and meadows, rivers and streams and seas of pure, glistening, crystal-clear water, magnificent buildings for the joy and benefit of us all, and our own individual homes where we can surround ourselves with still more beauty, and enjoy the delights of happy converse with our fellows.

But ugliness of mind and deed can produce nothing but ugliness. The seeds of hideousness sown upon the earth-plane will inevitably lead to the reaping of a harvest of hideousness in the spirit world. These dark realms have been built up by the people of the earth-plane, even as they have built up the realms of beauty.

No single soul is forced into either the realms of light or those of darkness. No soul could possibly take exception to anything he found in his realm of light, since discontent or disapproval, discomfort or unhappiness cannot exist in these realms. We are a supremely happy, united body of people, and we live together in complete harmony. No soul could, therefore, feel "out of place."

The denizens of the realms of darkness have, by their lives on earth, *condemned themselves, each and every one,* to the state in which they now find themselves. It is the inevitable law of cause and effect; as sure as night follows day upon the earth-plane. Of what avail to cry for mercy? The spirit world is a world of strict justice, a justice that cannot be tampered with, a justice which we all mete out to ourselves. Strict justice and mercy cannot go together. However wholeheartedly and sincerely we may forgive the wrong that has been done to us, mercy is not given to us to dispense in the spirit world. Every bad action must be accounted for by the one who commits it. It is a personal matter which must be done alone, even as the actual event of death of the physical body must be gone through alone. No one can do it for us, but by the great dispensation upon which this and all worlds are founded, we can, and do, have ready and able assistance in our tribulation. Every soul who dwells in these dreadful dark realms has the power within himself to rise up out of the foulness into the light. He must make the individual effort himself, he must work out his own redemption. None can do it for him. Every inch of the way he must toil himself. There is no mercy awaiting him, but stern justice.

But the golden opportunity of spiritual reclamation is ready and waiting. He has but to show an earnest desire to move himself one fraction of an inch towards the realms of light that are above him, and he will find a host of unknown friends who will help him towards that heritage which is his due, but which in his folly he cast aside.

CHAPTER SEVENTEEN

SOME FIRST
IMPRESSIONS

T O FIND oneself suddenly transformed into a permanent inhabitant of the spirit world is, at first, an overwhelming experience. However much one may have read about the conditions of life in the world of spirit, there still remains an almost illimitable number of surprises in store for every soul.

Those of us who have returned to earth to tell about our new life are faced with the difficulty of trying to describe in terms of the earth what is essentially of a spirit nature. Our descriptions *must* fall short of the reality. It is difficult to conjure up in the mind a state of beauty greater than we have ever experienced upon earth. Magnify by one hundred times the beauties that I have told you about, and you would still be far short of a true appraisement.

A question, therefore, that might come into the minds of not a few people would perhaps be this: What was it that struck you most forcibly and most pleasurably when you first arrived in the spirit world, and what were your first impressions?

Let me place myself in the position of one seeking information, and interview our old friends, Edwin and Ruth.

Edwin and I, as you will recall, were brother priests when we were on earth. Edwin had no knowledge whatever upon the subject of spirit return, beyond what I had tried to give him of my own experiences. He was one of the few who really sympathized with me in my psychic difficulties, one of the few, that is, who did not brandish orthodox church teachings in my face. He has since told me that he is very glad he did not do so. When he was on earth the "life to come" was a complete mystery to him—as it unnecessarily is to many others. He naturally conformed to the church's teachings, obeyed its "commandments," performed his duties, and, as he has since quite frankly admitted, hoped for the best—whatever that best might be.

But his earthly life had not consisted solely of religious exercises; he had helped others upon every occasion where help was needed and where he could possibly give it. Those services, unobtrusively performed, had helped him immeasurably when the time came for him to quit the earth world. Those kind actions brought him into the land of beauty and eternal sunshine.

His first impressions upon his awakening in the spirit world were—to use his own words—absolutely breathtaking. He had visualized, subconsciously perhaps, some sort of misty state as the condition of a future life, where there would be a great deal of "prayer and praise." To find himself in a realm of inexpressible beauty, with all the glories of earthly nature purged of its earthliness, refined and etherealized, with the enormous wealth of color all around and about him; to behold the crystal purity of the rivers and brooks, with the charm of the country dwellings and the grandeur of the city's temples and halls of learning; to find himself in the center of all such glories without an inkling of what had thus been in store for him, was to cast doubts upon the veracity of his own eyes. He could *not* believe that he was not in the midst of some beautiful, but fantastic, dream, from which he would shortly awaken to find himself once again in his old familiar surroundings. He thought how he would relate this dream when he returned to consciousness. Then he considered how it would be received—as very beautiful, no doubt, but just a dream.

And so he stood gazing upon all this wealth of beauty. That, Edwin said, was his first and greatest impression.

He had regarded as part of the same dream all that had gone before, all that had led up to his standing and gazing in wonder upon the scene that stretched out almost unendingly before him. How he had awakened upon a comfortable couch, in a very charming house, to see sitting beside him an old friend, who performed the same office for Edwin as did Edwin for me when he came to meet me.

His friend led him out-of-doors to see the new world. Then came his friend's most difficult task—to convince Edwin that he had "died" and yet still lived. You see, at first he took his friend and his friend's explanation to be part of the same dream, and he was nervously awaiting for something to happen that would break up the dream into returning earthly consciousness. Edwin admitted that he took some convincing, but his friend was infinitely patient with him.

The instant that he was assured that he was really and truly and permanently in the world of spirit, his heart knew no greater joy, and he proceeded to do what I afterwards did in company with Ruth—travel through the lands of the new life with the luxurious freedom of body and mind that is of the very essence of spirit life in these realms.

What most impressed Ruth upon her first awakening in the spirit world was, she said, the enormous profusion of color.

Her transition had been a placid one, and she had consequently awakened, after a very brief sleep, calmly and gently. As with Edwin, she had then found herself in a delightful house, small, neat and compact, and all her own. An old friend was beside her, ready to help in the inevitable perplexities that accompany so many awakenings in the spirit world.

Ruth is by nature rather reserved, especially, as she said, when it came to talking about herself. In Edwin's case I knew so much of his earth life that it was easy for me to draw upon my own knowledge of him. Ruth, however, I had never seen until we met here upon that occasion beside the lake. After much persuasion I managed to extract from her one or two details concerning her earthly life.

She had never, she said, been an active churchgoer, not because she despised the church, but because her own views upon the "hereafter" did not agree with what her own church taught. She saw too much of faith required, and too little of fact being given, and altogether she had encountered so much of the troubles and afflictions of others in her daily life that the vague, but rather terrifying, picture of the world to come, the dreadful "Judgment Day" that was so constantly held before her in the church's teaching, she instinctively felt to be wrong. The emphasis laid so strongly upon the word "sinner" with the almost wholesale condemnation of everyone as such, she also felt to be wrong. She was not foolish enough, she declared, to believe that we are all saints, but, at the same time, we are not all sinners. Of the many people she knew, she could recall none who could ever be so branded and condemned in the religious sense. Where, then, were all these people going after they had "died"?

She could never imagine herself sitting in judgment upon these souls and passing sentence upon them as "sinners." It would be preposterous to contemplate, Ruth added, that she could be more "merciful" than God. It was unthinkable. So she had built up for herself a simple "faith"—a practice that the theologian would at once say was highly dangerous and never for one moment to be encouraged. He would have spoken of the "peril" in which her "immortal soul" stood by entertaining such ideas. But Ruth never for an instant considered her "immortal soul" to be in "peril." Indeed, she went happily along, living her life according to the dictates of her gentle nature, helping others in her daily life, and bringing a little sunshine into the drab lives of others. And she was firmly convinced that when her time came to leave the earth-plane she would take with her into the new life the affection of her many friends.

She had no fear of death of the physical body, nor could she imagine it to be the terrifying experience that so many people anticipate and dread. She had no absolute grounds for this belief, and she has since concluded that she must have been drawn to it intuitively.

Apart from the glorious colors of the realm in which she found herself, what struck Ruth very forcibly was the astonishing clearness of the atmosphere. There was nothing like it to be seen on earth. The atmosphere was so free from the slightest trace of mistiness, and her own vision seemed to be so intensified in power and extent, that the enormous range of colors became doubly vivid. She had a naturally keen eye for color, and she had undergone considerable musical training when she was upon earth. When she came into the spirit world these two faculties had combined, and the color and music of the new land had burst upon her with aft the luxuriance of their superb beauty.

At first, she could scarcely believe her senses, but her friends had soon explained to her just what had happened, and as she had so few fixed ideas about the future life, so had she so little to unlearn. But, she said, it took her many days of earth time before she could fully grasp or absorb all the wonders that lay around her. When once she had fully realized the significance of her new life, and that all eternity lay before her in which to sample the marvels of this land, she was able to restrain her excitement, and, as she said, "take things a little more quietly." It was while she was in process of the latter that we first met.

Once, when the three of us were seated in the garden pleasantly discussing all manner of things, we espied, walking up the garden path, a figure that was well known to Edwin and myself. He had been our ecclesiastical superior when we were upon the earth-plane, and he was what is known as a "Prince of the Church." He was still attired in his customary habiliments, and we were all agreed—when we came to compare notes afterwards—that they eminently suited both the place and the conditions. The full-length style and the rich coloring of the robes seemed to blend most harmoniously with all about us. There was nothing incongruous about it, and as he was at full liberty to wear his robes in the spirit world he had done so; not because of his former position, but through long custom, and because he felt that he thus, in some small measure, helped to add to the colorful beauty of his new habitation.

Now, although the high office, which he held with distinction upon earth, has no counterpart or significance in the spirit world, yet he was well known to many here by name and by sight and by repute. This provided a further good reason for his retaining his earthly style of clothing, at least for the present. But the deference that his position upon earth had always evoked, he utterly cast aside when he came into the world of spirit. He would have none of it, and he was very insistent that all who knew him—and those who did not—should be strictly attentive to his wishes in this respect. He was very much loved when he was incarnate, and it is but natural that, with his advent into spirit lands, those who knew him should show the same respect as before. Respect is one thing, for we all respect each other in these realms; but deference that should be given to others of greater spirituality is another thing altogether. He early recognized this, so he told us, and from my own personal knowledge of his innate humility I could guess that such would be the case with him.

Our first meeting led to others, and many have been the occasions—and we shall enjoy many more—when he has joined Edwin, Ruth and myself, where we have sat in the garden, or gone forth together. It was during one of our peregrinations together that I asked our former superior if he would give me some brief sketch of his first impressions of the spirit world.

What struck him so forcibly when he found himself here was not only the immensity and beauty of the spirit world, but the very description of this world itself in relation to the earth world, and most particularly in relation to the life he had left behind him. First of all, there came the feeling, an almost crushing one, of having wasted his earthly life upon seemingly nonessentials, irrelevancies and a great deal of useless formularies and formalism. But friends had come to his rescue intellectually, and they had assured him that the time in its personal application had not been wasted, although his life had been encompassed by the pomp and pageantry of his office. However much the latter had engrossed those about him, he had personally never let them become an absorbing factor in his life. He derived much comfort from this reflection.

But what he found to be most mentally disturbing was the invalidity of the doctrines which he had perforce upheld. So many of them were tumbling in ruins about him. But again he found friends to guide him. And they did so in a simple and direct manner, such as would appeal to his alert mind, namely: to forget the religious teachings of the earthly life and become acquainted with spirit life and its laws. Discard the old, and accept the new. He had therefore made every endeavor to do so, and he had been completely successful. He swept his mind clear of all that had no foundation in truth, and he made the very pleasant discovery that, at last, he was in full enjoyment of absolute spiritual freedom. He found it was so much easier to obey the natural laws of the spirit world than to obey the church's "commandments," and it was very pleasant to be rid of the formalities of his earthly position. He could at last speak with his own voice freely, and not with the voice of the church.

Altogether, said our former superior, he thought that his greatest impression upon his arrival in the spirit world was this splendid sense of freedom, first of mind and then of body, and made so much the greater in the spirit world by the measure of its absence in the earth world.

CHAPTER EIGHTEEN

RECREATIONS

I HAVE USED the word "recreation" once or twice, but I have not given you any specific details upon this relatively important subject.

The merest suggestion that we should have recreations in the spirit world will, most assuredly, come to some minds as an unpleasant shock. Those same minds will instantly think of the many and varied sports and pastimes that are usefully and profitably indulged in upon the earth-plane. To transplant, as it were, such fundamentally earthly things into a world of pure spirit is inconceivable. Inconceivable, perhaps, because the whole idea is far-fetched, or because the spirit world should be regarded as a *higher* state. A state, that is, in which we shall leave behind us all our earthly habits, and live perpetually in a condition of high ecstasy, caring only for those vague, unsubstantial things that our respective religion hinted to us as being the reward of the good.

To entertain such suppositions about this life is to suggest that, by the very fact of our coming into the spirit world to live, we are at once in the presence of God, or that at least we are within the realm wherein God dwells, and therefore anything even remotely suggestive of earthly customs or manners would be rigidly excluded as too unholy for admission.

Such ideas as these are, of course, pure nonsense, since God is no nearer to us in the spirit world than He is to us in the earth world. It is *we* who are nearer to *Him*, because, among other things, we can see more clearly the Divine Hand in this world, and the expression of His Mind. That, however, is a deeper subject which it is not within our province to go into just now.

Many of us find our recreation in another form of work. In the spirit world we do not suffer fatigue either of body or mind, but to continue unremittingly in the pursuit of any one occupation, without any intermittent change, would soon produce feelings of mental dissatisfaction or unrest. Our powers of application to any given task are immense, but at the same time we draw a very clear line of limitation for any period of our work, in respect to the whole, and beyond that line we do not go. We will exchange our present task for another form of work, we can cease work altogether and spend our time reclining in our homes or elsewhere; we can occupy ourselves in study; or we can engage ourselves in the amusing recreations that abound in these realms.

When we have ceased our work for the time being, we are much in the same case as are you who are still upon the earth-plane. What shall you do to amuse yourself? You may feel that physical rest is necessary, and so you will incline towards intellectual recreation. And so it is precisely with us here. Intellectual recreation, which may take diverse forms, is amply provided for in the halls of learning, because learning can itself be a recreation.

Ruth and I have spent many happy hours in the library and the hall of art, but there have been numberless occasions when we felt the need for something more sturdy, and we have walked down to the sea and gone aboard one of the fine vessels there, and thence paid a visit to one of the islands. And here at the seaside we have one of the most entertaining of our sports.

I have already told you how vessels in the spirit world are propelled purely by the process of thought, and I have further indicated how it takes a little time to become proficient in the art of personally applying such propulsion. Such proficiency is ultimately achieved, but we can test our progress and receive valuable aid in our endeavors by taking part in contests upon the water.

A clear distinction must be drawn between such contests upon the earth-plane and those in the spirit world. Here we are assured, because we know, that all rivalry is purely friendly. There is no gain attached whatever, beyond the experience and the acquisition of greater skill, and there are no prizes to be fought for and won. At the end of every race we shall be sure of the greatest help to make us more expert in the increasing and handling of our vessel's speed.

One particular diversion that finds a very considerable measure of favor with us here is that of dramatic representation of different kinds.

We have beautiful theatres situated in environment just as beautiful, worthy buildings devoted to a worthy purpose. The architects who design the buildings do so with the same meticulous care as is shown in all their endeavors, and the results, as usual, reveal the degree of active co-operation that exists between the masters of the craft. The garniture within is the product of skilled artists from the Hall of Fabrics; the gardens without have the same devoted care lavished upon them. The result is as far removed from an earthly theatre as it is possible to imagine.

Before I speak further upon this subject I would like to observe that I am fully aware that there are people upon the earth-plane who totally disapprove of theatres and everything connected with them. In most instances such aversion is the outcome of religious upbringing. I cannot alter the truth, as I find it in the spirit world, to accord with certain religious views held by people still incarnate. I speak of those things which I have witnessed in company with thousands of others, and the fact of strong disapproval, by earth people, of what I have described as existing in the spirit world, in no way proves such things to be non-existent, and therefore my statement to be false. My position for observation is incomparably superior to theirs, because I have left the earth world and become an inhabitant of the spirit world. If our descriptions of the world we now inhabit were to be altered to suit every individual taste and every preconception of what the spirit world ought to be, we might just as well cease, forthwith, to give any further descriptions, since, after being so tampered with, they would be worthless. Lest I should have conveyed any false impression in saying this, let me add that anyone who expressed disapproval of all, or any, form of recreation he found here, such a person would never be asked to indulge in them. With others of similar views, he would find himself in a little community apart, there to remain, safely out of range of all supposed earthly things, and able to live in such a place as he thought "heaven" ought to be. I have met such people, and it was not long, as a rule, before they abandoned their home-made heaven, and walked abroad into the finer, greater heaven, which is the work of the Greatest Mind.

Each theatre of this realm is familiar to us by the type of play that is presented in it. The plays themselves are frequently vastly different from those that are customary upon the earth-plane. We have nothing that is sordid, nor do the authors of plays insist upon harrowing their audiences. We can see many problem plays where social questions of the earth-plane are dealt with, but unlike the earth-plane our plays will *provide a solution* to the particular problem—a solution which the earth is too blind to adopt.

We can go to see comedies where, I do assure you, the laughter is invariably much more hearty and voluminous than is ever to be heard in a theatre of the earth-plane. In the spirit world we can afford to laugh at much that we once, when incarnate, treated with deadly seriousness and earnestness!

We have witnessed grand historical pageants showing the greater moments of a nation, and we have seen, too, history as it really was, and not as it is often so fancifully written about in history books! But surely the most impressive, and, at the same time, interesting experience is to be present at one of these pageants where the *original participants* themselves re-enact the events in which they were concerned, first as the events were popularly thought to have occurred, and then as they actually took place. These representations are among the most widely attended here, and never are there more attentive and rapt members of the audience than those players who, during their earthly lives, played the parts, in stage plays, of the famous characters whom they are now seeing "in the flesh."

In such pageants the coarser, depraved and debased incidents are omitted entirely, because they would be distasteful to the audience, and, indeed, to all in this realm. Nor are we shown scenes which are, in the main incidents, nothing but battle and bloodshed and violence.

At first, one experiences a strange feeling in beholding, in person, the bearers of names famous throughout the earth world, but after a time one becomes perfectly accustomed to it, and it becomes part of our normal existence.

The most noticeable difference between our two worlds, in this matter of recreations, is created by our respective requirements. We have no need here to take bodily exercise, vigorous or otherwise, nor do we need to go out into the "fresh air." Our spirit bodies are always in perfect condition, we suffer no disorders of any kind, and the air, which cannot be other than fresh, penetrates into every corner of our homes and buildings, where it fully retains its purity. It would be impossible for it to become vitiated or contaminated in any way. It is to be expected, then, that our recreations should be more upon the mental plane than upon the "physical."

As most of the outdoor games of the earth world involve the use of a ball, it will be appreciated that here, where the law of gravity operates under different conditions from yours, anything in the nature of propelling a ball by striking it, would lead to quite hopeless results. I am speaking now of games of a competitive nature.

On the earth-plane skill in games is acquired by the mastery of the mind over the muscles of the body, when once the latter has been brought to a healthy condition. But here we are always in a healthy condition, and our muscles are always under the complete and absolute control of our minds. Efficiency is quickly gained, whether it is in playing upon a musical instrument, painting a picture, or in any other pursuit that requires the use of the limbs. It will be seen, therefore, that most of the usual games would lose their point here.

And it must be remembered that indoors or outdoors are precisely one to us here. We have no changes of weather during recurrent seasons. The great central sun is for ever shining; it is never anything but delightfully warm. We never feel the necessity for a brisk walk to set our blood circulating the better. Our homes and our houses are not necessities, but additions to an already enjoyable life. You will find many people here who do not possess a home; they do not want one, they will tell you, for the sun is perpetually shining and the temperature is perpetually warm. They are never ill, or hungry, or in want of any kind, and the whole beautiful realm is theirs to wander in.

It must also be remembered that viewpoints change very much when one comes to live here. What we deemed so very important when we were incarnate, we find is not nearly so important when we arrive in the spirit world. And many of our erstwhile earthly games seem rather tame and trivial beside our greatly increased powers in the spirit world. The fact that we can move ourselves through space instantaneously is enough to make the greatest earthly athletic skill recede into insignificance, and our mundane sports and games are in similar case. Our recreations are more of the mind, and we never feel that we must expend a superfluity of physical energy upon some strenuous action, for our energy is at a constant level according to our individual requirements. We find that we have so much to learn, and learning is in itself such pleasure that we do not need the number or variety of recreations that you do. We have plenty of music to listen to, there are such wonders in these lands that we want to know all about, there is so much congenial work to be done, that there is no cause to be cast down at the prospect of there being few of the *earthly* sports and pastimes in the spirit world. There is such a superabundant supply of vastly more entertaining things to be seen and done here, besides which a great deal of the earthly recreations appear sheer trivialities.

CHAPTER NINETEEN

SPIRIT PERSONALIA

W HAT DOES it feel like to be a spirit person? That is a question that has arisen in the minds of many people. If, in turn, one were to ask: what does it feel like to be an earth person?—you might be inclined to reply that the question is rather a foolish one, because I have been incarnate myself once, and therefore I should know. But before the question is dismissed as foolish, let us see what it can provide by way of an answer.

First of all, consider the physical body. It undergoes fatigue for which it is vitally necessary to have rest. It gets hungry and thirsty, and it must be provided with food and drink. It can suffer pains and torments through a great variety of illness and disease. It can lose its limbs through accidents, or from other causes. The senses can become impaired through increasing age; or accident, again, can cause it to lose the faculty of sight or hearing; or the physical body can be born into the world without either or both of those senses, and, in addition, it may be powerless of speech. The physical brain may be so affected that we are incapable of any sane action, and we have, in consequence, to be taken care of by others.

What a gloomy picture, you will say! That is so, but anyone can be the victim to some, at least, of the catalogue of disabilities I have mentioned. At least three of them are common to every single soul upon the earth-plane—hunger, thirst, and fatigue. And that by no means exhausts the list. But it will suffice for our purpose.

Now, eliminate, completely and entirely, every one of these unpleasant disabilities that I have enumerated; exclude, infallibly and everlastingly, the cause of them, and you should have in your mind some idea of what it feels like as a spirit person!

When I was upon the earth-plane I suffered from some of the ailments that are common to most of us, ailments that are not necessarily serious, and that we take rather as a matter of course; the minor aches and pains that most of the incarnate, at one time or another, manage to put up with. In addition to those minor ailments, I was, of course, conscious of my physical body by the intrusion of hunger, thirst, and fatigue. The final illness—the serious one—was too much for the physical body, and my transition took place. And immediately I knew what it felt like to be a spirit person.

As I stood talking to Edwin I felt, physically, a giant, in spite of the fact that I had just departed from a bed of sickness. As time went on I felt even better. I had not the slightest suspicion of a twinge of pain, and I felt light in weight. Indeed, it did not seem as though I were encased in a body at all! My mind was fully alert, and I was aware of my body only in so far as I could move my limbs and myself wherever I wished, apparently without any of the muscular actions that were but so recently familiar. It is extremely difficult to convey to you this feeling of *perfect* health, because such a thing is utterly impossible on earth, and therefore I have nothing with which to draw a comparison, or form an analogy for you. This state belongs to the spirit alone, and completely defies any description in earthly terms. It *must* be experienced, and that you will not be able to do until you become one of us here yourself.

I have said that my mind was alert. That is an understatement. I discovered that my mind was a veritable storehouse of facts concerning my earthly life. Every act I had performed, and every word that I had uttered, every impression I had received; every fact that I had read about, and every incident I had witnessed, all these, I found, were indelibly registered in my subconscious mind. And that is common to every spirit person who has had an incarnate life.

It must not be supposed that we are continually haunted, as it were, by a wild phantasmagoria of miscellaneous thoughts and impressions. That would be a veritable nightmare. No. Our minds are like a complete biography of our earthly life, wherein is set down every little detail concerning ourselves, arranged in an orderly fashion, and *omitting nothing*. The book is closed, normally, but it is ever there, ready to hand, for us to turn to, and we merely recall the incidents as we wish. I am now speaking personally, and as it governs the folk with whom I live in this realm.

The description that I gave you of that particular soul's memory in the lowest realms, brings into force other laws, as I attempted to show you. I am not prepared to say *how* it happens; I can only tell you *what* happens.

This encyclopedic memory, with which we are endowed, is not so difficult to understand when you pause to consider your own average earthly memory. You are not continuously bothered by the incidents of the whole of your life, but they are simply there for you to recall, when and where you wish, and they may arise out of the occasions of the moment. One incident will set a train of thought going in which the memory will have its share. Sometimes you cannot recall what is in your memory, but in the spirit world we can recall instantly, without any effort, and unfailingly. The subconscious mind never forgets, and consequently our own past deeds become a reproach to us, or otherwise, according to our earthly lives. The recordings upon the tablets of the real mind cannot be erased. They are there for all time, but they do not necessarily haunt us, because in those tablets are also set down the good actions, the kind actions, the kind thoughts, and everything of which we could justly be proud. And if they are written in larger and more ornate letters than those things we regret, we shall be so much the happier.

Of course, when we are in the spirit world our memories are persistently retentive. When we follow a course of study in any subject whatsoever, we shall find that we learn easily and quickly because we are freed from the limitations that the physical body imposes upon the mind. If we are acquiring knowledge we shall retain that knowledge without fail. If we are following some pursuit where dexterity of the hands is required, we shall find that our spirit bodies respond to the impulses of our minds immediately and exactly. To learn to paint a picture, or to play upon a musical instrument, to mention two familiar mundane activities, are tasks which can be performed in a fraction of the time that they would take when we are incarnate. In learning to lay out a spirit garden, for example, or to build a house, we shall find that the requisite knowledge is gained with equal ease and speed—insofar as our intelligence will allow; for we are not all endowed with keen intellects the moment we shake off the physical body. If that were the case, these realms would be inhabited by supermen and superwoman, and we are very far from that! But our intelligence can be increased; that is part of our progression, for progression is not only of a spiritual nature. Our minds have unlimited resources for intellectual expansion and improvement, however backward we may be when we come into the spirit world. And our intellectual progression will advance surely and steadily, according to our wish for it to do so, under the learned and able masters of all branches of knowledge and learning. And throughout our studies we shall be assisted by our unfailingly retentive memories. There will be no forgetting.

Now to come to the spirit body itself. The spirit body is, broadly speaking, the counterpart of our earthly bodies. When we come into the spirit world we are recognizably ourselves. But we leave behind us all our physical disabilities. We have our full complement of limbs, our sight and our hearing; in fact, all our senses are fully functioning. Indeed, the five senses, as we know them upon earth, become many degrees more acute when we are discarnate. Any supernormal or subnormal conditions of the physical body, such as excessive stoutness or leanness, vanish when we arrive in these realms, and we appear as we should have appeared on earth had not a variety of earthly reasons caused us to be otherwise.

There is a stage in our lives on earth which we know as the prime of life. It is towards this that we all move. Those of us who are old or elderly when we pass into spirit will return to our prime-of-life period. Others who are young will advance towards that period. And we all preserve our natural characteristics; they never leave us. But we find that many minor physical features that we can profitably dispense with, we shake off with our earthly bodies—certain irregularities of the body with which, perhaps, we have been born, or that have come upon us during the course of the years. How many of us are there, I wonder, when we are incarnate, who could not think of some small improvement that we should like to make in our physical bodies, were it at all possible! Not many!

I have told you how the trees in these realms grow in a state of perfection—upright and clean-looking and well-formed, because they have no storms of wind to bend and twist the young branches into malformations. The spirit body is subject to just the same law here in spirit. The storms of life can twist the physical body, and if that life has been spiritually ugly the spirit body will be similarly twisted. But if the earth life has been spiritually sound, the spirit body will be correspondingly sound. There is many a fine soul inhabiting a crooked earthly body. There is many a bad soul inhabiting a well-formed earthly body. The spirit world reveals the truth for all to see.

How does the spirit appear anatomically, you will ask? Anatomically, just exactly the same as does yours. We have muscles, we have bones, we have sinews, but they are not of the earth; they are purely of spirit. We suffer from no ailments—that would be impossible in the spirit world. Therefore our bodies do not require constant looking after to maintain a state of good health. Here our health is always perfect, because we have such a vibrational rate that disease, and the germs that cause it, cannot enter. Malnutrition, in the sense that you know it, cannot exist here, but spiritual malnutrition—that is, of the soul—does most certainly exist. A visit to the dark realms and their neighborhood will soon reveal that!

Does it seem strange that a spirit body should possess fingernails and hair? How would you have us to be? Not different from yourselves in this respect, surely? Would we not be something of a revolting spectacle without our usual anatomical features and characteristics? This seems an elementary statement, but it is sometimes necessary and expedient to voice the elementary.

How is the spirit body covered? A great many people—I think it would be true to say the great majority—wake up in these realms dressed in the counterpart of the clothes they wore when upon the earth-plane at the time of their transition. It is reasonable that they should, because such attire is customary, especially when the person has no foreknowledge whatever of spirit world conditions. And they may remain so attired for just as long as they please. Their friends will have told them of their true state of being, and then they can change to their spirit clothing if they so wish. Most people are only too glad to make the change, since their old earthly style of clothing looks very drab in these colorful realms. It was not long before I discarded my old clerical attire for my true raiment. Black is altogether too somber amongst such a galaxy of color!

Spirit robes vary in themselves almost as much as the realms vary. There always seems to be some subtle difference between one person's spirit robe and another's, both in color and form, so that there is an endless variety in the two particulars of color and form alone.

All spirit robes are of full length; that is, they reach down to the feet. They are sufficiently full to hang in graceful folds, and it is these very folds that present the most beautiful shades and tones of color by the effect of what on earth would be called "light and shade." It would be impossible to give you anything like a comprehensive account of the different additional features that go to make up the whole composition of spirit vesture.

Many people will be found wearing a girdle or sash around the waist. Sometimes these will be of material, sometimes they appear to be of gold or silver lace or tissue. In all cases of the latter, they are rewards for services performed. No possible conception can be formed of the superlative brilliance of the golden or silver girdles that are worn by the great personages from the higher realms. They are usually adorned with the most beautiful of precious stones, fashioned in various shapes, and mounted in beautifully wrought settings, according to the rulings that govern such matters. The higher beings, too, will be seen to be wearing the most magnificent diadems as brilliant as their girdles. The same law applies to these. Those of us of lesser degree may perhaps be wearing some such embellishment as I have just described, but in a greatly modified form.

There is an enormous wealth of spirit lore behind the whole subject of spirit adornments, but one fact can be plainly stated: all such adornments *must* be earned. Rewards are given only upon merit.

We may wear what we like upon our feet, and most of us prefer to wear a covering of some sort. It usually takes the form of a light shoe or sandal. I have seen numbers of people here who have a predilection for going bare-footed, and they do so. It is perfectly in order, and it excites no comment whatever. It is natural and commonplace with us.

The material of which our robes are made is not transparent, as some would perhaps be inclined to imagine! It is substantial enough. And the reason why it is not transparent is that our clothing possesses the same vibrational rate as the wearer. The higher one progresses the higher this rate becomes, and consequently dwellers in those elevated spheres will take on an unimaginable tenuousness both of spirit body and clothing. That tenuousness is the more apparent to us than to them, that is, externally apparent, for the same reason that a small light will seem so much the brighter by virtue of the surrounding darkness. When the light is magnified a thousand times—as it is in the case of the higher realms—the contrast is immeasurably greater.

We seldom wear any covering upon our heads. I do not remember seeing anything of the sort anywhere in this realm. We have no need for protection against the elements!

I think you will have concluded by now that to be a spirit person *can* be a very pleasant experience.

And in my travels through these realms of light I have yet to find a single solitary individual who would willingly exchange this grand, free life in the spirit world for the old life upon the earth-plane.

Experto crede!

CHAPTER TWENTY

THE CHILDREN'S SPHERE

ONE OF the innumerable questions that I put to Edwin, shortly after my arrival in the spirit world, concerned the destiny of children who, as such, passed into spirit lands.

There is a period of our earthly lives which we are accustomed to call "the prime of life." There is also a prime of life here in spirit, and it is towards that period that all souls either advance or return, according to the age at which their transition takes place. How long it will take rests entirely with themselves, since it is purely a matter of spiritual progression and development, though with the young this period is usually much shorter. Those who pass into spirit after the prime of life period has been reached, whether they be elderly or extremely aged, will, in due time, become younger in appearance, although they will grow older in knowledge and spirituality. It must not be assumed from this that we all eventually reach a dead level of commonplace uniformity. Outwardly, we look young; we lose those signs of the passage of years which cause some of us no little disturbance of mind when we are incarnate. But our minds become older as we gain knowledge and wisdom and greater spirituality, and these qualities of the mind are manifest to all with whom we come into contact.

When we visited the temple in the city, and, from a distance, beheld the radiant visitor whom we had come to honor, he presented to the eye the appearance of perfect—and eternal—youth. Yet the degree of knowledge and wisdom and spirituality which he diffused, and which we could feel with our minds, was almost overpoweringly great. It is the same, in varying degrees, with all those who visit us from the higher realms. If, therefore, there is this rejuvenation of fully grown people, what of the souls who pass over as children; indeed, what of those, even, who pass into the spirit world at birth?

The answer is that they grow as they would have grown upon the earth-plane. But the children here—of all ages—are given such treatment and care as would never be possible in the earth world.

The young child, whose mind is not yet fully formed, is uncontaminated by earthly contacts, and on passing into the spirit world it finds itself in a realm of great beauty, presided over by souls of equal beauty. This children's realm has been called the "nursery of heaven," and surely anyone who has been fortunate enough to have visited it will say that a more apposite term could not be found. It was, therefore, in response to my original question that Edwin proposed that Ruth and I should accompany him on a visit to the nursery of heaven.

We walked towards the boundary between the higher realm and our own, and we turned in the direction of Edwin's house. Already we could feel the atmosphere more rarefied, though it was not sufficiently pronounced to cause us any inconvenience or discomfort. I noticed that this atmosphere had a great deal more color in it, much more than in the depths of the realm. It was as though a great number of shafts of light were meeting and spreading their broad beams over all the landscape. These shafts of light were forever on the move, interweaving themselves and producing the most delicate and delightful blendings of color, like a succession of rainbows. They were extremely restful, but they were also filled with vitality and, as it seemed to Ruth and me, lightheartedness and merriment. Sadness and unhappiness, one felt, would be utterly impossible here.

The countryside took upon itself a much brighter green in its verdure, the trees were not so tall, but they were as shapely as every other tree in these realms, and they were growing as perfectly.

After we had proceeded a little distance the atmosphere became clear of the colored beams, and it more resembled that of our own sphere. But there was a strange and subtle difference which was puzzling to the visitor upon his first visit, and it arose, so Edwin told us, from the essential spirituality of the children who live there. Something akin to this is to be encountered when one is privileged to journey to a higher realm than that in which one normally resides. It is almost as though there were a greater degree of buoyancy in the air, apart altogether from a noticeable effect of elevation of the mind.

We saw many fine buildings before us as we walked along the soft grass. They were not of any great height, but they were broad in extent, and they were all most pleasantly situated among trees and gardens. Flowers, needless to say, were growing prolifically everywhere, in artistically-arranged beds, as well as in large masses upon the grassy slopes and beneath the trees. I noticed that in some instances flowers that have their counterpart upon the earth-plane were growing by themselves, those that were proper to the spirit world being separated from them. We were told that there was no special significance in this segregation, but that it was done solely to show the distinction between the two classes of flowers, the spirit and the earthly. Beautiful as the earthly flowers are that grow here, there can be no comparison with those that belong alone to spirit lands. Here again one is limited by earthly experience in any attempt to describe them. Not only are the colorings richer, but the conformations of the flowers and foliage present such an abundance of unparalleled beauty of design that we have no earthly example to adduce by way of comparison. But it must not be supposed that these magnificent flowers remotely suggested the rare hot-house bloom. Far from it. The superabundance of them, together with the great strength and variety of their perfumes, would instantly dispel any thought of rarity. It was no case of cultivating the beauty of the bloom at the expense of its perfume. They all possessed the quality common to all growing things here, that of pouring out energizing force, not only through the medium of their aromas, but through personal contact. I had already tried the experiment of holding a flower within the cupped hands—it was Ruth who had instructed me—and I had felt the stream of life-force flowing up my arms.

We could see delightful ponds and small lakes, upon the surface of which were flourishing the most beautiful water flowers in the gayest colors. In another direction we could see larger expanses of water like a series of lakes, with many small boats gliding serenely along.

The buildings were constructed of a substance that had all the appearance of alabaster, and they were all tinged with the most delicate colors, such as one is accustomed to seeing in the subtle blendings of an earthly rainbow. The style of architecture resembled, for the most part, that of our own sphere; that is to say, some of the buildings bore upon their surface the most exquisite carvings of such natural objects as abound in the trees and flowers, while others drew for their relief upon the normal features particular to the spirit world.

But what gave us the most enjoyable surprise was to see, interspersed throughout the woods, the quaintest little cottages such as one was always inclined to believe only belonged to the pages of children's story-books. Here were diminutive houses with crooked timbers—beautifully crooked—with bright red roofs and lattice-windows, and each with a charming little garden, all its own, surrounding it.

It will at once be concluded that the spirit world has borrowed from the earth world in these fanciful creations for the children's delight, but such is not the case. In truth, this whole conception of miniature houses emanated, in the first instance, from the spirit world. Whoever was the artist who received our original impression, she has been lost to the earth world through the course of the years. That artist is known to us here, though, where she continues her work in the children's sphere.

These little houses were large enough to allow a grown person plenty of room in which to move without appearing to knock his head! To the children they seemed to be of just the right size, without their feeling lost within them. I learnt that it was for this same reason that all the large buildings in this realm were without any appreciable height. By thus not making them too high, nor the rooms too large, they conformed with the child's mind, as yet not fully formed, where spaces seem greater than they really are, and where buildings too spacious would have the effect upon the little mind of seeming to dwarf it.

Great numbers of children live in these tiny dwellings, each being presided over by an older child, who is perfectly capable of attending to any situation that might arise with the other "residents."

As we walked along we could see groups of happy children, some playing games with their fellows, others seated upon the grass while a teacher was reading to them. Others, again, were to be observed listening attentively and with marked interest to a teacher who was explaining the flowers to them, and giving them something of a lesson in botany. But it was botany of a very different order from that of the earth-plane, insofar as the purely spirit flowers were concerned. The distinctions between the earthly flowers and the spirit flowers were amply demonstrated by the two orders of flowers being separated.

Edwin took us to one of the teachers, and explained the reason of our visit. We were instantly made welcome, and the teacher was kind enough to answer a few questions. Her enthusiasm for her work added to her pleasure, she said, in telling us anything we wished to know. As to herself, she had been in the spirit world a goodly number of years. She had had children of her own when upon the earth-plane, and she was still keenly interested in their welfare, and that had led her to take on her present work. So much she told us of herself. It was not very informative, and we knew as much without her having to tell us! What she did *not* tell us—it was Edwin who later gave us the details—was that she had made such a success with her own children upon earth, who now joined their mother in her work, that it had been obvious from the commencement just what her work would be in spirit lands. Needless to say, it was the very work upon which she had set her heart—the care of children.

It needed no one to tell us that she was admirably suited for such work. She radiated that charm and confidence, kindliness and mirthfulness of nature that so appealed to the children. She understood the child mind—she was, in fact, just a grown-up child herself! She possessed a wide knowledge of the most interesting things, especially of those things that appeal most to children; she had an inexhaustible fund of capital stories for her small charges, and, most important of all, she could be—and showed herself to be—at one with them. I do not think we had as yet seen anyone so superlatively happy as this gracious soul.

In this sphere, our new friend told us, there were to be found children of all ages, from the infant, whose separate existence upon the earth-plane had amounted to only a few minutes, or who even had had no separate existence at all, but had been born "dead," to the youth of sixteen or seventeen years of earth time.

It frequently happens that as the children grow up they remain in this same sphere, and themselves become teachers for a period, until other work takes them elsewhere.

And what of the parents? Were they ever the teachers of their own children? Seldom, or never, our friend informed us. It was a practice that would scarcely ever be feasible, since the parent would be more inclined to be prejudiced in favor of her own child, and there might be other embarrassments. The teachers are always souls of wide experience, and there are not many parents upon the earth-plane who would be capable of undertaking the care of spirit children immediately upon the transition of the former. Whether the teachers were themselves parents upon the earth-plane or not, they all undergo an extensive course of training before they are adjudged fit to fill the post of teacher to the children, and to conform with, and uphold, the rigidly high standards of the work. And, of course, they must all be temperamentally fitted to hold the position of teacher.

The work is not arduous, as you would judge it in the earth world, but it demands a multiplicity of special attributes.

The mental and physical growth of the child in the spirit world is much more rapid than in the earth world. You will recall what I told you about the absolute retentiveness of the memory here. That retentiveness begins as soon as the mind is capable of grasping anything at all, and that is very early. This seeming precocity is perfectly natural here, because the young mind absorbs knowledge evenly. The temperament is carefully guided along purely spirit lines, so that the possession of knowledge in one so young never takes upon it the obnoxiousness of earthly precociousness. The children are trained in strictly spirit matters first, and then they are usually taught about the earth world, if they have not already lived in it, or if their earthly lives were very brief.

The ruler of the realm acts, in a general sense, *in loco parentis*, and all the children, indeed, look upon him as a father.

The children's studies have an extremely wide range. They are taught to read, but many other subjects of the earthly curricula are entirely omitted as being superfluous in the world of spirit. It would be more exact to say that the children are given knowledge of a particular subject rather than taught it.

As they grow they are able to choose for themselves the type of work that appeals to them, and so by specializing in their studies the children can become equipped with the necessary qualifications. Some of them, for instance, elect to return to the earth-plane temporarily to work with us in the exercise of communication, and they make highly efficient instruments, and thoroughly enjoy their visits. Such visits have the advantage of adding widely to their experience. It increases their depth of understanding of the trials and tribulations—and the pleasures—of being incarnate.

There is always one question that arises in the minds of earth. People in connection with children who have passed on: Shall we be able to recognize our children when we ourselves arrive in the spirit world? The answer is, most emphatically, *Yes,* beyond all shadow of doubt. But how, if they have *grown up* in the spirit world and out of our sight, can that possibly be? To answer that, it is necessary to know a little more about one's self.

You must know that when the physical body sleeps, the spirit body temporarily withdraws from it, while still remaining connected to it by a magnetic cord. This cord is the veritable life-line between the spirit body and the earth body. The spirit thus situated will either remain in the vicinity of the earth body, or it will gravitate to that sphere which its earthly life, so far, has entitled it to enter. The spirit body will thus spend part of the lifetime of the earthly body in spirit lands. And it is upon these visits that one meets relatives and friends who have passed on before, and it is similarly upon these visits that parents can meet their children, and thus watch their growth. In the majority of cases the parents are not allowed within the children's own sphere, but there are plenty of places where such meetings can take place.

Remembering what I have said about the retentiveness of the subconscious mind, you will see that, in such cases, the problem of recognizing a child does not arise, because the parent has seen the child and observed its growth throughout the whole of the intervening years, in just the same way as the parent would have done if the child had remained in the earth world.

There must be, of course, a sufficient bond of attachment between the parent and child, or else this law will not come into operation. Where such does not exist the conclusion is obvious. That link of affection or kindly interest must also exist between all human relationships in the spirit world, whether it be with husband and wife, parent and child, or between friends. Without that interest or affection it is problematical whether there would ever be any meeting at all, except fortuitously.

The children's realm is a township in itself, containing everything that great minds, inspired by the greatest Mind, could possibly provide for the welfare, comfort, and education, and the pleasure and happiness of its youthful inhabitants. The halls of learning are as fully equipped as are those larger establishments in our own sphere. Indeed, in many respects, they are more so, since they have all the equipment for the diffusion of knowledge and learning to those who are possessed of neither in the slightest degree, and who must therefore start at the very beginning, as they would have done had they remained upon the earth-plane. This concerns those children who have passed into the spirit world in their extreme infancy. Children who leave the earth world in their early years will continue their studies from where they left off, eliminating from the latter all that are of no further use, and adding those that are spiritualistically essential. As soon as they reach a suitable age, the children can choose their future work, and study for it accordingly. What that work can be, I will recount to you later.

The whole question of infant survival had puzzled me considerably when I was incarnate. Ruth said she had no ideas upon the matter whatever, beyond supposing that children must survive, because she felt intuitively that grown people did so. The survival of the one would presuppose the survival of the other in a world of anything like law and order—which she presumed the spirit world to be.

Edwin was as perplexed as I was. You can imagine our surprise, then, when we were introduced into the children's realm, to behold the more than adequate provision made for the young folk who have passed into spirit lands in their tender years. It is a provision instituted under the greatest and wisest dispensation—that of the Father, Himself—involving no creeds or belief, no doctrines or dogmas, no ritual or formulary. It involves nothing more, in fact, but the plain act of undergoing the "death" of the physical body, and the operation of the same laws that govern us all, whether infants or aged—just the casting off of the physical body, and entering, for all times, the world of spirit.

And the children, as might be expected, have the same opportunities, the same rights to their spiritual heritage as we all have here, young and old.

And we all have the same great goal—perfect and perpetual happiness.

CHAPTER TWENTY-ONE

OCCUPATIONS

THE SPIRIT world is not only a land of equal opportunity for every soul, but the opportunities are upon so vast a scale that no person still incarnate can have the least conception of its magnitude. Opportunities for what?—it will be asked. Opportunities for good, useful, interesting work.

I hope that, by now, I have sufficiently indicated that the spirit world is not a land of idleness, not a land where its inhabitants spend the whole of their lives in a super-ecstatic atmosphere of religious exercises, formally offering up "prayer and praise" to the Great Throne in a never-ceasing flow. There is an uninterrupted flow, most certainly, but it comes about in a very different way. It surges up from the hearts of us all, who are happy to be here, and thankful withal.

I want to try to give you some slight idea of the immensity of the range of occupations in which one can become engaged here in these realms.

Your thoughts will at once turn to the many and varied occupations of the earth world, covering every shade of earthly activity. But behind the earth world's occupations is the ever-driving necessity of earning a living, of providing the physical body with food and drink, clothing and a habitation of some sort. Now, you already know that these last four considerations have no existence whatever with us here. Food and drink we never need; the clothing and the habitation we have provided for ourselves by our lives upon earth. As our lives have been on earth, so will our clothing and our domicile be when we come to spirit lands. We have, as you see, no *physical* necessity to work, but we do have a mental necessity to work, and it is because of the latter that all work is a pleasure with us here.

Imagine yourself in a world where no one works for a *living*, but where everyone works for the sheer joy of doing something that will be of service to others. Just imagine that, and you will begin to understand something of the life in spirit lands.

A great many earthly occupations have no application whatever to the spirit world. Useful and necessary as they are, they belong essentially to the earthly period of life. What, then, becomes of people who occupied such a position as I have just mentioned? They will discover, immediately they are fully aware of their new state, that they have left their earthly avocation behind for ever. They will see that the spirit world does not offer the same or similar work for them. But this does not cause regret or unhappiness, because the need for physical subsistence no longer exists with them, and in place of it such people feel gloriously free to engage themselves in some new work. They need never wonder what they are fitted for; they will soon find something which attracts their attention and draws their interest. And it will not be long before they are joining their fellows in learning some new occupation, and thoroughly enjoying themselves.

So far, I have merely referred to work in the abstract. Let us be more specific, and consider some of the business of the spirit world. First, let us take what we might call the purely "physical" side of spirit life, and for the purpose we might pay another visit to the city.

On the way there we walk through many beautiful gardens, which at some period have all been designed and created. Here, shall we say, is the first means of employment that we come across. Scores of people upon the earth-plane love gardens and gardening.

Some have engaged in the latter as their calling, and enjoyed doing it. What better than to continue with their work here in the spirit world, unrestrained by physical exigencies, free and unhampered, and with the inexhaustible resources of the spirit world at their command? Their occupation is their own. They can—and do—stop whenever they wish, and they can resume whenever they wish. And there is no one to exert his will upon them. And what is the result? Happiness for themselves, because by creating a beautiful work of horticultural art they have added more beauty to an already beautiful realm, and in doing so they have brought happiness to others. So their task goes on, altering, rearranging, planning, beautifying, building anew, and ever acquiring skill and still greater skill. Thus they continue until such time as they wish to change their work, or until their spiritual progression carries them on to fresh fields of endeavor in other realms.

Now let us go into the hall of music, and see what work we can find there. Someone, of course, had to plan, and others to build, the hall itself. I have already given you an account of the building of an annex to the library.

In all major building operations the method followed is the same, but the methods of the spirit world have to be learnt, and the work of the architects and builders, with their various expert assistants, is among some of the most important in the spirit world. As all descriptions of employment are open to anyone who has the taste for such work, that of the architect and builder is, likewise, free to all who express a preference for continuing their earthly occupation, or who wish to turn to something new. The wish to do so is really all that is required, although, naturally, an aptitude is a great help. But it is very surprising how quickly efficiency is gained by the stimulus of desire. The "wish to do" becomes translated into the "ability to do" in a very short time. Keen interest and predilection for the work are all that are asked.

Inside the hall of music we find libraries of music, where students are busy at their studies, and pupils with their musician teachers. Most of the people whom we meet thus are learning to be practical musicians; that is, they are learning to play some one or more instruments. And someone has to provide them with the necessary instruments. The hall of music does that, but somebody must create them for the hall of music. And so the instrument makers of the earth-plane find themselves at home in their craft if they wish to continue with it in the spirit world.

Now, it may be suggested that a lifetime on earth spent in one particular form of work would be quite enough for the average person, and that when he comes into the spirit world the last thing he would want to do would be to take up again his old earthly occupation with its interminable routine and drudgery. But bear in mind all that I have told you about the freedom of these realms, and the fact that no one is *compelled*, either by force of circumstances, or from the mere need of subsistence, to do any work at all in the spirit world. Remember that all work is undertaken willingly, freely, for the love of doing it, for the pride in creating something, for the desire of being of service to one's fellow inhabitants and to the realm in general, and you will see that the maker of musical instruments—to adduce one occupation among thousands—is just as happy as we all are in these realms. So he continues to make his instruments, brings happiness to himself and to so many other people, who will pleasurably and usefully bring joy to still more through the creation of his mind.

Incidentally, I should mention that it is not imperative that one should acquire a musical instrument solely through the hall of music. Any person who is skilled in the fashioning of such instruments would be only too willing to provide another person with anything he might require musically. In many a home here there reposes—and not as a mere ornaments—beautiful pianoforte, built by clever hands, who have learnt the spirit methods of creation. These things cannot be bought. They are spiritual rewards. It would be useless to try to possess that to which we have no right. We should simply find ourselves without it, and with no means of getting it. No one could create it for us, whatever it might be. If they were to try, they would find that their power would not function in that direction. If you were to ask me who or what governs these things, I could only tell you that I do not know, beyond knowing the fact that it is the operation of a spirit law.

Before we pass on from the hall of music, we might just look at the library. Here are musical scores by the thousand, together with the various parts from which the instrumentalists play. Most of the large orchestras here obtain their music from the hall of music. It is free for all to borrow whenever they wish, but someone has to duplicate it. And that is another important and productive occupation. The librarians who take care of all this music, and who attend to people's wants in this connection, fulfill another useful task. And so the details could be multiplied, covering the whole range of musical endeavor, from the person who does no more than love and enjoy music to those who are instrumentalists and leaders in the musical art.

In the hall of fabrics we shall find the same industry, the same happiness among all those who are working there. At any moment I am at liberty, if I wish, to join the students there who are learning to weave the most exquisite fabrics. It happens, however, that my interests lie elsewhere, and my visits to the hall are for purposes of recreation only. Ruth regularly spends a certain time there studying, and she has become an expert in weaving tapestries. It is part of her spirit-life occupation, and it is part of her recreation also. She has produced some beautiful tapestries, of which Edwin and I possess two choice specimens hanging upon our walls.

We can obtain all the different materials we need from the hall of fabrics, or, as in the case of music, we can ask some craftsman to make what we require. We shall never have a refusal, nor shall we have to wait an interminable time before we receive what we want. There are plenty of craftsmen to supply the needs of all of us.

In the same hall there are students learning the art of designing, and they are instructed by masters in the art. Experimentation is continually going on in producing new types of cloth and new designs. These various materials have nothing whatever to do with our own spirit clothes. That is a personal matter. The products of the fabric hall are used for general purposes; such as, for instance, in the garniture of our homes and in the larger halls and buildings. In the case of the historical pageants, which I mentioned to you, those who organize them exact a heavy contribution from the hall of fabrics for all their authentic costumes.

Now, I have given only two or three examples of what it is possible for a person to do here. There are thousands more, covering as great a field of activity as there is to be found upon the earth-plane. Think of the doctors who come into the spirit world, and still carry on their work here. Not that we need doctors, but they can work here with their colleagues in investigating the causes of sickness and disease upon the earth-plane, and they can help in alleviating them. Many a spirit doctor has guided the hand of an earthly surgeon when he is performing an operation. The earthly doctor is, probably, perfectly unaware of the fact, and would ridicule any suggestion that he is receiving assistance from an unseen source. The doctor in spirit is contented to serve without acknowledgment from him whom he serves. It is the successful issue that he is concerned about, not who shall have the credit. The earthly doctor, in such cases, makes some very illuminating personal discoveries when he finally comes into the spirit world.

The scientist, too, continues his researches when he comes here. In whatever branch of science he may be concerned, he will find enough, and more than enough, to engage his attention for a long time to come. And so with the engineer, and scores upon scores of others. Indeed, it would be impossible, or if not impossible, a little tedious, perhaps, to run through the long list of occupations so well known upon the earth-plane, of which we have a counterpart in the spirit world. But by now you should have some idea of what the spirit world has to offer. All that we have in our halls and our houses, in our homes and in our gardens, has to be made, to be fashioned, or created, and it requires someone to do it. The need is constant, and the supply is constant, and it will ever be so.

There is another department of industry, though, which is vitally necessary, and it is peculiar to the spirit world.

The percentage is low, deplorably low, of people who come into the spirit world with any knowledge at all of their new life and of the spirit world in general. All the countless souls without this knowledge have to be taken care of, and helped in their difficulties and perplexities. That is the principal work upon which Edwin, Ruth and I are engaged. It is a type of work that appeals to many of the ministers of the church of whatever denomination. Their experience upon earth stands them in good stead, and all of them—perhaps I should say all of *us!*—know that we are now members of one ministry, with one purpose, serving one cause, and all of us possessed of the same knowledge of the truth of spirit life, without creed, without doctrine or dogma, a united body of workers, men and women.

In the great halls of rest there are expert nurses and spirit doctors ready to treat those whose last earthly illness has been long and painful, or whose passing into spirit has been sudden or violent. There are many such homes, especially for the latter. These homes are a standing monument of shame to the earth world, that they should be obliged to exist at all. Passings may be sudden and violent—that is inevitable at present, but it is to the eternal shame of the earth world that so many souls should arrive here in woeful ignorance of what lies before them. These halls of rest have multiplied very considerably since I first came into the spirit world, and consequently the need for more nurses and doctors has been more pressing. But that is always supplied.

As this service belongs exclusively to the spirit world, we have special colleges where those desiring to take up this particular work can become fully conversant with it. Here they learn much that scientifically concerns the spirit body itself, and the spirit mind. They are given a general knowledge of the ways of spirit life, since they will have to deal with people who, for the most part, have no knowledge whatever of their new state. They will have to know the facts of intercommunication between our world and yours, since such numbers of people ask about this important matter the instant they realize what has taken place in their lives. It is astonishing how many of them want to rush back to the earth-plane to try to tell those they have left behind of the great discovery they have made of the fact that they are alive and in another world!

In numbers of cases people require a long rest after their dissolution. They may be awake during the whole of this period of rest, and those in attendance have to be a storehouse of information. The attention of such souls is usually about equally divided between the spirit world and the earth world. It requires a high proportion of general spirit-world knowledge, as well as tactfulness and discretion, upon the part of all the nurses and doctors.

By making mention of any particular occupation I do so entirely without prejudice to any other, and not because those which we have discussed have any pre-eminence over others. One or two of them have been chosen to present to you because they have the appearance of being so very "material," and to point what I have tried to demonstrate repeatedly before—that we are living in a *practical* spirit world where we are busy upon our own individual and useful tasks, and that we are not spending the whole of our spirit lives in a high state of religiosity, nor perpetually absorbed in pious meditation.

But what of the person who has never done a useful thing during his earth life? All I can say is, that such a person will not find himself in these realms until he has worked his way here. Entrance is by service alone.

To make a complete list of *all* spirit occupations would take a very large volume to do so, for they seem to be inexhaustible. Indeed, my mind becomes almost numbed at the thought of their countless number, and of my inability to do justice to so vast a subject. In the scientific sphere of labor alone, thousands upon thousands of people are happily employed, whether it be upon probing the secrets of the earth-plane, or in investigating those of the spirit world.

Science and engineering being closely allied in the spirit world, far-reaching discoveries are constantly being made, and inventions are ever being perfected. These inventions are not for us, but for you—when the time is ripe, and that is not yet. The earth world has given a poor exhibition of what has been sent through to it from the spirit world, by putting to base uses what has been given for its benefit. Man has exercised his own free will, but he has been exercising it in a direction that ultimately brings destruction. The mind of man is but in its infancy, and an infant becomes dangerous when he has free use of that which can destroy. Hence, much is held back from the earth world until man has reached a higher state of development. That day will assuredly arrive, and a torrent of new inventions will come pouring through from the spirit world to your world.

In the meantime, the work goes on, research, investigation, discovery, and invention, and it is work that absorbs great hosts of interested people, and provides them with useful employment in their spirit life. Nothing ever disturbs the ordered routine of our work. While the work continues, we may be retiring from it for a space, either to rest or to follow some other line of endeavor. We have no disputes, no domestic upheavals, no rivalries that produce dissatisfaction and unpleasantness. We have no discontented folk. We may have the urge to be doing something of greater moment, but that is not discontent, but the prompting from within that denotes the steps of our spiritual progression. The humblest of us is made to feel that whatever his work, however insignificant it may appear beside other and seemingly greater tasks, he is performing something vital and significant that will bring with it its own inevitable reward that none can withhold from us, none can take away. In the spirit world, to work is to be profoundly happy—for the many reasons that I have given you.

There is none here who would not endorse my words wholeheartedly and unreservedly!

CHAPTER TWENTY-TWO

FAMOUS PEOPLE

TO LEAVE this world and to take up permanent residence in the spirit world is not such a personal upheaval as some people might be disposed to imagine. It is true that for a great many all earthly ties are severed, but when we pass into the spirit world we meet again those of our relatives and friends who have passed over before us. In this respect we start a fresh period in our lives, apart altogether from the new life that begins with our entry into the world of spirit.

The meetings with relations and friends are something that must be experienced in order to grasp the full significance and joy of reunion. Such meetings will only take place where there is mutual sympathy and affection. We will not, for the moment, consider any other. These gatherings will continue for some while after the arrival of the new resident. It is natural that in the novelty both of surroundings and condition some time should be spent in a grand exchange of news, and in hearing of all that has transpired in the spirit lives of those who have "predeceased" us. Eventually that time will come when the newly-arrived individual will begin to consider what he is to do with his spirit life.

Now, it might be said that with most of us on the earth-plane we have a twofold existence—our home life and the life connected with our business or occupation. In the latter we associate, perhaps, with an entirely different group of people. It is therefore in the natural order of things, here in spirit, that much the same state of things should also exist. The scientist, for example, will meet, first of all, his own family connections. When the question of work is broached he will find himself among his old colleagues who have passed into the spirit world before him, and he will again feel more than at home. And he will be more than overjoyed at the prospect of the scientific research that stretches before him. It is the same with the musician, the painter, the author, the engineer, the doctor, the gardener, the stonemason, or the man who weaved carpets in a factory, to mention but a fraction of the many occupations both of the earth and spirit worlds. It will be seen from this that the question which puzzles many folk, namely, what becomes of the famous people in the spirit world?—practically answers itself.

Fame in the spirit world is vastly different from fame in the earth world. Spiritual fame carries with it distinctions of a very different order from the earthly distinctions, and it is gained in one way only—in service to others. It sounds almost too simple to be feasible, but such is the case, and nothing will alter it. Whether the earthly famous will reside in the realms of light immediately after their dissolution remains with themselves. The law applies to all irrespective of earthly position.

A certain inquisitiveness concerning the general fate of those well known upon the earth-plane is possessed by most people who are in their early days of psychic study. The mere fact of their being well known is sufficient. But none calls forth more curiosity than the historically famous people. Where are they—the masters in all branches of earthly endeavor, the names that are familiar in the history books? They must be somewhere. Most certainly they are. A good number of them are to be found in the dark realms where they have been living for countless centuries, and they are more than likely so to continue for more countless centuries. Others are in those exalted realms of light and beauty, where their noble lives upon earth have found their just reward. But there are many, a great many, who will find themselves within these realms whereof I have tried to give you some account.

I cannot do better than give you an example, of which, for our present purpose, I have gathered a few details.

It concerns the passing into the spirit world of a royal personage. I take this case because, although an extreme one, it demonstrates more clearly than any other the principles that govern life in general in the spirit world.

In this particular case we knew beforehand that this personage was about to come to the spirit world. His own countrymen were naturally interested in what was about to take place. His own family, in common with any other family here, were ready and awaiting his arrival. A short illness was the occasion of his passing here, and as soon as dissolution had taken place he was taken to the home of his mother, who had everything in readiness for him. The home is an inconspicuous one, similar, broadly speaking, to others here about. The news had spread that he had at last arrived. There was no universal rejoicing, such as might take place upon the earth-plane following a safe homecoming, but happiness was felt for all those who were directly concerned with the arrival in the spirit world of this well-known and much-loved figure. And there he remained for a time, enjoying a seclusion and freedom of action and a simplicity of life that had been denied him upon the earth-plane. He needed rest after his active life and the illness that terminated its earthly span. Numbers of people who had formed part of his official circle as well as his private circle, and who had passed on before him, had called to inquire after him, but they had not seen him as yet. There had been, of course, a grand family reunion, and as soon as he had rested sufficiently, he issued forth to see the wonders of his new life.

He retained to a noticeable extent his former and usual personal appearance. The signs of illness and bodily and mental fatigue had disappeared, and he looked some years younger. The rest had achieved its purpose as unfailingly as usual.

As he walked abroad he was recognized *for what he had been,* and respected for it, but he was still more honored and respected and loved for what he now was. Now, you may think that as soon as he met and mingled with his own countrymen, the latter would have shown some embarrassment, perhaps, and exhibited a general air of diffidence such as they would have done, perforce, upon the earth-plane. But during that period of recuperation much had been explained to him as to the conditions of life in the spirit world, its methods, its laws, and its pleasant customs. Such revelations had filled him with happiness, and he knew that as soon as he left the seclusion of his mother's house to venture abroad, he could do so with a freedom that is only to be found in spirit lands, where the inhabitants would regard him in the light in which he would wish to be regarded—that of a plain man desirous of joining with his fellow beings in their happiness and their rejoicings. He knew that he would be treated as one of themselves. When, therefore, in company with members of his family, he walked through these realms on the voyage of discovery that is such a common sight among the newly arrived, he did not experience in himself or cause in others any feelings of mental discomfort. No one referred to his earthly position, unless he himself broached the subject, and then there was no suspicion of inquisitiveness or ignorant curiosity.

You may think that one who had occupied so elevated a position upon the earth-plane would engender in the minds of others here thoughts of sympathy with such a change of relative position that had taken place. But no such feelings of sympathy are ever wished for, nor extended, in these realms in such cases, for the very good reason that the occasion for them never arises. We have left our earthly importance behind us, and we do not refer to it except to show, by our own experiences, to others still incarnate, just what to avoid. We do not revive our memories for the purpose of self-glorification, or to impress our hearers. Indeed, they would not be in the least impressed, and we should only succeed in making fools of ourselves! We recognize the truth here, and our true worth is for all to see. It is spiritual worth, and that alone, that counts, irrespective of what we were upon the earth-plane. Perspectives and view-points are completely altered when one comes into the spirit world. However mighty we were upon the earth-plane, it is spiritual worth only that takes us to our right place in the spirit world, and it is the deeds of our life, regardless of social position, that at our transition will assign to us our proper abode. Position is forgotten, but deeds and thoughts are the witnesses for or against us, and we become our own judges.

It is not difficult to see, then, that when this royal personage arrived in the spirit world, like others of his family before him, he found himself faced with no difficulties or awkward situations. It was just the reverse, for the whole situation seemed to simplify itself, and provided its own solution. Now, what applies in this extreme case, applies equally to all who were famous upon the earth-plane. But how does this affect some well-known scientist, let us say, or a musical composer, or a painter? To us—and to themselves—they will be learners, and humble learners, too, in whatever branch of science or art their earthly lives led them. To you, still incarnate, they are famous names, and when we have occasion to refer to them in speaking to you we use those names by which they are familiar. Here, in the spirit world, they dislike to be referred to as masters or geniuses. Their names, however famous, mean nothing to them personally, and they sternly repudiate anything that even remotely approaches the hero-worship that the earth world accords them. They are just one of ourselves, and as such they wish to be—and are—so treated.

In the spirit world the law of cause and effect applies equally to all people, regardless of their former earthly status. This law is no new thing. It has always been in existence, and so every famous name that is to be found within the chronicles of nations comes strictly within the jurisdiction of this law. The soul who passes his earthly life in obscurity, known only to one or two people, is subject to this same law just as much as the soul whose name is a household word among nations. In living in these realms one is inevitably bound, sooner or later, to encounter some person whose name is known to all upon the earth-plane. But these famous folk have no attachment to the earth world. They have left it behind them, and many of those who passed to here hundreds of earthly years ago are glad to have no occasion to recall their earthly lives. Such numbers of them suffered a violent transition that they are happy to consider their present only, and leave their past sealed up in their memory.

The people of the earth world may think it strange to walk through these realms and mingle with persons who lived on the earth-plane hundreds— and, in some cases, thousands—of years ago. A meeting of the past, as it were, with the eternal present. But it is not strange to us here. It may be so for the newly arrived, but then there are many other things that *may* seem strange— at first. Discretion is something we soon learn to exercise, and it is embodied in our never prying into the facts and circumstances of other people's earthly lives. That does not mean to say that we are debarred from discussing our earthly lives, but the initiative always comes from the person concerned. If he wishes to tell anyone of his life on earth he will ever find a sympathetic and interested ear awaiting him.

You can see, then, that our earthly lives are very strictly our own. The discretion that we exercise is universal among us—we show it and we receive it. And whatever our former position upon earth, we are united in these realms, spiritually, intellectually, temperamentally, and in such human traits as our likes and dislikes. We are one; we have achieved the same state of being upon the same plane of existence. Every fresh face that enters these realms receives the same heartfelt welcome, without reference to what he was upon earth.

One will meet many people here who were famous upon earth, in all sorts of places and pursuing all sorts of occupations, some of the latter a continuation of their earthly calling, and some, perforce, entirely new. All alike are approachable without formalities of any kind whatever. We need no introductions to men and women whom the earth knows as famous. Their gifts are at the disposal of all, and happy, indeed, are they to assist another who comes to them for help in any difficulties, whether it is in art or science, or in any other form of activity. The great, who have gained their greatness through the various expressions of their genius, consider themselves but the lowly units of a vast whole, the immense organization of the spirit world. They are all striving—as we are too—for the same purpose, and that is spiritual progression and development. They are grateful for any help towards that end, and they are glad to give it wherever possible.

The riches and honors of the earth world seem very tawdry and trumpery by comparison with the spiritual riches and honors that are ready to be won here. And those riches and honors are within the grasp of every soul the instant he enters the spirit world. They are his spiritual birthright, of which no one can deprive him, and it rests with himself just how long it will be before he gains them. Earthly greatness may seem very tangible while we are in the midst of it. Just how tangible it is can be seen as soon as our dissolution takes place. Then we find that it is spiritual greatness that is concrete and permanent. Our earthly prominence just melts away as we step into the spirit world, and we stand revealed for what we are, not for what we were.

Several of the earth world's famous people have spoken to me of their awakening in the spirit world, and they have told me of the shock of revelation they received when they beheld themselves for the first time as they really were.

But oft-times greatness of earthly position goes hand in hand with greatness of soul, and thus spiritual progression and development continue without intermission from the moment of dissolution.

CHAPTER TWENTY-THREE

ORGANIZATION

YOU WILL have gathered that the spirit world is a vast place, and, with the earth world in mind, you may conclude that it possesses an administrative organization in all respects proportionate to its demands. You would be right, for it does. But our needs are not as yours. With you in your corruptible world it is constant war with material decay and degeneration. With us in our incorruptible world we have neither the one nor the other. Ours is a state far beyond Utopian in quality. But it is a state where thought is its basic element.

I have recounted to you how, when I first saw my own spirit garden, I marveled at its orderliness and excellent preservation, and I wondered just how it was maintained thus, and who was responsible for it. Edwin told me that it would require *practically* no effort in its upkeep. By that he meant, as I have since learnt, that provided my wish remained constant for the garden to continue unaltered, and provided that I had affection for the flowers and grass and trees, the garden would respond to my thoughts and flourish under them. If I desired to alter the arrangement of the flower beds, and so on, I could easily ask some expert to come to my help—and he would be only too happy to do so. So much for the upkeep of my garden.

My house is provided for under the same law. And so it is with all gardens and houses belonging to other folk in this realm. These, however, are what you would call more or less private concerns. They are so in one respect, but the fact that I can find an expert gardener who can make radical changes in my house and garden; indeed, who can build me an entirely new and different home, with surrounding gardens wholly different from what I have now, shows that organization of some sort—and a very considerable one—must exist somewhere.

The united thoughts of the inhabitants of the whole realm will sustain all that grows within it, the flowers, and the trees and the grass, and the water, too, whether of lake, river, or sea—for water is fully alive in the spirit world. It is when we come into the city and travel through the halls of learning that the organization becomes outwardly more observable.

In the hall of music, for example, we find many students busy at work upon their lessons and studies. We find others engaged upon musical research, and delving into ancient music books; others will be arranging the music for some concert, consulting the shelves for suitable works, and sometimes discussing those works with their composers. There are many teachers, many able people ready to assist us in our inquiries or our difficulties, and they are all able to provide a solution to our problems, because the staff of this hall—as of all others—are themselves experts.

Nominally, the ruler of the realm is the principal of all the halls, and all major decisions would, of course, be referred to him. But he appoints competent people to the staffs of the halls, and extends to them a free hand in all their undertakings.

Each hall will have its own direct head, but it must not be thought that this "official" is an unapproachable, detached personage, hidden away from all sight, and only seen on relatively rare occasions. He is just the opposite. He is always to be seen about the hall, and he welcomes, personally, anyone who comes there, either as a learner, or as a "mere lover" of music, or to carry out musical researches.

I have recounted to you how we continue with our work for just that period during which we derive pleasure or profit from it. The moment we feel the need for a change of work or other diversion, we cease our work for the time being, and turn to whatever else we wish. The staffs of all the halls of learning are no different from others in this respect. They most certainly need change and recreation, and so we find that the staffs alternate in their personnel as occasion demands. As some retire, others take their places. It is the most natural thing in the world, and the most practical. We need never fear that when we call to see some particular expert we shall be disappointed because he is not there. We shall be able to have all the help we need, and if it is vitally necessary to consult the absent one, either an instantaneous thought will answer our question, or with equal rapidity we can visit his home. We need have no misgivings about our intruding upon him.

Now, when I tell you that the service in all these halls is going on unremittingly simply because we have perpetual day in these realms, I think you will appreciate that our conception of organization begins to assume its right proportions.

Many of the people attached to the halls of learning have been there a great number of years as you reckon time. So devoted are they to their work that although they have progressed and virtually belong to a higher sphere, they prefer to remain where they are for some considerable period yet. They will retire, from time to time, to their own realm, and then return to take up their labors anew. The moment will eventually arrive when they will relinquish their position altogether to reside permanently in their own sphere, and then others, equally capable, will take their place. And so it goes on, and has gone on for countless centuries, and so it will go on for countless more centuries—an unbroken continuity of service for others in these realms. And this rule applies to all the various halls of learning. The work of the spirit world functions unceasingly; the workers rest and change about, but the work never stops. The pressure of work may fluctuate, as it does with you upon earth. When we have our great celebrations and festivals, during which we are honored by the presence of visitants from the higher realms, it follows that large numbers of people will be present in the temple or elsewhere, and during that time there will be an appreciable diminution of some activities. We are naturally desirous of holding our festivals in company with one another, and we do so. But the services never suffer on that account. It so happens that the inhabitants in these realms are always considerate of others, and will never ask of others that which would entail a disappointment for them, such as would be the case if one insisted upon some attention in one of the halls when we were all, as it were, on holiday. This concerns the various halls in the city where any temporary cessation of work would be of no great consequence.

In the halls of rest, however, the doctors and nurses are always in attendance whatever else may be taking place in other parts of the sphere. Their devotion to duty is always instantly rewarded, for during the general celebrations of the realm, the illustrious visitors from the upper realms make a special journey to the rest homes where they personally greet every one of the staff. The latter can afterwards arrange amicably for their own family and friendly festivities.

All this administration belongs to the spirit world proper, so to speak, and concerns the spirit world alone. There are other services that concern the two worlds together, ours and yours. Such, for example, as the arrival, or the approaching arrival, of a soul into spirit lands. The rule is that all souls passing to here shall have some measure of attention. It depends upon themselves how much attention they shall have. Some are sunken so spiritually low as to preclude any approach to them that would be effective. We will not consider those for the moment, but only those who are destined for the realms of light.

Without anticipating what I wish to say regarding the interrelationship of our two worlds, we might, for our present purposes, consider a typical inquiry in the matter of transition, such as it affects a very large number of people here.

We will suppose that you are yourself in the spirit world, and that beyond knowing the truth of communication with the earth world, you have had no experience of the close ties existing between the two worlds. You have, we will further suppose, left behind you a friend for whom you had—and still have—a warm affection, and you wonder when he will be coming to reside permanently in the spirit world. Occasionally you have received his thoughts of affection arising from the earth-plane, by which you know that he has not forgotten you. You have, we will say, never tried to communicate with him because you know from your earthly knowledge that he would rather frown upon such ideas. Is it possible to find out just when he is likely to join you in the spirit world, and if so, how does one go about it? The answer to that question reveals the existence of one of the great organizations of these lands.

In the city there is an immense building which exercises the function of an office of records and inquiries. (In the earth world you have your multifarious offices of inquiry. Why should we not have ours?) Here a great host of people is available to answer all manner of questions that are likely to arise both from the newly-arrived and from those of longer residence. Occasions will occur when we need a solution to some problem that has arisen. We may consult our friends upon the matter, only to find that they are as uninformed as we are ourselves. We could, of course, make an appeal to some higher personage, and we should receive all the help we wanted. But the higher beings have their work to do in just the same way as we have, and we forbear to interrupt them unnecessarily. And so we take our difficulty to this grand building in the city. Among its many important duties is that of keeping a register of people newly arrived in this particular realm. It is a useful service, and full advantage is taken of it by scores of people who have an interest in that direction. But a still more important service is that of knowing beforehand of those who are about to come into this realm. This information is accurate and infallibly reliable. It is collected through a varied process of thought transmission, of which the inquirer sees little or nothing. He is merely presented with the required information. The value of this service can be readily imagined.

In normal times upon the earth-plane, when transitions maintain a fairly steady level, it is valuable enough, but in times of great wars, when souls are passing into the spirit world in thousands, the advantages of such an office are almost incalculable. Friend can meet friend, and together can unite in helping others who are passing into spirit lands.

Foreknowledge of terrestrial events both national and private is possessed by a certain order of beings in the spirit world, and when expedient this knowledge is communicated to others, who in turn pass it on to those principally concerned. Among the first to receive pre-knowledge of an impending war are the different homes of rest. The office of inquiry will be similarly informed.

You are anxious, then, to know when your friend is likely to be coming to the spirit world to reside; you want to know when his "death" is going to take place. Your first step is to go to the inquiry office. There you will be readily assisted to consult the right person for your needs. You will not find yourself passed from one "official" to another, nor will you be submitted to other forms of procrastination. All that will be required of you is to furnish the name of your friend, and you will be asked to focus your attention upon him to establish the necessary thought link. When this has been accomplished, you will be requested to wait for a brief period—in your time it would amount to only a few minutes. The requisite forces are put into action with astonishing rapidity, and we shall be presented with the information of the time of our friend's arrival. The actual date may mean very little to some of us, as I have already tried to make clear to you, because it is towards such an event that we cast our minds, and not towards the time of its taking place. At least, whatever our condition of proximity to the earth-plane, we shall be assured that when that event is close at hand we shall be informed of it without fail. In the meantime we shall be given a conception of the closeness of the event or otherwise, which we shall understand according to the measure of our knowledge of the passage of earthly time.

The organization that exists behind this one service should give you some idea of the vastness of the whole office of help and inquiry. There are many others. This same building houses people who can provide answers to the innumerable questions that arise in the minds of us here, especially among the newly-arrived, and its extent covers the whole range of spirit activity. But what is most to our present point, this office employs thousands of people, usefully and happily. Many souls ask to be allocated to work there, but it is necessary to have some training for it first, for however suitable may be our personal attributes, it requires absolute knowledge, in whatever department we wish to work, since we should be there for the express purpose of providing information to those in need of it.

Let us now pass to another example of spirit organization, and for the purpose we might visit the hall of science.

There are numberless people upon the earth-plane who are mechanically minded, and who pursue as a means of material livelihood one or other of the engineering arts.

Others are interested in engineering as a pleasant diversion from their usual work. The opportunities in the spirit world in this field alone are enormous, and such scientific work is carried on under conditions precisely similar to all other work here—without restriction, freely, and with the limitless resources and the perfect administration of the spirit world behind it. This form of work attracts thousands, young and old alike. All the great scientists and engineers are carrying on their investigations and researches in this world of spirit, assisted by scores of enthusiastic helpers from every walk of earthly life, as well as by those whose work lay upon those lines when they were incarnate.

Most of us here are not content with one type of work; we engage in another form of labor as part of our recreation. You see, we have the constant urge to be doing something useful, something that will be of benefit to others. However small that service may be, it will be valued as a service. To have only two forms of work with which to alternate is to give the lowest estimate. So many of us have a dozen channels through which we are usefully engaged. It must be obvious, then, that the supply of useful tasks is entirely adequate to the thousands upon thousands of us here. And each and every form of work has its separate organization. There are no such things as haphazard methods. Every type of pursuit has those in charge of it who are experts, and the administration admits of no muddle or fuss. There is no mismanagement, for everything runs with the smoothness of perfectly-constructed machinery under the operation of efficient hands.

It must not be concluded from this that we are infallible. That would be a totally wrong estimation, but we know that whatever our mistakes may be we are always sure that our perfect organization will come to our rescue and help us to put things right. Mistakes are never frowned upon as a piece of glaring inefficiency, but are regarded as very good lessons for us by which we can profit to the fullest extent. But because of this sympathy with our mistakes, we are not careless on that account, for we have our natural and proper pride in our work, which spurs us on to do our best always—and free from mistakes.

To attempt to give you anything like a comprehensive survey of the administrative organization of the spirit world would be a gigantic task, and quite beyond my descriptive powers, apart altogether from the impossibility of putting into material language what can only be understood as an inhabitant of these lands.

Perhaps one of the most striking features of life in the spirit world is that the organization of life is so perfect that there never seems to be any suspicion of hurry or confusion, in spite of the fact that we can perform so many actions of a "material" kind with the rapidity of thought, which latter is the motive force. This rapidity is as second nature to us, and we scarcely notice it. It is there, none the less, and it is because of it that our great system of life, and the organization of living generally, works so perfectly and yet so unobtrusively.

It is something of a proud boast upon the earth-plane that you have reached such an age of speed. By comparison with our rapidity of motion, why, you are scarcely moving! You must wait until you come to live here with us. Then you will know what real speed is like. Then you will know, too, what real efficiency and real organization are like.

They are like nothing upon the earth-plane.

CHAPTER TWENTY-FOUR

SPIRIT INFLUENCE

I T IS the habit of most men to look upon the spirit world and the earth world as two planes apart, separate and distinct. They regard the two worlds as being each independent of the other, cut off from each other, and both entirely uninformed or unaware of what the other is doing. That the spirit world could possibly have any influence upon the earth world to the latter's advantage is demonstrated to be altogether false by the state of universal disorder that exists through the entire earth world.

There is another school of thought, consisting of those who have made a superficial study of what they call occultism. These people believe that the earth world, being indisputably very earthy, and the spirit world being incontrovertibly very spiritual, the two worlds are for these reasons automatically inhibited from anything like intercommunication.

Both these lines of thought are unquestionably wrong. The two worlds, yours and ours, are in constant and direct communication, and we are fully aware of what is occurring upon the earth-plane at all times. I do not, for one minute, say that we all of us know what is taking place with you. Those of us who are in active communion with you are conversant with your personal affairs and with the affairs of your world in general. While the rest of us here, who have no further active interest in the earth-plane since we left it, may be unaware of many things in connection with it, those wise beings in the higher realms are in possession of all knowledge of what is transpiring upon earth.

I would like to indicate one or two channels through which the influence of the spirit world is exerted upon the earth world.

First, we might take that influence in a personal way.

Every soul that has been, and is to be, born upon the earth-plane has allocated to him—or her—a spirit guide. In past ages, some such idea must have filtered through into the minds of the early churchmen, since they adopted the pious notion of giving to every incarnate person an unseen protector whom they called a "guardian angel." These guardian angels sometimes found their way into contemporary art, where the artists drew a somewhat vapid individual habited in glistening white garments and supporting from his shoulders a pair of enormous wings. The whole conception would suggest by its very implications a remoteness, or a great gulf, between the guardian angel and the soul he was supposed to be guarding. He would, one might say, be unable to draw very near his charge because of extreme spiritual refinement upon the one hand, and repelling earthly grossness upon the other.

Let us turn from this inaccurate figment of the artist's brain to something a little more practical.

Spirit guides constitute one of the grandest orders in the whole organization and administration of the spirit world. They inhabit a realm of their own, and they have all lived for many centuries in the spirit world. They are drawn from every nationality that exists upon the earth-plane, and they function regardless of nationality. A great many of them are drawn from eastern countries, and from the North American Indians, too, because it has always been the case that dwellers in those regions of the earth world were, and are, already possessed of psychic gifts themselves, and were therefore aware of the interrelationship of our two worlds.

The principal guide is chosen for each individual on the earth-plane in conformity with a fixed plan. Most guides are temperamentally similar to their charges in the latters' finer natures, but what is most important the guides understand and are in sympathy with their charges' failings. Many of them, indeed, had the same failings when they were incarnate, and among other useful services they try to help their charges overcome those failings and weaknesses.

A great number of those who practice communication with the spirit world have already met their spirit guides and are in close touch with them. And fortunate, indeed, they are. The guides, too, are never happier than when they have established a direct link with those whose lives they are helping to direct. It would be safe to say that by far the greater number of spirit guides carry on their work all unknown to those whom they serve, and their task is so much the heavier and more difficult. But there are still others whose lives upon earth render it practically impossible for their guides to approach within any reasonable distance of them. It naturally saddens them to see the mistakes and follies into which their charges are plunging themselves, and to be obliged to stand aloof because of the thick wall of material impenetrability which they have built up round themselves. Such souls, when they at last arrive in the spirit world, awake to a full realization of what they have thus missed during their earth lives. In such cases the guide's work will not be entirely in vain, for even in the worst souls there comes an occasion, however transient, when the conscience speaks, and it is usually the spirit guide who has implanted the better thought within the brain.

It must never for one instant be thought that the influence of the spirit guide negatives or violates the possession or expression of free will. If, upon the earth-plane, you were to observe somebody about to take a false step into a stream of traffic upon the road, the fact that you put out your hand to stop him would in no way impinge upon his exercise of free will. A spirit guide will try to give advice when his advice can be got through to his charge; he will try to lead him in the right direction solely for his own good, and it remains for his charge, in the exercise of his free will, to take that advice or reject it. If he does the latter, he can only blame himself if disaster or trouble overtakes him. At the same time, the spirit guides are not there to live a person's life for him. That he must do himself.

It has become a habit among a certain class of individuals of the earth-plane to ridicule the whole establishment of spirit guides. There will assuredly come a time when they will bitterly repent their folly, and that day will be whereon they meet in the spirit world their own guide, who probably knows more about their lives than they do themselves! We in the spirit world can afford to pass by such ridicule as this, because we know that the day will inevitably come when they will arrive in the spirit world, and great is the remorse—and, in many instances, the self-pity—of those who have, in their supposed wisdom, made fools of themselves.

Apart from spirit guides, there is another prolific source of influence that derives from the world of spirit. I have told, for example, how earthly doctors' hands will be guided, in performing an operation, by the hand of a spirit doctor. In many other walks of life spirit inspiration is being carried on in the same way as it has been carried on since the dawn of time. Incarnate man can really do very little of himself, and he is the first to realize it when he comes here to live. Man can perform certain mechanical actions with precision and exactitude. He can paint a picture, he can play upon an instrument, he can manipulate machinery, but all the major discoveries that are of service to the earth-plane have come, and always will come, from the spirit world. If man, employing his free will, chooses to put those discoveries to base ends, then he can thank himself for the calamities that follow. Inspiration, devoted to whatever cause or pursuit, comes from the world of spirit, and from nowhere else. If it be for the good of mankind the source is equally good; if the inspiration is obviously not for the good of mankind, then the source is unquestionably evil. Man has it within his own hands as to which source of inspiration he will lend himself—to good or to evil.

You will remember how I have told you that a person is exactly the same spiritually the moment after he has "died" as he was the moment before. No instantaneous change takes place to turn an earthly lifetime of evil into good.

One orthodox church takes the view, which is also an infallible teaching, that those of us who return to the earth-plane and make our presence known, are all devils! It is a pity that the church is so blind, for it can be said that they are trying—ineffectually—to stifle the forces of good, while they are ignoring the real forces of evil. If they encouraged the forces of good to come to them, the forces of evil would soon be put to flight. The churches, of whatever denomination, suffer from abysmal ignorance. Throughout the ages right down to the present time they have gone their own blind, ignorant way, disseminating fantastic teachings in place of the truth, and paving the way, through the universal ignorance begotten of such false teachings, for the forces of evil to operate.

A minister of the church performs the services and offices prescribed by his particular sect, and he stifles all inspiration by holding to creeds and dogmas that are utterly false. If he were interrogated in the matter he would reply that he believed in inspiration—in a vague, remote way. In the long run he would find it much less trouble to borrow the religious thoughts of some other incarnate person, and rely upon his own cleverness for any original thought. But to suggest that the spirit world has any influence upon the earth world other than evil, would be totally against his principles.

It is a strange habit of mind that persists in the belief that it is always the forces of evil from the spirit world that try to make their power felt upon the earth-plane. The forces of evil are attributed with powers which, it would seem, are denied to the forces of good. Why? And why are the churches mortally afraid to "try the spirits"—as they are advised to do in the very book upon which they place so much reliance? They ignore this text, and point a warning finger to the supposed woman of Endor.

The spirit world works constantly to make its power and force and presence felt by the whole earth world, not only in personal matters, but through individuals into a wider sphere for the good of nations and national policies.

But so little can be done, because the door is usually closed to the higher beings of the spirit world, whose range of vision, and whose wisdom and knowledge and understanding are vast. Think of the evils that could be swept from the face of the earth under the immensely able guidance of wise teachers from the spirit world. The world of spirit does its best through the limited channels available. But it is safe to say that there is no problem upon the earth-plane that could not be solved by the help and advice and experience of those beings I have just mentioned. But it would involve one thing—an implicit adherence to whatever they advised or advocated. Many a leader, either of the nation's affairs or of religious thought, who is here with us in the spirit world, is filled with sorrow when be looks back upon the wasted opportunities for bringing about a revolutionary change for the betterment of his fellow countrymen. He will confess that he had the idea in his mind—he did not know then that it had been impinged thereupon by the spirit world—but he had allowed himself to be overruled. These souls sigh for the state into which humanity has degraded itself. Humanity has, in effect, allowed the evil forces to dictate to it. But the evil ones, so beloved by the churches, have appeared in a different direction from that which those same churches allege that they come. The men and women who practice communication with us in all seriousness and earnestness, and who enjoy happy meetings with their spirit friends as well as with noble teachers from the higher spheres, are accused of dealings with "devils." That is rubbish. The real devils are far too busy elsewhere, in places where they can produce far greater results to their own evil satisfaction.

You will say that my outlook seems rather pessimistic; that really, after all, the earth world is not so bad as I paint it. That is perfectly true, because we have managed to get through to the earth world just one or two of our ideas and thoughts and precepts. But it can safely be said that in spite of universal earth-world disorder, had we withdrawn every element of our influence, the earth world would, in a very brief time, be reduced to a state of complete and absolute barbarity and chaos. And the reason is that man thinks he can get along nicely by his own powers and volition. He is conceited enough to think that he requires no help from any source whatever. As for assistance from the spirit world—if such a place exists—it is unthinkable! If there is such a place as the spirit world, it is fully time enough to begin thinking about it when one arrives there. For the present, then, they are so superior that they know everything, and can manage their own affairs perfectly well without the help of a shadowy spirit world. And when many men arrive here in the same world of spirit that they scorned, they see their own littleness and the littleness of the world they have just left. But small though the earth world may be, man still needs help in conducting its affairs—and that is another discovery that he makes when he comes here.

The earth world is beautiful, and life upon it could be beautiful as well, but man steps in and prevents it. The spirit world is surpassingly beautiful, more beautiful than the mind of man incarnate can possibly imagine. I have tried to show you a glimpse or two of it. But your world looks very dark to us, and we try very hard to bring a little light to it. We try to make our presence known, our influence felt. Our influence is great, but it has yet to be increased far, far beyond its present range. When we and our world gain full acceptance you will then know what it means to *live* upon the earth-plane.

But we have a long, long way to go yet.

CHAPTER TWENTY-FIVE

THE HIGHEST REALMS

I HAVE SPOKEN to you, on a number of occasions, of the higher spheres. There are two ways, and two ways only, of penetrating into those lofty states. The first is through our own spiritual development and progression; the second is by special invitation from some dweller in those regions. Any other way is barred to us by the invisible barriers of spiritual impenetrability.

I would like to speak to you now about a special invitation that we received to visit those high realms.

We were seated in one of the lower rooms of my house, from which all the beauties without could be viewed to perfection. Across a glittering expanse of countryside could be seen the city in the distance, as clearly as though it were close by instead of some distance away. Edwin and I were chatting, while Ruth was seated at the piano playing some pleasant work that seemed to blend so harmoniously, not only with our present mood, but with all our colorful environment.

Ruth had never really recovered from her initial surprise when she first beheld the piano in her own home. She was an accomplished performer during her earth life, and she has since told us of the thrilling moment when she seated herself before her "spirit instrument," as she called it, and struck the first chord upon it. She said that she never precisely knew what was going to happen, or what description of sound would come forth with her striking the keys! She was consequently amazed at the result of her simple action, for the tone of her "spirit piano" was something that she could never have imagined possible, it was so perfectly balanced and of such ringing quality. Her surprises were not ended, however. She found that her dexterity had increased a hundredfold by her casting off her physical body, and that she had taken her technique with her to the spirit world. She further discovered that her hands, when applied to the instrument, just rippled along the keys without conscious effort, and that her memory was as sound as though she had the very music before her.

On the present occasion she was filling the air with dulcet sounds, and so helping all three of us in our rest and recreation, for we had just completed a particularly onerous task during the course of our usual work. We three worked together—we are still doing so at this moment of your time—and we usually take our rest and amusement together. In fact, Edwin and Ruth spend far more time in my home than they do in their own! Speaking for myself, I would not have it otherwise.

Suddenly Ruth ceased playing, and ran to the door. Wondering what had caused her to stop so abruptly, Edwin and I joined her. We were much surprised to see, walking across the lawn, two striking figures, of whom I have before made mention. One was the Egyptian who had given me such helpful advice when I was but recently arrived in spirit lands, and who had since taken such a kindly interest in my welfare. The other was his "master," who had accompanied the great celestial visitor upon that occasion in the temple in the city.

The Egyptian's "master" was a man with jet-black hair, matched in its color by a pair of eyes that bespoke the greatest sense of humor and merriment. I subsequently learned that our guest was a Chaldean.

We went forward eagerly to welcome our two visitors, and they expressed their pleasure in thus coming to see us.

We conversed happily upon various matters, and Ruth was persuaded to finish the work she had been playing when they arrived. At the finish they voiced their appreciation of her talent, and then the Chaldean broached the subject upon which they had called.

He came, he said, with an invitation from the great soul whom we had assembled to honor upon that memorable day in the temple, for us to visit him at his own home in the high realm in which he lived.

The three of us were silent for a moment. Ruth and I did not know exactly what to say beyond expressing our sense of the privilege that was contained in such an invitation. Edwin, however, came to our rescue, and acted as our spokesman. The Chaldean was much amused at our embarrassment, and he hastened to assure us that there was nothing to fear in such a meeting. That would be impossible, as we should see. I think what troubled us most, or, at least, puzzled us most, was the reason why we should be invited upon such a visit, and just how we were to get there. Indeed, we had no notion where "there" might be! As for our first question, the Chaldean said that we should ascertain that when we arrived at our destination. As to our getting to our destination, why, that was what he and his much-loved friend, the Egyptian, had come for purposely.

We tried to speak our feelings, but we failed; at least, that is how I felt about *my* attempt. I think Edwin and Ruth were really much more successful than I was, although the Chaldean helped us with his delightful lightheartedness and his keen sense of fun.

I truly believe that the Chaldean is the merriest soul in the whole of the spirit realms. I mention this specifically because there would seem to be an idea in some minds that the higher one's spiritual status becomes the more serious one has to be. Such a notion is entirely false. The reverse is the truth. Lighthearted merriment that comes truly from the heart, that hurts no one and is directed against no one to their detriment, but that is indulged in for the sake of making others merry, such merriment is welcomed and encouraged in the spirit world. There is no inscription: "Abandon all *laughter*, ye who enter here" written over the portals of these realms! To suggest that the greater the spirituality the grimmer one must look is altogether a horrible notion, and recalls too much the sanctimoniousness of some breeds of earthly religious piety. We know when to laugh and how to laugh, and we do so. We do not like mournful countenances with no mirthfulness behind them. So that when I tell you that our distinguished guest, the Chaldean, so elevated our minds with his gaiety—and he was very ably assisted, one might say aided and abetted, by the kindly Egyptian—you must know that he lost none of the grand dignity and stateliness of his high station. And it must not be thought that it was a case of laughing at everything he said before he had hardly spoken it! We are not living in a land of make-believe; we laughed because there was genuine cause to do so. It was not the spurious laughter of dependents upon another of greater position.

Edwin inquired when we were to make the journey. The Chaldean replied that he and his good friend the Egyptian had come to take us back with them now. I was still—we all were—in the dark as to the actual procedure in making such a journey, but the Chaldean soon took matters in hand by bidding us to "come along." And he led us towards the boundary of our realm.

As we walked through the woods and meadows, I asked the Egyptian if he could tell me anything about the great being whom we were about to visit. What he told me was very little, although I was certain that he knew very much more than he revealed! Most likely I should not have understood had he told me all he knew, so that he, in his wisdom, withheld further information. This, then, is what he told me.

The illustrious personage, towards whose home in the high realms we were making our way, was known by sight to every soul in the realms of light. His wish was always treated as a command, and his word was law. The blue, white and gold in his robe, evident in such enormous proportions, revealed the stupendous degree of his knowledge, spirituality, and wisdom. There were thousands who named him as their "beloved master," the principal among whom being the Chaldean, who was his "right hand." As to his special function, he was the ruler of all the realms of the spirit world, and he exercised collectively that function which the particular ruler of a realm exercises individually. All other rulers, therefore, were responsible to him, and he, as it were, united the realms and welded them into one, making them one vast universe, created and upheld by the Great Father of all.

To attempt to define the immense magnitude of his powers in the spirit world would be to essay the impossible. Even were it possible, understanding would fail. Such powers have no counterpart, no comparison even, with any administrative powers upon the earth-plane. Earthly minds can only conjure up those individuals who ruled great kingdoms upon earth, who held sway over vast territories, it may be, but who did so through fear alone, and where all who lived under him lived as serfs and slaves. No earthly king throughout the whole narrative of the history of the earth world ever presided over a state so vast as that presided over by this illustrious personage of whom I am speaking. And his kingdom is ruled by the great universal law of true affection. Fear does not, *could* not, exist in the minutest, tiniest fraction, because there is not, and cannot be, the slightest cause for it. Nor will there ever be. He is the great living visible link between the Father, the Creator of the Universe, and His children.

But notwithstanding the supreme elevation of his spiritual position, he descends from his celestial home to visit us here in these realms, as I have tried to describe to you on a former occasion. And it is permissible for others of incomparably lesser degree to visit him in his own home.

There is nothing unsubstantial, vague, or unreal about this regal being. We have beheld him on those great festival days that we have in the spirit world. He is not some "spiritual experience," some grand upliftment of the soul produced within us by some invisible means from some invisible source.

He is a real living person, as firm a reality as we are ourselves—and we are more real than are you upon the earth-plane, though you are not conscious of it yet! I am putting it to you in this almost blunt way so that there will be no misunderstanding of what I am attempting to recount. There are mistaken notions that the beings of the highest realms are so ethereal as to be practically invisible except to others of their kind, and that they are utterly and completely unapproachable; that no mortal of lesser degree could possibly view them and survive. It is commonly held that these beings are so immeasurably higher than the rest of us that it will be countless eons of time before we shall ever be permitted to cast our eyes upon them even from a remote distance. That is sheer nonsense. Many a soul in these realms has been spoken to by one of these great beings, *and he has been totally unaware of the fact.* We all of us have certain powers which are magnified as we pass from sphere to sphere in the progressive steps of our spiritual development. And one of the principal of these powers is that of matching ourselves, of adjusting ourselves, to our surroundings. There is nothing magical about this; it is highly technical—far more so than most of the scientific mysteries of the earth world. In the spirit world we call it an equalizing of our personal vibrational rate, but I am afraid you are now none the wiser—and it is not within my province to attempt to explain it!

The Egyptian supplied me with these few details, and I have supplemented them from my own knowledge, which is very small indeed.

In the meantime I have digressed a little.

By now we were close to Edwin's house, and we were rapidly passing from our own realm into a more rarified atmosphere. In a short while it would have caused us some discomfort to proceed further. We instinctively halted in our walk, and we felt that the crucial moment of our journey had come. It was, of course, exactly as the Chaldean had said: we had nothing whatever to fear. And the procedure was perfectly normal and unsensational.

First of all he came behind us and allowed his hands to rest upon our heads for a brief moment. This, he told us, was to give us extra power to move through space. We felt a tingling sensation immediately beneath his hands that was most pleasant and exhilarating, and we felt as though we were becoming lighter, although one would scarcely have thought that would be possible. We could also feel a gentle heat running through the system. This was merely the effect of the power, and was nothing in itself. The Chaldean placed Ruth between Edwin and me, and then he stood just behind her himself. He placed his left hand upon Edwin's shoulder and his right upon mine, and as he was wearing a mantle—which we saw was richly embroidered—it formed a perfect cloak about the three of us.

It must not be assumed that a dignified silence had fallen or had been imposed upon us during these preliminaries. On the contrary, the Chaldean and the Egyptian, in fact, all the five of us were chatting away merrily, the former contributing by far the largest share to our jocundity. This was no dreary pilgrimage upon which we were embarking. Far from it. It is true that we were about to be taken into realms, far, far removed from our own normal habitation, but that was no reason for a heavy solemnity nor for the assumption of an intense gravity which we did not feel. The Chaldean had done his utmost to dispel any such emotions upon our part. This visit, he said in effect, was to be a gloriously happy one. Let us have smiling faces, then, and lightness of heart. Mournfulness has no place in the high realms any more than it has in our own sphere. We shall be expected, he said, to present smiling happy faces that are a true reflection of our feelings within. But it would be impossible not to be cheerful when in the presence of the Chaldean and his companion. And I am sure we did credit to them both for all their assiduity on our behalf, for I think we did most surely present to others the very embodiment of spiritual gaiety.

The Chaldean told us that by placing his hands upon our heads it would also have the effect, in addition to giving us power to travel, of adjusting our vision to the extra intensity of light that we should encounter in the high realm. Without such counterbalancing we should find ourselves in very considerable distress. In this adjustment our sight was not dimmed from within, but a kind of film was superimposed without, just in the same way as upon earth you wear protective glass to shield the eyes from the light and heat of the sun. We did not actually wear any such apparatus, of course; the Chaldean merely applied his own powers of thought. What he did precisely, I cannot say, but the process, whatever it was, he had applied many times before, and it was, needless to say, fully effective.

The Egyptian next took our hands within his, and we perceived a fresh accession of power flowing into us.

The Chaldean asked us to make ourselves completely passive, and to remember that we were upon a journey for our enjoyment and not as a test of our spiritual endurance. "And now, my friends," said he, "our arrival is awaited. So let us be off."

We immediately felt ourselves to be floating, but this sensation ceased abruptly after what seemed but a second of time, and thereafter we had no sense of movement whatever. A light flashed before our eyes. It was extremely bright, but it was by no means startling. It vanished as quickly as it came, and coincidental with its disappearance I could feel the solid ground under my feet. And then the first vision of this high realm opened before our eyes.

We were in a dominion of unparalleled beauty. There is no imagination upon the earth-plane that can visualize such inexpressible beauty, and I can only give you some meager details of what we saw in the limited terms of the earth-plane.

We were standing within the realm of a king—that was evident to us at once. We stood upon an elevation some height above the city; our good friends had expressly taken us to this particular location to present us with this superb view. It would not be possible, they said, to spend more than a limited period here, and so it was the wish of the Chaldean's master that we should see as much as possible within that period.

Stretching before us was the wide stream of a river, looking calm, peaceful, and overwhelmingly lovely as the heavenly sun touched every tiny wave with a myriad tints and tones. Occupying a central position in the view, and upon the right bank of the river, was a spacious terrace built to the water's edge. It seemed to be composed of the most delicate alabaster. A broad flight of steps led up to the most magnificent building that the mind could ever contemplate.

It was several stories high, each of them being arranged in a series of orders, so that each occupied a gradually diminishing area until the topmost was reached. Its exterior appearance was, if anything, almost plain and unadorned, and it was obvious why this should be so. The whole edifice was exclusively composed of sapphire, diamond, and topaz, or at least, their celestial equivalent. These three precious stones constituted the crystalline embodiment of the three colors blue, white and gold, and they corresponded with the colors which we had seen before in the robe of our celestial visitor as we had seen him in the temple, and which he carried in such an immense degree. The blue, white and gold of the jeweled palace, touched by the pure rays of the great central sun, were intensified and magnified a thousand-fold, and flashed forth in every direction their beams of the purest light. Indeed, the whole edifice presented to our bewildered gaze one vast volume of sparkling irradiation. We at once thought of earthly topaz and sapphire and diamond, and we pondered how small stones of purity were only tiny objects that could be held between the forefinger and thumb. And here was an immense glittering mansion entirely built of these precious stones, and of such stones that the incarnate have never beheld—nor are they ever likely to behold while they are incarnate.

Our first question concerned the reason or significance of the especial fabric of the building that was before us. There was no special significance in the actual materials of which the palace was constructed, so the Chaldean informed us. The precious stones were proper to the realm which we were now visiting. In our own realm the buildings are opaque, albeit they have a certain translucence of surface. But they are ponderous and heavy by comparison with the upper realms. We had journeyed through many other spheres to reach this present one, but had we paused to observe the lands through which we had passed, we should have seen a gradual transformation taking place until the relatively heavy-looking materials of our own realm became transmuted into the crystalline substance upon which our gaze was now fastened.

But the colors most certainly had a special significance to which I have already alluded.

We could see, surrounding the palace, many acres of the most enchanting gardens laid out in such fashion that, from the distant and elevated viewpoint which we occupied, they presented a huge and intricate pattern as in some superbly-wrought eastern carpet. We were told that upon close view, or in walking through the gardens, the pattern would be lost, but that we should find ourselves in the midst of delicately arranged flower beds and soft velvety lawns.

Though we could scarcely remove our eyes from the superlative glory of the palace and its grounds, yet the Chaldean gently drew our attention to the remainder of the prospect.

It extended for miles upon countless miles—or so it seemed to us. The range of our vision was increased in these rarefied regions beyond all human conception, and so it seemed that literally an unending vista spread before us of more earthly miles than it is possible to contemplate. And all through this wide expanse we could see other magnificent buildings built of still more precious stones—of emerald and amethyst, to name but two, and far away, what looked like pearl. Each of the different buildings was set amid the most entrancing gardens, where trees were growing of unimaginable richness of color and grandeur of form. Wherever we cast our eyes, there we could see the flashing of jeweled buildings, reflecting back the rays of the central sun, the myriad colors from the flowers, and the scintillations from the waters of the river that flowed before us far away into the distance.

As we were gazing spellbound upon the scene a sudden flash of light seemed to come from the palace directly to the Chaldean, and it was acknowledged by an answering flash which he sent back to the palace. Our presence in the realm was known, and as soon as we had feasted our eyes upon the view, we were asked to walk within the palace, where our host would be waiting to receive us. Such was the message contained in the flash of light, as interpreted by the Chaldean. We, therefore, proceeded at once towards the palace.

By the same means of locomotion that had brought us into the sphere, we quickly found ourselves walking upon the terrace beside the river, and up a broad flight of steps that led to the main entrance of the palace. The stonework of the terrace and the steps were pure white, but we were much surprised by its apparent softness under foot, for it was like walking upon the velvet softness of a well-tended lawn. Our footsteps made no sound, but our garments rustled as we walked along, otherwise our progress would have been a silent one except for our conversation. There were, of course, many other sounds to be heard. We had not stepped into a realm of silence! The whole air was filled with harmony sent forth from the volumes of color that abounded upon every hand.

The temperature seemed to us much higher than that of our own realm. The Chaldean told us that it was really much higher than we could feel, but that our minds had been attuned to the difference of temperature just as they had been attuned to the intensity of light. A gentle breeze was pleasantly perceptible as it touched our faces with its heavenly scented breath.

As we proceeded through the palace entrance, I should dearly have loved to have lingered to examine more closely the remarkable materials of which the building was composed, but time pressed. Our stay could not be prolonged beyond our capacity to resist the rarity of the atmosphere and the intensity of light, notwithstanding the charge of spiritual force that the Chaldean and the Egyptian had given us. As we passed through, therefore, we had but a fleeting glimpse of the grandeur that encompassed us.

So beautifully proportioned were the various apartments and galleries that there was no overbearing loftiness to any one of them, such as one might have expected in an edifice of such dimensions. Everywhere that we cast our eyes we could see jeweled walls and jeweled floors. Upon the walls were pictures of pastoral scenes where the artist had utilized every gem known to mortal man—and many others unknown to him—as the medium for his work. These pictures were, in their execution, of a mosaic order, but the effect produced upon the beholder was one of liquid light, if I may use the term. The constituents of the pictures sent forth their rays of light in all the colors that the subject demanded, and the effect upon the eye was one of pure life. The colors themselves were exquisite, and contained many more tones and shades of tones than earthly pigments could provide. It seemed inconceivable that precious stones could exist that had such a wide variety of colors—but, then we are in the spirit world and in a high realm of the spirit world, too.

As we walked down the corridors we met and were greeted by the most friendly and gracious beings, who thus added to our welcome. Welcome, indeed, was the overmastering feeling that enveloped us as we first put foot within the palace. There was no coldness, but everywhere the warmth of friendliness and affection.

At last we paused before a small chamber, and the Chaldean told us that we had reached the highest point of our journey. I did not feel exactly nervous, but I wondered what formalities were to be observed, and as I was totally unaware of what description these might be—as we all were, except, of course, our two ciceroni—I was naturally a little hesitant. The Chaldean, however, immediately reassured us by telling us to follow him, and merely to observe those rules dictated by good taste.

We entered. Our host was seated by a window. As soon as he saw us he rose and came forward to greet us. First he thanked the Chaldean and the Egyptian for bringing us to him. Then he took us each by the hand and bade us be welcome to his home. There were several vacant chairs close to that in which he had been seated, and he suggested that we might like to sit with him there and enjoy the view. It was, he explained, his favorite view.

We drew close to the window, and we could see beneath us a bed of the most magnificent white roses, as pure white as a field of snow, and which exhaled an aroma as exalting as the blooms from which it came. White roses, our host told us, were flowers he preferred above all others.

We seated ourselves, and I had an opportunity, as our host spoke to us, of observing him at close quarters where before I had but seen him from a distance. Seeing him thus, in his own home and surroundings, his facial appearance was, in general, similar to that which he had presented when he visited us in the temple in our own realm. There were differences, however, as we saw him here; differences that were largely a matter of light intensity. His hair, for example, seemed to be golden when he came to us. Here it seemed to be as of bright golden *light*, rather than of the color of gold. He *looked* to be young, to be of eternal youthfulness, but we could feel the countless eons of time, as it is known on earth, that lay behind him.

When he spoke his voice was sheer music, his laugh as a rippling of the waters, but never did I think it possible for one individual to breathe forth such affection, such kindliness, such thoughtfulness and consideration; and never did I think it possible for one individual to possess such an immensity of knowledge as is possessed by this celestial king. One felt that, under the Father of Heaven, he held the key to all knowledge and wisdom. But, strange as it may sound, though we had been transported unfathomable distances to the presence of this transcendingly wonderful being, yet here in his very presence we felt perfectly at home, perfectly at ease with him. He laughed with us, he joked with us, he asked us what we thought of his roses, and had the Chaldean managed to keep us merry upon our way thither. He spoke to each of us individually, displaying an exact acquaintance with all our concerns, collectively and personally. Then finally he came to the reason for his invitation to us to visit him.

In company with my friends, he said, I had visited the dark realms, and I had recounted what I had seen there. He thought that it would be in the nature of a pleasant contrast if we were to visit the highest realm, and see for ourselves some of its beauties; to show that the inhabitants of such high realms are not shadowy unreal people, but, on the contrary, they are like ourselves, capable of feeling and exhibiting the emotions of their fine natures, capable of human understanding, of human thought, and as easily susceptible to laughter and free-hearted merriment as were we ourselves. And he had asked us to visit him in order to tell us himself that these realms, wherein we were now visiting, were within the reach of every soul that is born upon the earth-plane, that no one can deprive us of that right; and that although it may take countless years of time to reach those realms, yet there is all eternity in which to achieve that end, and that there are unlimited means to help us upon our way. That, he said, is the simple, great fact of spirit life. There are no mysteries attached to it; all is perfectly straightforward, plain, and unrestricted by complicated beliefs, religious or otherwise. It requires no adherence to any particular form of orthodox religion, which, of itself, has no authority to assure any single soul of its powers to secure the soul's "salvation." No religious body that ever existed can do that.

And so this realm of incomparable beauty was free and open to all to work their way thither from the very lowest and foulest realm. It may take eons of time to accomplish, but that is the great and superb finale of the lives of the earth world's millions of souls.

Our good friend, the Chaldean, then mentioned to his "master" that our stay had almost reached its limit. The latter said he was sorry to observe that it was so, but that such powers as had been invoked for us had their limitations, and so, for our comfort, we must work within them. However, he added, there are other occasions, and thus he extended further invitations to us.

We now rose, and I could not resist the lure of the view of the roses from the window. I gazed out once more, then we made ready to depart.

Our gracious host said he would accompany us to the hill from which we had had our first glimpse of his kingdom. We followed a different route from that by which we had reached the palace, and what was our delight when it led us directly to the rose bed. Stooping, our host culled three of the most choice blooms that mortal eyes ever beheld, and presented one to each of us. Our joy was still further heightened by the knowledge that with the affection that we should shower upon them, the blooms would never fade and die. My one anxiety was that in taking them to our own realm we should see them crushed, perhaps, by the unaccustomed density of our heavier atmosphere. But our host assured us that they would not, for they would be borne up by our thoughts of them and of the giver, and between the one and the other they would be amply supported, and would so remain.

At length we reached our point of departure. Words would not express our feelings, but our thoughts passed unfailingly to him who had brought us this supreme happiness, this foretaste of our destiny—and of the destiny of the whole earth world and the whole spirit world. And with a blessing upon us all, and with a smile of such affection, of such ineffable benignity, he bade us God-speed, and we found ourselves once more in our own realm.

I have tried to tell you something of what we saw, but words cannot be found to describe it, because I cannot translate the purely spiritual into earthly terms. My account must therefore fall far, far short.

And so also in those other matters of which I have treated. To give you a comprehensive account of all that we have seen in the world of spirit would fill many volumes, and therefore I have chosen what I felt would be of most interest and benefit. My earnest wish is that I have captured your interest, taken you away, for a moment, from the pressing affairs of earthly life, and given you a glimpse of the world beyond the world in which you are now living.

If I have brought a measure of comfort, or of good hope, then great is my reward, and I would say to you:

Benedicat te omnipotens Deus.

BOOK TWO

(1956)

MORE ABOUT LIFE
IN THE WORLD
UNSEEN

ANTHONY BORGIA

PREFACE

THE SPIRIT communicator of this book was known on earth as Monsignor Robert Hugh Benson, a son of Edward White Benson, former Archbishop of Canterbury, and he was at the height of his renown, both as preacher and author, when I first met him many years ago.

After he had passed from this life, I many times wondered as to his welfare. Through a spirit friend I was told that he was well and prospering, and that in time I should hear from him directly.

Such eventually proved to be the case, and there commenced a series of scripts given by him, the first of which, *Life in the World Unseen*, gave an account in some detail of his actual passing. He recounted how, at the close of his earthly life, he was met by a former colleague named Edwin, and taken by him to the spirit world, where his home awaited him, a counterpart of his house on earth. After a brief rest he commenced his explorations, under Edwin's guidance, of the land of his new life. During the course of their rambles they met a young girl of great charm, named Ruth, also a newcomer to the spirit world, who joined them, and the three have been together ever since, closely associated in work and pleasure.

In the scripts that have followed, Monsignor has dealt with an extensive variety of subjects in connection with the spirit world, not the least among them being his "theology," which underwent a wholesale and drastic revision.

His principal occupation is to meet people at their dissolution, and conduct them into the spirit world. Working with him in this are his friends, Edwin and Ruth.

It has been my privilege and pleasure to act all along as his amanuensis for recording the scripts. Through other sources of communication we have had literally hundreds of forgatherings, where he has brought with him a goodly company of spirit friends.

In the present script, recorded by me in 1951, Monsignor recounts how Ruth and he, but without Edwin on this occasion, embarked upon one of their visits to earth for "escort duty," in this instance to a young lad of eighteen years. Instead, however, of passing him into the care of other hands, as usually takes place, they invite him to stay with them in their home (where he first awakens to his new life), and thereafter, when fully recovered, they set out upon "escort duty" of another kind: through the realms in which they live, to see the wonders and meet some of the people.

ANTHONY BORGIA

CHAPTER ONE

A PASSING

YOU WILL have read, I hope, the few prefatory words that my earthly amanuensis has written concerning myself, so allowing me to proceed at once to my narrative without going over old ground.

It is now close upon forty years since I stood upon the threshold of a new life when the moment of my dissolution came. During the passage of the last decade I have been enabled to give some account of life as it is lived in these parts of the spirit world wherein I am happy to be living.

Life, you must know, is upon a gigantic scale here in the spirit world, how gigantic you can have very little conception until you yourself come to dwell among us. But because its magnitude is vast that is not to say that it is proportionately complex. Indeed, when one comes to compare the earth world with the spirit world, it is at once apparent how complex the earth world is, and how much simpler is life in the spirit world. This may seem an astonishing statement to make; nevertheless, it is a true one. That, however, is a subject which I will discuss with you later. And now, without further preamble, to my narrative.

Situated in the city, which is not far from my home here, is a large building which carries out the important functions of an office of records and inquiries. Here knowledge is to be obtained upon an infinite range and variety of subjects and affairs. Of all these, what closely interests us at the moment is that department which deals with the actual passing of folk from the earth to the spirit world. Part of my work consists of helping people at the moment of their physical death, people of all kinds, of both sexes, of any religion—or none—and of all ages, from young folk to the aged. Working in conjunction with me are my two old friends, Edwin and Ruth. Sometimes Edwin is not with us, but Ruth and I almost always work together.

Now you may wonder how we come to know when our services are needed, and who or what directs those services into the required quarter. The answer is a simple one: the office of records and inquiries. It is not part of our normal functions to be fully acquainted with all or any of the methods employed in the gathering of information by this central office. All that Ruth and I are called upon to do is to apprise this office with the fact that we are both free to undertake whatever task may present itself, and we follow the simple procedure of awaiting notification that our services are desired.

We were seated, then, upon a particular occasion in our house, which is itself a replica of my old home on earth, when word reached us that our presence was desired at the central office. We at once proceeded thither, and were greeted by one whom we had come to know very well during the passage of years, as he had come to know us.

This man is a genial soul, of great kindness and comprehension, and his knowledge of those who work for him is prodigious. For it is by the application of this knowledge that he is enabled to send upon their various missions those of us who are exactly suited to the specific task in hand.

There may appear to be a great similarity between one normal transition and another when viewed by earthly eyes, but from our point of view the variations are enormous.

They are as great, in fact, as the variations in human personalities. What to the earthly beholder is the end of life, is to us and the person chiefly concerned, the beginning of a new one. It is with the personality that we have to deal, and according to the personality, to the knowledge or ignorance of spiritual matters of the passing soul, so is our especial task governed and our course of action regulated. In short, every "death" is treated and served with strict regard to its essential requirements, so that we are allotted our various tasks with one eye, as it were, upon our capabilities, experience, temperament, and so on. Edwin, Ruth and I are decidedly of similar temperament, while our capabilities and experience have been augmented and broadened by long practice.

As you can imagine, a great deal of patience has at times to be exercised when we are confronted with minds that are tenacious of old beliefs and ideas that bear no relationship with the truth and facts and realities of spirit life, and it may take much arduous work to free the newly arrived person of so much that is mentally inhibiting and spiritually retarding. You will see, then, the wisdom of choosing instruments who are ably suited in all respects to the work in hand, so that a difficult or awkward case may not be rendered more so.

The spirit world never does things by halves, to use a familiar expression, and what might appear to be sheer preciosity to the incarnate is clear wisdom to us who have to carry out the work. No trouble is spared. We have infinity of time, a vast amount of patience, together with the services of a multitude of people always available. There is no bungling, there are no mistakes; nothing is left to chance. Our principal in the central office, therefore, knowing us, sends us upon our missions to earth with complete confidence in his choice of ourselves, while for our part, we have complete confidence that we are not being given a task beyond our powers of performance.

After a few friendly exchanges and kindly inquiries, our friend turned to the business in hand. A perfectly straightforward case, he informed us, and one that should present no unusual features. "It is the passing," he said, "of a lad, aged eighteen. A sprightly youth; mentally alert and receptive. I have kept this case for you both, as I think he will be useful to you later on when he has become accustomed to things. Would you care to take him to your home? It would be a good plan." We readily acquiesced.

We then plied our friend with a few questions so that we should be as fully charged with information as possible. It appeared that the lad's earthly end was approaching rapidly, that he had no prejudices concerning the subject of "life after death"; his religious instruction had followed the usual lines but had not left any very great impression. There was a happy toleration between him and his parents, but no such strong affection as would introduce any complications of an emotional nature. The parents would regard the early "death" of their son as part of God's will, and they would therefore submit in accordance thereto.

We were agreed that this certainly did seem to be a straightforward case enough, and we were not sorry, inasmuch as we had had a number of very trying transitions of late, and welcomed this fresh one upon easier lines.

You will no doubt wonder how we are directed at the outset of our "labours" to the actual "chamber of death," to use a most lugubrious phrase. Incidentally, what a wealth of gloom and lamentation it conjures up! It seems as though all the most doleful phrases are specially reserved for the simple act of passing from your world to ours. Of course you do not need to remind me that from the point of view of those who are parting from a loved one, it is no time for cheerfulness and "joy abounding." Yet were the truth known and realized, what a world of difference it would make, especially if that happy state of things were to exist to the end that all the mournful trappings so closely associated with transition were to be ruthlessly cast out. Is not the event, at the present day, sufficiently harrowing in itself without adding to its gloom by the adoption of so much black? This, I am afraid, is a slight digression. To return.

We are given the name, but not the address of the person upon whom we are to attend. Indeed, the whole procedure is far simpler, and gives a very good example of what I mentioned but a moment ago regarding the relative simplicity of life in our world as compared with the complexities of life in yours. Everything, you will say, must have a beginning, so that some indication must be given somewhere *by* someone *to* someone that the passing of a particular person is about to take place, within, shall we say, a matter of an hour or two of earthly time. It is hardly likely, things being what they are, that a direct message would be sent out to us from earth people intimating that assistance was required at an imminent dissolution.

It is not my purpose, at this moment, to trace matters to their source, and, strictly speaking, we who undertake this kind of work are not concerned with the minutiae of organization which terminate with our presenting ourselves at the side of the passing soul. That is part of the expert economic functions that are but a commonplace in spirit lands. This, however, can be said: the knowledge that a transition is about to take place, together with its precise location, is the result of a remarkable conveyance of information, passed from one to another, commencing with that important functionary, the individual's personal spirit guide, and terminating with us who undertake the work of escorting folk from the earth world to their homes in the spirit world. Between the former and the latter there is a clear concatenation of minds, if I may so express it, an exchange of information carried out by thought transmission, accurately and rapidly.

At the present moment, as Ruth and I were seated before our friend of the central office, all that remained was to receive our "sailing directions." These were given to us in this manner: our friend sent a message—by thought, of course—to the spirit person who was in attendance at the place of dissolution, to the effect that we were ready to assume charge whenever he deemed it advisable. This brought an instantaneous response. We could perceive the light as it flashed to our friend, and by a sort of confluence we were brought into the "thought-beam." We were now in direct *rapport* with our attendant friend "at the other end," as you would say. And now—to use very unscientific language—we had but to project ourselves along this thought-beam to find ourselves in the exact spot where our services were needed. How this happens, I have not the remotest notion. All that Ruth or I could tell you is what we do, how we do it, but not *how* it *happens*! Do you believe you could describe in simple terms—or any terms—precisely what you do when you think, and having done that, tell me how it happens? Try that "simple" experiment for yourselves, and then you will understand just what I mean!

We now thanked our principal for this new case, and upon his intimation that the time was close at hand, we immediately set forth.

Ruth and I found ourselves in a bedroom of a house of modest dimensions, unpretentious, and moderately prosperous as far as earthly possessions were concerned. A nurse was in attendance, and relatives were close at hand. It was evident that they believed the end was not far distant, and the doctor appeared to have done all that he could to make things easier for his patient.

There also seemed to be some evidence that a minister of their church had not long left the room. There were distinct signs that prayerful petitions had been sent forth, but these being couched in the usual terms of theological obscurity, and in addition being totally inapposite to the events about to take place, they were completely ineffective to achieve any purpose whatever beyond giving a doubtful satisfaction to those then present. This was a matter, however, that Ruth and I were quickly able—and qualified—to set right. We did so, asking for a downflowing of helpful power to supplement our own natural resources and abilities. It was instantly forthcoming, and was clearly observable in the bright beams of light that diffused themselves round about us.

It was plain to see that in a brief space our friend would be joining us. Accordingly, we commenced our small preparations. Ruth stationed herself at the head of the bed within easy reach of the lad's head, and placing her hands upon his brow, she gently smoothed his temples.

We are never certain that our ministrations are perceived or felt unless the "patient" reveals some sign or another that he—or she—has done so. In this case, it was patent that Ruth was making a decided impression, because coincidental with her placing her hands upon the boy's head, he turned his eyes with an upward motion as though seeking or trying to perceive whence the pleasant, soothing sensation came.

It was possible that he could actually see Ruth; if that were the case, so much the better.

We had both assumed a replica of our former earthly habiliments, Ruth being attired in a gay summery garment, looking very natural and normal, and altogether charming. It is necessary to emphasize this, since it was—and always is—our aim to appear as unlike "celestial beings," should our presence be observed, as it is possible to be. (When Edwin came to meet me upon my own transition, he revealed himself to me dressed in his customary earthly attire. Had he presented himself to me in his spirit clothes, there is every reason to believe that I should have been sufficiently terrified to fancy that if the worst had not come, it could not be long delayed!)

I perched myself at the foot of the lad's bed and directed my gaze upon him, and there were evident signs of his seeing me. I smiled to him, and gently waved my hand to reassure him. So far, things were proceeding very favorably—would that all passings were as serene.

The great moment in the boy's life had now arrived. I moved to a position at about the middle of the bed upon the side opposite to Ruth. The boy had lapsed into a gentle sleep. As he did so, his spirit body rose slowly above his inert physical body to which it was attached by a bright silver cord—the lifeline as it is termed. I placed my arms beneath the floating form; there was the slightest momentary twitch, the cord detached itself, retracted, and disappeared.

To the relatives in the bed-chamber, the boy was "dead" and "gone." To Ruth and me he was *alive* and *present*.

I held him in my arms, as one would a child, while Ruth again placed her hands upon his head. A gentle movement of her hands for a minute or two to ensure that the boy would be peacefully comfortable, and we were ready to start upon our rapid journey to our home.

Throughout the transit Ruth held one of the boy's hands, thus giving him energy and strength while I supported him in my arms. The journey, as with all such journeys, was soon over; we had left the dismal bedroom, and we were in our own beautiful land and home. Quietly and gently we laid the boy upon a very comfortable couch, Ruth seating herself close beside him, as I took a chair at the foot facing our new arrival. "Well, my dear," Ruth remarked with evident satisfaction, "I really think he'll do."

All there was for us to do now, was to await the awakening, which, in the nature of the case, would not be long delayed.

Our simple, but usually effective, arrangements had already been made. The couch upon which the lad had been laid was placed close beneath a wide open window in such a position that, without even the slightest movement of the head, a most enchanting view was to be seen of the gardens without, while through a gap in a line of trees, a distant view of our beautiful city was to be had, clear and colorful. Upon the wall immediately facing the lad there hung a large mirror, so that the reflection of the rest of the room, with all that it suggested in comfort and ease, could be observed with the merest turn of the eye. Children's voices could be heard in the distance, and the birds were singing with their customary vigor.

This was the pleasant situation awaiting our friend when he emerged from his short but refreshing sleep, and *this* is often the moment when our *real* work begins!

CHAPTER TWO

THE AWAKENING

RUTH WAS the first to speak when our friend had opened his eyes. "Well, Roger," she said, "how do you feel?" (Our friend at the office had given us the boy's first name, which was sufficient for all purposes.)

Roger opened his eyes still wider as he turned to Ruth. "Why," said he, "I saw you—when was it? A little while ago. Who are you?"

"Just a friend to help you. Call me Ruth."

"And you, sir. I seem to remember you were sitting at the foot of my bed."

"That's right," I said. "The memory will become clearer in a moment or two."

Roger started to sit upright, but Ruth gently pressed him back upon the cushions. "Now, Roger," said she, "the order of the day is that you just stay quietly there, and not do too much talking."

The boy stared out of the window.

"Lovely view, isn't it," I said, pointing through the window. "Feeling comfortable? That's right. Well, now, you are wondering what all this is about. Have you any idea what has happened? Only a hazy notion. But the great thing is that *now* you are feeling all right. All the aches and pains gone. Isn't that it?"

Roger nodded and smiled as the realization seemed to come upon him. "Yes, rather, thank you."

The boy was obviously not of the nervous sort, and there appeared to be no purpose in withholding the truth any longer. I caught Ruth's eye, and she nodded in agreement.

"Roger, my dear boy," I began, "I have some pleasant news for you. You were perfectly correct, you *did* see Ruth and me a little while ago. We were in your bedroom at home, and you were very ill, so ill that the doctor couldn't pull you through. So Ruth and I came to *bring* you through, through into another world, a lovely world. Do you follow?"

"Then, I've died. Is that it?"

"That's it, old fellow. You're not frightened?"

"No, I don't think so." He paused. "I never expected anything like this," he added.

"No, I don't suppose you did. Who does, except the very comparative few who know what's to come? Honestly, now, what did you expect?"

"Goodness only knows."

"Angels with large wings, and stern countenances, looking very frigid and remote? Suppose you had seen something like that, what would you have felt and thought? You needn't tell me; I'll answer the question for you. You would have thought that they had come to haul you off to be tried before some awful judge somewhere in the High Court of Heaven. And woe betide you if you had misbehaved yourself, my lad."

Ruth gave a merry peal of laughter, while Roger, who had caught the look in my eye and interpreted it correctly, laughed too.

"Let me tell you at once, Roger, that there are no judges, or even a single great judge, anywhere in this world, the spirit world. Any judging to be done, we do it for ourselves, and manage very nicely. You'll find you will become extremely critical of yourself, as we all do. We can be very hard on ourselves even. So whatever you may have thought about Judgment Day, dismiss the whole idea from your mind. There is no such thing, there never has been, and *there never will be.*

"Now I expect you are wondering what is to happen next," I went on. "The answer to that is simple: Nothing!—at least for a little while, until you feel refreshed, and then we might all go off together and explore things a bit. How does that appeal to you?"

"It appeals to me very much, but there is something I would like to know." Roger looked round. "Whose house is this, and who are you? I can see you are a padre, but the color of your cassock is not what I've ever seen before."

"As to the house, it is mine, though really it is ours, as Ruth lives most of her time with me and so does an old clergyman friend you will meet later. As to my clothes, these I am wearing are only replicas of my earthly ones which I have put on specially for *you.* I have proper spirit clothes, but suppose I had worn them—and Ruth hers—when we came to fetch you in your room, we might have looked like those grim, forbidding angels I spoke about just now.

And no matter how we set our faces into pleasant looks and smiles, there is no doubt there would have been a very frightened Roger. So, behold us as we used to be when we lived on earth, and now you look at yourself as you used to be on earth only a very short while ago." Roger glanced down at his clothes to discover that he was wearing a pair of flannel trousers and a brown jacket, while on his feet were a pair of substantial shoes. He caught hold of the material as thought to reassure himself that it was real. He even clutched his arm to make doubly sure he was solid! Then he placed one foot on the floor and stamped lightly with it.

"All pretty solid, eh, Roger?"

From a side-table Ruth fetched a huge bowl of fruit, and offered it to the boy. "You'll find these very real, too," said she with a smile. "Help yourself to what you fancy. They're lovely, and will do you a world of good. We keep them here especially."

We all three took some fruit, and Ruth and I waited to see the boy tackle his. First, he looked at it closely, turning it over and over in his hand—it was a plum he was examining—and seemed undecided what to do with it. There is, of course, only one thing to do with a fine, juicy plum, especially if it is one grown in the spirit world, and that is to eat it. Ruth and I did so, while Roger watched closely to see what would happen. He expected, no doubt, to see a torrent of juice run out and down our clothes. His eyes opened in astonishment when he saw the juice run out, certainly, and with equal certainty, disappear, leaving our clothes unstained. Thus encouraged, he followed our example, and was wild with delight at this seeming wizardry.

"Nothing is wasted here, Roger," explained Ruth. "Everything that is unwanted returns to its source. Nothing is destroyed. You couldn't *destroy* anything however hard you tried. If you find you no longer need or desire a thing it will simply fade away to all appearances, just evaporate before your eyes. But it is not lost; it will return to the source from which it came. If we didn't want this house and all its contents, it would vanish, and there would be nothing to see but the ground it stood on. It's the same with anything else you care to name. All things are *living* in the spirit world; we don't have such things as 'inanimate objects.' Things are managed much better here than on the old earth, don't you think—from the tiny bit you've seen of things so far?"

Roger thanked Ruth for her explanation. He seemed a little diffident in the matter of speaking, though, of course Ruth had recommended him not to talk too much yet. However, he turned to me after pondering Ruth's words, with something of an air of puzzlement:

"Were you a bishop, or something?" he asked.

"Oh dear, no," I laughed; "nothing so grand or exalted. You were going by the color of this garment I'm wearing. No, I was only Monsignor when I was on earth. Some of my friends there still call me by the old title. It pleases them, and does no harm, though really we have no such titles and distinguishing marks here. Still, if you would like to use the same name, do so by all means. It serves a useful purpose, and it's not "against the regulations." Ruth always uses it."

Here I would like to interpolate one or two observations which I think it expedient to make. What I am setting down for you is the account of an actual case, a real occurrence, though it is typical of many. The young lad, Roger, is a person of real existence, who came into the spirit world in the circumstances precisely as I am now giving you.

Again: exception may be taken to the conversation as I have recounted it to you. There are folk who will object that the whole of it is too appallingly flippant and trivial to merit consideration for one moment; that it is frivolous and third-rate, and such as would not, most certainly *not* be indulged in in any region that could be properly designated "heaven"; that "heaven" must surely be conducted upon lines far less commonplace and far more holy and spiritual.

It may be complained that anyone making "the awful change" from life to death and from death to eternal life—*"supernatural"* life—would have far graver things to think about and discuss than the conversational fripperies which I "allege" take place.

With a long experience of transitions upon which to draw, commencing with *my own*, I know this beyond peradventure: when the last earthly breath has been drawn, and life has begun in the spirit world, there is never the slightest inclination, at that vital moment, to think in terms of learned theological disquisitions or indulge in any "pious platitudes." Every soul who arrives in these or other realms of the spirit world completely untutored about life here, is concerned with one thing and one thing only: what is to happen next? just that. Because we are inhabitants of the spirit world we have not become grand rhetoricians, who speak only in long eloquent periods upon matters of the highest spiritual consideration. *Deo gratias* that we do not. We are normal, rational people, who speak and act in a normal, rational manner.

Suppose Ruth and I, in taking charge of Roger, had adopted a grave comportment and grim countenances, what do you imagine would have happened both to him *and us*? The lad would have been terrified, where, in good truth, no grounds for fear existed, and all for what purpose? Merely so that Ruth and I should appear and act as misguided folk believe we should appear and act, as became inhabitants of the world of spirit.

And what would have happened to Ruth and me? We should have been adjudged totally unfitted for the occupation we had adopted, and at once sent upon our way—*in disgrace*. However, such a thing could never transpire, since we should not be entrusted with this work were we to harbor such unthinkable notions. So it is, my dear friends, that in our conversation with Roger, *as with thousands of others* upon whom we have attended, we are just ourselves. After all, this is a world of life and activity and truth, not a sham, shadowy, sanctimonious mockery of existence. How glad we all are that it is so! We prefer *our* form of "heaven" to the strange conception current in some quarters on earth. Now to return to my narrative.

Roger had felt tempted to rise from his couch, a sure sign that he was gaining in strength and vigor. The fruit had made an improvement, as we knew it would. In matters of that kind there are no failures. At the same time, it would not have done to let him test his strength too far, and so for the time being, we recommended he should remain where he was. He was—and of course, still is!—a most amiable fellow, and was ready to fall in with all our suggestions. In such cases as these, that is, in the initial moments of the newly arrived, so much depends upon the little incidents, those homely things, of great implication in themselves, and outwardly so very reassuring and comforting.

Long experience has taught us that often the smallest, most insignificant incident can do far more to bring peace and mental quietude to the newcomer to spirit lands than would a hundred of the most brilliant dissertations. Therefore it is that we deliberately introduce the apparently trivial. And I cannot do better to exemplify this than by recounting what next occurred in our care of Roger.

The boy suddenly turned his gaze towards the window, attracted by the sound of fluttering wings upon the window-ledge, when he perceived a small bird had made its entrance into the room, and had perched itself only a foot or so from him. Roger remained perfectly still, as though scarcely daring to move lest he should frighten the small visitor away. Ruth, however, called to the bird, which immediately flew to her and perched upon her outstretched finger. The bird was dressed in a smart livery of pale gray feathers.

Roger was greatly interested when Ruth transferred the bird to his own finger.

"He often visits us here," I told him, "though he really belongs to two old earth friends of mine."

"Then what is he doing here?" asked Roger.

"Well, he was found by my friends in great distress when he was but a fledgling; they cared for him, watched him grow, but sad to say, he came to grief. Possibly he became a trifle too daring, overdid things, had some sort of sudden seizure, and died almost at once. A great pity. He was like you, Roger, young and had hardly begun his life. And exactly like you, Roger, he passed into these beautiful lands, and was cared for immediately, just as we try to do for all the human souls who come to us. That small bird, so very inconsiderable on earth, and the action of my two friends, equally inconsiderable, have not been lost. Their affection for that tiny atom of life has preserved that life for all time. At present he is part of the "household" of a mutual old friend, who already has other bird and animal friends of his own. They're a merry family, and we'll take you along to see him—and them. Don't you think he is a rather handsome fellow?"

"I do. What kind of bird is he?"

"When he first came to us here, he was a much darker gray, and not so big. But he has grown, and his color, as you see, is now almost dove-gray. What kind of bird is he, did you say? Why only a common sparrow."

Ruth was indignant that I should refer to him as in any sense common, and so I was compelled to recant—not for the first time since I came to the spirit world!

Roger was still playing with the bird, when Ruth espied two visitors coming towards the house. They were walking in leisurely fashion through the garden, often stopping to examine the flowers that were growing in profusion round the house. As they drew nearer, we recognized them as old friends who had often come to see us before. One, the taller of the two, was a Chaldean by nationality, the other an Egyptian.

I told Roger that not on any account was he to rise when these two visitors came into the room, as they both knew the purpose for which that couch was used, for it had had many and many a newly arrived person resting upon it.

Ruth and I went to the door to welcome our visitors, and cordial greetings were exchanged. The Chaldean's name is Omar, by which he is universally known. He is a man of striking appearance, the most remarkable feature being his raven-black hair, so much in contrast with the slight pallor of his complexion. He is, without doubt, one of the merriest souls to be met with in these lands, and he has a wide reputation for his keen sense of humor.

"Will you come in, Omar," I said, "and see our 'patient'?" He replied they would be delighted, and we moved two chairs nearer to the couch.

"Well, my son, how are you feeling? Happy? Rested?" Omar turned to us:

"Roger is wondering who I am. Perhaps he is wondering *what* I am."

"You see, Omar, you are really the first person he has seen wearing spirit clothes. Isn't that so, Roger?"

"Yes, it is, and well, I'm a bit confused. Your clothes," he said to Omar, "are so different from Monsignor's."

"Different from those he is wearing now because he did not want to frighten you. You are not frightened of me, are you, Roger? There's no need to be, my dear son, for I'm really harmless, and my two friends—your two friends—will vouch for me. Perhaps you think I'm an angel! Well, that's better than being thought a devil. Do you know, Roger, there are some charming people on earth who would call me one, yes, and you, too; in fact, all of us here! Do you think Ruth looks particularly satanic? Monsignor, now; there is certainly a hint of brimstone about *him*. Well, well, it's a good thing we can laugh, though, mind you, those same nice people would deny us *that*. Speaking for myself, I don't feel the least bit holy, and Monsignor is far too hardened a sinner ever to come within a mile of it."

Omar turned to me: "I must be off now," said he. "Give my love to my friends on earth." Then he took Roger by the hand, held it for a moment, and patted him on the cheek. "Bless you, my son," he said, "be rested, then get your friends to show you the glories of these lands. This is your own home land, now, you know. And just between ourselves, we're rather proud of it."

CHAPTER THREE

A First View

AS WE returned to the house after parting with Omar and his companion, we saw that Roger had left his couch and was now leaning out of the window. We waved to him, and he waved back.

"It looks as though he's completely regained his vigor," I remarked to Ruth.

"There's no doubt of it, I should say."

"And I should say what's completed his 'cure' is Omar's visit. Did you notice how he held the boy's hand? If that wasn't charging him with vitality I'm much mistaken. Now isn't that just like Omar?"

There was no question that a great change had been wrought in the lad for he stood in the doorway as we drew near with every appearance of youthful buoyancy. No longer was that slight languidness to be seen, so common in such cases.

"Well, Roger," said Ruth, "you look ready for anything."

"That's how I do feel, Ruth. Now, Monsignor, the old brain has got clear, and I want to know lots of things." He grasped an arm of each of us, and held us in a firm grip.

"Omar certainly *has* given you strength, judging by the pressure," I observed. He laughed, and it was good to hear him, for it showed more than anything else could, that the lad was now clearly himself, and that our task thenceforward would be the simple one of introducing him to the wonders of the spirit world, always an enjoyable occupation, in spite of the fact that we had gone through a similar performance times without number.

"Come along, my boy, and let's start on the roof."

"On the roof? What on earth do we want to go climbing on the roof for?"

"On earth, Roger, my lad, no reason at all. However, I know what you mean. Come along and wait till you get there before making any rude remarks about it. Now then, to the roof!"

We mounted the stairs to the upper floor. Here there is a passage, and about halfway along it is a small bay, in which a brief flight of stairs leads to a door on to a flat roof. Here was presented to the astonished gaze of Roger a most superb view of the countryside, a vast territory extending far away into the distance.

"Now, Roger; cast your eyes over this. Did you ever see anything like it, or even remotely approaching it in beauty?" The boy was silent for a minute or two as he turned in a full circle. "Gracious heavens," he said.

"And that's just about it," said Ruth, "those two words are a complete description, if ever there was one."

"Now, Monsignor, Ruth—I don't care which of you—but one of you *must* tell me what all this is. All those people, for instance. What are they doing?"

We could see many people interspersed about the countryside, some close at hand, others at a distance; some in small groups, others in larger, and individuals either seated or walking alone.

"All these folk you see are going about their various business, or perhaps no definite business at all. Look there at that little group sitting beneath the big tree. They may be doing all manner of things, from merely having a pleasant, gossipy chat among friends, or perhaps one of them is doing what Ruth and I are doing now for you—introducing you to the spirit world. Whatever it is all these folk are doing, no one will tell them they shouldn't be doing it—and move them on!

"Of absolute, positive idling, I don't think you'll find a trace, Roger, because no one, as far as I've been able to find out—and Ruth and I have poked about in all sorts of places—no one ever feels the slightest inclination to do nothing simply by virtue of an indolent nature. There *are* no indolent natures here. We are always occupied in some way, but that doesn't mean that this is a life of eternal work as opposed to the *old*—and still current—idea of eternal rest. We all, every one of us, have our time off, and no one will come and tell us it's time to start work again in the earthly sense. We have all the recreation we need and desire, and we come and go as we please. What Ruth and I are doing now, here on this roof, is a very pleasant form of recreation to us both, and a pleasant change from our chief occupation. It might look as though we were idling the time away—to anyone who didn't know. But, you know, Roger, there are millions of us here—with no overcrowding either, as you can see—so that even as there's plenty to do, there are plenty of people to do it."

"Well, that's simple enough, Monsignor, but that makes me wonder what I'm going to do."

"Then stop wondering, my dear," put in Ruth. "Good gracious, why you've only just arrived here. Wait till you've been here as long as we have, then you'll see there's not always such a terrific hurry to be getting on with something." "How long have you been here, then, Ruth?"

"Oh, getting on for forty years."

"And you, Monsignor?"

"About the same time. There might be ten minutes difference between us! You see we are really seasoned residents."

"How long has Omar been here?"

Ruth and I exchanged glances, and there was a roar of laughter.

"Omar has been in the spirit world some two thousand years, Roger. I think I had better withdraw what I said about being seasoned residents."

The lad enjoyed our trifling joke, and so was helped along the road of self-assurance and well-being.

"Now, Ruth, point out the sights to Roger."

"Do you see that large building with the blue beam of light coming down on it? That's a home of rest for people immediately after they have arrived here. You could have gone there. It's very beautiful, and you would have been well looked after, with every kindness in the world."

"Then why was I brought here?"

"You're not sorry, are you?"

"No, *no*; I could never be that."

"The suggestion of bringing you here came from the particular person who sends us on our various errands in helping folk, when they are crossing into this world. He thought it would be a good idea, and we shouldn't dream of questioning his wisdom. It would not be the first time this has happened, by any means; many people have caught their first peep of the spirit world while reclining on that couch downstairs. It is good for them, and it is good for us."

Roger pointed to the houses of all kinds that could be seen, some almost buried among the trees, others in more open ground. "Whose are those?" he asked.

"They belong to the folk here. Once you have the right to possess a home there is nothing to prevent you from having one. Everything is owned upon the same terms here, no matter what it is—even your spirit clothes. That does not mean that you might have to walk abroad naked, because by some chance you had not earned the right to possess clothes! The natural laws here work in a rational way."

I broke into the conversation: "It's not by any means everyone who owns a house here, Roger. Some people don't want to be bothered with one—though bothered is not the exact word to use, as no home, whether large or small, can possibly be any bother in the old earthly sense. But there are folk who don't feel the necessity for a house, and so they don't have one. Perfectly simple. To begin with, the sun is always shining in these and other regions, there's no unpleasant wind or cold. It's always the same steady, unvarying, genial warmth you can feel now. So there's nothing from which we need protection as on earth, in the way of the elements. As for privacy, well, there are myriads of spots—you can see some of them from here—that will provide all the solitude you are ever likely to want."

"What are those large buildings in the far distance?" our friend asked.

"Those are the various halls of learning in the city. In fact, that is the city. Everything in the way of knowledge is to be found somewhere there, and a thousand accomplishments can be gained there. You can become a technician in any of the varied occupations that are all part of the life of the spirit world."

So we went on, pointing out innumerable things to Roger, explaining this, providing reasons for that, and bringing a clearer understanding to a young mind that had left the earth—as so many do—with no knowledge whatever of the most important part of the Universe—the spirit world. He could see, spread out before him into seemingly illimitable space, the stupendous countryside, with the bright verdure, the rich colors abounding upon all sides, the gentle undulations leading to the glistening water of lake or river. The carefully laid-out gardens, the flowers, the birds, all heavenly nature—with the blue sky above.

I suggested that we now move downstairs. Roger admired the neatness and solid comfort of the various rooms he peeped into on the way down, and when we had at last reached the lower room that he now knew so well, he broached a matter that we could see was on his mind.

"Where, Monsignor, shall I have to live?"

"You won't *have* to live anywhere in particular, Roger," I answered. "You may live where you like, though I understand you have no house of your own. You could have one if you wished, but do you? It would be rather like living in solitary state, although you would have plenty of visitors one way and another. You couldn't really be lonely here, and you have but to step outside your door to find people who would soon drive any loneliness away. Still, Ruth and I know what you mean, so I would like to make this suggestion if it falls in with your own ideas in the matter. Would you care to live in this house with us? You see the size of it—there's plenty of room, and to spare. There are all sorts of little things to interest you, without having to go outside. Stay here for as long as you wish, and be sure of one thing: never will you outstay your welcome.

"We cannot foresee the absolute future, and time, as you will have guessed by now, is of little consideration. Ruth and I, with Edwin, whom you've not met yet, have been doing this work, among other things, for years now. We seem likely to continue for more and more years yet. We are none of us tired of it. Even so, if we changed our work, we should still wish to have our house here.

"Spiritual progression is another matter, Roger. When we go higher—or farther along the road—we may move into other quarters. We need not think of that at present. Join our small household. In other words, stay where you are. That shouldn't be difficult as you have no 'goods and chattels.'"

The boy started to express his gratitude, but we stopped him. There was no need for words; his thoughts were sufficient.

"That's settled, then," said Ruth, "and now, Roger, tell us what you think of things."

Our friend seated himself in a comfortable chair, and looked considerably puzzled. "What I can't make out," he said, at length, "is how all this you've shown me squares up with religion? I wasn't taught much, and never knew exactly what to expect. . . ."

"You're not the first to wonder that, Roger. Millions do the same. Ruth and I did so. We were in no better case than yourself. What it comes to is this: when you are on earth, this whole spirit world is regarded as the 'life after death,' the 'next world,' and is treated solely from the religious standpoint, except by a comparatively *select* few. I call them select because those few possess the truth—not all the truth, naturally, but sufficient for absolute comfort. The religions of the earth have assumed rights over this life to which they are not entitled. The passing from earth to the spirit world is not a religious affair whatever. It's a purely natural process, and one that cannot be avoided. Living a good life on earth is not a religious matter. Why should it be? Have you seen signs of that sort of thing here, Roger? Yet who will dare to say we are not living good, decent lives here?

"Then take the total number of religions on earth. There are thousands among the Christians alone, and all believing something different from each other."

"I read somewhere that no one religion possessed all the truth, but that each had a bit of it, so that taken all together they'd have the truth between them. Isn't that so, Monsignor?"

"That is so. I've heard of that theory, but think what it involves. First, how are you going to tell what is the truth among all the rest of the claims of any one particular church? Is one to be content with that one fragment, if it can be discovered, or try to do the impossible, and join all the religious bodies spread over the earth, and so become possessed of all the truth—though you'd have the deuce of a job in sorting the false sheep from the truthful goats?"

The boy gave a loud laugh.

"You can laugh, Roger, my boy, but that's what it comes to in the end."

"Sitting here in this chair, in this room, actually in the spirit world seems an awful long way from sitting in a church on Sunday, as I used to—sometimes."

"Only sometimes?" put in Ruth; "that was naughty in one so young!"

"I know what you're thinking of," I said; "that Sunday churchgoing, with the clergyman, and the choir singing, and the sermon—and the collection, don't forget that! Especially the sermons that didn't seem to have any bearing on what you know *now*. How could it have, coming from the average minister? How could you expect a person—or a parson—to be able to instruct others on a particular subject, or on any subject, when the instructor knows literally nothing about it? That's the real trouble. Ignorance, or lack of knowledge. Yet it is his job, the minister's job, to know. *I* should have known, but I didn't. A person in my position on earth should have been able to tell a person in Ruth's position, or yours, Roger, all that we know at this moment. There are abundant opportunities for finding out.

"What a mournful, miserable business it all is, when you come to think about it. Here is this magnificent world we're living in, and yet on earth it has been shrouded and obscured with a multitude of extraordinary beliefs, conditions, limitations, misconceptions, and I don't know what else besides. The one cannot be reconciled with the other. Like oil and water, they do not mix. Unlike those two substances, there is nothing with which to emulsify them, so to speak. They are not to be fused.

"Odd, isn't it, how the religions of the earth have assumed authority over us—so they think? They cannot regard us in terms of solid reality, of rational living, of breathing, working, playing, helping one another. They would look upon that bird you have there, Roger, as being too outrageous, too preposterous to bear thinking about, even remotely. Yet that little gray fellow is part of life in these lands, and a beautiful part of it, too. How many folk have their animal friends on earth as part of their very lives? Thousands, but the same thing would be denied us here, if some people on earth had their way. It's not *religious*; it's not what one would look for in spiritual realms. It's not the kind of thing that God would allow, because it's too *earthy* and frivolous. It brings us back to that appalling angel I spoke to you about, Roger, when you had opened your eyes as you lay on the couch.

"The whole thing can be summed up in this way, Roger, my boy: the earthly religions know nothing about this world at all, about the life we live. They do not seem to be able to conjure up in their minds any sort of vision or image of what it might conceivably be. But they are certain of what it cannot be—upon what authority no one knows—that it cannot be anything like *this* at all. No man on earth would be prepared to suggest—if he were sane—that the only thing to look forward to is a life of doing nothing for all eternity, in a place or region that was simply vaporous, a void. The very thought of such an existence—and it would be barely that—would fill him with deep horror, and decide him that he would not *wish* to survive under such ghastly conditions. And no one could blame him.

"Now, Roger, let's go out and do a little visiting. Bring the bird with you. He could show you the way, without us. Come along."

CHAPTER FOUR

A VISIT

O UR WALK through the countryside was another revelation to Roger, not alone for its beauty and enchantments, but from the many friendly greetings that we received upon all sides. These latter, in the main, came from folk who were complete strangers to us, and whom the boy thought were part of a wide circle of friends, but we explained that had he been alone, he would have had a similar experience.

"We don't wait for formal introductions here, Roger," Ruth told him. "In fact, we don't need them at all."

We passed much on our way that excited the interest and curiosity of our friend in his new life, a great deal of which I have already recounted to you, until, at length, we reached our destination.

This was a somewhat large dwelling placed amid the most beautiful gardens, with many flower-beds, glistening pools of water, and innumerable trees. The house itself was a square-built edifice with broad windows and a central doorway, but without any marked architectural ornament upon its exterior surface. It seemed to combine, from outward appearance, the dual purposes of a home and a place of work.

The material of which the building was constructed was, I hardly need add, of that pure spirit-world order that veritably lives in its superb tones of coloring, as compared with the heavy dullness of earthly "bricks and mortar."

This was the first view at close quarters that Roger had had of anything like a large building, and he could not resist the impulse to pass his hand over the surface of the "stone."

"It's real enough, Roger," said Ruth.

"Yes, but it's warm," he replied; "at least, it's not cold!" We smiled in concert, for every new friend's enthusiasm has something fresh about it, in spite of the fact that we have experienced this same thing over and over again.

By this time our arrival had been perceived, and our host was awaiting us at his front door. He was an American Indian of handsome and imposing appearance, tall and dignified. He gave us a warm-hearted welcome as we presented Roger to him. We explained that he was but newly arrived, and that we had brought him to these realms, and were now disporting ourselves by acting as his ciceroni.

"And so," said our host, with a merry laugh, "you are including me among the sights."

We hastened to disclaim any such uncomplimentary intention, which only made our friend laugh the more as our explanations seemed to become more involved! At last Ruth said that we had better desist as the patch was rapidly becoming worse than the hole.

It should be mentioned that our host had learned sufficient of our mother-tongue for all practical purposes in connection with his work, and in here setting down his words I have therefore omitted all such slight linguistic "irregularities" that cause his friends—and admirers—on earth such immense joy, and which, incidentally, equally amuse the speaker of them! Most of our conversation has taken place by the thought process—we are old friends—so that he reveals himself to us as the learned, cultured expert that he is.

In common with the great majority of his race, he has retained his picturesque name, with some slight adaptation to spirit world conditions and circumstances, so that he is known widely in these and other realms of light as Radiant Wing, the first part of that appellation being the adaptation to which I have just referred. It is self-explanatory in that it should—and does here, of course—convey to the onlooker its meaning through the flow of light that leaves the tips of his head-dress.

My friends of earth may wonder why feathered headdresses should be worn in such a place as the spirit world. The answer is simple: all that is beautiful is preserved, and because some feature, in itself beautiful, appertains to the earth, that is no reason why we should be denied it in these lands. The fact is that we are *not* denied it, nor shall we deny ourselves anything because, or for fear that, folk on earth may disapprove.

If the truth be told, we care not a fig for what the earth people may think of what we do or do not, and we are certainly not going to take orders from such inferior minds, or, indeed, from any kind of mind on earth! No person is forced in these lands to submit to anything of which he disapproves. He is at liberty to seek elsewhere in the avoidance of offence to his fastidious susceptibilities. Equally, he is always at liberty to emerge from his obscurity or seclusion if he eventually feels that he was mistaken. The latter is what always happens!

The headdress, then, of our host is very fine, displaying a series of rainbow tints in the most delicate shades. The feathers of which it is constructed have not been taken from a bird. They would have to be taken from a *living* bird, if taken at all—an impossible and revolting supposition—as there are no *dead* birds in the spirit world. The feathers, therefore, are wholly fabricated from spirit-world substance, and fashioned by skillful hands and minds into an absolute verisimilitude of the real article. It should be added that such a headdress is not worn constantly, but upon the more formal occasions.

We had already explained to Roger that Radiant Wing's principal work was that of a healer to incarnate folk, which he carries on through the agency of an earthly instrument. He is, in addition, a great experimenter, ever searching for new methods in the application of the various resources at his command in many different combinations.

Our host invited us within, and knowing something of my proclivities for gathering information concerning the activities of our life here, he assumed, he said, that we wished to see something of what was going on in his particular department.

We found ourselves in a very pleasant apartment which was, by all appearances, his own particular "den," and there explained that apart from his actual healing work, he also trained others in the art, mostly young people, many of them, he informed us, just about Roger's age.

He then led us into his "laboratory," and we were introduced to a number of young men—his students and probationers, as he described them.

It was a spacious chamber, upon one side of which were reposing many varieties of flasks, vials, and small jars, each of them containing some substance in a wide range of colors. There were many large diagrams depicting the different parts of the human body, while a number of anatomical models in full color were displayed in other parts of the room.

"You will understand," our host explained, "that it is essential for us to know all about human anatomy and the functions of the body, together with the many ailments that earth people suffer from, before we can even begin to heal them. We are no different in this respect from the doctors on earth. Our methods of treatment, of course, are entirely different. We use materials and forces which the earth doctors do not possess. They belong purely to the spirit world.

"*Our* methods are very much simpler. For example, look at the glass vessels on those shelves. They contain various ointments for healing an enormous number of complaints. The colors you see have little significance of themselves in the matter of actual healing. They are used to distinguish each unguent, and the especial value of the color is revealed when we mix one component with another, for as soon as we start blending the color naturally changes, just as the artist's colors change as he blends his pigments. So you see we are able to know at once the precise amount of any one substance that is mixed with another by the tone of blend. In this way we can modify by increasing or diminishing one substance or another according to the particular requirements of the case we are treating.

"For those with an eye for color these mixtures are a very great pleasure and joy, for our blendings produce an almost unlimited range of beautiful tones.

"Apart from learning the ABC of the healing art, my student friends here also help me to find new blends, and from this we may find a new healing balm for our earth friends in their bodily ailments. What you see on the shelves are merely samples of the spiritual substance. As we attend each case, wherever it may be, our materials are always freshly compounded. By our previous experiments and knowledge, we shall know what color or blend to use, and so our medicaments are in their right proportions.

"That is but one part of our method of treatment. Another is by light ray, and that we cannot put in flasks and bottles upon our shelves. We *can* show you what happens, though." He turned to Roger. "Did you, my son, see from Monsignor's house a large building with a bright blue ray streaming down upon it? You did. That blue ray has a soothing effect upon earth people as well as upon us here. Let me show you. Draw closely round me, my friends."

We gathered about our host in a small circle. In a moment we perceived a bright blue beam of light descend upon us, and we instantly felt its most soothing effect—not, of course, that we were in *need* of it!

Radiant Wing then had the beam reduced to a small pencil of light, bringing it to focus upon each of our hands in turn.

"You see," he said, "we can direct the light on to any area, and in any width we wish, from a broad beam to this small ray. It depends upon the nature of the trouble we are working on."

It was fascinating to watch him maneuver and manipulate the light wherever he wished it to fall.

"Now here is another kind of ray. Watch."

The blue beam ceased, and in its place a bright red one descended.

"This," he explained, "is a stimulating light; it provides energy: it builds up not only an affected part after treatment, but the whole body, and that is greatly needed on earth at this moment. Our friends of earth need not fear that we shall run short!"

There was a distinct feeling of warmth with the red ray, and Roger remarked upon it.

"That is so, my son. Usually some warmth is needed with the application of the red ray, but we have special heat-rays, where we work with heat alone. The colors of these rays are more for distinguishing purposes, though the color does help. But the force is really in the ray itself rather than in the color.

"Well, now, I think you've seen everything, except a demonstration of our work, and that, I'm afraid, we can't show you here. But I must introduce you to my family. Come along into the garden."

Our host opened a door that led directly into the garden, and we stepped out of doors. Turning to our left, we found ourselves in a most exquisite garden. It was very broad and with two long walls upon either side. Our friend explained that these were not to establish his "territorial rights," but merely to hide from first sight the grounds that were upon the other sides. In addition they formed a perfect background to the tall plants and flowering shrubs that were growing immediately in front of them.

Equally spaced throughout the length of the walls were fairly wide openings beneath rounded arches, the whole of which produced a most pleasing antique effect. There were many grand trees flourishing in the full vigor of their heavenly growth, free from the winds that deform so many trees on earth, and here displaying their *true* form in unblemished nature.

In the center of this haven, there was a lily-pond sunk below the level of the ground, with wide steps leading down to a paved surround.

We could see no evidence of the family, but in response to a call from our friend, there came bounding across the large tract of grass upon which we were standing, two beautiful creatures, one a large dog, and the other a puma.

I have omitted to mention that as we emerged from the laboratory, the small bird that Roger had retained in his hand, then flew away in a direct line to a huge tree. He now emerged bringing with him, as it were, a raven and a macaw.

Radiant Wing held out his arms, and the two birds at once perched upon them. The small bird flew back to Roger.

"What do you think of my family?" Radiant Wing asked. "The dog, the raven, and the macaw are my own. The small bird you have there, my son, belongs to friends who are still on earth, and this lovely puma, as well, belongs to one of them, who is also my instrument on earth."

The colors of the macaw contrasted vividly with the blackness of the raven and the soft gray of the sparrow.

Roger was obviously a trifle timid of the puma, no doubt from his recollection of the same kind of animal on earth, but our host at once reassured him.

"You need have no fear, my son," said he. "See, she is without her wildness, and wishes harm to no one."

Ruth had stooped down and was stroking and playing with the lovely creature, which was as gentle as a lamb.

"She is not the only one of her kind here, by any means," continued our host, "but their dispositions are all the same—harmless and gentle. You see, the two chief earthly factors are gone from all the animals in these lands—the need for food, which makes them prey upon others, and fear of both their own creature-kind and of human kind. Remove these two, and there you have the result. They are a great joy to us—and to themselves. Try for yourself, my son."

Roger bent down beside Ruth, and in a moment had lost his misgivings in stroking the puma's thick fur.

"She is the mad one," said Radiant Wing, "and continually keeps all the others 'on the stretch.' Watch her now with the little bird."

Roger held up his hand and the sparrow flew into the air only a short distance above the ground, but high enough to be provokingly out of reach of the puma. At this height he flew in a somewhat erratic manner, hither and thither, without appearing to be upon any direct course. The puma immediately gave chase, and as the bird followed a zig-zag way so his companion on the ground tried to emulate him. The acrobatics she was obliged to perform sent us all into roars of laughter, while we could but admire the nimbleness of the agile creature on the ground. The latter made the most astonishing leaps into the air, evidently sure of catching her small friend on the wing, but she was foiled upon every occasion by the bird moving an inch or two higher, or to right or left.

"What would happen," asked Roger, "if the puma actually caught up with the bird?"

"Why, nothing," answered Radiant Wing with a laugh. "It would be impossible, even if they were not the very best of friends, which, of course, they are. There are no enemies here." The game was quickly ended, however, by the bird swooping down upon the puma, and alighting upon the latter's head, who trotted back to us, and rolled herself over on the grass in evident satisfaction with her performance.

Radiant Wing again turned to Roger: "Now you know where I live, my son, I hope you will visit us whenever you wish. My boys and myself will always be delighted to see you. Or, if you wish, just walk into the garden and enjoy yourself with my family. You may not always find all of them here; sometimes these two," he slightly raised his arms with the two large birds upon them, "and the dog go with me when I'm on my earth missions. But you know the small bird, and friend puma is most times hereabouts, and ready to play."

Roger was delighted with this invitation, and thanked our friend warmly, as did Ruth and I, for spending so much time upon us and our new charge.

CHAPTER FIVE

SPIRIT INTERCOURSE

A S WE strolled along after leaving Radiant Wing, it was easy to see that Roger was fairly deep in thought, no doubt pondering what he had seen both in the house and in the garden of our friend.

At length he spoke. "What astonishes me, is that all this is unknown to the world. How all this can be going on without somebody knowing about it, is more than I can understand."

"By the world, you mean the earth, Roger. No, all this is not entirely unknown to the earth people. Some of them are aware of it, but by comparison with the earth's millions, only a very few."

"And how do *they* know?"

"Because they have been told, friend Roger. *We* have told them. I don't mean Ruth and I, though we have done our microscopic share in the work. But the telling has been going on for years. The earth has never been left high and dry, without someone to tell them about all this. Latterly, the flow of revelation has increased, but you must remember that one of the greatest ecclesiastical establishments on earth has long ago decreed that all revelation ceased when the last of the apostles passed from the earth. Since then— silence. Do you think that sounds at all likely from what you have seen, so far, of the way things are done here?"

"*No*, I do *not*."

"Yet, that is the fact. Others believe that to know, or even try to know, anything about the 'afterlife' is against Holy Writ. So there is another 'dead-end.' 'We are not meant to know. If we were we should have been told'—that's what those folk say. Yet they *have* been told—officially; and in the very book that they say is against this knowledge. Strange, isn't it? Those people read that book piously—perhaps too piously—and fail to perceive that it is crammed, literally crammed with psychic lore of every kind. They will swallow whole accounts of it, but because those phenomena still happen, *now*, they will have nothing to do with them. If it was right in those far-off days—and it was— then it must be right now—which it is. Officially, of course, there is silence."

"Wouldn't you think it to be in the interests of any religion to know, or at least to try to find out?"

"Yes, Roger; that's what you would think. The position on earth is rough- ly this. Of the two principal Churches, one says decisively, dogmatically, that anyone is a fool who denies the existence of psychic phenomena of all kinds, but with equal insistence says that the cause of them is none other than the devil himself, or some of his satellites. That is what Omar meant when he said that there are nice people on earth who would call him—and all the rest of us—just plain devils. Isn't the whole notion too utterly preposterous for words?"

"It is, but can't something be done about it?"

Ruth and I smiled at the healthy, vigorous enthusiasm of our young friend.

"Roger, dear," said Ruth, "your feelings do you great credit. We both know exactly how you feel. Monsignor and I had the same experience. We should have liked to have taken people's silly heads and banged them to- gether, and tried to knock some sense into them, but we were restrained—by wiser minds than ours."

"Now," I said, "let me tell you what happened with the other important Church I mentioned. That Church held an inquiry into the whole subject of communication with the earth, ordered by no less a functionary than the Archbishop himself. They investigated very thoroughly and deliberated very carefully, and compiled a report of their findings The majority were in favor, and declared that communication did in fact exist. Splendid. Now, Roger, if you are fond of a joke—we know you are—get ready to laugh loudly: *the whole report was officially suppressed.*

"Peculiar, isn't it, how people do not want to know about us and the life we are living here? Of course there are very naughty people who say that if that report had been against us, it would have been published with a flour- ish of trumpets to help it on. I haven't told you the actual sequel yet. The Archbishop who ordered the inquiry and then ordered the report to be sup- pressed, has since come to live here himself.

"It's a difficult job, my Roger, to try to undo some things we wish we had never done. That good prelate has all my sympathy, for I too left behind me things which I had rather left undone. By great good fortune I have been enabled to put them right; not entirely right, you must understand, but sufficiently so to make very little difference. And where I spoke with vigor when I was on earth, I have since spoken with extra double-strength vigor to make up for it. I can feel now in my mind a great calm and contentment that were lacking before. When we get home I will show you a volume that was the cause of the earthly trouble many years ago. It was terrible stuff!"

Ruth laughed. "Don't get overheated, my dear," she said, "there are much worse things on earth than that old book—*and* more foolish!"

"Both those Churches take a peculiar interest in this world—a *religious* interest, of course. Neither knows what precisely to expect in the way of an afterlife. An afterlife there must be, naturally, but they can suggest nothing that does not imply some description of an essentially *religious* life. In effect, it means that the earth life is the *real* material life, and that the afterlife is conducted upon holy lines of some sort. Certainly the whole atmosphere will be pious, and totally unlike what man has been accustomed to on earth. They are right in the latter; this life is totally unlike the earth life, but not in the way they mean.

"What's to be the end of it all, then? Will the Churches eventually find the truth? That is a large question. As they are at present constituted, nothing could be done. They are perfectly contented as they are. The first of the two I mentioned claims to be the one true Church, and infallible. There would not seem to be much hope there. The second Church possesses no authority whatever. Within broad limits—very broad ones—its members can think and believe what they like. The bishops have little or no authority over their clergy in matters of 'faith.' There are some ministers who wholeheartedly support the spirit world as it really is, because they have spiritual knowledge derived directly from us. Even if this particular Church pronounced in our favor officially, it by no means follows that the clergy and the laity would do the same thing. There are some who have this knowledge, and uphold the Church as well—with all its strange doctrines. In that they are trying to face both ways at once. But when they come here, they must eventually face only one way.

"You can see, Roger, what difficulties are in the way when it comes to official acknowledgment of the true manner of life in the spirit world. That is why the truth is in the hands of unofficial folk. You see what a lecture your simple proposition has brought upon you!"

Ruth suggested that we sit down for a while. We found a spot beneath a tree upon slightly rising ground, where we could see in the distance a glittering expanse of water.

"Doesn't it seem an awful pity, Roger," said Ruth, "that so many millions of people on earth should know nothing about this lovely land? And doesn't it seem outrageous that officially they should be 'warned off' from knowing anything, and for the most silly, stupid reasons? What harm, what possible harm could there be in knowing all about us and the life we live? One would think we are absolute outcasts, or peculiar people it were better not to have anything to do with. It makes me furious."

"Now, don't you get overheated, my dear," I said. "This wholesale ignorance isn't a new thing. It's been going on for hundreds of years. That's the real trouble. It's been going on too long, so that people have got into the one way of thinking—mostly the religious or theological way. You know, Roger, it's not so very surprising that hundreds of people, when they arrive here and find out the truth, go about like a 'mighty wind,' and want to go back to earth to shout the truth at last to the folk they've left behind them. Some of them actually do go back, but the result is dismal—on both sides. Their voices cannot be heard—that is, heard in the very place where they want them to be.

"Take yourself, my boy. Ruth and I could lead you to a little spot on earth where we could make ourselves known among old friends. We could introduce you to them, and ask if they would convey a message for you to your people at your old home. Very well. What would happen next? Remember your relations would be complete strangers to our friends, and presumably your people know nothing about communication between the two worlds, or if they know, do not believe it can be done. What do you suppose would be the result when our friends presented themselves at your parents' house, and said they had a message from their Roger? You know best what would happen, because you know them. As a matter of interest, Roger, what *would* happen?"

The boy thought a moment. "They would be civil, at least," he said, "but a bit grim. Probably think your friends cranks, if not altogether mad."

"They don't *look* like cranks, Roger, so they might be able to escape that. But mad—yes, perhaps; though they don't give any evident or unmistakable signs of that either. What next?"

"They might think it in shockingly bad taste."

"Ah, that would be difficult to overcome. Bad taste that our friends should intrude upon their bereavement, and so on. Then what?"

"I rather fancy your friends would be shown the front door. After that, they would discuss it between themselves, and go off to see their vicar. He would listen civilly, and tell them he *had* heard about such things, but that they were far better left alone."

"That's about it, Roger. The same old story all over again, and one we have to recount, and keep on recounting, to people as they arrive here in their thousands, and want to go back to earth to speak.

"The chief trouble with the Churches is that they cannot make the truth about this world fit in with their theology. They don't realize that they are going about things the wrong way. They must make their theology fit the truth, and that means a wholesale clearance of everything that does not accord with it. At present they prefer the shadow to the substance; they prefer creeds and doctrines and dogmas. They are not realists—far from it.

"Let us put the matter plainly, even crudely, if you wish it. Here are three of us, human beings who once lived on earth. We have passed through the experience of dying, and now we are seated in the spirit world upon some delightfully soft turf beneath a beautiful tree, with all the lovely countryside round about us, and reaching for miles away into the distance. It is all unquestionably real and solid. It is no 'spiritual experience' in the religious sense, but an 'everyday' experience of a very ordinary nature. We are here—all three of us—because, by virtue of man's spiritual heritage, it is our right to be here, and *not* because of what we believed on earth, or through the merits of any particular Church to which we belonged. Ruth will tell you herself that she gave up going to church altogether. Yet she is here with us, and she will tell you she was an awful heathen in the eyes of her Church. Another Church would call her a heretic and a schismatic, and doomed to who-knows-what terrible place for her sins.

"As for myself, I was a priest of the Church, and should have known better, but didn't. You, Roger, are young, but I believe you did not become exactly a pillar of your Church. Now between us, and strictly from the theological point of view, you two should not be here at all, if this place is reserved for folk like me. If my theology, and all the doctrines and dogmas I rigorously upheld and preached about, have brought me to this particular region of the spirit world, then you two have no business to be here at all. You can't say, theologically speaking, that either of you is the least fitted to be in my company, for you, Ruth, on your own terrible confession, were no churchgoer at all latterly in your earth life, and you, Roger, were only half-hearted in it. It's extremely difficult for me to adjudicate between you, and settle who is the worse sinner. You're both pretty bad, it would seem, and I have no business to be in your company, or you have no business to be in mine. But the stubborn fact is that you *are* here, and so am I.

"What is the conclusion? There's only one: that something is wrong somewhere with all the theology. The theology doesn't fit the facts.

"Let's go further. When you were on earth, Roger, did you go about your daily life in a 'pious' frame of mind—it sounds a silly question to ask, but did you?"

"No, Monsignor; I certainly did not."

"Of course, you didn't; no rationally constituted person does. One may have pleasant thoughts, kindly thoughts, and do pleasant, kindly actions, but that is not going about and behaving in a 'pious' manner, and generally being sanctimonious and altogether objectionable. Now, how do you feel about things at this present moment? Any different?"

"Not a particle."

"And so, if a bulletin were issued it might read like this: 'no change has been reported in Roger's condition other than his now feeling *perfectly* fit in bodily health. He is in the most cheerful spirits (as well as being with them), and is at this moment thoroughly enjoying himself—if his face is any indication of the state of his mind. He is pleased to inform all theologians that he does not feel the least particle pious or holy, and is most thankful that he feels himself, and nobody else.' Would you subscribe to that declaration, my lad?"

"I would, indeed, Monsignor. I wouldn't swap this back for the old earth."

"*Exchange*, Roger, *exchange*. You must understand that 'swap' is a word that would never be used by a disembodied entity; that you would be expected to speak the most perfect language, entirely free from all slang and vulgarisms, and that everything you say must be profound in nature and weighty in substance. That's how we are expected to behave by most of the earth people—the uninstructed ones. Now the great point is that there are no evident signs of piety or holiness, or even of religiosity to be seen here, nor do we go about quoting scripture or other uplifting texts to one another, and behaving in a thoroughly unnatural manner.

"In brief: we are not living in a religious institution or a religious world as a whole, but in a sane, sensible world, of incomparable beauty, where we can work and play, as we wish, and laugh to our heart's content, and where, moreover—and this is vitally important—*where we can be ourselves*, and not be as others on earth would mistakenly have us to be.

"Isn't it odd that when I had plenty of pulpits at my disposal to preach from, I had nothing much to say—as I see it now? And now I *have* a great deal to say, I have no pulpit."

CHAPTER SIX

SPIRIT LOCOMOTION

W E HAD been walking along in leisurely fashion when Roger turned to me: "Is walking the only means of getting about?" he asked. "I can't see any roads anywhere, and the countryside seems to stretch for miles."

"It does stretch for miles," I replied, "thousands of them. What you mean, Roger, is: where's the transport system and what is it? The answer is that we each of us carry our own transport system about with us, the most efficient and the most rapid in the universe. That is in addition to walking. So far we have relied upon our two legs since we brought you here, but the time has obviously come when we must show you something of what we can really do here.

"Personal locomotion is done by the thought process, and it's perfectly easy to do when once you're shown how; then it becomes second nature. It may sound like a contradiction in terms, but the thought process of locomotion hardly requires thinking about when once you're accustomed to it.

"Can you remember when you first learned to walk on earth, Roger?"

"No, I can't say I do."

"I don't suppose there are many who can. But there did come a time when you could keep upright successfully and without tumbling down. Since then you have walked many miles on earth, and some distance here as well. Do you ever think about it?

"Suppose you are sitting in a chair and you wish to rise and cross the room, you simply rise and walk without thinking of all the muscles that have to be controlled to get your limbs on the move. You do all that without thinking, though there must be some thought somewhere, obviously, or else you would remain rooted where you were. What particular line does the thought take: that you must walk, or that you wish to rise, or that you want to cross the room, or all three? It doesn't matter. Basically, the desire is to get across the room—the other side of the room is your destination. And that's all you need to consider here in using the thought process to move yourself about.

"At first, you must make a really conscious effort; you must think about it. A little practice, and you'll find that no sooner do you think, than you are wherever you wish to be. Sounds rather fantastic, don't you think?"

"It does a bit."

"It's the sort of thing skeptical folk on earth like to poke fun at, and generally ridicule. Such a splendid joke, and causes roars of laughter. The same folk should take out their Bibles and study them a little more, and then bring their wits to bear upon what they read there.

"A great many of our ways here form a constant source for derision among the incarnate, Roger. Taking the earth as the standard for everything, including life itself, they cannot imagine anything better or different. Of course, they'll regard 'heaven' as a place or condition of perfection, but of perfection of what, they know not, and cannot imagine. I would say seriously to such people not to pour scorn upon our spirit lands and the way we do things unless they are prepared to provide better. If there is any single feature or factor or law to which they take exception, let them at once suggest a better or finer or more sensible, and all of us here in the spirit world will gladly listen, and see that their suggestions reach the right quarter.

"We need not, of course, worry ourselves unduly about these folk. If there is anything of which they disapprove when they come here, they are at liberty to depart, to remove themselves, leaving us in the enjoyment of our own mode of life, while they betake themselves elsewhere and create their own bleak void—and live in it."

My two companions had such a merry twinkle in their eyes, that I subsided into laughter.

"You know, Roger," said Ruth, "Monsignor feels very strongly on some subjects. He caught the public eye and ear when he was a priest, and since coming here he has done the same thing again in a very different way. He knows how hard it is to get people to shake off old and wrong beliefs for the truth, and it really vexes him. That is perhaps one of the penalties, if one can call it so, for being in such close touch with the earth. I'm not, though I visit it occasionally with Monsignor purely to watch proceedings and give a greeting to our friends there.

"Thoughts are very real, Roger," she continued, "and can reach us here from earth as easily and as surely as they can reach us here between ourselves. And ours can go to the earth people too, though they don't always notice them."

"Perhaps that's what accounts for the feeling I've had. I don't know how to describe it, but there seems to be a sort of pulling, if you follow; a kind of urge to go—well—I don't know where. Oh, this is all terribly vague. I've felt peculiar; not ill, but restless, I suppose."

"Poor Roger," said Ruth; "I think we can diagnose your 'complaint' without difficulty. The trouble is caused by friends or relations, or both perhaps, sending out a few thoughts of grief. It's natural they should be sorry you've left them, though their sorrow is not deep, or else you would have felt it very keenly yourself, and that would have been troublesome. I doubt if this feeling will get stronger, but if it should, tell us, Roger, and we'll help to dispel it. You have no personal regrets yourself on any account?"

"None whatever, Ruth, thank you."

"Good; that's a great help."

"We seem to have wandered a trifle from Roger's question. Do you recall, Ruth, soon after we had arrived here, how we discussed the quaint notion of 'angelic beings' having wings? Strange idea, isn't it, Roger? The only thing one can imagine is that long ago, people, especially artists, must have wondered how 'angelic beings' managed to get about. Legs would seem preposterous, out of the question, by being far too mundane. I mean for perambulating purposes. But if one eliminates the use of legs, what remains? Nothing, so far as I can see, and I suppose that is how it struck the artists.

"Angels must be able to move; they can't be rooted to one spot for all eternity. That, one supposes, led some genius to invent huge wings for all inhabitants of the spirit world. I believe Satan himself was endowed with a pair, as, of course, it was essential for *him* to be extremely mobile so that he could, get about comfortably and quickly 'seeking the ruin of souls' as one pretty prayer expresses it.

"Can you think of anything more clumsy and ponderous than having an enormous pair of wings fastened upon you somewhere in the region of the shoulder-blades? I can't."

"I should imagine," said Roger, "that a large flock of angels would stir up an awful breeze when in flight."

"Roger, I'm afraid you're being highly irreverent in referring to a large number of angels as a flock."

"Well, what would they be, then?"

"I really don't know; it's not easy to find a word for what doesn't exist, except poetically, perhaps. But you are severely practical when you say that a great concourse—that is more elegant than flock, Roger—would disturb the atmospheric conditions, and that's something the artist fellows never thought of. It is astonishing how the idea originally caught on and has persisted even to the present day. The conventional way of portraying a being from this world—and they still don't look upon us as human; only half—human—is with two large wings. Even symbolically it's a pretty poor idea. As a means of personal locomotion, wings would be useless, an impossibility, and we should be anatomical monstrosities. We're obviously not built for such apparatus, the wonders and marvels of the spirit world notwithstanding.

"Angels with their fantastic wings being another of the many extraordinary misconceptions of the true way of things in spirit lands, it really is no wonder that in the end, with all these falsifications, the people of earth regard us as sub-human. The higher we go in spiritual advancement the less human we become, it would seem, and the more grim. Did either of you ever see a picture of an angel, or a piece of sculpture of one, especially in a cemetery, where the artist had put a smile upon the face of his subject? Smiling is not 'heavenly' enough. Isn't it too awful for words? Aren't you very glad, Roger, that things are as they are, and not as they might be if some folk were given a free hand?"

"I should jolly well think so," the boy agreed.

"A loud *Amen* to that," exclaimed Ruth.

"Otherwise," I added, "we should have to get all the doors heightened to allow sufficient clearance for our wings. Truth is better than fiction, in this case, Roger, and the truth of moving ourselves about these lands by the process of applied thought is the simplest and best. Now suppose you try."

"What do I have to do?"

"Only a little thinking. You needn't be alarmed. Everyone has to try at some time. Ruth and I were delighted with the results when we first managed, and you will be the same." We were sitting on the grass at the time, and I suggested that Roger desire himself to be at a tree we could see, some quarter-mile distant.

"You need not make a gigantic effort of will, old man," I said. "Merely think firmly that you would like to be under that tree yonder—or anywhere else you fancy. I suggest the tree because it's not too far off, and you can see us easily from there. As 'a good outset is half the voyage,' Ruth and I will send a thought with you. Now, then; off you go."

Of course, he vanished from our presence, as we knew he would, and we saw him beneath the distant tree, where he waved to us. We waved back, and then joined him.

"Well, did you enjoy the journey, Roger?" asked Ruth.

The boy laughed. "There was nothing much to enjoy; one second I was there, the next here. But it is wonderful though; there's no getting away from that. What a marvelous feeling of independence it gives you. Wouldn't I love to have been able to do this back on earth. My goodness, it would have frightened the life out of mother, though."

"Yes, it has its possibilities on earth, and its impossibilities. There it would revolutionize life. Here it is part of life, and has been, ever since there's been a spirit world."

"Here is something that occurs to me," said Roger. "Would it be possible for me to lose myself. I mean, suppose I got out of touch with either you or Ruth; what then?"

"You mean," I replied, "suppose Ruth or I were to take you to some spot far away from this particular locality, and then disappear and leave you to your own devices?"

"Yes, that's it."

"Then your own devices would get you out of your difficulty very nicely, Roger. Don't be disturbed, though. We shouldn't dream of abandoning you on a door-step, so to speak, and leaving you for someone else to find!

"This is precisely what would happen. Suppose for a moment you could not conjure up in your mind any sort of recollection of our house, there is yet the connecting link between ourselves—the three of us. And if the worst really came to such extremes, you would have but to concentrate your mind upon either Ruth or myself, and you would see and feel an instantaneous response. So that, wherever we happened to be, you *could* come to us. I say you could come to us, but it by no means follows that you would, because we might prevent you—or send someone to do so. You see, my boy, Ruth and I penetrate into some very unpleasant quarters of the spirit world, places that we have not mentioned to you yet, and it would not do for you to approach them.

"Wherever Ruth and I might be, you would always be in touch with us in mind. Of course, you have not forgotten our house, its arrangements, and surroundings, so really the matter doesn't arise. Merely for the sake of argument, if you did forget, there's Radiant Wing's home and his delightful family. You could hardly fail to recollect all that we saw there, and so you would have that refuge in case of failure of memory, and *he* would look after you.

"But there's one thing to be considered, though perhaps we have not mentioned it specifically, and that is the impossibility of memory failure.

That resolves your difficulty finally and completely. You've *not* forgotten our home and all its appurtenances, have you?"

"No, indeed not; it's all very clear in my mind."

"Exactly; and so it will remain. You cannot forget, because the memory is itself unfailing in operation. I know one can imagine all kinds of difficulties or perplexities of the same sort, but they have no substance, and cannot be otherwise. To lose one's self, for instance: impossible. To forget something or other: equally impossible.

"You spoke about a transport system, Roger, no doubt having in mind the usual earthly services and arrangements: trains, buses, cars and so on. As you see, we don't need any of those for carrying us about these lands."

"Yes, but suppose you want to move house. How do you shift the stuff?"

"Why, we shouldn't find much difficulty, no difficulty, in fact, in moving it. We may not be giants here, Roger, but we do have powers—and we use them when called upon to do so. We could, between us, move all the furniture in our house with the greatest ease, and feel none the worse for it afterwards. We shouldn't have blisters on our hands, nor strained backs! We could transport the whole contents of our home a dozen times over, while the earth folk were thinking about it—and without fuss and breakages!

"We do move house when we feel we should like to live in another part of these realms. We are not necessarily tied to one spot, or unable to move without many formalities. The fact is, once we have chosen a spot in which to have our dwelling we mostly stay there, at least until such time as we leave the realm altogether. But we don't become stale, as it were, or tired of our surroundings, for the reason that there are always changes of some sort going on, large or small, to alter or enhance the precincts of our dwellings. For instance, our house, as you see it at this moment, is not exactly as it was when I first arrived. With our various activities we thought we should like to enlarge it for convenience sake, and so we had an annex built, the fairly large apartment we showed you, with the tapestries on the walls, the long table with the chairs round it, something in the style of the 'great hall' in the ancient mansions on earth—and in the spirit world, too. That was one alteration.

"The gardens themselves have undergone all manner of rearranging. That in itself is a delightful occupation carried out by real artists in horticulture and garden design. So you see, the movement of our goods and chattels presents no problem. We don't require great lorries and vans. The mere effort of one person can move the largest piece of furniture, because all things, everything, in this world is endowed with life. There's no such thing as inert matter, as I told you. Between us we could remove the entire contents of our house—or any other house—without the least trouble.

"Now, Roger, would you care to go and see the city at first hand? You've only seen it from the house so far. Come along. Walk—or otherwise? Otherwise, then, by all means."

CHAPTER SEVEN

THE CITY

"NO ONE seems to be in a hurry," observed Roger.

"That's because no one is in a hurry."

"Oh, of course; that never occurred to me!"

"Just so."

"If there's any need to hurry, one can be 'there' as quick as thought. If there's no need, there's no hurry."

We had reached the environs of the city, and we were on ground sufficiently elevated to give the boy a capital introduction to the "metropolis" in one comprehensive view. From where we stood he could see the many stately buildings, each with its surrounding gardens and miniature lakes, radiating, as with the spokes of a wheel, from a grand central building. He remarked that there were no roads as such, but instead were broad thoroughfares *paved* with superb grass.

Upon the dome of the central building he perceived a brilliant shaft of pure light descending, and inquired what it was.

"That domed building, Roger," we told him, "is where we meet upon the more formal occasions to welcome the great personages from the higher realms. It is not precisely a temple, though one might call it that for want of a better name. Nor is it specifically a place of worship, as it would be regarded on earth. We hold no services there. When we forgather there to meet these great visitants, the whole assembly is never very long. Their visits are brief as a rule, though naturally we are seated comfortably a little while before they arrive, and remain a little while after their departure. But brief as the whole proceedings are, all that is necessary is accomplished within that short space. No time is wasted upon 'non-essentials' or upon useless formularies! The bright beam you see descending upon the dome is permanently there."

"It must be an immensely strong light to be able to see it in this broad daylight."

"It is a strong light, have no doubt about it, and considering the source whence it comes, that's not surprising. It comes from the greatest Source of all, my Roger. Yet the light itself is not blinding, is it?"

"When we first talked to you about a city, you hardly expected anything like this, did you, Roger?" asked Ruth, "though that's rather a silly question," she added, "because you didn't expect anything in particular—like so many people."

"I don't know what I really expected. I suppose I had something in mind comparable with an earth city."

"The secret is that we are much simpler here than the earth can ever be—unless the earth radically alters its general mode of life. Bethink you, Roger, of the myriads of things we don't need here. In an idle moment you could compile such a list of commodities that are not required for life in the spirit world as would reach the dimensions of a stores' catalogue!

"Think, now. Start with the domestic arrangements of a house. Food, for instance. We don't need food, so that means the elimination of a huge industry comprising all the various departments of eating and drinking, and all the vessels and utensils for manufacturing it, cooking it, and serving it.

"Our clothes are provided for us by the operation of a natural law—another vast industry dispensed with."

"The transport system you have already seen here!"

"Conspicuous by its absence."

"Very much so."

"Then think of all the trades and professions that have no counterpart or equivalent in these lands."

"Undertakers, for instance," suggested Roger with a laugh.

"Or politicians," added Ruth.

"Don't forget priests and parsons—even bishops," I said. "Perhaps it would be as well not to be too specific. The undertakers are more pleasantly employed here, and the politicians more usefully!"

"As you can see, Roger, of shops there are none," Ruth pointed out, "because there is no commerce of any kind."

"Then what do you do when you want something?"

"Such as—?"

"Well—" He reflected a moment. "I don't seem able to think of anything," he finished, with more surprise to himself than to Ruth and me. We laughed.

"That's rather odd, isn't it Roger? You don't seem to want anything. Those clothes you are wearing are the clothes you arrived with here. By the way, whenever you feel you would like to change to your spirit clothes proper, you can do so at once. As you are attired now, everyone knows you for a new arrival. If you wish to appear as a 'seasoned resident,' the same as Ruth and I, you'll have to put off the old and put on the new. So there, at least, is something you would want—spirit clothes to make the change."

"If there are no shops or tailors, what's to be done?"

"Nothing, or at least very little. You would like to discard the old style of attire, Roger?"

"I should very much."

"Then do so, my dear boy."

"Yes, but *how*?"

"I'm afraid we can't tell you *how* it happens, but look at yourself, Roger. Your eyes have been on the view before you. Now glance a little nearer."

The boy did so, and was astonished to discover that his old earthly habiliments had given place to bright spirit clothing, full and free, and in absolute keeping with the surroundings. Ruth and I did the same, and for the first time Roger saw us in spirit attire.

"Now you can see, Roger, how we should have appeared in your bedroom had we not returned to our former earth clothing. It *might* have frightened you."

"I'm sure of it," he said. He raised a fold of his garments, and examined it closely, and remarked that it did not seem to have been made by human hands.

"No, Roger; no hands were employed upon the creating of these garments, but Ruth and I must tell you, honestly, that we do not know what natural process comes into operation in the making of them. There are many things we must know first, and so we take things as we find them. Did you, when you were on earth, try to analyze every mortal thing that came your way in life, and try to discover how it was made, and a hundred other reasons or causes for its existence? I'm sure you did not; neither did Ruth nor I. There's no reason why we should carry out minute investigations here into the existence of the many things that are part of our very life. It's problematical if we should be any the better for knowing.

"Our spirit garments are in a class by themselves, though. Do you see that large building a little to the right of us? That's called the hall of fabrics. In there you can inspect thousands of the most wonderful materials and cloths, some of them representing the fabrics that were upon earth—all parts of the earth—during the course of hundreds of years. Others are types of material peculiar to the spirit world alone, both in design and in texture.

"You saw the tapestries hanging on the walls of our home. They were made by Ruth herself in the hall of fabrics. When we were first shown over that hall, Ruth saw numbers of happy folk weaving tapestries, and was immediately taken with the same idea. Since then she has become expert in the art, as you saw at home."

"It was nothing," said Ruth; "you could do the same, Roger, if you had a mind that way. That's one of the principal functions of these places, to teach you to do all manner of things expertly."

"The hall of fabrics cannot supply you with spirit clothing, Roger," I said.

"It makes me feel terribly ignorant to see all these halls stuffed with knowledge."

"Then don't let it, my dear boy. After all, one can experience much the same emotion standing in the presence of a couple of dozen volumes of an encyclopedia, if it comes to that. We are not born with a vast deal of knowledge all ready to hand, as it were. Ruth and I felt the same way about it when we were shown all these wonders of knowledge; and so does everyone else. We're all in the same boat, Roger, so we can all be nicely ignorant together!"

"I must say the people don't seem upset about it."

"These halls of learning are mostly devoted to what on earth are called the arts," I explained, "by which I mean painting, music, literature, and so on. Great stress is laid upon those. There are, of course, many others. On earth the arts are regarded more as adjuncts to life than necessities. They could be dispensed with, though the earth would then be more drab than it is already. Here they are vital and are given a wide field. To begin with, without all those industries that we tried to enumerate just now, there is a corresponding freedom for other and far pleasanter occupations.

"There's one thing, Roger, that you won't see here among the arts, and that is musical monstrosities or art abominations masquerading as masterpieces. They have not been thrown out—they were never admitted, and never will be. No shams here, my Roger. 'Abandon all pretence ye who enter.'"

"What does a person have to do to get taken on in one of these halls, Monsignor?"

"Why, walk through the front entrance, and you'll be left in no doubt. You'll be welcomed with the greatest warmth, and set upon the path of studying whatever it is that has taken your fancy. That's how Ruth began, almost, with her tapestry weaving. She asked could she join the others and be taught the art, and forthwith, without *any* formalities whatever, she did so."

"And was never so happy in my life," put in Ruth. "Charming people, patient and kind, especially if you are 'all fingers and thumbs,' as I was when

I began. Monsignor has spent an enormous amount of time browsing among the books in the principal library. That's a terrible place once you are interested in it. There are millions of books there upon every subject under the sun. Have you ever tried to look up something in an encyclopedia, Roger, especially one that has good illustrations?"

"Yes, rather; a hopeless business, there's so much dallying on the way."

"Then you can imagine what it's like there in the library. If Monsignor were ever reported missing in these regions, that is the first place where a search party would call."

"Let us go closer and inspect some of these buildings," I suggested.

"Are we allowed to go in as we like?"

"Exactly as we like, Roger. No permits required, no opening and closing times, as they are open all day—and that's not difficult as we have no night!"

"Are the same people on duty all the time, then?"

"Oh, dear, no; that would sound like eternal work instead of 'eternal rest.' You could say truthfully that the work is eternal, but the same people are not employed upon it in an eternal succession without personal remission. We have no division of night and day, but the work is carefully divided among the staffs so that they can have their periods of change and recreation, and everybody is perfectly satisfied."

Roger remarked that the buildings were of no very great height as judged by the usual earthly standards.

"Well, no; two storeys of moderate height are sufficient here, as there are no problems of space limitations. We don't have to build upwards; we have unlimited room to spread ourselves, and the result, you must confess, is excellent."

Roger expressed his unbounded delight with the beauty and charm of the whole creation with its broad thoroughfares of superb grass, the many flower-beds and trees, the pools of crystal-clear water that provided an exquisite setting for the many fine edifices that comprised the city itself.

"Doesn't it strike you as odd, Roger, that all this beauty, this superlative beauty, should be rather sneered at by so many of the uninstructed on earth? Doesn't the earth recede into something like dingy insignificance beside all this splendor? Yet earth folk, a great many of them, regard *their* world as *the* world, by which all is judged, assessed, or appraised. The smoky, dirty cities and towns of the earth are made the criterion, and this lovely city is treated by them with something that seems remarkably like contempt, if not ridicule."

Ruth and I between us pointed out the purposes to which the various halls were devoted, and at length Roger expressed his desire to investigate the interior of the hall of engineering, which also included chemical research. We passed in, and were greeted by the man who is "in charge" of the myriad activities that are in constant performance.

"Why, Monsignor," said he, "and Ruth, too. This is a pleasure; we've not seen you for a long time. What can I do for you?"

I explained our errand, and presented Roger to him.

"Of course you've come to the right place, my dear friend." We smiled at this little pleasantry, as it has become almost a tradition that the man in charge of each of these great halls will, in similar circumstances, say precisely the same thing—a justifiable pride!

Perhaps of all the halls of learning, this, of engineering and chemistry, concerns the earth most closely, since it is here that so many of the earthly engineering and chemical discoveries have their origin. Many new substances are invented in the spirit world that are subsequently transmitted to people on earth for the benefit of all.

As we passed from room to room we could see chemists and their assistants experimenting with a variety of substances which in time will, when combined, form an entirely new product exactly fitted for its purpose. We were shown how, by synthesis, exact replicas of earthly materials were compounded, since it would be of no use whatever to invent a new substance of purely spirit materials which would not—could not—have any application to earthly uses. The scientist on earth must use earthly materials, and the spirit world scientist must therefore work in a precise counterpart.

It so often happens, our guide told us, that a mere hint to an earthly scientist is enough to set him upon the track of a dozen or more other discoveries. All that the scientists here are concerned with is the initial discovery, and in most cases the rest will follow.

Here also were new substances to be used as building materials for houses or large edifices, and for many other types of building construction. New compounds were in process of being made that would eventually be converted into fabrics of all kinds, light and heavy, for personal clothing, for example, or for upholsteries in houses and homes.

In the mechanical sections old principles were being applied in new directions, to result in better and safer and more commodious means of transport, with greater comfort.

Many inventions we saw, of all kinds, from some simple device for use in the home, to the large machine to be used in one industrial process or another.

Life on earth has become far too complex, and people are spending far too much time in purely material pursuits, usually to the exclusion of the spiritual. Life on earth, therefore, must in the end become simpler, and in doing so will become more enjoyable. The spirit world has much to send to the earth to achieve this end. But the earth world has first to put itself in good order. What is of major importance, the people of earth must learn to banish war from off its face, must learn not to turn to evil purposes that which was transmitted to it for peaceful purposes. In the latter lies disaster; in the former lies happiness.

It is for man himself to choose.

WE VISIT A CHURCH

W E HAD left the city and were walking along the edge of a wood when Roger, pointing into the distance, said, "That looks remarkably like a church."

"It is a church," said Ruth, "but with a difference."

"Would you care to go to inspect it?" I asked, and Roger answering in the affirmative, we turned in that direction.

The "church" in question had all the appearance of its familiar country counterpart on earth, excepting, of course, that of age. It had antiquity of form without showing the effects of the ravages of time, and there was now no occasion for us to tell the boy that physical decay, brought about by the elements and the passage of years, was a condition that did not exist in the spirit world, and though an edifice might look as though it had been erected but yesterday, it may have been standing many hundreds of years.

The "church" we were now visiting was no exception to the rule. In point of fact, I do not believe that, in the spirit world, there *are* any exceptions that are supposed to prove a rule! There were, however, other features about this "church" that Roger might have passed without realizing their full implication, and so, as we drew close to it, we asked him if he saw anything unusual about it.

The lad had a very keen eye and was quick to seize upon the principal characteristic.

"Yes," he observed; "the 'church' has a familiar look about it, but its surroundings are so unusual that it almost makes the 'church' itself look different."

"Good for you, Roger," I said. "You've only recently come from the earth, and so earthly things are still fresh in your mind, as it were. You can make comparisons with greater fineness.

"The 'church' you see here is a complete exemplification of what *could* be done on earth, if an effort were only to be made, in making the churches there things of real beauty in their externals. The whole of this has been built, including the fabric itself, to show exactly what can be done even in a limited space. As you can see, the territory round the building is spacious, but nevertheless, it has not been used to its full extent, so as to preserve, as nearly as possible, the customary conditions on earth, where space is usually somewhat limited."

As we drew near we could see a low brick wall running irregularly round the church grounds in imitation of an earthly situation where other land rights encroached. The wall was trim and neat without being too plain and uninteresting. We passed through a lichgate, walking on a wide path that had been made of composite substance to give the appearance of asphalt, for in a matter of pure utility, a grass path would have soon worn "threadbare" under the tread of many feet, and our reproduction had to be exact.

Flowers being in constant bloom in these lands, we had perforce to strike a compromise between what would be a general appearance in summer and that in winter. To do this many evergreen trees and bushes were introduced, and the flowers were so planted that horticultural anachronisms were avoided as far as each bed was concerned. Some flower-beds were left empty to suggest the extreme of winter when few, if any, flowering things are possible out of doors.

Running along one side of the grounds was a small brook carefully confined to a straight course, and which had its source in a small cascade, while the sides of the brook itself were lined with flowers. Here and there were lily-ponds, while the whole was encircled with many fine trees. In imagination, therefore, one could see the great possibilities of such an arrangement on earth, making full allowance for the infinitely greater beauty of a spirit-world counterpart. Such a scheme and its fulfillment are here, and could be emulated upon earth with the removal of the unsightly and unnecessary burial grounds so often to be seen about church buildings, and so often nothing but a wilderness of weeds and neglect.

Roger noticed at once the absence of a burial-ground, to which so much importance is attached on earth, nor could he see anything in the way of a notice-board.

"Ruth told you there was a difference, you remember, Roger. There are differences within, as well as without. In truth, this is only a church in name and appearance; a sample of what could be done if earth folk had a mind to bring about a few alterations. It is only the outside, the surroundings, that we are offering as an example, for this is not a 'place of worship' in the earthly sense. In other words, there are no services held here, though what takes place inside is really of more value than what goes on perennially in so many of the earthly churches. Still, we won't pursue that line of thought. . . . Let us go inside."

We found the building empty of people when we entered. It was a fair-sized structure built on the lines of a "parish church," and as it was no church in the strict meaning of the word, there was much absent that would otherwise have been conspicuous: the font, for example, and the pulpit. But what struck Roger most forcibly was the absence of a high altar.

The sanctuary itself remained the same, with the usual flights of steps leading up in a series of "orders," to the highest, where there was a broad space upon which were a number of handsome chairs, the chief of which, placed in the center, being slightly more ornate than its fellows. Above them was a fine lancet window, containing some exquisite colored glass. Instead of the familiar religious pictures, the glass represented pleasant rustic scenes such as one sees depicted in tapestries and the like.

On the wall immediately above the chairs were two inscriptions worked in mosaic, and placed side by side. Roger's attention was immediately attracted to these, and turning to me asked, "why are those two beams of light coming down on the texts?"

"They're not coming down, Roger; they're *going up and out*."

The lad read the Latin inscription aloud: *"Gloria in excelsis Deo, et in terra pax hominibus bonae voluntatis."*

"Correct, Roger, but if you will forgive me, your pronunciation of the Latin is appalling!"

"That was the way I was taught," he laughed.

"Of course you were, my dear fellow. So was I, at first. That's another example of the cult of the hideous on earth, the rule being: if possible always choose the ugly!"

"Oh, come, Monsignor; things aren't altogether as bad as that."

"Not far from it, then. You know what those words mean—if not, they've been conveniently translated for you: 'Glory to God in the highest, and on earth peace to *men of good will*.' Note the last, Roger. Different from what you were used to, perhaps, on earth. It's the better rendering, because it means so much more. Peace, my dear boy, will never come to the folk of earth without there is good will *first*. If there were universal good will, there would be universal peace. If anyone doubts it, let it be tried.

"The light you see might be going either way, might it not, but as it happens it is ascending. It came about in this way. This whole building with its gardens, was originally put up by the folk living hereabouts to serve as a pleasant place to receive the numerous teachers, and so on, who come from time to time from the higher realms to help us in a multitude of ways. Hence the chairs there, where the altar-stone would normally be. The principal visitor will occupy the central chair, as you would guess, while the others would be taken by those who come with him.

"Look round you, and what do you see; or rather, what don't you see?"

Roger turned about him: "No memorials on the walls," he enumerated, "no religious pictures, no hymn-board, no candles or other ornaments. In fact, it's just the empty shell of a church, but with comfortable chairs instead of hard pews."

The side windows were also of colored glass, and the rays of light passing in upon both sides produced the most delicate rainbow tints that met and mingled.

"Those two texts that you see, were put there at the express wish of the folk who were responsible for the whole building. As with the rest of us here, they have a wholesome horror of war, the most detestable scourge that ever could assail the people of earth. So they tried to think of some way in which to show their general concern, and at length they hit upon the scheme of taking that familiar quotation and emblazoning it upon the walls, right behind and above those high visitants when they are seated there, and in full view of every person as soon as he enters. They had it worked in mosaic, exquisitely, as you can see, in those bright colors, and made of it a permanent prayer by their thoughts. That is what you see ascending in that light, and it is never allowed to grow weak or feeble. You will always find it bright and strong. An infinitely small drop, my dear fellow, in an immense ocean of good thoughts; powerful enough in its way, though not powerful enough to stop or prevent war.

"You will have seen by now, Roger, that in these lands nothing is left undone merely for want of trying. Whatever the outcome of any enterprise, however hopeless it may seem from the start, yet an attempt will be made. We have our failures, and we have our successes too. War, my boy, is a large subject, and not a cheerful one, especially to you who are sampling the delights of the spirit world. Ruth and I don't want to depress you."

"You won't do that, Monsignor; I like to know things, even if they're not too pleasant."

At the "west" end of the building there was a deep narthex upon which was reposing a large organ. It was not an instrument of advanced design or construction, and the pipes were arranged in their conventional order.

"A nice instrument, Roger. Anyone who wishes is at liberty to play upon it. Come along upstairs, and examine it, and perhaps Ruth will play us a tune."

We mounted the stairs, and found ourselves in a wide gallery.

"There can't be electricity here, so would you like me to pump for you, Ruth?" Roger suggested.

"There's no need to do that, thank you, my dear," said Ruth, "You're right about our not having electricity. We've something much better."

She pointed to a box-like receptacle on the floor a short distance from the organ.

"In there," said she, "is all we require. All I have to do is set that little machine in motion, and the air is sent along the trunk to the instrument."

"Yes, but what makes the machine go?"

"Thought, Roger, thought; that's all," answered Ruth with a smile. "You know, you've hardly any notion yet what thought can really do."

"No, I'm beginning to realize that!"

Ruth seated herself at the manuals and played a short piece that had been specially composed for her by one of our master musician friends—a light, frolicsome little work, rather in the nature of a scherzo. When the final note had sounded, Ruth left the organ-seat, and taking Roger by the arm said, "Now come and see what we've done."

We left the building, and observing Ruth and myself gazing upwards above the roof, Roger did the same and was astonished to see, high up over the building, a huge sphere like a bubble, gently rotating upon its axis. Its colors, a delicate blue and pink, interweaved themselves without losing their identity.

"We should move a little farther away," I said, "then Roger will see the full effect. At present we're too much under it." We took up a position about a quarter of a mile distant where the full effect was superb. To Roger it was somewhat awe-inspiring to see this apparently fragile form suspended in the air with "no visible means of support."

"All music, Roger, makes a form of some kind when it is performed," Ruth said, "no matter what instrument it is played upon, though if I had played that piece on the piano, we should not have got such a large one as that. But we should have made a form; perhaps not as lovely. I've never played that piece on the piano, so I can't say what exactly would have happened. It was written for the organ, where one can get sufficient volume and variety of tonal effect. It's very beautiful, isn't it?"

"You know, Ruth," said Roger, "that's more frightening, even, than anything I've seen so far, though frightening isn't what I mean really."

"No, old fellow, I know it isn't. I suppose awe-inspiring is the right term—it's a peculiar emotion whatever one calls it."

Ruth and I both felt the same when we first experienced it, and even now we've not entirely grown out of it. I don't believe we ever shall. I hope not. If we did fail to respond there would be something wrong somewhere, and it wouldn't be the fault of the music. No, there's no question about it; we shall always feel some deep emotion whenever we hear and see music written by such masters as we have here, and they are masters, Roger."

The lad was looking at Ruth with something like deep admiration, a kind of "heroine-worship," one would say, that she should be able to achieve such a remarkable feat. For her part, Ruth was amused, and not a little touched by the lad's warmth of feeling, but she hastened to wave aside any credit to herself.

"What *I've* done is nothing, Roger. Anyone who can play can produce the same result. A mechanical instrument could do it, but no mechanical instrument could compose the music—that's where the credit must go, to the composer."

"Did I understand you to say that a *master*-musician wrote the piece *specially* for you?"

"That is perfectly correct, Roger. Another surprise? It shouldn't be, you know, because, if you come to think of it, all those famous composers who have died, must be somewhere, mustn't they?"

"Yes, of course; that's rummy—I never thought of that."

"Ah," I remarked, "I suppose that's because most folk regard musical composers as being only half human, if even that. That's why so many of them were half-starved when they lived on earth. When they left it, the people suddenly remembered them, and put up statues and monuments to them, and their works suddenly became very valuable. Things are a trifle better now on earth, and a composer need not actually starve, but if he has written some really good things they will be much more valuable after he's dead. At the present moment, the earthly geniuses are notable by their absence. The real geniuses are all here. You've had an example, this minute, of the real genius. Even without being able to see that piece, it is a delight merely to listen to it."

"How long will that ball remain there?" Roger asked.

"Normally," Ruth told him, "it would fade in a moment or so, but Monsignor and I put our thoughts together to charge it with a little more permanence so that you could see it in all its glory. When there are orchestral or other works following one another quickly, if the forms stayed too long they would all be mounted in a jumble on one another, and their shapes would be lost."

CHAPTER NINE

A QUESTION OF AGE

"THERE'S ONE thing that puzzles me," declared Roger.

"Only one thing?" I queried. The lad is so good-natured that he never minds our mild bantering.

We had returned to our house after our visit to the "church" and Ruth's brief organ recital, and were sitting comfortably in the downstairs room where Roger caught his first glimpse of the spirit world.

"What is it that puzzles you, my dear fellow? State your case, as the lawyers say, and perhaps Ruth or I can throw some light on the matter."

"It's this: how is it that everybody looks so young? I've not seen any old people anywhere."

"Oh, yes, you have, Roger; but not in the way you mean, of course."

"If I'm being too personal, Monsignor, tell me to mind my own business, but what would your age be?"

"You need have no fear about being too personal, my dear boy, in this matter of ages. We're not the least touchy over here. Even Ruth won't mind your asking such a question, and as you may know, the women folk on earth are sometimes a little sensitive on the subject! But here, no one cares, because one ceases to give the thing much thought. Still, it has its interesting side, especially to people like you and me, Roger and Ruth, too—who like to 'look into things' a bit.

"Well, now, as to my age. When I came over here I was forty-three, and I've been here for thirty-seven years—I know that because I have active interests in the old earth, and so have kept track of the passage of time. So, then, a simple sum, and you have the answer."

"Good gracious," the boy exclaimed. "Then you are eighty!"

"Just so—a young man of eighty!"

"But you don't look anywhere near it."

"I hope not. As a matter of fact, I scarcely look any different from what I appeared to be when I arrived here. A few alterations for the better, perhaps, but otherwise, no change."

"And how old would you say I am, Roger?" asked Ruth.

"Careful, Roger," I interposed, but he would not venture a guess.

"If you had said a hundred it wouldn't have upset me in the least. But I'm not that yet. Put it at about sixty-two, and you'll be right."

"You don't look a minute older than about twenty-five," returned Roger.

"Which was just my age when I came here."

"Then what on earth age must I look?"

"Hardly beyond an infant in arms," laughed Ruth. "No, Roger, you look the same as you looked on earth, as far as age goes. In health, of course, vastly different, at any rate from those last few days. Poor dear, you were a very ill Roger then, but there's no comparison now. Your mother would see in you now the lad she used to know."

"You see how it is," I said. "In the spirit world age in years doesn't count. What happens is that the period known as the prime of life is the normal and permanent age. If one arrives here before that time, as you did and as many other do, even tiny infants, then you proceed gradually towards that prime of life, and there you remain. If you should come here after you've reached it— one may have gone far past it into the eighties and higher—then you revert, you return to the prime of life. In other words, you become younger."

"That seems a sound idea."

"It is a sound idea, but then all the ideas here are sound." We joined in laughter at our own condescending approval of the spirit world.

"Still, Roger," I continued, "for all our fun, the law that brings it about is a just one, and that's what you really meant. It's just in every way: for those who have passed the prescribed span on earth and for those who left it in early or very early infancy, or when they were your age, or Ruth's—and if it comes to that, mine as well almost.

"But I'll tell you one thing: you'll find it extremely difficult to guess a person's right age, which is to say, how long they have been in the spirit world, with the addition of the few years lived on earth.

"The longer you've lived in these lands, the shorter does the earthly period seem to become by comparison. Take Radiant Wing, for example. You couldn't possibly guess how long he has been here. If you had a little more knowledge—which, of course, will come to you as you go along—there would be certain indications that would help you in your guess."

"No, I couldn't fathom how long he's been here. He looks in his prime—a young man. Yet when he speaks, and when you look at him closely, you can see that, without appearing old or elderly in any way, there is something that suggests weight of knowledge, or something like that."

"Difficult to define, Roger, very. There's many an occasion, on seeing someone here, that you might say to yourself—if you should ever be so disrespectful—'he's no chicken.' But there would be nothing to indicate positive agedness in such outward signs as wrinkles and lines, and all the other familiar landmarks of passing, or passed, years. How old would you say Radiant Wing is?"

"I can't hope to guess."

"He's turned six hundred."

"It's amazing, isn't it?"

"Not really. You remember Omar is two thousand if he's a day. His Egyptian aide is even older—in the region of five thousand years. What is it the psalmist says? *Longitudine dierum replebo eum*: I will fill him with length of days.

"This is an ageless world, Roger, and some of us, at any rate, would appear to be the same. No lined faces, no white or graying hair, no suggestions of that additional weight with which on earth we manage to burden ourselves, or on the other hand, no indications of shriveling up and wasting away; no slowing down of our movements, or alterations in the pitch of our voices; no loss of mental vigor. No second childhood. Eliminate this melancholy catalogue, and you have us as we are, restored to a second prime, those of us that need it, instead of advancing into a second childhood."

"How old would you say the spirit world is, Monsignor?"

"My dear fellow, that is a question! You know what is said: eternity can have no beginning. And eternity, as with immortality, is something that cannot be proved. The only thing you can do in this particular instance, is to try to find out what is the consensus of opinion on the matter, and there you will find that we are all of one mind, and that is that this world and ourselves with it, are eternal. We have the feeling of absolute permanence. If it were not permanent, then what is the use of all this? What is the use of continuing at all?

"No, my boy, everything here in these lands cries out against there being an end to this glorious life, and the still better life that lies in front of every one of us. And we, in these realms, have the assurance—did we need it—of those stupendous souls in the very highest realms. If they are not telling us the truth, which is an infamous and preposterous supposition, then there is no truth.

"But we have our own powers, Roger. There's that to be considered. We can ourselves create. You've not seen us really on the job, yet, doing that. Wait till you see one of the experts running up a house for someone to live in, and as with a house, so with a palace or anything still larger. We make all this for ourselves with that power that comes from the great Source. Doubtless, you might argue, suppose the great Source cut off the power, withheld it, what then? That idea is equally preposterous. The power has been sent down ever since the spirit world existed. And that brings us back where we started!

"There does come a time when figures cease to have much significance for the ordinary person. When you contemplate the astronomical proportions into which the nations' finances have developed, when money is reckoned in thousands of millions, these figures can convey nothing whatever to the average mind. It's doubtful if they convey much to the people who are responsible for them. At any rate, the earth folk are now accustomed to such rows of almost unending digits, that when universal ages are brought in, they should cause no surprise.

"The most one could say, Roger, in answer to your question as to the age of the spirit world, is that it existed before the earth world. That we know from high sources. Well, then, if the earth first came into being between three thousand and five thousand million years ago, as it has been computed, then that figure *may* convey something to your mind. I'm rather afraid it won't. It doesn't to me."

"Nor to me," said Ruth.

"Just so. All it can do is to suggest a gargantuan number of years. If the spirit world were in existence so long ago as that—*and we have every assurance that it was*—then there are existing people in these lands, *somewhere*, who can claim *at least* that gigantic number of years as *their* age. And that makes the rest of *us* seem like—what? A grain of sand in a whole vast desert of comparative spiritual stature."

"This is staggering, Monsignor."

"Yes, Roger, if you allow it to be, but the truth of the matter is, in practice, we don't. It's breathtaking when regarded in a row of figures, in thousands of millions, but what seems to me the most shattering and crushing of all, is the knowledge, upon universal proportions, of those personages I spoke about. You've not met or spoken with one yet, Roger. Ruth and I have, in common and in company with many others in these lands. We have even visited the high abode of the greatest of them all. The time will certainly come when you will have that privilege, too, Roger, here in these very realms, even in this very house. Omar is himself in personal attendance upon him; is, in fact, his right hand.

"You see what you've brought on your young head by asking a simple question!"

"I realize now it was a foolish thing to ask."

"Oh, no, my dear fellow; by no means. The difficulty is to find an answer, and it's right you should satisfy your mind, as far as possible, upon things as they occur to you.

"There is, as you will guess, an enormous amount of things that are not told us not because they are deep secrets, but because we have much to learn first. The fact is, that with our necessarily limited knowledge and powers of comprehension, we should fail to understand them in our present state of advancement.

"It is like your school books, Roger. You were obliged to start at the beginning. A peep at the end of them would reveal things far beyond your then capabilities, and so would convey no meaning whatever. We are in no different case here as regards innumerable problems or questions. So we jog along, and find we're none the worse off for not knowing the answers. Everything fits into its proper place in these lands, and none of us would be handicapped in our progression by lack of knowledge. The knowledge will be there at the right moment. In the meantime, there's no harm in our having as many discussions as we like among ourselves—as we're doing at this minute. If it's possible for us to have light thrown upon them—subject to the limitations I have mentioned—then the light will come, you can be sure of that.

"This is a sensible world, Roger, as you will have gathered; though if some earth folk were to be relied upon, or believed, in their wild fantastic notions, this would be one of the silliest places in the universe. How would you like to exchange this life for one that has all the appearances of a long continual Sunday?"

"I should hate it."

"So would we all. But there *are* people on earth who regard that mode of existence as being the very height of spiritual felicity—Paradise, in fact.

"There is another point about this longevity of the spirit world and the prime of life. And that is, some of us would tend to change rather in outward appearance if by chance we should be old or elderly when we came to the spirit world. On the other hand, there has been very little change in both Ruth and me, on account of our respective ages at transition. You, Roger, will naturally move onwards towards the prime of life period, and some change will no doubt take place. Not much, but some.

"The prevailing earthly fashions or modes would have some little effect, at any rate in men, for there have been times on earth when bearded gentry were the rule. Now you may have noticed we don't indulge in such facial adornments here, though if you wished to grow a patriarchal beard down to your waist, or any other kind, there is nothing whatever to prevent you. There's no law 'agin it.' It might require some considerable courage. Certain of our friends might make very pointed remarks if I were to cultivate any facial decorations."

"I should, for one," said Ruth.

"Which I should at once ascribe to pure envy! You can see, Roger, how it is. Identity isn't lost, but it certainly can become obscured, as you might say. The man—or woman—when he is old looks very different from when he was young, and the man with a beard looks vastly changed without it. And those changes are not long in taking place. One soon shakes off the physical characteristics that belong to the earthly side of life, and puts on the spirit-world personality. Thereafter, longevity makes no difference.

"Take the comparative ages of Omar and his aide: there's a difference between them that can be reckoned as three thousand years of earthly time. Could you honestly say which of the two is the elder?"

"No, Monsignor; impossible."

"It is the same with millions more of us."

"What would happen in the case of people whose features are very well known on earth?"

"Do you mean historical figures or contemporary?"

"I was thinking of both."

"In the case of historical people, there are all sorts of factors. One is that there may happen to be no accurate picture of them on earth to which reference can be made. Artists have tried at different times, and built up some semblance from records containing a description of the particular person. Most of them are inaccurate—the pictures, I mean.

"So that you might find yourself talking to people here, and be totally unaware of the fact that on earth they were once very famous people. Their identity has, in such cases, become completely submerged, as far as externals go. Of course, the person himself is still that person, although greatly improved, as we all hope to be! The old painters did their best, and turned out faces that were at least human—which is more than can be said of so many of the present earthly painters! But the originals have changed beyond all recognition.

"What, after all, is earthly fame, of one sort and another? It depends upon what the fame rests. It is possible to see on the earth at present many whose fame rests upon a reputation of utter fatuity. That's not so much their fault as that of the empty-headed people who give them such generous support.

"There are people, too, whose earthly reputation and fame were of a very unsavory kind, but who have since risen to the realms of light, and are profoundly glad that their portraits on earth are inaccurate delineations. Recognition, therefore, fails in these lands."

CHAPTER TEN

A LESSON
IN CREATION

"HOW," I asked Roger, "would you regard this house and everything that's in it, and all that you can see from these windows? As something pretty solid?"

"I certainly should," he answered. "Why do you ask?"

"Because, my dear fellow, there are people on earth who will have it that all this is a *condition* built by thought, and therefore having no concrete existence, as they would term it. Odd, isn't it?"

"I think I can understand it, in a way," said Roger, "because when I woke up on your couch, it did occur to me that it might be a dream."

"Then what happened?"

"Well, I saw you sitting at the foot of the couch, and there was Ruth at my side, and you spoke sense."

"Thank goodness for that!"

"You know what I mean."

We laughed at the boy's confusion. "Of course, Roger. You mean that the whole situation was sensible, and not the sort of crazy things that usually happen in dreams."

"Yes, that's it. At once it was all very real. You remember I put my foot on the ground. After that there could be no suggestion that everything here is not real and solid."

"Real and solid, Roger; that is the vital point. The trouble would seem to be that folk on earth have not yet fully realized the true significance of the power of thought. Within limits they have some idea, and a good idea, but it's my opinion that they don't carry the matter far enough.

"Take your mind back to the time when Ruth and I came into your bedroom on earth. We just came in, as it were. Nothing was solid to *us*. The walls meant nothing. And we meant nothing to you—as yet. Even when you did see us, we were pretty unsubstantial. The whole of these lands were as yet invisible to you, though you did begin by seeing us.

"Then what happened? One life ended for you there, and another began—in your bedroom, or to be precise, in the spot where your room was situated, and we took charge of you for the time being. Had you remained awake—it was Ruth put you into a nice little nap—you would have seen what we two saw—a vapory room, with rather vapory people in it. We could have said with similar justification, that the room was only a condition, and not a state. But we know differently. That room was real and solid to your folks there in it. You had changed your condition, from earthly to spirit life, but you had not turned yourself into a state, nor had we done it for you. You see what I mean?

"Now, had you anything in mind about a future life? No, you've told us you hadn't, so that you could not have found yourself in some kind of thought creation of your own, based upon what you supposed the spirit world to be."

"No, but couldn't I have found myself in some kind of state or condition that someone else had *created*?"

"Well said, my lad. That's precisely what did take place. So that, to use definite terms, it must be a solid type of place that others can see and feel and experience—and enjoy."

"Then where comes the difference between this and the earth?"

"The difference lies in the fact that here there is no solid earth condition to interpose itself between us and our thoughts. Whatever is created or made on earth has to be thought about first, planned, perhaps drawings made if it is something a bit elaborate, and then fashioned by machinery or by hand, as the case may be. Here we dispense with the intermediaries, as it were, and let thought do the job, which it does very capably.

"Thought has direct action here. That's where the real difficulty is. Because thought has such direct action, folk on earth think that the results must be intangible, dream-like, and capable of being, or liable to be, dispersed upon the slightest provocation, or upon none at all. Our thoughts in these lands have far greater power and scope than on earth. To make things concrete on earth, one had to get past the thinking stage. Here one is always in the thinking stage because that is the last stage, if you follow me.

"Immediately upon the thought there follows the concrete article. I don't mean for one moment that we merely think of what we need or desire, and hey presto, there it is. Dear me, no. This house, Roger, was carefully thought about, planned, and then the masons and builders got to work. But *their* work was performed by thought alone. There were no intermediaries in the form of the procuring of materials, and the erection of scaffolding, and so on. Those friends *thought*, and thought produced this very real and solid house. And here it will remain.

"We're not sitting on nothing. We're sitting in comfortable chairs, and they are resting on the floor. This is not a thought condition we're living in—and a good thing, too!"

"Then if you want to make something, you have to learn how to make it; is that it, Monsignor?"

"Very much so. Do you think you could make a table like that, this very minute?"

"I'm sure I couldn't."

"No, neither could Ruth nor I. Ruth makes tapestries—you've seen some of them here, Roger; but she makes them on a machine, itself made by an expert, with materials also made by experts. But they're none the less real for that. How do you suppose the flowers and things come?"

"I haven't the faintest notion."

"Would you care to see some being made?"

"I should, very much indeed."

"Then let us go and call on the man—or one of them—who does it."

As we made our way thither, we explained to Roger that the friend upon whom we were calling keeps what on earth would be called a nursery-garden; that when he was incarnate he had done similar work.

"I imagined," said Roger, "that the flowers grew here in much the same way as on earth—from seed, and so on. That doesn't appear to be so from what you say. What happens, then?"

"Let us wait until we get there, Roger, and our friend will tell you all about it. Look, now; you can see where the gardens are."

In front of us we could perceive great tracts of brilliant colors, each color separate, stretching far away in field after field. There were trees of all kinds in every stage of growth, from mere saplings to veritable patriarchs. We followed a path that led directly to a large house.

As I had already sent a message to the "owner" of the nursery, he was awaiting our arrival. Roger was therefore surprised when the opening words of our friend clearly indicated that he already knew of our impending visit. Ruth briefly told Roger about the thought process of sending messages, to which he replied by saying that that was something further that had to be investigated!

We introduced Roger to our host as a new arrival who was following the usual procedure of seeing things for himself!

"So you've come to see the flowers made, young friend. Well, you've come to the right place," he said with a merry twinkle.

Roger had by now completely overcome any shyness he may have had, and plied people with questions with a right good will. He commenced operations at once upon our gardener friend.

"Do you supply the flowers for all these lands?" he queried.

"Oh, no. Only for this area, as you might call it. There's lots more people doing the work in other parts. This is just one. Now where shall we begin? First come and see some of our products."

Surrounding us were hundreds of flower-beds each containing a different kind of flower, and each arranged in orderly rows.

"We don't make any attempt to be properly artistic in what we call our stock beds, though, mind you, the colors themselves attract great admiration, as well as the long lines of flowers and plants. It is the masses of flower and color that folk find so fascinating. Our own gardens, over yonder, we laid out for pure pleasure purposes."

We noticed particularly the enormous number of blooms that grew upon a single stem of each plant.

"You see," explained the gardener, "in the old earth plants the flowers fade in due course, and seed pods form, so that you might have half the stem with blooms and half with seeds. You can see for yourself that, without this happening, and the whole stem being filled with blooms for its right length, there's no comparison. There's nowhere else but here—I mean, the spirit world—where flowers could be grown like these.

"Cast your eye on those hollyhocks. Did you ever see such beauties as those—with blooms from the top reaching down all that way? And no fading or dying. That's how we make them and that's how they stay."

As far as we could see were bed upon bed of such perfect flowers as incarnate eye never beheld. Ruth and I had visited this beautiful place often before, but to Roger it was new, and such a revelation as to hold him almost speechless.

There were flowers of every variety known on earth, all the old cherished blooms that have been familiar to earth folk time out of mind—the "old-fashioned" flowers" as one liked to regard them: the hollyhocks and pansies, the snapdragons, Canterbury bells, and wallflowers, stocks, and a hundred other kinds. As may be imagined, the scent from this great collection was superb; not overpowering, but sufficient to make its presence pleasantly felt, and enjoyable.

"You can understand this work is more like a holiday when we compare it to the labor that would be required on earth for such large gardens as these. I doubt if there are any as big as these on earth, and these aren't the biggest by any means. Still, we have everything that may be called for here.

"As I was saying, it's more like a holiday here. We're not bothered with all the troubles of things on earth, the weather, for instance—most of all the weather; or the right soil; and everything to do with the planting, and so on. It's a long process on earth from the moment the seed is planted to the time you come to pick the blooms for the market. But here, bless you, we *make* our plant with its blooms already on it, in all varieties and mixtures of colors. We can have single blooms or double, as we fancy, or as others fancy. And once we've made them and planted them out, well, there's nothing more to do, so to speak. But we're not idle for all that—even if it's merely showing people round."

"You would think, Roger," I said, "that our gardener here had precious little to do. Don't be deceived. He is the genius behind all our gardens, the designer-in-chief. He and his colleagues, brothers in the art, are responsible for the loveliness of the many gardens you've seen."

We followed our guide along path after path, from flowerbeds to avenues of trees and shrubs. The super-abundance seemed overwhelming, but our friend assured us that everything we saw would be put to good use, and was not there merely for display.

Roger put a question to him: "If the flowers and trees never fade and die," he asked, "how is it so many are wanted? The demand must be enormous."

"You're right; the demand is enormous. Some people like to expand their gardens, or put in new beds. That's one way we come in. Then there's the gardens in the city. They're often reconstructed or otherwise changed about. So we come in again. Then people feel the urge to change what's growing in their gardens, and we supply them with new stuff, bringing back here what they have discarded. When you come to look around you, you can see there's still plenty of room to make more beds—and fill them. Now come indoors, and see some of our treasures."

We were shown into a spacious apartment containing many shelves filled with large volumes. Our friend took down one volume and opened it at random. It showed a picture of a tulip, exquisitely drawn in color. It was not an artistic reproduction in the strict sense of the term; it was a purely botanical picture, without background, and revealed full details of the flower and its foliage, so that anyone viewing it would know exactly how the flower was composed. Especially true was the coloring of it, so we were informed.

"It is from these paintings that our pupils learn all the details of the flowers before they commence the actual process of creation. Before you can begin to build a flower, or anything else, if it comes to that, you must know precisely all the details necessary for a faithful reproduction. 'Near enough' is not good enough. It's got to be perfect. And the only way to make it so is to know by heart every twist or turn of the object that is to be created. You could take it right off the drawing, so to speak; in fact, that is what the beginner always does. But afterwards, he will study the picture—or an original, if he prefers it—and that leaves him free, when the work commences, to devote his whole mind to the object in hand.

"In all these volumes you will find colored pictures of every flower we make here, both the earthly kinds and those that belong to the spirit world alone.

"In addition to these books, we have the prints hanging separately on the walls in another room. That's done for the convenience of anyone who wishes to view them without looking through the volumes. Come across the hall into the big room."

We entered a very large chamber where, hanging upon the walls, were magnificent pictures of every type of garden to be seen in these lands. It was impossible to assess the greater beauty of any one over that of another. They were all equally wonderful.

"Most of these gardens," our host pointed out, "have actually been built somewhere or other in this area. Inventive faculties don't seem to have any limit, as you can see.

"Some of these sketches have been presented to us from other nursery-gardens, in the same way as we pass on drawings and sketches that portray some particularly happy novelty. A regular exchange goes on, for you know, young friend, in these lands we are always on the move in things. We don't 'stick in the mud'!"

At length our gardener friend led us into a smaller room where there were a number of young people busily occupied, and we were told that these were pupils in the art of horticulture.

We perceived that Roger had all this time been immensely attracted and interested in what he was being shown. Not that he had exhibited any signs of boredom hitherto, but here there was an especial attraction, which, to the eyes of Ruth and me—and the gardener—showed very plainly that he would like to take up this work himself.

Our friend at last brought us to the climax of our visit: the actual creation of a flower.

For this purpose he seated us around him, while he placed upon a table a small vessel similar to the ordinary flower-pot. Into this he poured some "soil," and without further preliminary, he requested us to watch the vessel upon the table.

At first there was little to be seen beyond a slight haze of light round about the pot. Gradually, however, this formed itself into a distinct shape, which one could see was the outline of a stem with a flower upon it. This became more and more firm, until there was the complete adumbration of a flower, even to the color, though this latter was as yet rather pale. But there was sufficient formation to be able to observe unmistakably the kind of flower it was, namely, a tulip.

The gardener rose from his seat, took up the pot, and examined it minutely, before he pronounced his satisfaction, and then passed it round for us to inspect.

It was a beautiful object, shapely yet delicate, so that one could see clearly through it. I handed it back to its creator, who placed it upon the table once more, and with one final effort of concentrated thought brought the flower up to its full solidity and color, with apparently little effort.

"There you are, Roger. There's a nice flower for you. Can you see anything wrong with it?"

The boy replied that he could see absolutely nothing whatever the matter with it.

"There is, though. Monsignor and Ruth know, but we've not let you into the secret yet."

Roger re-examined the tulip, but again confessed himself unable to detect anything amiss.

"As a flower merely to look at, it's the best we can do, but there is something missing: there is no animation to preserve it. We can't give it—or any flower—*that*. That *must* come from another realm, and we don't ask for it until we are sure that what we have made is fitted to receive it.

"Oh, we make our mistakes, you know; especially my young pupil boys and girls. You expect to have some mishaps when you're learning, but no harm is done. We return the elements to their source, and begin again.

"Sometimes we find a petal, for instance, has not been shaped truly; perhaps one side of the bloom is a shade higher than the other, or the color may not be exactly as we want it. And so we have to begin again.

"My students find an enormous amount of pleasure in their learning, but the greatest satisfaction comes when they are fully proficient, and can turn out a flower or plant as perfect as the picture."

"How does the animation come?" asked Roger. "Do you have to perform some sort of service for it?"

"Do you mean a religious service?"

"Yes, something of the kind."

"Oh, no. What we do is to send to that higher realm I mentioned, where someone receives our message; after that, all we know is that there is a rapid descent of the power we ask for. Of course, originally, it comes from *the* Source, but it is passed on to us from another personage. It is a natural process and procedure, and the fact that we have created the flower or plant is sufficient. Our desire for its complete animation is fulfilled; our request is answered without fail, and without question. We shouldn't ask for it for an inferior article, though we could have it even for that, but our natural pride wouldn't allow us to do so.

"At first I examine all my pupils' work. If any slight modification or improvement is needed, that can be done, but if it's too bad for improvement, then it's started anew, and the misformed work is discarded.

"It's very simple when once you are in the running of it, so to speak. As with many other things, it's easy when you know how."

"I shouldn't like to say *that*—at least as far as I'm concerned," I said. "I'm convinced I should turn out a flower such as had never been seen before, and was never likely to be seen again."

"Oh, come now, Monsignor. Would you like to try for yourself?"

"Indeed, I should not. I should be far too nervous, especially with the three of you gazing at me—and waiting for trouble." They laughed at my frank expression of plain cowardice.

"As a matter of practice, we don't go about it that way. Every new pupil retires with me into our little sanctum, where we make our experiments and first essays at creation in seclusion. So there's no embarrassment at all."

"Of course, my dear friend, I know that, but all the same I don't somehow think I should make a great success of it," I affirmed.

"Would there be, do you think, a vacancy of any sort for another learner," asked Roger, "because, if so, I should very much like—?"

"To become one," said the gardener, finishing Roger's sentence for him. "There's plenty of room, and to spare. But before we go into that, let me finish off this tulip. It won't take a moment. So."

He held the tulip in his hand, and instantly we saw a flash of light descend upon it. It came and was ended almost before one realized it.

"Now," said he, "we have something very different. Smell." He gently waved the flower to and fro before us, and we were at once aware of the most subtle perfume.

"Place your hands round the bloom, friend Roger." Roger did so. "Why," he said, "it's alive! I can feel the—what is it; sort of electricity?—running up my arms."

"No, it's not electricity, but it *is* power. That is actually the life you feel, and it's passing some on to you, for your benefit. We've not finished yet. Put the pot on the table, then take hold of the stem of the plant and give it a little shake, as though you were trying to shake a drop of water off the petals. That's the way."

As Roger performed this simple action, a most perfect sound issued forth, as of the striking of a small silvery bell, of clear and sweet tone.

He repeated the experiment over and over again, such was his surprised delight.

"Do all the flowers make that sound when this is done to them?" he asked.

"All the flowers, and many other things beside. The water, for instance. You can bring out some lovely sounds from that when it is disturbed. But before the tulip was given life, it was silent.

"Well, now, you would like to join us. We shall be delighted to have you whenever you feel disposed to come. Ruth and Monsignor are showing you round for the present. There's plenty of time. See the world—our world—first, eh Monsignor?"

"That is so, Roger," I said. "Do you feel you want to start here immediately?"

"Oh, no, not this instant."

"Good; then we can continue our perambulations, and see some more, and then our friend will be happy to make you one of his pupils. I can give you any details that you might want to know, without taking up too much of our friend's time." And so that matter was pleasantly settled, and another happy soul made happier still.

CHAPTER ELEVEN

THE MAN
IN THE COTTAGE

"YOU MENTIONED other places, Monsignor," remarked Roger, "places that are not pleasant, as these are."

"That is so, Roger," I replied.

"Where are they?"

"As to their precise location, well, that is not so easy to define. As I expect you've noticed, the four points of the compass have no significance in these realms or anywhere else in the spirit world. That, as you will remember, was a matter that might have cropped up when you once asked if it were possible to lose one's self here. Still, we could soon take you to those unpleasant places. Do you really wish to see them?"

The boy was silent for a moment. "Perhaps I had better be guided by Ruth and yourself; I mean, guided by your advice."

"Then, my dear boy, if you wish for our suggestions, I'm sure Ruth will agree with me that it were much better that you keep away from the dark regions for some time yet."

"Monsignor is perfectly right, Roger. Don't go there. You know we will do anything for you that we possibly can, but those beastly regions are not for you yet. Later on, perhaps. Accept our word for it—there are thousands who could corroborate us—that you wouldn't feel at all happy about it afterwards. You know how, on earth, deep curiosity would lead us towards looking at something or other we were pretty sure we should afterwards regret having seen. We would give in, and our first impressions become verified. Here's just such another instance."

"There's this can be said, Roger. Those dark realms are not the theological hell to which people are condemned for all eternity—once in, never out again. Every person, who at present is an inhabitant of those terrible places, has the free choice to emerge from them whenever he changes his mind. He can work his way out in precisely the same way as *we* can work *our* way from these lovely lands into still lovelier. The law is the same there as here, and applies to us all—there and here. And here is a living witness to what I say.

"Do you see that trim cottage over there, Roger, with the two tall trees near it? Well, I'm revealing no secrets when I tell you that the dweller in that cottage once lived in an awful hovel, not actually in the dark realms, but in the dismal, bleak regions that lie close to them—the sort of twilight of the dark lands themselves. Ah, our friend has seen us."

We had perceived the owner of the cottage sitting in his garden, and now he was waving to us.

"Shall we take Roger to see him, Monsignor?" Ruth suggested.

"That would be a capital notion, my dear, if Roger doesn't mind listening to our friend's story. It's not a long one, nor is it frightening or anything of that sort. But I must tell you this, that it was largely due to Ruth that he was able to turn the corner, as it were, and emerge from his unhappiness. So you can readily imagine that he regards Ruth as something only very slightly less than an archangel."

Ruth laughed.

"Well," said Roger, "I think that the gentleman is entirely right. He's a very good judge, anyway. I can easily understand how he feels, for both of you have done so much for me already, even in this short period."

"No, my boy. We've done nothing that millions of others would not have done. But we must spare Ruth's blushes.

"I'll tell you what, Roger. If you feel like listening to our friend's story you will be doing him a very good turn, because he feels that he owes so much for the help he's been given that he can't do enough in return, and telling others about his rehabilitation, he believes, is some small way of showing his gratitude. Bless him, his heart's in the right place, and you'll find he doesn't spare himself, either."

"I thought for a moment you were going to say 'doesn't spare the horses.'"

"Roger! How *could* you!" exclaimed Ruth. "If Monsignor ever puts that down on paper—and he's liable to—what would some of the earth folk say?"

"'Trivial rubbish,' my dear; all of it," I said. "I hope you won't think, Roger, from what I've said about our friend here that he's a trying old bore. Far from it. But in this case I think you'll find his simple story will answer a number of questions for you without your having to ask them."

"And if I didn't know otherwise I should say that will save you a great deal of bother, one way and another," said Roger with a grin.

"Glorious, Roger; that's a good one against Monsignor," said Ruth.

"He included *you* in that statement, Ruth," I pointed out.

By this time we were within hailing distance of our friend, and he came rapidly towards us.

"Ruth—Monsignor," he cried with evident delight; "this *is* a pleasure. It seems a long time since I saw you both. And who is our young friend? I've not had the pleasure of seeing him before."

We introduced Roger, and explained that one of the reasons why we had not seen him of late was that we were showing Roger round his new land.

"How are you?" asked Ruth.

"Why, my dear, I never felt better in my life. Is it possible, do you think, for us ever to feel better than we do now?" "That's something I should very much like to know as well, sir," said Roger.

"There you are, my dear. Here's this young gentleman firmly supports me in my demand. Now then, what does that wise head say?"

Our friend slipped his arm through Roger's.

"Why, I don't know," Ruth answered with a smile, "but I don't see how we could feel any better than we do already. Perhaps it's all a matter of comparison."

"That must be it, and compared with what I *once* felt, this is perfection. It might be called 'Paradise regained,' if I were at all sure that I ever had it to lose and regain. But come inside, and let our new friend see what a spirit world country cottage looks like."

This small dwelling was as neat and trim inside as it was outside, and everything was arranged with the greatest taste and refinement, and with yet an eye upon solid comfort and enjoyment. In the apartment which we entered directly from the garden, the furniture was of the ancient style, well constructed and pleasant to behold. It was kept in a high state of polish, and reflected the large bowls of flowers that were everywhere displayed. The other rooms, both upstairs and down, were similarly appointed, and altogether the whole dwelling revealed the natural pride and devoted care of its owner.

"I have no shame in telling you, Roger, my friend, that this is a very different place from the one I inhabited when I first came into the spirit world, as Ruth and Monsignor will tell you, and, of course, Edwin. Where is Edwin, now? Why isn't he with you?"

"He has been very busy of late," Ruth replied, "and none of us has seen much of him beyond a fleeting visit. Roger was one of our own cases—do you like being referred to as a case, Roger?—and we thought we would take time off and show him things."

"Doing for him, what Edwin did for you and Monsignor. Do you remember your first visit to *me*?—but of course you do. *I* shall never forget it."

"If you feel so disposed, tell Roger about it."

Our friend reflected for a moment. "Why, yes, if you wish, he said, "but he should know first how I came to live in such a place, such an awful place, as that was.

"When I lived on earth, Roger, I was a successful business man. Business was my preoccupation in life, for I thought of precious little else, and I considered all means right in my dealings with others, provided such means were strictly legal. As long as they were that, I deemed the rest did not matter. I was ruthless, therefore, in gaining my ends, and coupled with a high degree of efficiency, I achieved great commercial success.

"In my home, there was only one person to be thought of, and that was myself. The rest of the family did as they were told—and I did the telling.

"I always gave generously to charity when I thought I should derive the greatest benefit and credit for myself, for I did not believe in anonymity as far as I was concerned. If any donations were to be given I saw to it that my name was sufficiently prominent. Of course, I supported the church in the district where I lived, and at my own expense had some portions added to the building, with proper emphasis upon the donor.

"The house I occupied was my own, and of such size and situation as befitted my position in the world. In every respect, Roger, I regarded myself as a god. It wasn't until I came to the spirit world that I discovered that I was one—made of tin, the sorriest, shabbiest god that ever existed.

"I was only a year or two past middle-life when disease overtook me, and at length I 'died.'

"I have every reason to know that I was given a magnificent funeral, with all the customary trappings, suitable mourning, and so on, though I have since learned that there was not one soul who cared a brass farthing that I had gone. On the contrary, they were glad. Some declared that the devil had got his own at last. Others said that I was the one justification for the existence of hell, and that the earth was the sweeter for my removal. Such was the fragrant memory I left behind me. And where was I, do you think, Roger, during all these sad lamentations at my departure?

"I awoke to find myself in the dirtiest, wretchedest hovel you can imagine. I could take and show you the place this moment, for it's still standing. The house—the hovel—was small, and seemed all the more so after the large establishment I was accustomed to on earth. It stood in a horrible, bleak spot, without garden or any living thing round about. The inside was in keeping with the outside, poorly, meanly furnished.

"Seeing it for the first time, some might have thought that poverty was the trouble. So it was—*poverty of the soul*—for I had never done anything for anyone on earth, except it be for my own ultimate benefit, not theirs.

"The very clothes I was wearing were threadbare and soiled. In this dingy hole I found myself, smoldering with rage that I should, in some inconceivable fashion, have been reduced to such a state of squalor. I didn't seem able to leave the premises; I felt glued to the house. I gazed out of the windows, and could see nothing but barren ground, with a belt of mist not far away. A grim, dismal outlook, in a literal sense. I stormed and raved, and it was in this situation that Edwin found me.

"He came to me one day, and I treated him as I had been accustomed to treat those whom I considered my inferiors on earth. Now Edwin was the last person to be spoken to in that fashion. You've not met him, have you, Roger, my boy? A quiet, kind personality, but firm. He stood no nonsense from me, I can tell you, but in my then frame of mind he could make no headway.

"I was consumed with anger, an anger that was aggravated by the fact that I did not know whom to blame for my present situation. The last person I thought of blaming was myself. However, I found some measure of consolation in assigning the responsibility where I fancied the largest share of it should rest, and that was upon the Church, for I felt I had been misled. Had I not given generously to the Church, and had I not been led to believe that my donations, and they were upon a considerable scale, would stand me in very good stead when my time came to depart from earth? I considered I had been done a grave injustice, and that the Church, of which I regarded myself a most ornate pillar, had flagrantly misled me, and that I was called upon to pay for its mistake.

"To whom was I to turn in my difficulties? I was perfectly well aware of what had taken place; in other words, that I was 'dead.' But the mere knowledge of that was of precious little use.

"I suppose I must have emitted some kind of thought in request of assistance. Whatever it may be, I perceived a man coming towards the house, and that man was Edwin. It was the first of many visits he paid me, and every one with the same result. I was adamant. I was also extremely rude. But Edwin was not the sort to be intimidated by one such as me, and he gave me as good—better, in fact—as I gave him! He could always have the last word, so to speak. He simply marched out of the house and left me when I became too intractable.

"At length he returned, but this time not alone, for he brought with him two friends (and another whom I had sometimes seen in the area), the same two friends who are looking after you, Roger—Monsignor and Ruth.

"Glancing back now, I know that visit was the turning point. Ruth and Monsignor stood in my room, very discreetly in the background, while Edwin spoke to me. I began to feel a trifle less angry, and my eyes were continually drawn towards Ruth, when I had first glimmerings of light, if I may so express it.

"Ruth's presence served to remind me that I had a daughter of my own, though I had treated her equally abominably with the rest. There was no physical resemblance between Ruth and my daughter, it was more one of temperament, as far as I could judge. Whatever it was, I already began to feel differently. That, combined with all that Edwin had spoken to me on so many occasions, had its effect. After my visitors had gone, a terrible loneliness came over me, as well as deep, dark remorse, so intense that I cried aloud in my despair for Edwin's presence now, which I had so often spurned with contempt, for I had put in some good thinking.

"You can imagine my joy and surprise when I perceived Edwin coming towards the house almost upon the instant of my cry. I met him at the door, and as he would tell you himself, I was a changed man.

"The first thing I did was to thank him for coming so expeditiously—and I was not much accustomed to thanking people for anything. The next, was to apologize to him for all I had said and done to him. But he waved my words aside with a brilliant smile upon his face that clearly bespoke his great pleasure that, at last, I was on the way to being something very different from the inflated egoist and spiritual blackguard that I was when I arrived in the spirit lands.

"Edwin at once sat down with me and proceeded to discuss ways and means of getting me out of the hell-hole that was my abode. A course of action was decided upon. Edwin did the deciding, for I put myself entirely in his hands, and for the present it was arranged that I should remain where I was for a brief while, and that I had but to call him and he would come.

"After he had gone, I gazed round upon my house, and in some extraordinary manner it seemed much brighter than it was. It was unquestionably less dingy, and my clothes were less shabby, and that discovery helped to make me feel a great deal happier.

"I will not bore you with all the struggles, hard struggles, I had to make up for all that was past. It was hard work, but I never lacked friends. I don't need to look farther than this room to see two, at least.

"Well, Roger, you see me now, as unlike my old self as day is to night, still working hard, and glad of it. My work? Why, doing for others what Edwin did for me—and for the same kind of people! It's easier to handle them when you've been one of them yourself," our host added with a chuckle.

"There's one consolation," he went on; "they've pretty well forgotten about me on earth. Otherwise they'd think of me as being far worse than old Scrooge, and would point out that, at the last, Scrooge reformed and became a decent citizen, while I went to my end unrepentant. Perfectly true, but they don't know that I've changed my views somewhat since then, and they'd not know me for the man I was.

"Still, maybe they'll find out one day, and, my word, there'll be surprises all round!

CHAPTER TWELVE

PHILOSOPHER'S FOLLY

"WOULD YOU, Roger, describe these realms of the spirit world as a dreary imitation of the earth?" I asked our young friend.

"Good gracious, *no*. Whoever said they were?"

"The particular gentleman I have in mind, though not the only one of his kind, lives on earth, and is regarded by his friends, and one or two people who make money out of him, as a philosopher. The truth is that he knows a little about something and never hesitates to say a great deal about everything. His friends and admirers naturally consider him a perfect oracle, and pause upon his every word—I believe that is the expression. He is always ready with pontifical declarations upon every subject on earth. Sooner or later a subject not on earth is bound to crop up. Somebody will ask him if he believes in a 'hereafter,' and if so, what manner of place does he think it to be. That is the moment when the trouble begins.

"The great philosopher—and there are many whose title is accorded them upon the flimsiest grounds—knows nothing about the matter whatever, but that is no hindrance, and so he refers to literature dealing with the subject which he has never read, but has only heard about very sketchily. One of his most fatuous utterances is embodied in the question I put to you a moment ago: that the spirit world is a dreary imitation of the earth, which in his estimation, is a vastly superior place in which to live.

"Another objection which he raises concerns the quality and substance of the spiritual teachings that are sent to the earth from time to time.

"Do you remember that scriptural text, Roger, about loving one another? Good sound stuff that, eh?"

"Oh, yes. I heard sermons on the text, sometimes, when I went to church."

"Which, I believe, was not very often. I'm referring to the church-going, not to the sermons on the text."

Roger and Ruth both laughed. Our wit and humor may not be of a high, scintillating order, but then, it is not meant to be. Among ourselves we utter the same kind of pleasantries such as would be, and are, customary among friends in their own domestic circles on earth. And, I would have you know, we like to have *our* domestic circles here in these lands of the spirit world. We prefer to retain our mild jokes, however *small* they may be judged to be. Humor is the essence of this life. We take pleasure in making our friends and companions smile, as we ourselves are pleasured at *their* sallies. In other words, we are human, despite earthly ideas to the contrary. Doubtless much of what I am here setting down for you will be regarded as trivial rubbish. At least there is this to be said for it: it is not nearly as trivial or such rubbish as most of the grandiose utterances of earthly philosophers when they give their opinions of the spirit world and of us who live in it. What those same gentry think about affairs when they themselves come to live here, is another thing altogether.

"Now, Roger; when you heard those sermons on brotherly love, you thought it was good sound teaching, and beyond dispute, didn't you?"

"Yes, certainly."

"And you were right. The original precept came from a man who *knew* what he was talking about. And our great philosopher would have been in complete agreement with the preacher in this case, that brotherly love is essential, and so on. It is essential, and spirit teachers have 'harped upon that theme' time out of mind, and they will continue to do so, as long as there is an earth world to speak to. But what do you suppose is the comment upon such spirit world teachings when considered by at least one of these renowned philosophic gentlemen?"

"I've no notion."

"It's this: *'frowzy religious uplift.'* Elegant, isn't it? Can't you observe the stupendous mind at work? The parson preaches brotherly love to him from his pulpit, and he is suitably impressed and in full agreement. The spirit teacher tells him about it, and it becomes frowzy uplift."

"Monsignor feels rather keenly on the subject, Roger," observed Ruth, "as we all do here, because sooner or later one of these gentlemen is bound to come our way, and that means hard work, and very tedious work for whoever is deputed to look after him."

"You see, Roger, the trouble is not alone with these gentry themselves. Their pernicious views are read and absorbed by their rather tattered following, and treated as profound truths, so that if nothing intervenes in the meantime to make them alter their opinions, there will be others arriving here in a similar state of ignorance."

"In other words," said Roger, "the mistakes of the earth have to be put right here."

"That's exactly it. In your own case, it was an absolute holiday for Ruth and me. What so complicates individual instances is where the new arrival knows nothing about this life, but has *wrong ideas* about it. You knew nothing, and fortunately had no ideas at all. I don't say that in derogation you know that, my dear fellow. What you did have was a clear mind, free of all silly notions—even to the extent of harps and wings.

"One of the most senseless charges brought by these learned gentry is that all the communicators from the spirit world are English, so that, in effect, the spirit world is wholly English, to the total exclusion of all other nations."

"People of other countries might say the same."

"Exactly. The Frenchman, for instance, might say that the whole spirit world seems to be French because in France all the spirit communicators are French. The very same thing could be said throughout the whole earth world. Can you imagine what would happen if a company of these highly intelligent and skeptical philosophers were to meet, one from every nation? They would each be in somewhat of a difficulty, for each would wish to establish his country's claims upon patriotic grounds, so to speak, but at the same time would lodge the complaint that the spirit world seemed to belong to his country alone. The proceedings would possibly have that familiar appearance to be observed in international conferences for the preservation of peace."

"I suppose people of other nations die in the same way that we've done."

"You suppose very rightly, my boy. A statement of the obvious, but not so obvious that our philosophic sages are able to perceive it."

"Is this part of the spirit world English, then?"

"What would you think purely from appearances?"

"I should say, subject to the differences between this world and the earth, that there is a most decided leaning towards the old home landscape."

"There is; and the houses bear a resemblance as well. We've not traveled very far afield as yet. So far you've not seen hills of any great height, nor have you seen mountains. But they are here. As to the people, whom have you met so far?" "Well, there's Ruth and yourself, and you have spoken of Edwin."

"All three of us English like yourself."

"Then there is Radiant Wing, and Omar and his friend."

"Exactly. The first an American Indian; the second, Chaldean; and the third, Egyptian. That's almost international in itself. You left out our cottage friend. He's another Englishman.

"The question is: among what nation did you—or would you—expect to find yourself after leaving the earth?"

"Why, it has never occurred to me. Among English people, I suppose."

"Do you speak any other languages than your own?"

"Not one. A smattering of school Latin, perhaps."

"It would have been decidedly awkward for you if you had awakened to find yourself among the Chinese, for instance."

"Probably scared the life out of me."

"Dear me, why? The Chinese are delightful people, kind and thoughtful, and always ready to help. You see, my dear fellow, that what you say points the stupidity of these philosopher gentlemen in their false notions that the spirit world must be an exclusively English one. There isn't one of them who would not feel much the same about it as you have this minute described.

"Ruth and I have met some of them, and they were profoundly glad to hear *their own* tongue, the English tongue, spoken in the same way as we spoke to you. And the same thing applies to the Frenchman, and the Chinaman, and all the rest.

"As you know, personal communication by the thought process obviates any difficulty in the language question. That process is without nationality. But when folks are awakening in these lands they use their vocal organs, and so do we. That's natural.

"What were your own impressions when you opened your eyes in our room beside the open window?"

"Well, I certainly had an at-home sort of feeling. The room was the kind I was familiar with, and the view through the window was most certainly familiar too."

"Precisely. That's as it should be. So you see, there's law and reason behind all this, and nothing that the 'wise' folk of the earth can say or think will alter it."

"Then the other nations must be living somewhere else—that's a foolish thing to say. Of course they must."

"They are, Roger. Every nation on earth has some position and location in the spirit world. People like to be among their own kind, and there's no reason why they should not be. Would it be right, do you think, or good policy, to force people of one particular nation or national temperament upon that of another? Not at first, at any rate.

"Then, as to the country itself. Nations prefer their own type of country however delightful that of others' may be. Here, they can find it. And *that's* right and natural too."

"What about Omar and his friend?"

"Ah, they come into another category. Where *they* live nations have no significance, for the people themselves are above or beyond nationality. Radiant Wing is just such another. In the realm proper to *him*, he loses his precise nationality though not his racial individuality, if you understand what I mean."

"I'm afraid I don't."

"That's not your fault. It's mine! What I mean is that Radiant Wing will retain his particular cast of features, in the same way as Omar will, but that the nation of which he was a former member will have no significance for him, to the extent that Radiant Wing and Omar regard themselves as of no nation and of all nations, as it were."

"There's no end to the objections which these philosophic geniuses raise upon one matter or another."

"I noticed that Omar and his friend both spoke English, and without a trace of accent too."

"That is one of the objections I referred to. Can you think of any reason at all why Omar shouldn't speak English, or any other language?"

"None whatever, if he wishes to."

"*If he wishes to.* There you have it, Roger. If his particular work would be made easier, or indeed, made possible, by his doing so, then do it he will.

"As it happens, Omar has friends on earth, mutual friends, as a matter of fact. It became necessary for him to speak with those friends. At first he spoke no English, and they certainly knew no word of Chaldean. What was to be done? It was obvious from the outset that they couldn't learn Chaldean, but it was equally obvious that he could, with the greatest facility, learn the English language. He did so without the slightest inconvenience to himself.

"You know what the memory can do here, Roger. Once something goes into the mind, there it stays. Why, Omar could learn any language well, so as to speak it fluently, while the earth folk were thinking about it. You will recall that Radiant Wing knows sufficient of our native tongue to make himself comfortably understood for the purpose of his work on earth. Omar also wanted to make himself understood, but in a different way, and more extensively. He wished to cover a wide range of matters as lucidly as possible, and so he went deeply into the task of learning English. The very same thing applies to us all here. If you, my boy, wish to learn any language, whether to use it actively—I mean, conversationally—as well as to read literature in that language, there is no power that can stop you. You are at liberty to begin this moment. Thousands of us don't, though, because there is no reason for us to do so.

"You know, Roger, the higher you go up the spiritual ladder, the less you think about nationality—and language, as such, unless there is work to be done on earth that involves the use of another tongue than your own."

"How does one get to another country here?"

"In several ways. Shanks's mare is one of them."

"*Monsignor;* what's this? How can you reprove Roger for using slang, when you use almost as bad yourself?" exclaimed Ruth laughing.

"You see, Roger, what a thoroughly bad influence you are. Here have I been carefully picking my way through the language so as not to use a single word or term that would be frowned upon by those folk on earth who think we should speak as though we were addressing an ecumenical council or something equally boring. Ah, well. 'Evil communications corrupt good manners,' I suppose.

"Here is no difficulty in getting to other countries in these realms, or to be more exact, to those parts where folk from other earth lands have their dwellings.

"You were thinking of frontiers mostly, weren't you? There are no frontiers. You may come and go as you please, and what's more, you'll be as welcome there as the inhabitants of those parts are welcome here. In fact, if you wander along you would hardly perceive you were 'there,' except for some slight difference in the landscape perhaps, and in the dwelling houses.

"There is only one kind of barrier you'll come across in this world, and that is the barrier between one realm and another, and that's invisible, or practically so. An increase or diminution of the light, as the case may be. If there were not that, certain unpleasant, extremely unpleasant, elements would be tempted to overrun the regions next above them. And perhaps some of us would be tempted to develop ideas above our station, as the phrase used to be. It is a natural law that works in this way, and like all such laws it works without any breakdown, fuss, or trouble. That's the beauty of it. No question of difference of opinion, or insistence upon rights. There's no arguing with a natural law. I've yet to hear of anyone arguing with the law of gravity on earth. It would be a one-sided argument in any case, and probably end in disaster.

"As far as at least these particular realms are concerned, you might call them Cosmopolis with every justification, for you'll meet people of every nationality under the sun here, some of them coming and going, and some staying."

"I can understand the coming and going, but how staying?" Roger asked.

"The best way to answer that is to give you a practical demonstration, though you've had one already, without knowing it."

"Have I?"

"Yes; our old friend Radiant Wing."

"Doesn't he belong here, then?"

"Not by any means."

"This is rather puzzling."

"Shocking."

"Monsignor is a terrible torment to you, Roger. Don't take any notice of him. I know what he means. Come along and we'll take you on another visit."

"That's right. A visit that would be worth a fortune if it could be made on earth."

With which cryptic utterance we took our young companion upon a social call at some distance from our home.

CHAPTER THIRTEEN

A HOUSE
IN THE FOREST

"NOW, MONSIGNOR, will you please explain to me, in simple words if you wish, what you meant by 'some staying,' when you spoke of people of other nationalities?"

"That's right, Roger," said Ruth; "be firm."

"Of course, my dear fellow. There's no mystery. What I meant was that it is sometimes the case that people dwell in certain realms here, when, by virtue of spiritual progression, they are entitled to live in a higher one."

"Then why do they stay here?"

"Because, Roger, there may be very sound reasons for their staying. Some may elect to abide here for purely private reasons, reasons of affection between two individuals. It may transpire that two people, between whom there is a strong bond, might belong to different planes of progression, and therefore inhabit different realms. In such cases it is not uncommon for the one entitled to live in the higher realm to remain with the one who has not yet advanced, until such time as the latter has progressed, and then, together, the two mount to their new realm, and so continue unseparated. That's one instance.

"There's another, and I believe more common one, and that is where a certain occupation keeps people so absorbed they prefer to work in the less high realm. Our friend Radiant Wing is such a case. They are working for humanity still incarnate, Roger, and although they spend a great deal of time here in these regions, yet they constantly travel to their own homes in the higher realms, and so they are residents of both realms. They're leading double lives!"

"Doesn't that sound too awful for words!" exclaimed Ruth.

"Doesn't it! And thousands of folk on earth are leading double lives too, if it comes to that. Their waking time spent on earth, and their sleeping time spent in the spirit world. There's a grand meeting of friends and relatives that way, Roger. But that's another story."

We had already covered some distance when we reached a part of the country that was well-wooded, and we entered a very pleasant pine forest. At length we came upon a clearing, and before us was a most attractive house, of no great height, but broad, as though several bungalows had been placed together to form the one structure. There were several large masses of banked flowers to be seen, but no attempt had been made to lay out the grounds surrounding the house into anything like formal gardens. There was an element of wildness about the place, without, however, any suggestion of disorderliness. To the beholder it seemed to betoken a haven of rest and quiet, though this was not in any sense exceptional, since it is possible to attain absolute rest and quiet even in the heart of the city without the slightest difficulty.

Ruth and I had visited this house upon many occasions, but it was new to Roger, and so, in respect thereof, our host was waiting for us at his house-door.

"Well, my dear Monsignor, and Ruth, too," said he, "you've come at the right moment, for I've something for you—at least, for Ruth."

We introduced Roger, and briefly explained our proceedings and mission. There was an exchange of warm greeting between our friend and Roger, and we were at once invited within doors.

"Call our friend *Peter Ilyich*," I whispered to Roger, "and look for surprises."

One of them was not long in presenting itself. We were shown into a spacious apartment that was both sitting-room and work-room. Close to a wide window there was a large table upon which were disposed many sheets of music-manuscript, some of which had already been written upon, while a further quantity of unused paper was ready waiting, and it was evident that actual work was in progress.

Along one wall was a commodious couch upon which an old friend of ours was seated, and who rose upon our entrance. He was presented to Roger as Franz Joseph, and then resumed his seat.

What instantly attracted the attention of our young lad was Franz's companions. For upon the couch there was our undoubted old acquaintance, the puma, with whom Franz Joseph was now playing, while upon the arm of the couch was to be seen the little gray sparrow, who was industriously employed exercising his lungs in a vast deal of twittering.

"You've met before, it's plain to see," said Peter Ilyich, for the bird had at once flown to perch upon Roger's outstretched finger.

We asked Peter what the pair were doing here in his house.

"Why," said he, "I was at their home one day, and witnessed their amusing capers. While I was doing so, some music ran through my head that exactly fitted their antics. I thought it was rather too good to miss, and so I borrowed the pair of them from Radiant Wing, so that I could have them on the premises here, and watch them at my leisure. He has very kindly given me a sort of indefinite lease upon them. Their performances are never exactly the same. I expect you know, Roger, that Radiant Wing is Curator-in-Chief and Friend-at-Large to them, acting by special commission for his two friends on earth, who between them are the particular friends of these two 'imps of mischief.' I was at work on that music when you arrived."

"Does that mean that we've seriously interrupted you?" asked Ruth.

"By no means, dear lady," answered Peter. "When I said I had something for you, I was referring to this very piece of music. The piano version is already completed. I thought perhaps you would like to have it. What I'm working on now is the orchestral arrangement, which I believe will be decidedly effective. It will differ only slightly from the piano version. Fuller, and with a few more frills and so on. Is Roger interested in this sort of thing?"

"Yes, very. I played the scherzo you wrote for me, on the organ—the sphere, you know, and he was full of delight, and questions. That's one of the reasons for our present call, apart from wishing him to meet you. He doesn't suspect—at least I don't think he does—who you are, though Monsignor did caution him to look for surprises. He's had one already with the two pets. I'm sure he doesn't know who Franz is either."

"Well, you know, my dear, we *have* changed a little since we came here."

Roger was amusing himself with Franz, the puma, and the bird, and was oblivious to our conversation.

Presently Ruth called to him. "Roger, dear," said she, "you remember the piece I played for you at the church? Peter has written another for me."

Roger joined us at the table, and was now gazing very earnestly from Peter Ilyich to a bust standing upon a side table. It was of a man in middle age, and wearing a neatly trimmed beard. Peter was amused at Roger's obvious attempt to match the two.

"You feel you can trace some relationship, Roger?" queried Peter. "You're perfectly correct. That was how I looked when I was on earth. It's not vanity that leads me to keep that bust here, but solely the beauty of the workmanship."

It was an exquisitely wrought piece of sculpture.

"It was done by someone who knew me as I was, and preferred to model it on those lines," Peter continued. "Do you think I've improved, Roger?"

"My goodness, sir," answered Roger, "that's an awkward question. If I say *yes*, it would imply there was room for improvement. If I say *no*, you haven't improved—oh, heavens!" The boy was lost in confusion, and there was a burst of laughter from the rest of us, not the least from Peter himself. He was, of course, now in his prime of life, in precisely the same way as Franz had reverted to a similar period of external youthfulness.

Roger was very apologetic for his seeming curiosity, but he could not resist asking Peter what was contained in the many large volumes that were to be seen upon the shelves. To those unacquainted with the manuscript of orchestral scores, the volumes might have an unusual appearance in their size. It was explained that they constituted the works of our present host Roger was astounded at their enormous quantity.

"There is nothing remarkable about that, my dear friend; said Peter. "You see, it's some considerable time since I first came here to live, and I've not exactly been idle in the meantime. It amuses us greatly when we hear the announcement made on earth before a broadcast performance, that 'this is the last work composed by so-and-so.' *The last work*. Naturally, one knows what is meant, but it sounds so funny to us, especially when one glances at those shelves. Is it positively believed, I wonder, that once we've left the earth, we've stopped composing?"

I hastened to assure him it was so.

"That is why they put up statues and monuments to us, my dear friend," said Franz Joseph. "They think we are finished and done for; not a note left in us. And now they are perfectly certain they know what was in our minds when we wrote any piece, large or small. If any of us had given the plain reason: to keep off starvation, they wouldn't have approved of that. Not nearly mystic enough. Ah, well. *This* is the life. What do you say, my friends?"

There was no need to affirm our complete agreement! "Now, Peter," Franz added, "play your new piece. I should like to hear it again myself."

Peter went across to a grand piano standing in a corner—a handsome instrument—and commenced to play. I will not essay the impossible by attempting to describe what our friend played. To give a description of any piece of music in mere words is a useless and fruitless task, as it conveys to the reader precisely nothing. The most that can be done is to give a series of musical technicalities and details which in the end indicate precious little. Suffice it that the music that was played followed in broad outline the physical movements of the two pets, the bird and the puma, in the amusing performance we witnessed when we called upon Radiant Wing. The music rose and fell, as it were, in imitation, or emulation, of what was taking place between the two, together with the many sudden twists and turns, first this way, then that way. Beyond this, it is not feasible to go, in *words*, except that the piece was in every respect a *scherzo*, as might be rightly supposed from the nature of its "program."

At the end of the playing Ruth expressed her delight, as did we all, especially Franz, who paid its composer the very sincere tribute of a brother artist.

"Now about the orchestral arrangement," said Ruth; "when shall we be able to hear that?"

"Very shortly, I hope," Peter replied. "It will be included in a program of other works, of course. Shall I let you know?"

"Most certainly, please."

Roger had been standing with his back to the bookshelves while the music was being played; now he turned, and was to be observed reading the titles upon the volumes. Ruth and I joined him, feeling that at any moment he would make an interesting discovery.

The works were arranged in orderly manner according to their nature, with all the compositions written while Peter was on earth grouped together. He ran his forefinger along the titles, naming them over to himself. *Suite in G*, he read; *Symphony No. 6*, when Peter said, "That work is always announced as 'the last work the composer wrote.' That is the line of demarcation, Roger, between what I wrote on earth and what I have done since."

It was plain to see that the latter heavily outweighed the former by innumerable volumes.

"Yet this is nothing," he continued. "It is the same with all of us. Take Franz Joseph, there, he has written volumes and volumes of music. Opus numbers run into four figures here, Roger, and if we hadn't wonderful memories, we should be at a loss to know how much we had actually composed."

"Is it easier to compose music here or on earth?" asked Roger.

"Oh, here, without a shadow of doubt. Consider how free we are from everything that might be—and so often was—a hindrance. Franz mentioned starvation, for instance. Call it plain hunger in this case, and all that it means.

In other words, caring for the necessary bodily wants. We're entirely free of that. Public apathy—there's something else that's thankfully missing here. Difficulty of getting one's works heard or acknowledged. No trouble about that either—here. Somewhere pleasant to live: this little place is an example. Franz lives in a delightful house where he is as happy 'as the day is long'—and it's a very long day here, Roger, as I expect you've noticed. Now what else is there?"

"No music critics," said Franz with a chuckle, "though fortunately for me I did not suffer much from those peculiar people. Not, I would have you understand, that my music was so perfect, but because I lived at a period when musical criticism was not the subject for every ignoramus who thinks he knows something about music, as I believe is the custom now on earth. Your native land was very kind to me, my friends, and still is," he said, addressing the three of us by the bookshelves.

"And to me, too," said Peter, "though they *will* look on us as *dead*. Only think what a sensation we should cause, my dear Franz, if we could collect the rest, and go marching upon some concert platform on earth, one after the other, or arm-in-arm. There would be a riot. Think of the money we should make, or somebody would make out of us."

"The second is more likely," exclaimed Franz.

"Then the critics would begin operations. They would cut our symphonies and things into small pieces, and put them under the musical microscope; show us exactly where we went wrong, what we ought to have done, and what we were thinking about when we wrote them. And nobody would be able to understand a word any of them said, least of all themselves. But they would all be completely satisfied, and fancy themselves to be vastly superior people. No; I don't think it would be so amusing after all. It's safer here. We're among friends, we are free of all troubles and cares, especially that awful bugbear, the fear of writing ourselves out. We can always have a hearing whenever we wish, without going hat-in-hand to some objectionable fellow who wants to exploit us. And it's nice to be among ourselves as composers and musicians, and be pleasantly rude to each other with the greatest good will in the world, and knowing that no unpleasant intent is involved. It's a pity there are no composers to speak of, on earth, at present."

"Are there any at all?" asked Franz.

"It seems a good many years since any came to join us here," replied Peter. "What do you say, Monsignor?"

"Well—" I began, but Ruth stepped in.

"You know, Peter," she said, "that given half a chance, Monsignor will let fly. Ever since he first became acquainted with all of you, and came under your combined tuition for practical purposes, some of the practical purposes have taken the form of outspoken words about the earth's present composers."

"It's this way," I explained amid the laughter that Ruth caused, "if I am to give a true picture of this world, I must speak the truth. Obvious and elementary, but so it is. The fact is that there are *no* master-composers at this moment on earth. I say that advisedly and without qualification. The composers at present there living are not worthy of the name. You truly observed, Peter, that it's a good many years since any real composers came to join us here. Composers have undoubtedly come here, but they were compelled to leave their musical monstrosities behind them. And there are others yet to come and the same thing will happen to *them*.

"You know they say on earth that all spiritual revelation has ceased. The same folk would be speaking the truth if they said that the composing of pure music has ceased."

"We have heard about it," said Peter, "but is it really as bad as all that? The music, I mean."

"It is indeed. I've not exaggerated. Ruth will bear me out; she's heard some of it. And Roger has only recently left the earth. Did you ever listen to any of what the earth people call 'modern' music, Roger?"

"I did—but not for long. It was more than I could stand."

"We have heard about it from time to time," Peter remarked, "but never suspected that it was as terrible as you say. What do the beloved critics say about it?"

"Beautiful things: they hail it as the work of great geniuses, and bamboozle the public into thinking that the particular piece they're reviewing is full of lovely melodies, when it would take more than a searchlight—if you know what that is, my dear friend—and a microscope to find even the slightest trace of one. It's impossible to discover what isn't there. It is the same with art. You've no possible notion of the appalling daubs that are bought at the most fantastic prices for public exhibition. To say that they are nightmarish is to put it mildly."

"But how do you account for their acceptance?"

"Perhaps upon two grounds: either a form of insanity, or a huge hoax. But the same acceptance is given for the revolting pictures as for the revolting music. That is the way of the earth at the moment—the cult of the hideous, the monstrous, the gigantically ugly. The poison has seeped its way into all the fine arts."

"Dear me," said Franz, "I *am* glad we are out of it, and none too soon by what you say, Monsignor!"

We were amused by Franz's remarks, since he has been many years in the spirit world, long before the present decadence began to assail the arts. Peter Ilyich has also been some considerable time here.

Peter came and stood beside Roger, who had resumed reading the titles of the music scores.

"May I take one down?"

"By all means, my dear fellow. Do what you like here," Peter replied. "No formalities, you know."

"I know, sir; Monsignor and Ruth are always telling me, but I've not got altogether into the way of it yet."

"It will come with practice, Roger," smiled Peter. "Begin now."

"It is pretty marvelous. Everything, I mean. You know they have been showing me round, and everybody's so awfully decent. Kind, I mean. You get the feeling that you're the most important person when you're being shown anything. And Ruth and Monsignor seem to have wasted a terrible lot of time on me."

"Not wasted, Roger; not wasted," said Peter. "Never that. Nobody ever wasted time here, because there's no time to waste! That sounds ambiguous, doesn't it? Might mean anything."

"Here is something you must know, Roger," I said, taking one of the scores from the shelf. "Do you read music at all?" "Not very well, I'm afraid."

"Well, then, see if you recognize this tune."

I hummed an air known the world over, much to the amusement of Peter.

"Good gracious," cried Roger, "that's from—"

"From the book Monsignor is holding," said Peter.

I passed the volume to Roger, who looked from the music to Peter, then turned to the first page where he read the title and composer's name, and appeared rather breathless.

Franz, from his seat on the couch, watched what was going forward. "So, Roger," said he, "you have discovered his awful secret at last. Does he, do you think, come up to expectation?

Or did you expect someone far handsomer—like myself, for instance?"

"The point is, can one be handsome *and* clever?" asked Peter.

Oh, yes, there's no doubt of that," returned Franz. "I need not tell you where to look. Just use your own judgment. I shan't blush."

"Well, Roger. We said you would have some surprises, and we've kept our word. Now, I think we must be off. Word has come that someone is on his way to see me. So we'll make for the house."

We thanked Peter warmly for his "hospitality," and Ruth reminded him of the new scherzo. He promised to let us know when it was to be performed orchestrally, and said that he would call for us, when we might all go together to hear and see the first public performance.

As we walked through the woods, Roger expressed his delight and amazement that it should be so simple a matter to be able to talk and joke with a man whose name is a household word in the realm of music, in both worlds.

"Franz Joseph is equally well known, Roger," said Ruth "He's an amazing man. He wrote more than a hundred symphonies when he was on earth."

TWO VISITORS

"**I**'VE NOTICED," remarked Roger, "that no one seems to use surnames here. I don't know even yours, or Ruth's."

We had returned to our home directly following upon our visit to the house in the forest, and our conversations there with our two friends had evidently set up a train of thought in the mind of our protégé.

"Why, no, Roger," I replied, "that is so; but then our surnames have no significance in this world. In fact, to the new arrival, there might almost appear to be some irregularity in the employment of names generally; no fixed custom or order about it. Here it is always a matter of personal identity, and not family identity.

"There is at least one fixed order of names here, and that is with the names that are of purely spirit-world origin; names that are formed or built up in accordance with rules. Each one of them has a distinct meaning, and belongs to no earthly language. Names of that kind are *given* after they have been earned, and are only to be obtained through beings of the highest realms.

"As far as identity goes, you might take our Ruth as an example. Everyone hereabouts—and in many other quarters—knows her as Ruth, and it's a recognizable earthly name, as are many others.

"Mine is a designation, rather than a name, and on earth is an ecclesiastical title. You will recall that I mentioned that we have no titles here. This is no breaking of the rule, because the title, *Monsignor*, which I held on earth, is always used by folk *by itself*, and never with my name conjoined to it. Our friends on earth started it, though they do sometimes use my Christian name. So the word *Monsignor* is impersonal as a title, but attached to me as a name for practical reasons."

"I noticed neither of you bothered to know my surname," said Roger.

"That is so. There's no need. You're already known as Roger, as you have seen for yourself."

"The same thing applies to Franz Joseph and Peter Ilyich, does it?"

"The same, exactly. We've simply lopped off their surnames, and they're not a scrap the worse off. What's most important is that no one complains about the custom, or rule, if you like to call it that. Everybody's happy.

"Do you remember, Roger, when we were chatting about age and identity, the difference that returning to the prime of life might make in one's personal appearance, so that a person might not be recognized for the individual he once was. Names will have something of the same effect, as you can see.

"When the higher personages go to the earth to speak to friends there, they are usually known by some name that has been specially chosen or invented for them. We have a very case in point. You heard me say to Peter and Franz that word had reached me that someone wished to see me?"

"Yes; I thought perhaps you were making an excuse for coming away."

"Roger," protested Ruth; "what would the earth folk say if they thought that telling fibs was the common practice in 'heaven' for ending social calls?"

"As a matter of fact, old fellow, we don't need to tell them—which saves one an awful lot of worry and fuss."

"Then what would you do if you wanted to get away from anywhere because you were a bit sick of it?"

"I can't say that situation has ever arisen that I know of. What do you say, Ruth? Can you recall any such?"

"No," Ruth answered, "I can't say I do. We never seem to have such awkward situations."

"Because, my dear, they don't exist—and couldn't. No boredom, no question of outstaying one's welcome. All this, Roger, arises from your suspicion that we were telling whoppers so as to get away from Peter and Franz gracefully. The fact is that while we were there a message was 'flashed' to me, that was all. It was not urgent, otherwise I shouldn't be gossiping here like this. The message came from someone who constantly visits the earth to speak to many friends there, and as we were upon pleasure rather than business. I responded at once that we were available. Had the message come when Ruth and I were upon 'escort duty,' the same kind as we performed for you, Roger, I should have sent back word of what we were doing, and in *no circumstances* would we have been expected to place ourselves at the disposal of anyone else, *however illustrious*. On the contrary, we should more likely get into trouble for leaving our work of the moment. Everything works upon lines of sound common sense and reason in these lands, Roger."

"Pity it doesn't do the same on earth," observed Roger, dryly.

"You may well say that. The visitor I'm telling you about is an eminent personage from the high realms, but his identity has been concealed under the simple yet effective name of *Blue Star*, and it's derived in a sensible, straightforward fashion from the fact that part of his personal insignia, if I may call it so, consists of a magnificent jewel, made in the form of a star of brilliant blue precious stones, more precious, my Roger, than anything that could be found or made upon earth. We'll ask him to show it to you when he comes."

"He doesn't wear it always, then?"

"Not always in these realms, not visibly, that is."

Being seated before one of the windows I was in a position to observe our visitor the moment he made his appearance in the garden. Roger guessed my reasons for so seating myself, for he asked, "Is it customary for people on visits to come the long way round? I mean, to walk through the grounds rather than 'think' themselves into the room?"

"Yes, Roger. That is the method we've employed all along in the few calls we've made round about. There's no law about it, you know; merely what good sense and good taste dictate. If the need for one's presence were vitally urgent, then we might use the thought method of getting us wherever we wanted to be, and so appear right in a person's presence without delay. But in all ordinary circumstances we behave like ordinary folk, and so present ourselves, walking upon our two legs, and, if necessary, we should knock on the front-door—though I don't ever remember doing that part of it.

"You'll find, Roger, as you go on, that you'll instinctively do the right thing. So don't let that detail trouble you. Calling upon our friends on earth is a different matter altogether. We went very quickly to your room to fetch you, and there were no formalities about knocking to be let in. If we *had* knocked, and by some chance your people *had* heard us, they would have been terrified, I expect."

"I should think they would. Most likely thought I was making a dreadful end, and that someone worse than the old gentleman with the scythe had come to take me away."

"Ah, here is our visitor, and he's not alone," I said, as I perceived two people walking through the garden.

"Who can the other be?" Ruth remarked, as she came over to the window.

In a moment they drew sufficiently near to be recognized.

"Why, it's Phyllis," Ruth cried, and hurried out into the garden.

"Ruth and Phyllis are old friends," I explained to Roger, and then went to greet them.

"Well, my children," said Blue Star; "we were on our way to do a little work with our earth friends, and this young lady suggested that we make a detour, and pay a call. You were not at home when you received my message, I understand."

"No, Blue Star. We had taken our friend to see Franz and Peter."

"Ah, yes, that is good."

"Could you spare a moment to see Roger? I've been telling him about you."

"Not revealing all my dreadful secrets, I hope," said Blue Star with a laugh.

"Come along in and meet Roger," said Ruth to Phyllis; "he's such a nice boy. He was our last 'case,' and now we're having a holiday together showing him the sights."

There was a marked contrast between the two girls, for Phyllis has dark hair, while Ruth's is a bright golden. Roger rose as we entered the room, and I presented him to Blue Star and Phyllis.

"Well, my son," said Blue Star, "you look happy and well, and that is not surprising, is it?"

"No, sir," the lad replied with a smile.

"Call me Blue Star. Everybody does; and why not? It's my name, after all—or one of them. Some of us have several names. On earth, I believe, if one has too many names one is apt to be regarded with suspicion, but here it is different. The name I had on earth has caused the most trouble, I fancy. But that is not *my* fault, but the fault of the people who have used it a shade too freely."

Blue Star smiled. His voice had a soft timbre, and he spoke carefully, it seemed to me, and with deliberation. Young though he looked in years, yet his voice revealed a man whose advent into spirit lands had come centuries ago. It is a distinctive quality that makes itself apparent to the practiced ear, where all outward signs of the ravages of earthly time have long since vanished. I learnt very early in my life here, that to try to assess people's ages is a dangerous task!

"I wonder, Blue Star, if I might ask a favor of you," I said, "for our young friend here?"

"Certainly, Monsignor. If it's possible for me to grant it, you have but to ask."

"We have been telling Roger about names here, and I explained the origin of your own."

"And now you wish a practical demonstration, and to see the origin—is that it?"

Blue Star threw open one half of the rich cloak he was wearing, and displayed upon the inner garment the superb star that we had described to Roger.

"Come close, my son, and examine it properly. It is very beautiful, isn't it. I doubt if you have ever seen anything like this on earth, eh?"

"Oh, *impossible*, Blue Star."

"You see the wonderful characteristics of spirit world precious stones, my son. They need no reflected light; their luster, their brilliance come from within themselves. If you could, by some means, take this star, or any other jewel, into the dark it would shine out like the sun in beautiful color. Monsignor, I believe, has described it as 'living light.' That is absolutely so. The jewels on earth, lovely as they are, rely upon reflected light for their beauty and their effect. Take a priceless diamond, shall we say, into the dark on earth, and all its glory is gone. There are many, many other wonderful jewels in the spirit world besides this one, my son, and all of them made of this same 'living light.' As I expect you know by now, these cannot be bought in the spirit world."

"No, Blue Star; I understand that. Monsignor and Ruth have told me a great deal already."

"No buying and selling here; only earning. And isn't that true justice? It places us all upon an equal footing, and each of us has the same level chance to earn many wonderful things—like this blue star, for instance. Has Monsignor told you much about these jewels?"

"No, Blue Star, nothing," I interposed. "It wasn't until your message came that the subject cropped up."

"The only reason I asked is because one doesn't want to tell you what you know already. Well, then, my son, I expect you wonder what they represent. In strict truth, they represent nothing but their own worth and beauty. They are what we would call adjuncts to our life, and are personal rewards for various services rendered."

"Something like the orders they have on earth."

"Something, my son, but not much! You see, these are not the insignia or jewels of exclusive orders, such as I understand exist on earth. Here they are open to all, without discrimination, who care to earn them, and they are not for certain privileged people as the custom is in some cases on earth. We carry no letters after our names because we are holders of such awards. That, I think, is a good idea, because some of our names would appear very odd decorated in that way; and then there is no call for us to proclaim that we are holders of such an award.

"You are fond of beautiful things, I can see, my son, since you find infinite delight even in this one example of spirit world beauty. You did not, by chance, see the jewels that Franz Joseph and Peter have? No, of course not. They would hardly show them to you unless you asked them. They and their brothers-in-art have many exquisite examples among them. All for services they have rendered to us here with their grand music. Why, now, I seem to be doing a great deal of talking. Is it a good habit, I wonder, or a bad one? What do you say, Monsignor?"

"Well, Blue Star, it can be a bad one; not here, I admit, but on earth, especially if one says the wrong things, as I did, from many a pulpit!"

Blue Star laughed. "I can say I do a fair share of talking now, on earth," he said. "There is one thing people cannot accuse us of here: that we get too talkative in our old age. I expect, Roger, at first, you felt you could hardly speak at all as the wonders of these lands were unfolded to you by our friends."

"That is so, Blue Star. I've mostly felt tongue-tied, or else kept my mouth closed, and eyes and ears open."

"An admirable thing to do on occasion, my son. When we were on earth some of us spoke when it would have been better and wiser to have remained silent, and some of us remained silent when we should have spoken."

"I am guilty under both counts, Blue Star!"

"Are you, indeed, Monsignor?" said Blue Star smiling. "The person I was thinking of was not you, but myself! Now, Roger, you will never guess where Phyllis and I are going when we leave here, which must be in a moment or so, for time draws on. Ah, that surprises you, doesn't it? How can time draw on? Not here, but on earth, whither we are bound. Monsignor often comes with us, but not on this occasion. We are to journey to some friends on earth where Phyllis and I, and others, will exercise our awful propensity for talking, and try to cheer our earthly friends. Goodness knows, they need cheering—the whole earth needs it. And the people there could have it, if only they would all turn to us. It's a gray old place the earth, eh, Roger, after this brightness and color?"

"One day," said Phyllis, "we'll take you to see our earth friends. Do you think you would like that, Roger?" Phyllis asked with a captivating smile.

"I'm afraid I don't know much about that sort of thing," Roger replied with evident caution.

"No, of course you don't. You can't expect to discover everything in five minutes, can you? You wouldn't have to go alone, you know. There's any number of us, and we usually go in a party."

"I rather think that Phyllis has a particular partiality for parties," said Blue Star with a laugh.

"Franz and Peter and others from the musical quarter often go with us. And Radiant Wing, too, and heaps more."

"Not to mention old Blue Star, himself," said our eminent visitor.

"Blue Star, don't say *old*," said Phyllis indignantly.

"Thank you, my dear child, but my comparison with the rest of this present distinguished company, I am not exactly a youth."

"I expect you feel like one," said Roger.

"Ah, yes; that's another thing. Now, my child, we must really be off. It has been very pleasant to have this little idle chat with you all, though doubtless, according to earthly notions, we should have been discussing deep, deep questions that no one here wants to discuss at all, and trying to explain things that have no explanation. It would have been highly edifying, but extremely dull. I much prefer our own brand of small gossip. It's more entertaining, and I am sure it will do us much more good."

And so with a wave of the hand our two visitors left us on their journey earthwards.

CHAPTER FIFTEEN

THE RULER
OF THE REALMS

"**W**HAT IS so astonishing," observed Roger, "is that there don't seem to be any signs of government anywhere."

"Would that be a complaint, Roger, or a compliment?"

"Certainly not a complaint."

"Then we'll take it as a compliment. No, however hard you look, you'll see no signs whatever of any form of government. It is there, nonetheless. I dare say you were thinking in terms of legislatures, acts of parliament, by-laws, orders-in-council, decrees, and many more horrors of ordered life on earth.

"Now I'll ask *you* a question, Roger. Have you seen anywhere notice-boards or notices telling you you must not do this or that, or informing you what the office hours are, or warning you with the old, familiar 'trespassers will be prosecuted,' or even 'keep off the grass'?"

"No, not one—anywhere."

"And you never will, for they don't exist here. Unique, don't you think?"

"Very much so."

"From which you will gather," said Ruth, "that we are all beautifully behaved."

"The truth is, my boy, that our 'government' is by natural laws, and therefore the best in the whole universe. Better, a million times, than anything that could ever be devised from man's ingenuity. Natural laws need no enforcing; they enforce themselves.

"The natural laws on earth are not so easily perceived. Few, for instance, can see the natural law at work when thoughts are emitted. We can here, and their effect. Obviously, some of those laws have no effect whatever on earth. If you had tried to shift your physical body by the power of thought, as you are able to do now, Roger, you would have remained where you were. Still, the natural laws are not the only means of what might be called government here. We have rulers."

"That's more what I was thinking when I asked you about governments."

"Each realm has its ruler. That's not a strictly accurate term, though we *do* use it."

"Doesn't he rule, then?"

"No, that's just it. He doesn't. He *presides*, and that is very different. I'm talking about the realms of light now. You can see for yourself how much pleasanter and easier it makes life. No falling of one government merely to make way for another equally bad or stupid or ineffective. No political fanatics with insane and inane ideas, and, what is most important, no individuals holding office who are totally unfitted for it. If the people of earth would like to settle some of their worst problems, the spirit world could give them a hint or two on how to do it."

"Monsignor is now getting on to a subject where he would like to have one of his pulpits back," said Ruth.

"I would, indeed, my dear; but suppose it were possible, suppose for one moment it could be done, how many would heed a word I could say? Why they would not take a scrap of notice of the wisest heads in the whole spirit world. Small use for me, then.

"Some of us, as you know, are in pretty close touch with events and affairs on the old earth, Roger, and some of us can see which way they are drifting. Can you not imagine, then, how the great beings in the highest realms must regard the situation, when supreme wisdom is to be had for the asking, if only incarnate man were not so blind?

"Look how the Churches are wasting their time and energies upon the sheerest trivialities. It is all so pitiable and dreadful. You've seen a little of this world, Roger, and one or two people in it. You're young, and fresh from the earth. You can surely see that the spirit world is right, and the earth world is wrong in so many things. Isn't the course a simple one as it presents itself to your mind?"

"You're perfectly right, Monsignor. It does look simple *from this side of life*."

"Have things changed so much, then, since I was on earth, would you say?"

"I can't say from my own experience, you know, Monsignor," Roger said with a smile, "because you were there before my time. But from what I've heard people say, there's been a lowering of standards in many ways on earth."

"They cannot have gone up very high if the best that can be done is to produce two world wars, and then talk about a third. And what about the Churches?"

"Oh, they still disagree among themselves."

"Precisely. All this springs from your mention of government over here. I was telling you about the rulers who preside over the realms. Many of them have been living here thousands of years. It requires the highest attributes to become one: for example, knowledge of humanity and sympathy, under-standing, and discretion; patience, kindness, and spirituality. Those are a few that are demanded. A ruler's knowledge is prodigious. At least that is how it would appear to earthly eyes, but you know now, Roger, how memories work here. It's safe to say that the ruler of a realm has a vast knowledge of the people under his care, and that is what makes him so very different from other folk. For one thing, the rulers belong to realms higher than those over which they preside.

"But over, and above, the rulers is one who is the greatest of them all, and *he* is the ruler of all the realms of the spirit world."

We were sitting in a "back" room during this conversation, when we heard a familiar voice calling: "May we come in?"

"That's Omar's voice," Ruth cried, and we jumped up and ran to the door.

Omar it was, and with him his constant companion, the Egyptian.

"This is a surprise, Omar! Have you come on business or pleasure, or both?"

"Oh, pleasure," replied Omar; "business only ages one, so I avoid it as much as possible. That is what keeps me young. How is Roger?"

Roger being very able to answer for himself, did so:

"Wonderful," said he.

"And you look it, my son. That is capital. The medicine has done you good, and the patient is now fully restored. Well, now to the real purpose of my call. I have a message for you to say that as my 'master' is coming to this realm shortly, he would be pleased if he might visit you for a moment. There, that is my commission; simple and brief. I think I can guess your answer."

"It needs no guessing, Omar. This is a private visit, I take it—to the realm, I mean?"

"Oh, yes; at least, as private as one can make it, and that's not easy, as you know."

"This is splendid news, Omar. I need not say how grateful we are, and especially am I happy on account of our youngster, here."

We exchanged a few more pleasantries, and Omar and his companion took their departure.

"Roger," I said, "this is something I never expected would happen so soon, though, in truth, one never knows."

"Who is this personage that's coming?" he inquired.

"Do you remember you once asked us if we knew how old the spirit world is, and that we told you about *one* being, at least, who was in existence himself before the earth was? You remember, of course. Well, it is he who is coming, and incidentally, it is he who is the ruler of all the realms of the spirit world, that I spoke about only a moment ago.

"You know, Roger, there are folk on earth who believe that the beings of the highest realms never by any chance leave those realms, because it would be too appallingly distasteful for them to leave the rarefied state in which they live. That is absolutely wrong. Those marvelous beings can, *and do*, journey into the different realms. It sometimes transpires that an individual may be speaking to one such personage and be totally unaware of it."

"Who *is* this being," Roger asked again; "surely not—?"

"I know what you were going to say, my boy. No, he is not the Father of the universe, though one can understand the inference you might be tempted to draw even from the little we've told you.

"He is known by sight, Roger, to every single soul living in the realms of light. How many thousands there are who name him as their 'beloved master'—and that includes Omar himself—it is impossible to say.

"He exercises over *all* the realms the function that the individual ruler exercises over the realm to which he is appointed. He unifies the whole of the realms of the spirit world into one gigantic universe, over which reigns the Father of us all. You cannot have the remotest conception, my Roger, of the magnitude, the immensity of the powers possessed by him, and yet, with it all he is the most gracious being it is possible to contemplate. His position is one of absolute regality, if one can so term it, while he himself is indescribable.

"You will be able to judge for yourself, very soon, the enormous degree of knowledge, spirituality and wisdom he possesses. The colors denoting these three attributes are blue, white, and gold, and he has them upon his robe in enormous proportions. You saw for yourself how Omar has these three colors in no inconsiderable degree himself. Even so, there is this still greater."

"This is a little frightening, Monsignor, to put it mildly. I was rather used to taking a back seat when I was on earth, and this looks like another occasion when it might be advisable to do it again. In other words, *bolt* before your visitor arrives."

"*No, no, no*, Roger. Stay, *stay*, you *must*."

"At any rate, I might be in the way."

"Oh, come, Roger, my dear," interposed Ruth; "you've stayed with us so far, and our advice has been good, though I do say so."

We had got thus far in our deliberations when we perceived two old friends walking across the grass, for we had remained out of doors after the departure of Omar and the Egyptian. The present callers were none other than Franz Joseph and Peter Ilyich. Cordial greetings were exchanged, and we hastened to tell them of Omar's visit and its purpose.

"Of course, you will both remain?" I concluded.

"My dear friend," said Franz, "you would have some difficulty in trying to dislodge either of us."

"Roger feels a little nervous," I told them.

"Dear me," said Peter; "that won't do. Still, I can understand. Now I'll tell you what to do, Roger. Wait until he comes, and then if you feel 'stage-fright' coming over you, well, you know the method of quickly removing yourself. But you won't. The minute you see this visitor, you will want to stay. That's how Franz and I felt on *our* first occasion of seeing him. We have seen him many times since, and spoken with him. We have so much to be thankful for, as it is from his high realm that the arts derive their inspiration, even to reaching as far as the earth. Many of us, since we came here, have had the opportunity to acknowledge and be grateful for what was given to us in those days on earth. Isn't that so, Franz, old friend?"

"Indeed, it is. We little knew on earth whence our ideas were coming."

Ruth, meanwhile, had placed a rather handsome armchair in the main room, a task that she always insisted upon assuming to herself upon all such occasions.

As we assembled before the house, we could perceive a distinct brightening of the light upon the outskirts of our small "estate," and we knew this for an unmistakable sign that our visitors were near. We therefore walked down the wide path that is flanked by broad beds crammed with flowers of many colors, and which led directly from the house towards where we should meet our visitors. Another moment, and we saw them approaching.

Our guest was walking with Omar and the Egyptian upon either side of him, the latter carrying a large bouquet of superb white roses. This, as we discovered later, was composed of a number of small bouquets.

Omar was the first to speak.

"Well, my dear friends," said he, "we meet again, and Franz is here, and Peter. That is well."

Our visitor took the hands of each of us, and spoke a word of kindly greeting. Franz and Peter had each taken an arm of Roger to give him assurance, and the picture presented by this action at once amused our visitor, for it chanced that our two friends had taken a somewhat firm hold upon Roger's arms.

"What is this, my children?" he laughed. "You look to be holding the boy to prevent his escape from us." Ruth explained that Roger was a little nervous, since his experience was so far rather limited.

"Come, now, Roger, my child," he said, "what is there to fear? Would you be fearful of *me*? Give me your hand—so. Now banish hence all fears, never to return. It sounds like an incantation, doesn't it?"

Roger's confidence was restored immediately, and he was himself once more.

"I think it will be safe now to release your prisoner, Peter and Franz."

The two appeared somewhat confused because neither of them had realized, nor had Roger, that they were still linked in arms. The rest of us enjoyed this little episode, trifling enough in itself, but filled with kindness and humanity, and revealing, as clearly as the noonday sun, that even the highest personages from the highest realms of the spirit world are not impossible beings, grim and forbidding, humorless and unsmiling, but that they breathe forth the very essence of all that is warmhearted and human.

Roger never for an instant took his eyes from our illustrious guest, who was habited as he usually is upon such visits: that is to say, in a gossamer-like white robe, bordered with a deep band of gold, over which he wore a rich cloak or mantle of brilliant blue, fastened by a great pink pearl. His hair was golden, though when this is seen in the high realm where he lives, the golden *hue* becomes golden *light*.

What seemed to attract Roger most of all was the countenance of our visitor, for following upon what we had told him of his immense *age*, as measured in earthly time, and running into millions of years, yet could Roger perceive no signs of the passage of time. Yet most assuredly when he spoke to Roger, the latter knew that there stretched behind him eons of time, while he presented the outward appearance of eternal youthfulness.

At length we repaired indoors; our guest seated himself in the special armchair, while we occupied a half-circle round him—seated also, I need hardly add, for upon all occasions we behave like rational human beings!

Our guest spoke to each of us in turn, and here again, lest I should be misunderstood, let me hasten to affirm that our conversation was also upon rational lines. We were most certainly not like a group of school-children being submitted to an awful inquisition by some bloodless inspector! We were free to speak when we wished, subject to the demands of ordinary good manners. And what is most important, we had many an occasion for laughter—and we laughed. No conversation could possibly be without humor where Omar is present, and he was capably aided and abetted both by Franz and Peter. Roger marveled greatly at their apparent boldness, but he soon learned that did he wish to express his own thoughts upon any subject, he was expected to do so.

Our guest thanked the two composers for all their work, as well as that of their colleagues, and assured them of his ever continued help and inspiration. It was interesting—and to Roger a revelation; another among so many!—to hear the three discussing a number of musical technicalities with lively vigor. At last he spoke directly to Roger about his future, and astonished the boy by displaying much interest in, and especially knowledge of, his affairs.

"Information reaches me from many quarters," he said; "it was Omar who told me, and Monsignor who told Omar, that you have shown a keen interest in the creation of flowers."

Roger explained how we had visited the nursery-gardener, who had cordially invited him to join his pupils whenever he wished.

"That is good, my son. As you have seen for yourself, there is an abundance of useful things for you to do, the doing of which will bring great happiness to yourself, and provide for your progress and advancement through the realms of this world. You will have seen, too, my son, how we all perform our different tasks for the general welfare without thought of personal reward. Yet the rewards come none the less, lavish rewards—and so you will discover for yourself.

"Whenever you feel so disposed the work awaits you, but that is not to say you must curtail your present explorations. No one in these or other realms would wish—nor, indeed, would they have the right—to put a definite term upon your desires for knowledge gained at first hand in this way. But there does came a time when the activity of the mind is such that there is a compelling wish to be doing something actively rather than to be a mere witness passively, as it were, to what is going on around you.

"You will never want for wise and willing friends to help you in whatever way you need. You have already in this brief period, gathered friends about you, from whom nothing can separate you, for you now live in a world where no such separation can take place. We are always here, even as you are.

"If you wish to study music, or follow any of the other arts, we can promise you such teachers as the earth cannot provide, for here we have the *masters*, the real masters, two of whom, I am happy to see, are with us here.

"Then, Roger, my son, take up your new work whenever the inclination comes upon you, with the full knowledge that the work performed in this world is never wasted effort.

"Now, my friends, the time has come for us to leave. Before doing so, I would like to leave a little memento of our visit." Here the Egyptian passed into his hands the bouquet of roses.

"Accept these, my friends, with my love and blessings. Perhaps, Roger, you will help to create some roses as lovely as these. Remember me when you do so, and you shall have my thoughts, for the white rose is my favorite flower. Our friends here have seen them flourishing in my own gardens. I think, Omar," he concluded, "we will return at once. And so, my dear children, the blessings of the Father upon you, and my love remain with you."

So saying, our guests took their departure.

"Well, Roger, my dear fellow," I said, after a moment had elapsed, "aren't you glad you stayed?"

"Aren't you glad we didn't let you get away?" said Peter and Franz together.

But Roger was unable to "come to earth" for a while. When he did, he was sufficiently wild with excitement to take us each in turn and "waltz" us round the room. Both Franz and Peter being equally elated, seated themselves at the piano, where they instantly played a duet with great zest, while Ruth and Roger continued to dance throughout the apartment.

At length, we became a little less boisterous, though the feeling of elation is such on these occasions that some form of outlet becomes a positive necessity.

What we had enjoyed was no "spiritual experience," such as the religiously-minded on earth might consider it to be. An overwhelming experience, it would be foolish to deny, and its spiritual value it would be equally foolish to ignore, but the emotions we felt were deliriously bright, cheerful, happy, exhilarating emotions; never pious or sanctimonious, nor so awe-inspiring as to leave us bereft of all sense of complete enjoyment—for the latter is what was intended by the visit, and not something done solely for the "good of our immortal souls." Those same immortal souls would derive superabundant benefit in a natural way, without overlaying it with unnatural, impossible religiosity.

Hence, then, our "exuberance of spirits"—in more senses than one—and hence, also, the way in which we demonstrated it, and were completely unashamed in the doing thereof.

We continued to talk for some long while after our three visitors had left, and we discussed with Roger his now expressed wish to begin work with the gardener, while between times he could pursue his explorations on all such occasions as he felt inclined. We assured him that were either Ruth or I engaged upon our own work at such periods, he would not lack ciceroni to take our places. Indeed, both Franz and Peter offered to deputize for us whenever required.

Nothing therefore remained to be done but to apprise our gardener friend of the advent of a new pupil. This was at once put in hand in a simple fashion by our setting out in a body for the nursery, where a great welcome was accorded Roger, together with many assurances that in a brief space he would soon learn to create many beautiful flowers in general, and *white roses* in particular, which was now his one, overpowering desire.

EPILOGUE

O UR RAMBLES and visits were temporarily halted when Roger became a student at the nursery-garden, and at first we saw little of him. He quickly gained proficiency, as two fine white rose-trees, standing one on each side of the wide path before our house, give eloquent testimony. Thereafter he relaxed his studies somewhat, and we were able to forgather more often, subject to the exigencies of our own work.

He has established a study for himself upon the upper floor of our home, replete with technical volumes, where, at the present moment, he is engaged upon a close study of a particularly intricate floral formation. He is also occupied upon some horticultural plans based upon careful measurements which he took of our own small domain, from which Ruth and I deduce that the gardens round about our home will in due season undergo considerable alteration and rearrangement, an achievement to which we look forward with pleasurable anticipation.

The friends he has made have derived benefit in numerous ways from Roger's newly acquired skill. Radiant Wing reports that a quantity of the most colorful and perfectly formed flowers are now enhancing his own gardens, and several suggestions made by Roger have been carried out with eminent success, within the gardens themselves, to the great satisfaction of their owner.

Both Franz Joseph and Peter Ilyich are in constant receipt of exquisite posies and bouquets of flowers for the further adornment of their respective homes, while Peter avers that the grounds around his house in the forest have lately come beneath Roger's speculative eye, and to his manifest delight, Peter has invited him to accept *carte blanche* in carrying out whatever "improvements" he wishes to make.

Our friend who lives in the cottage has not been neglected, and Roger is a frequent visitor there, the two having become fast friends.

I would like to make it perfectly clear, lest misunderstanding should arise, that our young friend Roger, the brief chronicle of whose life so far in these lands of the spirit world, is the subject of these writings, is no imaginary person, created merely as a character upon whom to hang certain spiritual facts. He is a real person whose passing and immediately subsequent story are precisely as here recounted. That story is an excessively simple one, such as could be narrated of countless thousands of other young folk, of either sex, as well as of older people. It is in no way exceptional or unusual, and although Roger could be said to typify numberless others, none the less he is Roger, a young man of great charm, and of whom we all grow increasingly fond. His merry pranks and lightness of heart are our constant joy, while behind his gaiety are great kindliness, a firm determination, and a mind capable of deep thought. He is equally at home with those who can count many "years" to their age as he is with the very young; for on numerous occasions he has accompanied Ruth and myself to the children's realm, where Ruth is always looked for eagerly both for herself and her musical accomplishments, and where I have gained some small reputation as a storyteller. Here, in this enchanting region, Roger is in his element among the little ones.

Such is the lad's enthusiasm for his work that he deems it his duty to entice Ruth and me into taking up the study of floriculture, in addition to our other occupations. Should he succeed in his efforts, we shall insist that Roger himself takes us as his pupils and teaches us the art of which he is now such a capable exponent.

One last word remains: it is almost inevitable that the charge will be made that the modest experiences and the mild conversation that have been here recorded are so inconsiderable as to be of little moment in the great spiritual scheme of life "hereafter," and that upon all occasions only matters of the highest importance and greatest application would ever be considered by "discarnate beings."

The spirit world is at all times a place where human beings can live in such comfort and happiness as they were meant to do *from the beginning*. We do *not*, therefore, spend our eternity in constant "prayer and praise," because that, as a mode of life, would be no life at all, not even mere existence. We do *not* occupy our time—or waste it—in profound theological discussions upon obscure theories, nor upon the more commonplace ones, for the simple reason that we have something much better to do, in every way more profitable, and infinitely more entertaining and enjoyable. Our conversation is at all times rational, natural, *and* normal. We do not speak to one another in terms of religious texts and scriptural quotations, nor are we endowed with wide knowledge and keen intellectual perception the instant we set foot in the spirit world at our dissolution. We are deeply thankful that we are ourselves, and not as others would have us to be.

And so to conclude: the friends who have passed before you in these pages have begged to conjoin themselves with me as I say to you:

Benedicat te omnipotens Deus.

BOOK THREE

(1959)

HERE
AND
HEREAFTER

ANTHONY BORGIA

PREFACE

SINCE THE first of our scripts was published there has been a steady stream of letters from readers all over the world, each of them showing an immense interest in psychic science and, in particular, in the subject matter of the scripts themselves. So much so, indeed, that our readers have constantly asked for still more information upon this important subject.

In compiling the scripts, our communicator's chief problem, he has always said, is not so much what to say, but what to omit, since, he says regretfully, with the limitations of space it is impossible, in describing the life and people of so vast a place as the spirit world, "to get a quart into a pint pot."

It is inevitable, therefore, that much interesting matter should be omitted altogether or have but fugitive reference to it. With this in mind, but chiefly in view of the great number of requests for additional information, our communicator has dictated this present volume, which was completed in 1957, and I use the word dictated in its literal sense. As with the previous scripts, I received the dictation by means of clairaudience. Should this fail, as at times it is almost inevitable that it should, then direct inspiration was resorted to—it mattered not which, for both were equally effective.

For my part, every care was exercised to ensure absolute accuracy and authenticity, and to this end I was anxious that the scripts should have some sort of independent verification, at least, my share of them. This I was able to do through the services of a non-professional trance-medium of the highest integrity, during the course of twice-weekly circle-sittings. I was thus able to talk directly to the communicator, who gave me his verbal assurance independently that I had taken down correctly all he had to say.

Interested readers may be wishful to know, perhaps, how the communicator views the results of his achievement regarding the previous books and their penetration into many lands. He says with warm appreciation: "I am delighted with the results that have far exceeded my expectation."

A voluminous, worldwide correspondence has itself been a "revelation," our readers being folk of all ages, from a youthful 20 to an equally youthful 80 years of age. Throughout all the letters, I have been almost overwhelmed by the writers' many expressions of appreciation and gratitude, of cordiality and warmth. "*Life in the World Unseen*," writes one minister of the Church, "has given me much inspiration. Thank you most sincerely." And the wife of a clergyman wrote to say: "I have read your indescribably lovely book through twice already, and hope to read it many times more." It is not surprising, therefore, that our communicator should have feelings of justifiable gratification.

Here and Hereafter is, in fact, complete in itself, and while it is not a sequel to the two previous books, it bears a thematic relationship to them by responding to our readers' oft-repeated entreaties (in the words of Goethe) for "light, more light."

ANTHONY BORGIA

INTRODUCTION

I T SEEMS incredible that the organized body known, collectively, as "the Church," while speaking repeatedly and familiarly of heaven, confesses to knowing nothing whatever about that future state. (A clergyman once wrote to me that nine-tenths of his congregation did not believe in a hereafter at all.)

On the other hand, one Church in particular claims to know a good deal about hell, one of its most important features being that once a person has got into it, there is no getting out of it. One's residence there is for all eternity. A priest of this Church was once asked if he really believed in hell. "Oh, yes," he replied, "but I don't believe anyone ever goes there!"

The Church has made the hereafter into a place of mystery, and the whole subject of a future state has been wrapped round with a mantle of religiosity, until people have come to look upon it with fear, with awe, with skepticism, with ridicule, with horror, and with a variety of other emotions according to their several temperaments or upbringings.

Death can come to a person slowly or rapidly, but it *must* inevitably come sooner or later. There is no dodging it. It has been going on since life began. Would it not be a relief to many minds, then, if they knew something, even if only a little, about the possible or probable state of their being after they have made the change from this life to the next? In other words, what sort of place is the next world? The only way to find out is to ask someone who lives there, and to record what is said. And the latter is precisely what has been done in this present volume as in the two that have preceded it.

It is again necessary to say that I first came to know the communicator of this book, Monsignor Robert Hugh Benson, many years ago. A son of Edward White Benson, former Archbishop of Canterbury, he was then at the summit of his fame both as author and preacher.

By telling others, who are still on earth, of his experiences in the spirit world, he will have attained more than his purpose if he is able to cast out of people's minds the fear of death and the hereafter.

ANTHONY BORGIA

CHAPTER ONE

THE THRESHOLD

WHEN WE first began to set down the joint experiences of Edwin, Ruth, and myself of our life in the spirit world, I was told that there would be some who would take exception to what I had to say upon one particular incident or another. Indeed, that was almost bound to happen among thinking people whose eye I should be fortunate enough to catch.

The thoughts of many persons still upon earth have come to us here in the spirit world as a consequence of the narration of those experiences.

Some there are who have thought to themselves, and, indeed, voiced the opinion to their friends, that the descriptions I have given of the spirit world, or rather, of that part of it with which I am acquainted, are almost too good to be true. An ideal state, they would say, that is too wonderful to exist in actual fact. The picture I have painted, they would continue, is an imaginative one, and has no existence outside the imagination.

Now, that attitude of mind is not confined to the earth. People who are newly arrived in the spirit world express exactly the same opinion upon thousands of occasions. They simply cannot realize the concrete existence of all the wonders and beauties and marvels that they see around them. At least, they cannot do so at first. When they do realize it, their joy is supreme. So that, if seeing these entrancing things brings with it an initial and temporary disbelief, then it is not surprising that mere descriptions of them should engender something of a similar disbelief among people still upon earth.

But the validity of my descriptions still remains, whatever adverse opinion or disagreement may be expressed upon them. I cannot alter the truth. What Edwin, Ruth, and I have seen, millions of other folk also have seen, and are still seeing—and enjoying. We would not have one tiny fragment of these conditions altered. They are our life, and they afford us the greatest satisfaction and happiness. When the time comes for any one of us to depart for realms higher above us in spiritual progression, we shall never for a single instant regret the period we have passed in these realms. They will always remain a fragrant and happy memory; and it will always be permissible for us to return to these realms whenever we so wish.

There is an enormous number of people throughout the entire earth that prefers to leave the whole subject of an "afterlife" alone. These people regard it as an unhealthy subject, and treat the very thought of "death" as morbid. If such people were truly honest with themselves they would admit that such a state of mind merely increases their fear of "death" and the "hereafter," instead of reducing it. They believe that by sweeping the question completely from their minds they will also have dismissed the real fear that so many people have—an instinct, they would say, of self-preservation. Others who are more fortunate and who have no such fears, will divide the unseen world into two principal departments, namely, a place where the wicked will go when they leave the earth, and a place where the not-so-wicked—in which category they would, perhaps, place themselves—will eventually find themselves.

The average earth-dweller has no notion what kind of place "the next world" can possibly be, usually because he has not given much thought to the matter. How those very same people regret their indifference when they eventually arrive here in the spirit world! "Why," they cry, "were we not told about this before we came here?"

Now, all this arises from the fact that the average person does not know of what he himself is composed. He knows he has a physical body, of course. There are not many who can easily forget it! But leaving the earth in the common act of "dying" is a perfectly natural and normal process, which has been going on continuously, without intermission, for thousands upon thousands of earthly years.

Man will proudly point to the vast achievements that these passing centuries have seen. He will tell you of the world-shaking discoveries he has made, and remind you of the countless inventions for the greater happiness and well-being of man on earth. He will tell you how "civilized" he has become by comparison with his ancestors of medieval times. He will tell you that he has exact knowledge of this or that, and that many years and vast sums of money have been spent in acquiring that knowledge. But officially, man has neglected the most important study of all—the study of himself, and, arising from it, the study of his ultimate destination when, after his very,

very brief span of life on earth, the time comes for him to leave it at "death" and to journey forth—where?

It is commonly understood that man is composed of body, soul, and spirit. The physical body he is fairly conversant with, but what of the soul and spirit? Of these two man knows little indeed. What he does not realize is that he is a spirit, first, last, and always. The physical body is merely a vehicle for his spirit body upon his journey through his earthly life.

The mind belongs to the spirit body. Every human experience, every thought, word, and deed, that go to make up the sum of earthly human experience is infallibly and ineradicably recorded upon what is called the subconscious mind through the agency of the physical brain, and when the time comes for man to leave the earth, he discards the physical body forever, leaves it behind him upon the earth, and passes into the realms of the spirit world. His spirit body he will find is a counterpart of the earthly body he has just left behind him. He will then find that what he called the subconscious mind when he was incarnate has now assumed its rightful place in his new scheme of existence. And it is not long before it begins to show its particular attributes to its owner. By its principal ability of ineffaceable and infallible recording, this mind reveals itself as a complete and perfect chronicle of its owner's life upon earth. The revelations, therefore, that are attendant upon the person newly arrived in the spirit world can be sufficiently startling.

It is customary among certain minds of the earth to regard the spirit world and its inhabitants as vague and shadowy, extremely unsubstantial and speculative. These same minds regard the dwellers in spirit lands as a class of subhuman beings who are immeasurably worse off than themselves simply because they are "dead." To be upon earth is normal, sound, and healthy, and infinitely to be preferred. To be "dead" is unfortunate—but, of course, inevitable—very unhealthy, and anything but normal. The "dead" are much to be pitied because they are not alive on earth. This line of thought tends to place an undue importance upon the earthly life and upon the physical body of man. It is as though it were only at the point of "death" that man takes upon himself any spiritual nature, whereas, in truth, that spiritual nature has been present within him since the moment of his drawing his first breath upon earth.

The whole process of leaving the earth—of dying—is a perfectly natural one. It is merely the operation of a natural law. But for thousands of years the generality of people have lived in entire ignorance of the truth of "dying" and of the "hereafter." And in this, as in so many cases, ignorance, or lack of knowledge, means fear. It is fear of the future following upon "death" that has surrounded the act of transition with so many mournful and morbid solemnities and doleful trappings.

Sorrow is but natural in human hearts at the parting of loved ones and in their removal from physical sight, but sorrow is aggravated and increased by the lack of knowledge of what precisely has taken place. Orthodox religion is largely responsible for this state of affairs. The one who is mourned has gone to an unknown land where, presumably, an omnipotent God reigns supreme, ready to mete out judgment to all who enter that world. It behooves us, therefore, orthodoxy would urge in effect, that we should do all that we can to placate this Great Judge, that He may deal mercifully with our departed brother. Such a situation, it would be further urged, is no time for anything but the gravest demeanor, the most solemn behavior.

And how does the departed soul view all these adjuncts of "death"? Sometimes with disgust, sometimes with amazement at their stupidity, sometimes, and especially with those whose sense of humor is well-developed, with undisguised mirth!

And what of all the paraphernalia of "death"? Has it availed the departed soul anything? No, nothing. Black garments, drawn blinds, ponderous solemnity, hushed voices, and countenances of exaggerated gloom are utterly worthless to help the soul upon its way. Indeed, the reverse can, in many cases, be the result. But of that I will speak to you later. For the moment I wish to show you that "dying" is the operation of a simple and natural law; that it is healthy and normal to consider the subject, and discuss it, and find out all about it.

Surely the greatest stimulus to enquiry should be occasioned by the thought that every single soul born upon earth must, at some time or another, face the death of his physical body. Let us begin, then, by briefly sketching the operation of physical death.

The spirit body exactly coincides with the physical body, and during waking hours the two are inseparable. When sleep takes place the spirit body withdraws from the physical body, but the former is attached to the latter by a magnetic cord. I call it a magnetic cord for want of a better name. It is a veritable life-line. Its elasticity is enormous, since the spirit body can travel either throughout the earth during sleeping hours, or throughout the spirit world subject to special conditions and limitations. However vast the distance between the sleeping physical body and the temporarily released spirit body, the magnetic cord can span the distance easily and perfectly and without any diminution of its active agency, which is to sustain life in the earthly body.

The life-line will, as its length increases, become exceedingly fine and almost hair-like in appearance.

Just so long as the magnetic cord is joined to the earthly body, just so long will earthly life remain in the physical body. But the moment that dissolution takes place the life-line is severed, the spirit is free to live in its own element, while the physical body will decay in the manner which is perfectly familiar to you upon earth.

The death of the physical body, then, is simply the severance of the magnetic cord, and as far as the physical body is concerned it is closely akin to ordinary sleep. There does not seem anything very dreadful about this straightforward process if a little thought is given to it.

I have already spoken to you concerning my own passage to this world of the spirit. It was easy and comfortable, and I was certainly not aware of any distress when the actual moment arrived for the magnetic cord to break from my physical body. As far as I was concerned there was no shock or struggle, no unpleasant circumstances of any description.

Since my own advent into spirit lands, I have talked with many friends upon this matter, and not one of them was aware by any internal or external incident that their magnetic cord had parted from their physical bodies. In this respect the actual process of dissolution is painless. Whatever suffering is endured by the person whose transition is imminent, is purely physical. That is to say, it is the cause of physical death, from disease, for example, or accident, that may bring pain and not the actual death itself. If doctors can relieve the pain, and there is no reason why in all cases they should not, then the whole course of dissolution would be entirely painless. Why should the severance of the magnetic cord be a painful operation? If it were, it would surely suggest that there were some fault in the heavenly scheme of things. But there is no fault, and "death" is painless.

And now, what happens next? Just this: the person who has just passed into spirit lands goes to his own *self-appointed place.*

At the very outset, this would seem to suggest that I have overlooked what is known as "judgment," where every man shall be judged according to his merits and rewarded or condemned—received into heaven, or sent to hell.

No, I have not overlooked it, because there is no such thing as being judged at any time, either by the Father of the Universe or by any single soul that lives in the spirit world. There is no Judgment Day.

Man, himself, is his own judge. His thoughts, his words, and his deeds, registered upon his mind, are his only judge, and according to how his earthly life has been lived, so will his place be in these lands of the spirit world. This is another natural law, and like all the laws of the spirit world, perfect in its operation. It requires no interpreters of it, no exponents of it. It is self-acting and incorruptible, and, what is most important, it is impartial and infallible.

The old idea of a Recording Angel, whose especial function is to inscribe in a great book all our good deeds and all our bad deeds, is poetic enough, but completely wrong. We do our own recording for ourselves, and this is one instance at least when we speak truly! We cannot hide our bad deeds, but, also, we cannot conceal our good deeds. I am using the word deeds in a general sense.

What really counts in our earthly lives is the motive behind our deeds. Our motives may be of the highest, but the actual deed may have a poor external appearance. And the reverse is equally true. For example, a man may give vast sums of money for some charitable purpose with the sole thought of personal publicity and self-aggrandizement. While the gift itself may do great good to those upon whom it is bestowed, the motive behind the gift will not be to the giver's spiritual advantage. But if this same donor were to perform a small service to another person in difficulty or similar circumstances, all unwitnessed by a third party, and with the sole intention of helping a fellow mortal in distress, such unobtrusive and stealthy service brings a rich reward to him who performs it. It is motive, always, that counts.

The richest services are most often those that are performed without a fanfare of trumpets. So many of us here in the spirit world are surprised when we discover that some small service that we have done—and immediately afterwards forgotten—has helped us in our spiritual progression to an extent that we should scarcely have thought possible. But here we see things in their proper light, that is, in their true light, because they are registered within ourselves in their true light.

So you see, we need no one to condemn us. No one could condemn us more strictly, more exactly, more truly and efficiently than we do ourselves. When we come to the spirit world at our dissolution we thus find ourselves in the precise environment for which we have fitted ourselves. That environment may be one of darkness or of fight, or it may be one of gloomy grayness. But wherever it may be, we have ourselves to thank, or blame for it.

But, you will naturally ask, having in mind certain orthodox religious teachings on the subject, are those who dwell in grayness or darkness confined to those regions for all eternity? No, no! Never for all eternity. They will remain there for just so long as they wish. Indeed, some of them have lived in the dark realms for thousands of years, but thousands of years is not eternity, although it may seem like it sometimes to some of the inhabitants of those regions. But every soul so situated in darkness is free to terminate his sojourn there whenever he sees fit. The choice rests with himself.

If the denizens of the darker regions show no aptitude towards spiritual progression and so lifting themselves out of the darkness, then they will remain where they are. No one forces them to stay there. They themselves elect to do so.

The instant that one of the unhappy inhabitants shows the most minute tendency to lift himself out of the sad conditions of those dark realms, such tendency becomes a wish that others higher up can see, and every help is given to that soul to place his feet firmly and strongly upon the upward path of progression. That pathway may be steep and difficult, but neither so steep nor difficult but that some one cannot help him to surmount all the obstacles upon the way. This is spiritual progression in the fullest sense of the word. It is open to all.

We in this beautiful realm of light are all working for our spiritual advancement. It is not restricted to those who live in the dark regions. The people who inhabit the magnificent spheres above this wherein I dwell, are all moving forward and upward in their triumphant progressional march. It never ceases, and spiritual progress is the birthright of every single soul.

The whole crude conception of being damned for all eternity arises from a totally wrong conception of the Father of the Universe, a grotesque conception that has found its supporters throughout the centuries, and that has, in consequence, put fear into the hearts of mankind. It is a man-made belief without the slightest foundation in fact. And it is not long before a newcomer to the spirit world finds out that the whole idea of eternal damnation is an utterly impossible one.

And now, here is something that Edwin, Ruth, and I discovered early in our joint endeavors. When newly-arrived persons, who obviously could never qualify for eternal damnation, are told that such a thing does not, never did, or ever will exist, they exhibit an immensely strong sense of relief. They usually explain that this feeling of relief is not, as it were, on their own behalf, but partly on behalf of all those others less fortunate than themselves, and partly from the far-reaching possibilities and prospects that this absence of eternal damnation suggests to their minds.

They see at once that the whole spirit world lies before them in equal right with their fellow human beings, and that the God of whom they were always rather frightened when on earth is a Father of unlimited and illimitable benevolence, and One, moreover, who could never breathe vengeance upon any one of His children. That in itself is an illuminating discovery which is of great service to the newcomer to spirit lands, since it at once opens his mind to the truth.

A moment ago I told you that the person who has just passed into the spirit world goes to his own self-appointed place, but you hear of individuals, who are new arrivals, wandering about aimlessly, apparently lost, and who do not seem to know what has befallen them. Can it be that they do not know that they have passed on?

Such is the state of spiritual enlightenment of the earth that in many cases these folk are completely unaware that they have "died." That means simply that they have never ceased to live; there has been an unbroken continuity of life for them, as indeed there is for all of us. This situation frequently arises among people who pass into the spirit world suddenly and perhaps without warning. Their lack of knowledge of conditions existing in the spirit world produces this state of bewilderment, and if there is added to that ignorance also the fact that, during their earthly life, they never gave any heed to a future life in the spirit world, then their situation becomes a doubly unhappy one. But there is in the spirit world a vast organization of all its immense resources, and it must not be thought that these bewildered souls are left to shift for themselves. They are soon taken in hand by others long resident in spirit lands—as you judge time—who devote their spirit lives to such work. Edwin, Ruth and I have for years been engaged upon this identical work, so that I can speak from particular experience.

Our task is often a difficult one because it is not always easy for the soul to grasp what has happened. The mental equipment of the individual may cause a reluctance to accept the truth. On the other hand, those who are mentally alert will soon see for themselves the exact situation.

If only knowledge of the laws and conditions of spirit life were universally diffused throughout the earth world, what a wealth of difference it would make to each soul as he came to reside in these lands.

Was anyone ever so ill-equipped for a journey as is the average person for the journey into these spirit lands?

It is a journey that all, all must take, and how many even bother to think about it during their earthly life?

This voyage is inevitable, without failure, but so many thousands of people are perfectly content to dismiss from their minds all thought of it until the times comes to take it. Many have no chance even at the last moment to think about it, so sudden is their transition.

How many people living on earth would be foolish enough to undertake a journey with their eyes blindfolded, not knowing how far they were traveling, or whence, or to what conditions of living? Yet so many are willing to embark upon the first great voyage of their lives in absolute ignorance of all these factors. We in the spirit world are constantly seeing these bewildered souls arriving, and we do our best for them. We have then no need to chide them, for they are the first to blame themselves. And as often as not, they do so in good round terms!

I think if one were asked what was the most common mental state in which the majority of people arrive in the spirit world, I should be disposed to reply from a fairly extensive experience, that they arrive in a state of bewilderment and complete ignorance of the fact that they have passed from the earth world.

Speaking for myself, I was more fortunate than a great many, for I did know what was happening from my slight acquaintance with psychic matters. Even slender knowledge is of help in such cases, and I was glad of it then.

Relatives and friends, who have passed on before us, can help in such extremities, and they frequently do so. But some mutual interest must exist first, even if it does not reach to the state of affectionate regard. Affection is the great linking force in the spirit world. Without it a gulf comes between people. If you have never given a thought while you are on earth to those who have passed into the spirit world before you, or otherwise shown any friendly interest in your "deceased" family and friends, there is not much incentive or encouragement for such relatives and friends to display any concern on your behalf. Mutual interest, affection, or regard provide the active living link between individuals. Without them a gulf develops, and each and all of the parties will become detached and wander away to other interests and attachments.

The circumstances in which a person can pass into the spirit world vary so enormously with individual cases that it would be next to impossible to describe all of them to you. It would take volumes to do so. I can only, therefore, speak to you in general terms. These circumstances vary not only from the personal point of view, but the very state of life upon earth will help to diversify the actual transitions.

In ancient days great plagues would send thousands of souls into spirit lands in most distressing conditions. In modern times one has no need to point to the devastating wars that cast people loose into the spirit world with shocking suddenness. In many cases such sudden dissolution is a great shock to the spirit body undergoing it. But here again the spirit world has risen to every contingency. Homes of rest exist here especially for the treatment of people who have undergone a sudden transition.

The shock which is sustained is not exactly the same as would be the case of a shock merely to the physical body, though it is nearly enough like it for your understanding. But the results can be entirely dissimilar. In the rest homes of the spirit world a cure is certain to be brought about without any possibility of doubt, and upon full recovery the victim of the shock is not one whit the worse for the experience. The memory of it remains, though only perhaps dimly, without any recurring reactions upon the mind of an unpleasant nature. And there are no resulting fears implanted in the mind such as would be the case with the physical body.

Many people have passed into the spirit world in what the earth would call a dreadful manner—and dreadful it might be in earthly eyes—yet when they have come to tell me about their rapid transition, their "sudden death," they have treated the whole episode with a light heart, and often are perfectly ready to joke about the matter. Indeed, I have heard friends remark that they entered the spirit world in a most undignified manner! And that, I think, demonstrates the precise difference in the way in which "death" is regarded by us here in the spirit world and by you still upon earth. Here we view things in their proper perspective, while ignorance has distorted things so much upon earth. The "death" of the physical body is a tragedy to the earth world. To the spirit world it is the operation of a natural law unattended by any mournful solemnities. While the physical body is being consigned to its earthly abode accompanied by all the ceremonial trappings and dismal black habiliments of minister and mourners, the spirit body containing the real and everlasting substance of personality has gone to its proper abode in the spirit world.

In these realms we receive our friends amid great rejoicings. Another friend has come to join us. We wear no black, we do not recite long gloomy prayers or perform harrowing ceremonies. Nor do we have a reception committee of "angels," as many people are disposed to imagine is, or ought to be, the case. We merely behave in a normal rational human manner as one would expect from normal rational human beings. We are not pontifically welcomed among the "elect." We are not made free citizens of these realms because we have been "saved" through believing in some strange, obscure theological creed. We are not here because we have been "redeemed" through the offices of another. We are here solely because we have, by our lives on earth or by our progress in the spirit world, earned the right to call ourselves citizens of these realms. We are here because no one can keep us out! Once we have the right to be here, no one can gainsay that right, no one can dispute it, no one *would* dispute it even if he could.

Many people here regard their advent into spirit lands as their second birth, and they keep up the celebration of the second birthday with a deal more vigor than they ever did their birthday on earth.

In speaking of the magnetic cord, I mentioned that during sleep the spirit body sometimes visits other places either on earth or in the spirit world. It is not everyone, however, that travels during sleeping hours. It depends entirely upon individual circumstances. When no visiting takes place the spirit body is content merely to linger in the vicinity of the sleeping physical body until such time as the resting period is ended. With some people a desire to visit other parts of the earth is uppermost in the mind of the sleeper. The reason for doing so will vary according to his tastes or circumstances.

Visits to the spirit world are frequently made for some more important purpose, because there is so much useful work that can be done upon such visits.

These visits are usually made by people who are conversant with spirit truths, and who are eager to add to their knowledge. While these visitations are in progress they can meet and converse with such of their relatives and friends who have passed into spirit lands before them. Old relationships are renewed; indeed, it would be more accurate to say that they are continued since they have not been interrupted. The visitor can gain useful help and guidance upon his earthly affairs from people who, from their superior position in the spirit world, are able to offer assistance.

How often have you heard people on earth remark that they will "sleep on it" when they are confronted with some problem that needs solution? Invariably the morning brings to their problem the answer that they have sought. And in the great majority of cases the solution has been afforded them after they have held a consultation with their friends in the spirit world during their sleeping hours. Most people have some problem or another that is upon their minds, but not all of them come here during sleep for guidance in material matters.

Hundreds of individuals, who are in active communication with the spirit world, come to us here when they retire to rest upon earth, and with their knowledge of the laws of the spirit world they can give *us* material help of no small consideration in a variety of ways. They become temporarily one of our community of friends, enjoy the delights of these realms, enter into our affairs as one of us—as they will be permanently one day—work with us, indulge in our recreations, and so forward their own spiritual progression in a score of different ways.

Imagine the rejoicing when regular visitors to our realms at length come to take up their permanent abode with us. The information and knowledge that they have been accumulating during the years, but which, during their waking hours on earth, they will scarcely recollect, will now take their place in their minds and memories as useful experiences. These experiences will establish the continuity of their existence since their birth on earth, instead of transplanting them into the spirit world with the feeling that they must start life anew.

Many souls who are mourning those who have passed into the spirit world, leaving sad hearts behind them, can bring comfort and consolation to themselves even if only in a limited degree, by nightly visitations and meetings in the spirit world with those whom they mourn. Many a soul so afflicted has arisen from his bed in the morning with an unaccountable feeling that comfort has come to him in some mysterious fashion. This means of lessening the distress of separation is but another instance of the perfection of the dispensation that is the very foundation upon which the whole spirit world is built and upheld.

But such means of consolation is only a by-product, if one can so term it, of that larger knowledge of spirit truths. It is only a very limited means to an end, since it merely provides a rather unsubstantial antidote to acute sorrow and sadness. While it will reduce both the sorrow and sadness it does not provide the certain knowledge that all is well with the one who is being mourned. Active communication will alone provide that, and it is infinitely to be preferred to any presentiments in the matter.

The spirit world disapproves of mourning in every shape and form. Genuine, heartfelt sorrow is a human emotion that none of us is secure from, but so much mourning is spurious. Here we can see just what is taking place in the minds of the mourners. Mourning as a rule is utterly selfish, because people are not sorry for the soul who has passed on except in so far as it is thought that he is now infinitely worse off "dead." The great majority of people are *sorry for themselves* at the physical separation, not happy and glad that their friend has gone to a greater, grander, more beautiful life. Of course, I am now speaking of those who are destined for the realms of light. With those whose destination here is in the realms of darkness we are not treating at the moment.

Even where the sorrow is perfectly genuine and inspired by true affection, every effort should be made to curb it. The soul newly arrived in spirit lands will feel the determined drag of the thoughts of those who are left behind, unless those thoughts are constructive thoughts for the present and future well-being of the friend who has gone.

Thoughts of the wrong kind will draw the soul back like a magnet and prevent it from making a steady and natural transition into its proper sphere. It is no exaggeration to say that it would be immeasurably better, things being what they are upon earth, if mourners on earth were to pass into a complete state of physical insensibility for some days after the passing of a friend into the spirit world. There would then be no danger of the thoughts of others circumscribing the actions of the newly-departed soul.

The strong attachment to the physical body that exists in the minds of so many people would be largely broken down if those same people were to become fully acquainted with spirit truths.

Our friends who are in communication with us and who have knowledge of the facts of life in the spirit world, have given to the physical body *its* proper position in relation to *their* life on earth and their life *after* in the spirit world. They know that their physical body is a vehicle for their spirit body while upon earth. When the time comes for them to leave the earth world, and with it their earthly body, the latter is treated as something that is for ever done with. It has become utterly useless to them. It has been cast off—and our friends are never sorry to cast it off! What then becomes of it they are not the least bit concerned. They have no reverence for it. But so many people enshroud this cast-off body with a holy solemnity to which it is not entitled. The "dead," it would be asserted, should have a proper respect paid to them; the "dead" body should be similarly respected.

Let us put the matter in another light. Who is there upon earth who has any deep respect and reverence for some old, useless, worn-out, shabby garment? It is finished and done with. Away with it, and let us see no more of it. In the spirit world we have a new garment, fresh and lovely; it fits us perfectly, and it seems to our eyes faultless in form, color and mode. It suits us now as no other garment possibly could. We have fashioned it ourselves from imperishable material, and by comparison with it our earthly garment was dull, drab, and dreary in color, coarse in texture, ill-fitting, perhaps, in places, and although it served its purpose among surroundings that comported with it, we have now something infinitely better. In some such words would we describe our spirit attitude to the physical body that is "dead."

Old customs and old traditions, though they may be themselves worthless, take a deal of killing. It has become the custom to surround the disposal of the physical body after "death" with melancholy rites, begotten of the general disposition of regarding transition, from the earthly point of view, as a major disaster. But there are other and greater reasons for wishing that "funeral rites" were either considerably modified or entirely abolished in their present form upon earth.

From the moment of passing until the physical body is finally committed to the earth, and frequently for some time afterwards, the thoughts of the mourners are concentrated in *sorrow* upon the departed one. The various performances that comprise the "last rites" add force to this sorrow, enhance it, and give it greater directive power. Where this feeling of sorrow is genuine it will unfailingly reach the recently departed soul.

The spirit body may take some days of your time before it becomes completely separated from the earthly body, and it may be hindered very much by the combined thoughts of the sorrowers who are participants in the dismal rites. Instead of departing from the earthly sphere, the discarnate one will be attracted to the scene of obsequial activities, and more than likely will be saddened himself by what he is witnessing and by the sorrow of those he has left behind. He will feel a heavy weight within him of the separation that has come about, and perhaps being ignorant of what has befallen him, he will be doubly distressed, and even trebly distressed by the fact that he speaks to his friends but they cannot hear him. And how great a difference a little knowledge would make!

What we in the spirit world, who are actively associated with newly-arrived people, would like to see is the complete abolition of all attendance at burial grounds and similar places of all relatives and friends, leaving the physical body to be disposed of in a hygienic manner by those who are properly constituted to do so, and entirely unattended by anyone else. If it is felt that a religious service is right and becoming, by all means let there be one, but wholly purged of all erroneous doctrines and beliefs concerning the afterlife. No gloomy dwelling upon inappropriate themes from the minds of writers of hundreds of years ago. *Dies irae, dies illa* has most emphatically no place in the spirit world, and still less has the outrageous idea, embodied in the customary prayers, of asking for "eternal rest" to be granted to the departed soul. We shudder at the very thought of what our state in the spirit world would be if the prayers of others had been granted! The very thought of doing positively nothing but "rest" for all eternity fills us all with horror at such a "soul-destroying" prospect. If it were possible to destroy the soul, one would be disposed to imagine that this would be the quickest and easiest way of doing it!

Let there be prayers for the departed one, by all means, but let them be free from all suggestion of gloom and *doom*. The minds of those present want to be elevated, not depressed, and nothing could be more depressing than the calamitous forebodings that are voiced in so many of the prayers on these occasions.

The departed one has not gone to another world to be marched in front of a stern judge, a judge, moreover, not so stern and unrelenting but that our lamentations will not bring some mitigation in the sentence to be pronounced. Indeed, the prayers should be brief and very much to the point. And here I can again speak from particular personal experience.

Let the prayers be addressed to the Father of us all, that help may be sent to the soul who has passed on, and that the Father will also aid those who are offering their ministrations to the newly-arrived one. We need divine assistance in our work just as do you upon earth, and often are our powers taxed to their utmost when we come to aid those who are making their advent into spirit lands as permanent residents. Long recitations from the psalmists, however beautiful may be their theme, are perfectly useless to us and to the newcomer we are helping. They produce no effect whatever upon the endeavors we are making.

A short prayer, efficiently directed, asking for help, will bring an instantaneous answer. That response will be invisible to you on earth, but to us here it means a downpouring of light and power that we most need for the case in hand. Pray that the soul may soon receive the light of understanding of the new situation in which he finds himself, if he is entirely ignorant of spirit truths, and that he may be happy and contented in the life upon which he has just embarked.

We have found by experience that where prayers are offered such as I have suggested in bare outline to you, we are enabled to carry on our work in the easiest, most effective, and most straightforward fashion.

It may be objected that on such occasions it is next to impossible to be anything but utterly downcast, and that prayers, to a certain extent, must be in the same minor key; that anything approaching lightness of heart is out of the question, not only from the situation itself, but in respect for the feelings of others. There is a very simple remedy for this: a knowledge of spirit truths.

Consider the matter thus. In most cases the mourners are lamenting the departure of someone for a destination that is unknown to them—and, they would say, that is unknowable. They are a little frightened, not necessarily for their departed friend, but for themselves when their own time should come, because, by what they are witnessing, they are forcibly reminded of what inevitably lies before them and before all men. Unfortunately their knowledge is limited strictly to the fact of the death of the physical body. After that has taken place, what happens? They know not—and it scarcely bears thinking about, because that sort of thing is unhealthy and morbid. But the fear remains just the same, so that in the very presence of "death" they are apprehensive. And being apprehensive, they have no time for being anything else. The mournful obsequies are therefore completely in tune with their present emotion. They feel solemn, and diffident, and somewhat cowed, but they have the great consolation of knowing that they are alive while their friend is "dead."

Now transitions have been taking place since the world began thousand of centuries ago, but mankind in general is content to remain in ignorance of what is to happen to him when he leaves the earth for the spirit world. He either asserts that it is impossible to know, or else he prefers to abide in his ignorance. And yet if he had but the knowledge of even the simple facts such as I have detailed to you, what a wealth of difference it would make to his mind. It would drive out that dreadful fear of the unknown "hereafter" which can be, and is, such a crushing nightmare to sensitive minds.

I am disposed to believe that not only is it fear of the unknown that distresses people, but also the thought that physical dissolution is a painful process. A study of the facts and truths of life in the spirit world is the best antidote—indeed, it is the only antidote—for fears such as I have mentioned. Great faith may go a long way, but faith can never take the place of facts. And then instead of giving the departing soul a harrowing, sorrowful send-off, with a knowledge of the truth the same soul could be given all the help he needs in a powerful, bright and happy God-speed.

It is unquestionably a bad practice, too, to frequent burial-grounds for the purpose of attending to the upkeep of graves and tombs. It is not difficult to see why this should be so in the light of what I have told you upon the subject in general. Such places will start a train of depressing thoughts concentrated upon the one whose grave is being visited. The latter will be the recipient of such sorrowful thoughts as both the place and the circumstances are bound to engender, and these thoughts will exert a drawing influence upon certain types of mentalities that is extremely difficult to resist. The soul will be unable to combat the seemingly irresistible urge to visit the place whence the thoughts are coming, which in this case is the worst of all places—the tomb of the cast-off physical body. We do our best to ward off such thoughts, as it were, but we cannot go beyond certain limits, and where the person insists upon exercising his free will and wishes to be left to decide for himself in the matter, then we are bound to withdraw and allow the soul free passage.

Many people will, however, listen to our reasoning, and so save themselves an infinity of distress and unhappiness. If for no other reason than this, it would be the best thing upon the earth if cemeteries, graveyards, and all the visible and outward appurtenances of burial were entirely abolished. Large numbers of people would then be forced to relinquish what is a thoroughly bad practice from every point of view. It is unhealthy for mundane as well as spiritual reasons, and can be the unconscious means of bringing distress to the newly-departed individual.

From the fact that a mourner is spending time at the grave, indulging in melancholy thoughts of the soul who has passed on, and contemplating that a few feet of earth are now separating them, and so on, you will infer, in such a case, that the mourner has no acquaintance with spirit truths, or else he would never think that the departed one really lies there himself. We in the spirit world know that a soul who gradually yields to such melancholy importunities of thought as are being sent out from the earth, knows very little of spirit truths. And being in such case, when a soul returns to the earth and stands in the presence of the mourner and tries to talk to and comfort the one who is left behind, he becomes acutely disturbed in mind when he discovers that his voice cannot be heard on the earth. His words are falling unheeded upon the air. The thoughts of sorrow and despair pass and re-pass in a constant stream until at last both persons become exhausted with the emotional strain. The mourner will eventually leave the graveside, the newly-arrived spirit will return whence he came, and both are filled with inconsolable sadness. The whole performance has done no good whatever; on the contrary, it has had a very bad effect upon both parties. And what is still worse, the episode will be repeated and repeated until we on our side can instill some reason into our distracted friend, and show him the futility of the proceedings. Better counsels will eventually prevail, and the visitations to the resting place of the physical body will cease. In the meantime, the soul has passed through a period of untold misery that could have been avoided if only those who were left behind upon earth had possessed themselves of the necessary knowledge of spirit truths.

You can understand that we are not pleased with the willful stupidity of some earth folk who persist in closing their eyes and ears to the truth, and so causing an enormous amount of misery to friends and relatives who have passed into the spirit world before them. Their blind ignorance in refusing to look at the facts of spiritual truths, their blatant assumption of mental superiority over the whole subject of spirit life, their self-satisfied attachment to their own erroneous views, all these, taken together or individually, have the effect of giving us work to do in the spirit world which a knowledge of the truth would render totally unnecessary. We should then be enabled to carry on with other work than correcting the mistakes of the earth. The earth has, in fact, a completely exaggerated idea of its own cleverness. You need to be resident in the spirit world to see just how foolish mankind upon earth can really be! Here the mistakes are plain for all to see, and we are sometimes amazed at the ignorance displayed.

It must not be supposed that I am claiming infallibility for the people of the spirit world. Far from it. But man, when he is incarnate, has so many opportunities of learning about the life in the spirit world that has before him. He willfully passes the chances by with an airy wave of the hand, because he knows better. When he comes to the spirit plane of existence he knows better still, and bitterly laments the wasted opportunities of his earthly life. And there are few worse things than remorse. But we can come to the rescue in this as in so many other things, and help the soul to overcome the remorse for his earthly mistakes.

We are certainly not infallible here in the spirit world, but by virtue of our altered state we can see just a little farther ahead than can you who are still incarnate. When we perceive that our friends on earth are about to make some mistake or other that will eventually be to their disadvantage, we are naturally anxious to offer a word of caution or advice, and so save them from the consequences. Alas, man is so often deaf to our promptings, and the false move is made. Eventually, when our friend arrives in the spirit world, he sees the mistakes he has made and how he could have prevented them had he but listened.

Death always seems to the beholder of it to be such a solitary business, as perforce, it must be to some extent. But our help is always at hand, though help comes usually after the severance of the magnetic cord when the spirit body is free from the earthly body. The severance will take place in a perfectly natural manner, just as the leaf will fall from the tree. It is then that the moment comes for us to step in and offer our assistance. I say *offer* assistance because we do not force our services upon anyone. However, in all our experience so far, our offers of help have never been scorned. On the contrary, people are only too glad to leave themselves entirely in our hands.

Incidentally, we three, Edwin, Ruth, and I, have made literally countless friends through the instrumentality of our work. So many of them regard us as the first face upon which they cast their spirit eyes when death had closed their physical eyes. They regarded us then as friends in need, who had come to save them from heaven knows what nameless ordeals, and, if for no other reason than this, our work is repaid a hundredfold by the look of heartfelt relief upon their countenances and by the exuberance of their gratitude as we explain some of the pleasant things that are awaiting them. And never was gratitude more genuine!

The actual process of physical death must be undertaken alone, and in this sense it is a solitary business. But as soon as the spirit body is free then we can begin.

So far I have been speaking of people who are destined for the bright realms of the spirit world. Equally, assistance is offered to those whose lives on earth have brought them to the dark realms. It is a safe rule to say that no person passing into the spirit world at dissolution does so unattended. There is always *someone* there. But in so many cases we are prevented from giving any help by the spiritual state of the soul we are approaching. In fact, approach becomes impossible, and so we can do nothing but watch the soul depart upon its way into darkness. Naturally, if we can perceive the tiniest glimmer of light issuing from such a soul, we do our best to fan it into something more resembling a flame.

You must know that spirituality means light, literally, with us here in the spirit world. And absence of spirituality means darkness. The soul in the latter case will be just a dark image, the darker it is the more repulsive and hideous, like the life it led upon earth and which is the cause of the blackness. But a dark life may have been relieved in some minute instance by a good action, some kind action, and that will provide the small glimmer of light to which I referred. We can work upon that, as it were, recall it to the mind, and try to show to its owner the difference between this tiny gleam and the rest of its dingy, dark habiliments.

If the soul will listen to reason, then we can make some headway, and so increase the light by the owner's willingness to cleanse the rest of himself. If our words fail to affect the soul in any way, then, perforce, we must let it go upon its way until better thoughts and ideas and wishes come upon the soul in its darkness.

You can understand that this is exacting work for us, in spite of the fact that we do not suffer from physical fatigue. Nevertheless, we cannot continue in such enervating conditions without feeling mentally rather jaded, and so we emerge once more into the light of our own realms. In the meantime, others will take our places, so that no transition is left unattended, no matter where it may be, or in what circumstances, or howsoever caused; whether it be upon land, beneath the land; on the sea or under it, or in the air above the earth. We cannot always achieve our purpose in being present; that is not our fault, but that of the person who has just left his physical body behind him.

A person who is uninstructed in spirit truths can be remarkably obstinate in clinging to his old earthly ideas of what exactly should have taken place when he "died." Some may have no views upon the matter whatever, and so may be more amenable to reason and logic. Others may be good folk, but are completely dominated by orthodox religious views, and this type, if anything, is perhaps among the worst of them all to deal with!

There is, over and above these, a certain type of religious mind that causes us a great deal of trouble, and it is associated with those people upon earth whose religion is of a very crude, elementary description, founded upon a literal interpretation of the scriptures according to their own primitive ideas.

They consider themselves among the "elect" who are going to be "gathered up" in some mysterious fashion into the celestial realms, there to be suitably rewarded for their great "faith. Their whole religious concept is just as vague in its content and meaning as is this my description of it. The basis is "faith" in particular scriptural admonitions and precepts and prophecies. They verily believe that their "creed" will see them through their earthly life into the next world. They believe they will be met by a heavenly host and escorted to their home among the "elect."

It never occurs to these people that a life such as they imagine for themselves in heaven would, if realized in all its completeness, become a veritable nightmare to them. They picture themselves spending all eternity in some form of simple worship, which incorporates a vast deal of hymn singing and conversational quotation from the scriptural books.

You can imagine for yourself something of the shock that awaits such souls when they arrive here in the spirit world, to find that they are totally mistaken in the true state of things. At first they will gravitate to others of their own kind, if we find it impossible, for the moment, to convince them of their errors. At length, their home-made "heaven" will begin to bore them, until they become thoroughly dissatisfied with their life and surroundings. Then we can step in and introduce them to a normal, natural way of living in the spirit world.

It is strange—is it not, my good friend?—that we should have to expend so much labor, undertaken by so many of us here, in explaining to people, ordinary, normal, pleasant, amiable people, the very truth of their being alive in every sense of the word!

We have to explain *ourselves* first of all, which may sound stranger still. We have to convince the newly-arrived one that we are not "ghosts," unsubstantial beings whose sole function in the world is to frighten people. We have become accustomed to being asked the question, "Who are *you?*" when we first approach some soul just arrived and in difficulties. And we are obliged to explain that we are very much creatures of "flesh and blood," and that we have come to help them if they will allow us to do so.

Sometimes the homeliness of our attire and its familiar appearance bring some measure of confidence and assurance to their minds. Our voices, too, seem to be perfectly ordinary and recognizable. For you must know that any suggestion of our appearing as "celestial beings" would most likely terrify the newcomer and defeat our purpose before we had even commenced to work. Indeed, we are so very matter-of-fact, displaying no suggestion of religious tendencies in our conversation, and speaking to them and treating them as though their present situation were a perfectly commonplace state of affairs—which it is to us, but not to them—that it is not long before an intelligent, receptive mind will grasp the situation in its fullness, and be glad to resign himself to our care.

You will, no doubt, have heard or read of cases of people being "earthbound" and wondered how this comes about and what "binds" them to the earth.

In such cases where I have accosted earthbound people, I have always ascertained that the soul so circumstanced was totally unaware of any other state of existence to which he could depart from his present surroundings. He was ignorant of other realms higher or lower than that which he was occupying. Usually, these unfortunate people are tied to their earthly environment whatever it may be. That attachment may be one of sentiment, where a great affection was entertained for the earthly home, or place of residence, or work. The attraction may be a morbid one, where some misdeed has been committed which draws back the guilty one to the scene of its perpetration. Perhaps this latter is the most familiar to earth people under the designation of "haunted" places, and many people are puzzled by the fact that in a large number of cases the subject of the "hauntings" has remained in operation for hundreds of years.

What makes the matter still more puzzling is when the individual who is responsible for the "hauntings" has all the appearance of being a goodly soul, without any intention of harming or alarming a single person.

What is it that causes him to stay in this spot for these hundreds of years when, presumably, he could be much better employed elsewhere in the spirit world? The answer is that in many instances he *is* so employed. But you will remember that upon earth there is a familiar saying that it takes all kinds to make a world. Similarly, it takes all kinds to make a spirit world.

Bear that in mind, and remember, too, that a person is exactly the same the moment after he has "died" as he was the moment before. No magical, instantaneous change takes place either of mind or body, We pass into the spirit world with all our earthly likes and dislikes, all our fancies and foibles, all our idiosyncrasies, and with all our religious errors fast upon us. We are just as we were on earth, though it does not follow in every instance that we will behave just as we did on earth. In the spirit world we have more freedom of expression, and gravitating, as we do, to our own temperamental and spiritual kind, we are not diffident of giving open expression to our thoughts and feelings, and thus presenting, at last, a true picture of ourselves as we really are. Some minds are quick to grasp new ideas and new truths. Some are quick to grasp truth in place of falsehood or untruth. People of this mental caliber soon readjust their views, and so become in harmony with their new life and surroundings. They will "settle down" for the time being, at least, in their environment.

A great number show no further interest in their old earthly life and mode of living, but will concentrate all their energies upon the larger world that is opening out before them. But there are people who had, while on earth, and still possess now that they are in the spirit world, a sentimental attachment to some place or building. For some reason with which, strictly speaking, they alone are concerned, they show no particular wish to sever that attachment; their interest remains as strong as when they were dwelling therein on earth. They are keenly sensitive of its welfare and vicissitudes, and they take their leisure hours in constantly visiting and revisiting the scene of their former pleasures or activities. At length a time will come when they will grow tired of these journeyings back and forth, with very little actual purpose behind them beyond satisfying a certain curiosity. Then the visits will cease altogether, and the soul will be really free at last. For such ties have no value in them spiritually when the visitor, who is sometimes seen, sometimes only "felt," and at other times both seen and "felt," merely returns to satisfy his own interest and curiosity.

To return to the earth with the specific purpose of helping former colleagues or friends is another matter altogether. Many such people as I have mentioned to you are simple-minded folk who display a certain stubbornness on occasion, and are consequently deaf to our suggestions of terminating their "haunting" of some particular dwelling on earth. But, in common with us all, if they choose to exercise their free win to its full extent, we are powerless to intervene, and they must pursue their own course. Individuals of this sort are only partially earthbound. They live in their own proper realm in the spirit world, making frequent and solitary, but regular, visits to the place that draws them so powerfully.

The "hauntings" of an unpleasant nature where some crime of violence has been committed, or where some wrong has remained unredressed, fall into a different category altogether. In most instances, individuals remain rooted to the locality. They may still be in the same frame of mind as upon the original occasion of their misdeed. They may be consumed with the desire for vengeance or retribution, or for some form of violence. So strong will be the concentration of mind and so powerful the emotion, that the whole incident or series of incidents will be projected from this harassed mind in the shape of thought-forms, and these will assume the precise details, with exact precision, of the original occurrence. The memory will have recorded the details faithfully, and the mind will have released them, and it can go on releasing them with unfailing exactitude. Any person whose psychic powers are developed—and sometimes those that are not—will see what is taking place before them and thereby causing the "haunting."

Occasionally, so powerful is the thought concentration of the earthbound soul that the whole phenomenon will, as it were, be forced into the earth world for anyone to see or hear who should come within range of the manifestation. That such hauntings should go on for hundreds of years in the same place with similar exactness in each repetition, is not very remarkable when one considers the wide diversity of human minds. The harmless sentimentality of the visitant to old scenes of earthly endeavor can possess a degree of emotional feeling just as strong and binding upon the mind as that of the perpetrator of some crime whose thirst for revenge, shall we say, caused the crime which is now holding him so tenaciously to the earth.

In cases of the latter kind, people on earth could afford the spirit world very valuable assistance in relieving of their burden the minds of these tortured souls, or, at least, in giving them some amelioration of their unhappy condition. But so great a number of these occurrences are treated as something to "investigate," firstly, to see if the alleged haunting is really true, and then, after establishing the fact that something "queer" does take place, to study the thing with the view, if possible, to seeing what it is all about. After that, long reports are made from eyewitnesses' accounts, the veridical nature of the phenomena is proved, and there the matter rests.

In the meanwhile, the soul who has been the cause of this learned investigation still languishes in his misery. If at the very outset the investigators would interrogate the object of the disturbances, and would pray for aid to be sent from the higher realms of the spirit world, not only would unpleasant disturbances be thus terminated, but what is more important, the unhappy cause of them would be helped in his misery and his foot set upon the path of progression.

It is always so much easier, and produces much better results, for people still on earth to tackle these cases in the first instance. The person who is responsible for the haunting is so much nearer the earth, and is consequently more easily approached by you than by us here in the spirit world. When he has fully grasped what has happened and what he is doing, then we can take charge of him and lead him away from the environment that is causing the distress.

The mode of one's entry into the spirit world as a permanent resident is the same in every case—through the severance of the magnetic cord, although the physical cause may vary in such ways as are perfectly familiar to you: accident, illness, or old-age. But what may happen to us immediately after the cord is severed may vary infinitely according to the multiplicity of human temperaments which go to make up the populations of the earth, and according to the wide divergence in degrees of spirituality possessed by the new arrivals. Circumstances diversify individual cases to such an extent that it would require many volumes to recount even a part of the experiences of others in the matter of arrival in the spirit world alone. We can only treat the matter in a broad sense.

Among the physical causes of dissolution it would seem that illness would account for the largest number in normal times. What happens to the individual in such cases depends upon several factors.

For example, the length of the illness, and its painfulness or otherwise, and the mental make-up of the individual. Long illness has a tiring effect upon the spirit body—it would be more accurate to say an inhibiting effect upon the spirit body—and when, at last, the physical body is cast off, the spirit body usually goes to one of the numerous halls of rest with which the spirit world is plentifully supplied. There the new resident will pass into a state of pleasant sleep, ultimately to awake fully refreshed and reinvigorated.

The time, as you regard it, taken to achieve this course of treatment varies, of course, to meet individual requirements. With some a comparatively short space of time will serve; with others it might take months of your earthly time.

In my own case, I was ill for only a brief while upon earth. When I passed into the spirit world I did so without losing consciousness. I was able to gaze upon my physical body which I had just vacated, and a friend and colleague of my earthly days, who had passed on before me, came to me at the instant of my departure from earth, and took me to my new home in the spirit world. After a brief survey of my new abode, my friend recommended that I should take a rest in view of the fact that I had just quitted a final bed of sickness. I did so in my own house. I allowed myself to lapse into a most delightful state of slumber, feeling that I had not a care in the world. When I awoke I felt in a vigorous and perfect state of health such as I had never experienced before. I do not know precisely how long I lay sleeping, but I was told it was very brief; indeed, of much less duration than the illness that had caused my passing into the spirit world.

In considering the painfulness or otherwise of the illness that causes death, I think that the length of the illness and its painfulness could be linked together, for they both give a form of fatigue to the spirit body, though this fatigue must not be thought of in terms of earthly physical fatigue. The two are not really comparable. With us there is no heaviness of the limbs, no aching joints, no leaden weariness that makes the very movement of ourselves a misery to us; nor yet must it be thought that our fatigue is comparable with your earthly mental tiredness, where you have the inability to focus the mind upon anything except for the briefest possible time. Nor, again, do we lack interest in our affairs, or feel restless and ill at ease. The word fatigue is the best that I can find. There really is no word that adequately describes the condition.

With you, who are incarnate, physical energy will be expended during the course of your daily life until such time as it is necessary for you to rest. Rest is essential to you if you are to continue to function upon the material plane of the earth. When you retire to rest and to sleep, and while your spirit body is absent, your physical body is replenished with the energy that keeps you alive and active. Your body is, as it were, charged with force enough to carry you through your day and beyond it, if necessary. It constitutes a reservoir of force.

With us it is different. Force is continuously flowing through us from the source of all life. We are a channel for this inexhaustible energy which flows to us according to our needs of the moment. We have only to ask for a greater supply of force for some special purpose or for the accomplishment of some particular task upon which we are engaged, and it is immediately forthcoming. We have no need to recharge ourselves through the medium of sleep as do you. Our fatigue—for want of that better word—is more in the nature of a desire for a change from what we are doing, whether it be pleasure or work which is occupying our energies.

A desire for a change from what we are doing is a natural one common to both our worlds, yours and ours, but with us prolonged activities never lead to literal tiredness of the limbs or of the mind. We could pursue the course of our work far, far beyond the limits that are imposed upon you of earth without any loss of efficiency in our task. We could, and we do, work for a number of hours that would seem incredibly long to you, without the slightest ill-effect either to ourselves or to our work.

There seems to be an idea among certain schools of thought upon earth that in the spirit world we are employed upon the same work for all eternity. Possibly this strange notion is but a variation of the absurd idea of a spirit life of "eternal rest," upon which I have already spoken to you. The spirit world is not static, neither are all its inhabitants forever occupied upon the same tasks, unremittingly and never changing. The work may never cease, but there are regular occasions when we cease to work. Among the glories of the life in the spirit world are the opportunities for as constant change as taste demands. We do not stagnate, or travel in a groove from which we cannot extricate ourselves. The desire for change of some sort comes upon us—and we change forthwith. That is our fatigue as near as it is possible to describe it to you.

The rest of the newly-arrived person is frequently advisable, or necessary, to allow of adjustment of the spirit body to its new conditions of life. It has been accustomed to being very securely fastened to the physical body where it can receive whatever unpleasantness the physical body may be submitted to during the course of its earthly term. An alert mind can quickly throw off these physical repercussions and adjust itself to the new life. Other types of mind will be slower and more leisurely. The long and painful illness will be one of the unpleasantnesses to which I have just referred, and although an alert mind can soon clear itself of recent experiences, still it may take a little time, and so a period of rest is undergone.

In no sense is the spirit body impaired by any earthly illness that caused its permanent transference to the spirit world. But earthly illness reacts upon the mind, which in turn bedims whatever natural brightness the spirit body may possess. It is purely a matter of thought and has no reference at all to the personal brightness of spiritual progression. No ill-health or illness can take that away. A period of rest will therefore restore the spirit body to its proper and natural tone, both of color and harmony with its life and surroundings.

With us rest is a very elastic term. One may take rest through so many varieties of ways. Indeed, it is perfectly commonplace to see someone busily at work here displaying all the industry in the world, to discover that in reality he is resting! So that anyone may be resting for all there is to show to the contrary.

How is a person affected whose death is sudden and perhaps violent as well, which would include the person who is precipitated into the spirit world without warning, or that knowing the end of earthly life is imminent yet undergoes a violent transition? How would such a person fare?

It calls to mind the phrase that was once such a favorite with certain types of mind: launched into eternity. What dreadful images this stupid phrase must have conjured up in the minds of so many people. The awful tragedy of "death" which all men must face. The terrible uncertainty of what was to happen after they had "departed this life." The fearful prospect of being marched before the Great Dread Judge. Most of them having been told that they were "miserable sinners," the best that could be hoped for would be "mercy," provided that they "believed on" something or other that was so obscure in its meaning that they could not make head or tail of it, but which nevertheless possessed some magic means of "saving" them. Which was it to be—Heaven or Hell? Most probably the latter, from their obvious failure to reach the impossible standard set by their religious "teachers." Of what is there to be frightened in eternity? To us one of the greatest and most glorious truths is the very fact of this same eternity. But of that I will speak in due course. For the moment our question is waiting to be answered.

In speaking of people passing into the spirit world suddenly, you no doubt will recall where, for example, failure of the heart's action is the cause, and where accident or some deliberate action causes an instantaneous transition. In the latter instance you would be forcibly reminded of what takes place during the evil times of war upon the earth. Such transitions as these are not what could be considered in any way normal had other conditions prevailed. Normal transition, from the point of view of the spirit world, is that wherein the spirit body becomes gradually and easily detached from the earthly body in a slow and steady process of separation. The magnetic cord, in such cases, will become detached from the earthly body gently, it will fall away naturally, just as the leaf falls from the tree in the autumn. When the leaf is in full life and vigor it requires a strong action to dislodge it from the tree. And so it is with the spirit body. In the young the cohesion is firm, but it gradually lessens as age increases. When people on earth reach the autumn of their lives, like the leaf of the tree, the spirit body is less firmly attached to the physical body.

One reads of people reaching a great age upon earth, and then one day, in apparently good health, they are found to have "died" in the chair in which they were sitting. They have, in fact, gone quietly to sleep in a normal healthy fashion, and the magnetic cord has separated itself also in a normal healthy fashion. That is an ideal transition. When, therefore, the earthly body suddenly collapses and the organs cease functioning, as in the case of some illnesses, there is not a great deal of shock transmitted to the spirit body.

A person so situated will be in a state of great bewilderment which will be increased by lack of knowledge of the ways of the spirit world. Orthodox religious views will also add their considerable weight to the general confusion of mind. And even in cases where a good sound knowledge of spirit life is possessed there is bound to be some little momentary confusion in the mind. That is impossible to avoid. The mind may have been focused exclusively upon material affairs, and it would require a second or two to apprehend what has happened—to collect the faculties, to use the earthly term. How easy our work in the spirit world would be if all transitions were in the latter category.

It is when we come to transitions where the physical body is literally disintegrated, blown into fragments in a second of time, that the greatest distress and discomfort are caused to the spirit body. The magnetic cord is snapped off, or wrenched away, almost as though a limb of the physical body were torn from its socket. The spirit body finds itself suddenly dispossessed of its earthly tenement, but not before the physical shock of disintegration has been transmitted to the spirit body. Not only is there extreme bewilderment, but the shock has something of a paralyzing effect. The person so situated may be incapable of movement for the time being. In many instances sleep will intervene. He will remain in the place of his dissolution, but we come to his rescue, and carry him away to one of the rest homes specially provided for such cases. Here he will receive treatment from experts, and ultimately the patient will recover his full health beyond any shadow of doubt. The cure is certain and complete. There is no such thing as a relapse or a recurrence of the indisposition. Perhaps the most difficult part of the treatment comes when a full consciousness is restored and the patient begins to ask questions!

What effect, you might ask, does maiming of the physical body have upon the spirit body? None whatever, as far as the full complement of limbs and organs is concerned. Disintegration may be sudden, or it may take a number of earthly years through the normal processes of decomposition. Whichever way it may take place, the result is the same—a complete, or almost complete, disappearance of that physical body. The physical body is corruptible, but the spirit body is incorruptible. And what applies to the whole in the latter also applies to the limbs and organs; in fact, to every part of the spirit body. The loss of one or more limbs of the earthly body, the possession of diseased organs, physical malformations, any subnormal or supernormal conditions of the physical body, any or all of these states leave the spirit body entirely unaffected. Whatever has happened to the physical body, the spirit body will always maintain its complete anatomy.

But the spirit body can assume very hideous *spiritual* malformations. These have nothing whatever to do with the formation of the physical body, but are due solely to the kind of life that its owner has led upon earth. The malformations are various expressions of the hideousness that is resident within the mind, on many occasions that have found their outward expression in evil deeds of every description. These, however, do not come within the purview of our question.

People who believe that after their "death" there will be a bodily "resurrection" are often times puzzled in mind as to what will happen if they are not possessed of their full number of limbs, or, what is worse but more common, if their earthly body completely vanished in the course of time, or is instantaneously disintegrated. The trouble comes from the use of the word resurrection. Such people imagine that the normal procedure is for the physical body to rise up from its grave if it should possess one—at some future and unspecified date, whereupon it would find itself in the spirit world. It is fondly supposed that missing limbs would be restored and impaired faculties renewed, or if necessary, the physical body would be reintegrated after the fragments, in some inconceivable manner, have been collected and reassembled after their total disappearance.

The whole conception is, of course, fantastic. Once dissolution has taken place, the physical body is finished with as far as its former owner is concerned. It has no place whatever in the spirit world. It cannot enter there. And there is no magical process in existence that can so alter its constituents or form or mode of being as to be able to penetrate into spirit realms of any degree of height or lowness, of light or darkness, whatsoever. A profession of faith that such a thing is possible is of no avail; it simply cannot happen because it is against the laws of the spirit world. And these are natural laws, not laws that have been enacted by someone and can therefore be suspended or annulled at will.

To carry the matter still further, there is no such thing as resurrection of either the physical body *or of the spirit body*. As far as the spirit body is concerned, there is no "rising." There is simply a continuity of existence. From the moment that life is given to the physical body, the spirit body is also in existence. The earthly body comes to the end of its life; it ceases to function and so to provide an earthly vehicle for the spirit body, and the spirit body is released and *continues* its life in the spirit world, in its proper element and its true home. No resurrection has taken place. Nothing of the sort is needed. It has nothing to wait for, no Day of Judgment or other unpleasant prospect. The spirit body is free at last, unencumbered by its heavy earthly body; free to move and breathe, and enjoy the beauties of the realms of light.

And now, I think we have lingered long enough upon the threshold of the spirit world, and it is time that we passed through the great portal into the realms of light, where we can discuss other matters not so closely connected perhaps with the actual dissolution of the physical body.

Let us consider the spirit body and discuss some questions of its life in the spirit world, and perhaps in the process we may be able to smooth away a difficulty or two.

CHAPTER TWO

THE SPIRIT WORLD

I MENTIONED THE word eternity to you just now. It is a word that implies so much but that in reality conveys so little to the average earthly mind.

The earth dweller would say, in effect, that eternity is like immortality—you cannot prove it. How can it possibly be proved that a certain state of existence—namely, that of the spirit world—will continue forever, *without end*, to employ perhaps a more emphatic term? Just so. It is a difficulty that we all appreciate in the spirit world. And I would hasten to say that I am not going to attempt to prove it!

But I can do this. I can set before you one or two considerations that will serve to draw your mind towards the major differences between your incarnate state of existence upon earth and our discarnate state of existence in the spirit world. And in doing so there may emerge just a faint glimmering of what the word eternity can suggest.

If you will give the subject a brief moment's thought you will be forcibly reminded of the *impermanence* of life on earth. Living, as you do, with reality—for so you would term it—manifested to you so very obviously in life itself and all that goes to constitute living upon earth, with, for example, the buildings that surround you, the ground upon which you walk, the food you eat, the clothing wherewith you cover yourself, your daily occupations and recreations, your comings and goings over short distances and long; confronted as you are with all these evidences of being—and many others besides—yet you know that upon one day in your life the moment will come when you must leave all these "realities" behind you to undergo the natural process of the dissolution of the physical body—in a word, when you will "die."

But before that event occurs, and during the whole of your life on earth, you will observe the process of disintegration going on all around you. Firstly, yourself. You will become older, the signs of which are sufficiently familiar to you to need no mention of them. Your clothes are constantly wearing out and need replacement. The furnishings within your home undergo the same process and require the same remedy. Your very house is in a constant state of decay, though not always visible to the eye, until one day repairs of one sort or another will be demanded. Call to mind, also, the many articles of daily use that by accident you can break—even your own bones are not immune from that! So that there is constantly going on around you this action of decay. Everything about you on earth is corruptible. There is, then, a palpable state of *impermanence*. However much the decay may be arrested, you still have the certain fact of the eventual termination of your earthly life, which in itself sets the seal upon mundane impermanence.

Now let us contrast all this with life in the spirit world and with the dwellers therein. Perhaps one of the most heartening, reassuring of feelings that we in the spirit world can harbor is the feeling of *permanence*. Firstly, as to ourselves. We are incorruptible. We have shed our earthly and corruptible bodies as we entered the spirit world, and we stand as we truly are, incorruptible. We do not age. On the contrary, *we grow younger* if we should happen to have passed our prime of life when we left the earth. That in itself is something in which to make one rejoice, but most of all, to make one feel secure and *permanent*. Our clothes do not wear out, or deteriorate in any way. Our homes are governed by the same law of incorruptibility. In my own home, for instance, I have never been obliged to make replacements or renovations in any single detail, whether of interior furnishings or structurally, since I first came to take up my residence here upon leaving the earth.

And it is the same with all other folk in these realms. I have made alterations, certainly; we all do that, but not because of decay or breakage, or wear and tear. What alterations we make are carried out for the pleasure they may bring to us and our friends.

The imposing buildings which are such an outstanding feature of these realms—among so many outstanding features—are as clean and fresh and sparkling as upon the day when they were first erected. And when I tell you that no spot of decay or deterioration or dirt or dinginess can ever be detected upon any one of them, and when I also tell you that a great many of them have been standing there for *thousands of years*, I think you will agree with me that we are fully justified in considering ourselves and all that is about us and surrounding us in the agreeable light of *permanence*.

These few details I have given you are not one tithe of the numberless signs of permanence which are forever presenting themselves before our minds. So that, if we cannot prove that our life here in the spirit world will continue for ever, we have abundant evidence for entertaining the strong probability that it *will* do so. And I assure you that nothing can give us cause for greater satisfaction than that. For us the words, "for all eternity," would form a fitting clause in our charter of spiritual freedom.

I have often spoken of the magnificent buildings in the spirit world, but I have not so far made any reference to the particular form of architecture they favor. In fact, we have all types, from the earliest forms known to you on earth down to those of the present day. A type that is a great favorite among us here is that which is commonly known to you as Gothic. But all ages are represented. It would not be accurate to say they are reproduced, because here we can call upon people of a former age to erect buildings in the exact pattern of those of their own times. Beautiful though the various styles of architecture may be, and they *are* beautiful, yet to my mind the materials of which the buildings are composed, with their exquisite colorings, are still more lovely. Even the plainest structure, one that is perhaps almost devoid of external embellishment, is nonetheless a delight to see. All buildings, from the unpretentious cottage to any one of the stately halls of learning, look clean and fresh. But in addition, the materials of which they are constructed have a semi-translucence, an alabaster-like appearance with a superb variety of delicate colorings that seem to change their tones as the beholder changes his viewpoint. Some of them give the impression of being composed of mother-of-pearl in the most pleasing and restful shades of colors and tints. These colors are, of course, neither too vivid nor too brilliant where buildings are in fairly close proximity to one another. When more widely separated they can take on a more brilliant hue without disturbing the harmony of, or conflicting with, an immediate neighbor.

Whatever form of spirit world architecture you may care to consider, you must always remember the two extra factors of the materials of which they are made, and their wide range of gentle colorings.

There is one class of building that we do not favor, and that is the great gaunt barrack-like structure, rectangular or of any other shape, with rows upon rows of cheerless windows. Such buildings would not comport with the warmth and geniality of these realms, and would seem altogether too cold and forbidding, in spite of the luster of our building materials and their diversified colors, to find any response from the dwellers here. And without the cordial response of the inhabitants of these realms nothing would remain in evidence very long. It is because we like what we have here that we have it, and that it survives.

If I were to say that we have in the spirit world that type of domicile known to you on earth as "family mansions" it would no doubt conjure up in your mind the private ownership that is entailed in possessing a large mansion on earth.

Of course, there is ownership in the spirit world. Indeed, why should there not be? Ownership, however, is gained in a different way from that of the earth. There is only one right of ownership in the spirit world, and that is the spiritual right. None other will suffice; none other even exists. According to our spiritual right, gained by the kind of life we have lived upon earth, and afterwards according to our progression in the spirit world, so can we possess.

Many people arrive here to find themselves richly and abundantly provided with spirit-world possessions that are far in excess of those which they owned upon earth. And the contrary is often the case. Possessors of great earthly effects can find themselves spiritually poor when they come here. But they can gain the right to possess more, far more than they ever could own on earth, and of far greater value and beauty.

But to return to the large mansion-houses of which I spoke. These are not erected through a wish to indulge a mere desire of possession, though naturally there is nothing discordant with the harmony and laws of these realms to take a delight in whatever we may possess, from the smallest trifle to the largest building. These mansions are usually built up from smaller houses by making structural additions from time to time. But the latter are made with a very distinct purpose, a purpose that has for its intent not the enlargement of the building for its own sake, but to carry out some useful, interesting, or helpful intention that will be of service to many others in these realms.

One particular house I have in mind first began its existence as a moderate-sized dwelling somewhat similar to my own home. The owner of it is an artist and musician, and when he first started his new life here, he had a great ambition to make his house a small center for other artists and musicians, a meeting-place where kindred souls could forgather, the artists to discuss their art as it exists in the spirit world, and the musicians to perform such works as their fancy chose.

Gradually this little scheme took upon itself larger dimensions, far larger than were originally contemplated, until the house became much too small and insignificant for the worthy purpose to which it was being devoted. Additional rooms were built, and the whole house was extended in one direction and another. Finally, an apartment was added that resembled the "great hall" customary in large mansion-houses on the earth. Since that time it has extended its hospitality to scores of friends, and there is never a period when the house is devoid of visitors. It is a beautiful residence to look upon; a delightful one to reside in, and we have often joined one or other of the numerous assemblages there when we have taken a holiday from our work.

Instances could be multiplied where such great mansions have their existence here, each of them devoted to some serviceable purpose for the entertainment of us all. They are not halls of instruction, the latter being of an entirely different nature both architecturally and in the purpose for which they are used.

The mansion-houses are the homes of individuals in precisely the sense that my house is my own home, but their great size is due solely to the design for which they were erected, namely, hospitality and entertainment, recreation and pleasure.

As to the ownership of the ground upon which these houses stand, the ownership, such as I have explained to you, resides with the occupier of the house. As the house is extended in size, so also is the area of the grounds which are attached to it. The larger the mansion, the larger the tract of ground which surrounds it. Anything in the nature of cramping would materially detract from the grandeur of the edifice.

All these mansions are set in the most beautiful park land where it is possible and permissible to wander to one's heart's content. There are no petty restrictions, no exerting of "rights," no prohibiting notices, for there is nothing—and no one—to prohibit! The inhabitants of the mansions know that there will be no unwarrantable intrusion simply because we observe all the courtesies that it is common to expect among those who respect each other for their spiritual worth.

The woods and park lands are a dream of enchantment to wander in, and many are the occasions when we have strolled through them, or rested beneath the trees, while the deer, friendly and unafraid, have come to us and made themselves acquainted. They are beautiful creatures, enjoying such freedom as only the spirit world can give them, and they form an integral part of the superb landscape.

"Do we have churches in the spirit world?" is a question, I am persuaded, that will form itself in many minds, because what you call the "afterlife" is associated, in some form or another, with religion. An "afterlife" is a concomitant of religion, and while the state known vaguely as "heaven" may be a tenuous reward for the "good," there is always "hell" with which to threaten the "wicked."

If an ecclesiastical edifice is an indispensable adjunct to religion upon earth, then the establishment of churches would benefit the peculiar state of the "afterlife," whatever it may be. That is what many people think, and this attitude of mind finds outward expression in the spirit world. Yes, there are churches here, and very beautiful they are.

They are, of course, in keeping with all other buildings, being constructed of the same kind of materials, and having the same degree of care lavished upon them. Some people are considerably surprised to find such places here when they make their advent into spirit lands. I can number myself among them. Others, as I have hinted, more or less expected to find churches fully established in whatever "heaven" to which their earthly religion had safely conducted them. The discovery helped to make them feel more "at home" in their new surroundings, and they very soon become active members of the community attached to the church.

In these realms one will find churches of most of the denominations with which you are familiar. My own former religion is fully represented, and what is known as the Established Church also. But there are others besides, each with its own buildings. I have been into many of them. They all possess a calm, restful atmosphere in which it is very pleasant to spend a few thoughtful moments. When there is stained glass in the windows beautiful effects are created by the external light as it pours in from all quarters, while the rays meet and blend into colorful rainbow shafts.

Some of the churches are exact replicas of buildings that are in existence now upon earth. Others are what the earth would call restorations of once famous abbey churches, and so forth, that have fallen into ruins on earth. Here they have risen in all their architectural glory to grace the countryside with their presence.

The church buildings vary in size from what would be considered a small chapel to great cathedral churches, all of them erected and upheld by their devoted congregations.

How such things come to exist in the spirit world may cause you some wonder, since one would have thought there was no place for further religious differences and creedal distinctions. Most people do so think, but there remains a large residue who are still firmly wedded to their old earthly religious persuasion. Religious beliefs can take a very secure hold upon the minds of some persons. When they arrive in these realms they are fully convinced that their particular beliefs are alone responsible for their being where they are, which they regard as "heaven," their just reward for their true faith. The fact that they led good lives in the service of others on earth they would sweep aside as of very little account in the great reckoning which has taken place. It is their faith, and their faith alone, they aver, which has brought them to these realms of heaven. They cannot be made to see that their great faith has availed them nothing; that they are where they are, not because of their faith, not in spite of it, but utterly regardless of it, and that it is their life of service to their neighbor, just that and that alone, which has brought its reward. The faith persists, sometimes elaborated with ritual and ceremonial, sometimes left plain and unadorned, simple and rather crude. And while it so persists their spiritual progression and evolution are at a standstill. They remain where they are in an environment of their creation.

The laws that allow of their religious practices are strict and must be obeyed. Adherents to each form of religion must confine their practices solely to themselves. There must be no endeavoring to convert others to their beliefs. Their outlook, as you can imagine, is foreshortened. They can and they do enjoy their "heaven," homemade though it be, until one day spiritual enlightenment will come to them. Then they will emerge from their restricted, circumscribed life into the greater world that has been round about them all the time, had they but realized it. They will leave their useless creeds and dogmas behind them, and march forward upon the road of spiritual progression and evolution. They will then regard their churches as beautiful structures put to an entirely wrong use. They now see that as they regularly stepped out of their churches at the conclusion of a service, they stepped out into a world of truth, of truth which was not resident within the church's four walls.

Now a word as to the ministers who conduct the services in these churches. They are men who were clergymen on earth. There is no lack of ministers for different churches. In fact, the supply is largely in excess of the actual demand. But that makes no real difference, since a number of ministers can work together in the same church, and so provide a fuller and more elaborate ceremonial in such establishments where it is performed.

After their earthly labors, their work here seems very light to them. Indeed, they have precious little to do beyond conducting their services. But then, you must remember that they consider themselves in "heaven," and to take a few services and spend the remainder of the time in comparative idleness is simply the "eternal rest" of which they spoke so glibly when they were upon earth. The members of their congregation are eternally resting, too, so that they are happy enough in their own limited way. They have arrived where they are through the kind of life they led when on earth, and here they have stayed while a sort of spiritual somnolence has descended upon them. They live that life of "piety" which they thought so much about, and they are thankful for the church's help in getting them where they are.

The clergy are of all ranks in ecclesiastical orders, from learned prelates to simple parish clergymen. We have attended several of the services in these churches and listened to the sermons. It was an interesting experience.

Orthodox religion upon earth has much, very much to answer for. It forges many spiritual fetters which bind up the minds of countless souls upon earth, so that when they come here, we in the spirit world have to find means to strike off the irons that shackle them, so to release them to that freedom of spirit which is the natural, right, and proper mode of living in these lands.

When the earth becomes truly and completely enlightened in the knowledge of life in the spirit world, all these churches will be put to a different use. They will cease to be repositories of creeds and dogmas, and become true temples of the spirit world. And in the true temples of the spirit world something very different from what you call "communal worship" takes place.

In the center of the city in these realms there is a great temple, a magnificent structure. It forms the very hub of the city from which everything radiates in every direction. It is a huge edifice, capable of seating thousands of us without any fear of crowding or other unpleasant conditions. It is encompassed by the most beautiful gardens, and as soon as one comes within the precincts one feels the most astonishing flow of power that emanates not only from the great wealth of flowers, but from the very building itself. This outpouring of force never diminishes.

Now, this is a temple of thanksgiving, not of worship as the earth understands it and professes to practice it. We do not congregate here to offer up so-called "sacrifices"; nor do we perform elaborate ritual and ceremonial. Indeed, we do not perform either the one or the other at any time. We are not wearied by long and mostly unintelligible readings from ancient writers of a date so remote that they have no application to our present purposes and needs. We do not recite gloomy extracts from psalms which the majority of people do not understand. We do not sing hymns with whose sentiment we are either entirely out of tune or disbelieve in altogether. And lastly, we are not treated to the recitation of long, wordy, fulsome prayers that mostly breathe blatant flattery in their every sentence, and propound the most abstruse theological doctrines, as to the meaning of which one is utterly at fault. We perform none of these useless exercises. Instead, we meet here on special occasions, not by rule, not by habit, not because it is a duty, not because it is the "right thing to do"; we meet here not because God "demands" corporate worship as His right, not because some spurious authority proclaims that we must do so—or take the consequences.

We meet because on the special occasions to which I have just referred most illustrious beings from the higher realms come to visit us in this temple, beings who are close to the Great Source of all life and light. They bring with them some of the transcendental fragrance of those higher states of existence, and we are permitted to bask, as it were, in the radiance of the power and light they bring. Such power and light are partly of themselves and partly from their exalted realms, but chiefly from the Great Source of all.

The principal visitant on these occasions gathers together our heartfelt thanks for all that is given to us, for all that we possess, and he transmits them to the Giver.

Such a "service" is simple and unpretentious, and above all things it is short. Most of these gatherings last not much longer than fifteen minutes or so of earthly time. But into that brief space of time is concentrated an act of inspiring beauty such as the longest, most elaborate, and most spectacular church ceremonial upon earth could never achieve in hours of pontifical pageantry with little or nothing underlying it.

We can please ourselves whether we shall be present or not, and we are not thought any the worse for being absent. Sometimes many of us *are* absent upon important work at the time of these visits, but we enjoy the benefit of them on another occasion, and in the meantime our thoughts go out to the visitants. But it is the same in this as in all things here. Once you have experienced some of the delights of these realms you never wish to forgo further such experiences, if it can possibly be helped.

We have other and smaller temples distributed throughout the realms, where there is carried on upon a smaller scale the same description of visitation that takes place in the great central temple. Some of the smaller temples are fashioned exactly like the churches with whose form you are familiar upon earth. This is an ideal realized—a church as you know it, devoted to its true purpose, and not merely a stage upon which is enacted a great deal of worthless ceremonial which has no spiritual significance and certainly no spiritual effect.

Upon earth an act of religious "worship" implies in the minds of most folk an act of propitiation to a God who constantly demands it as His right. The Great Father of the Universe then ceases to be a Father and becomes an omnipotent being of uncertain temperament and most uncertain temper. Self-abasement, conciliation, worship, adoration, and a multiplicity of other emotions are what orthodox religions tell you *must* be your attitude towards the Great Creator. And to crown this gross and libelous conception of the Father of the Universe, you are told that you should—indeed, you *must*—love Him.

Orthodoxy, in one form or another, has claimed a monopoly of the "life hereafter," and therefore all that appertains to it has been regarded in a strictly religious sense. The spirit world has thus become a world of piety, of sanctity, of righteousness—how the latter word is relished by some types of churchmen! Heaven, these same churchmen would say, is a holy place, a place sanctified by the presence of angels and saints, where a continuous stream of worship ascends to the Great Throne above. And so on earth you must have Divine Worship, and it is the *duty* of every citizen, according to his religious persuasion to attend once a week at some place of worship. A great many do so without the remotest notion of what they are doing or the reason for doing it. They have only the crudest ideas concerning a Supreme Being, such ideas as they have are derived from their religious teachers.

At last, when they pass into the spirit world, they bring all their crude notions with them. But as there are no laws here against thinking what you like, they continue so to think along the same old lines. Perhaps it would be more accurate to say that they do not think at all. But we who have our spiritual freedom know just what the term worship is worth.

We do not worship, as the earth understands the term. We pour out our eternal thanks for the happiness that is ours, a happiness that is itself magnified by the thought and the knowledge that still greater happiness lies ahead of us all. We are consumed with the deepest and truest affection for the Great Being who so lavishly bestows so many good things upon us.

After this slight digression, let us return to our discussion of architecture. Of all the types of buildings to be found in the spirit world, and those which will interest my friends on earth, the most numerous, by far, are the dwelling houses, the private houses and cottages in which we live. They are of all kinds known to you on earth. But the appearance of our houses is very different from the appearance of earthly houses. The principal distinction is, of course, in the building materials, as I have indicated to you in the case of the churches here.

Although we have houses constructed of brick or of stone, as well as the half-timbered variety which is so popular here, your mind will inevitably be drawn to your own acquaintance with such buildings upon earth. But bear in mind what I have told you about the quality of the materials, with their particular and colorful external appearance, and you will see wherein lies the very great difference between your houses and ours. But there are other and important distinctions.

You must know, then, that we are never crowded for space here. You will never see rows upon rows of dwellings, each contiguous with its neighbor upon both sides, each built upon precisely the same plan and design, and altogether presenting to the eye a dreary, unimposing, unimaginative line of depressing uniformity. In these realms each house stands completely detached in its own grounds or garden. There is adequate space in which to move freely around and about the house without the constant feeling of being hemmed in.

Of the gardens surrounding our houses I will speak to you in a moment or so.

In the spirit world we are not governed—or hampered—by certain conditions of the first importance which must be considered when building an earthly house. Firstly, upon the outside of our houses we have no unsightly pipes to carry off rainwater or the water that is used for domestic purposes; nor do we have gutterings upon the edges of the roof. We have no rain here— or snow. So that feature will be absent in our houses, and they look all the better for it, as you can imagine.

Now as regards the aspect of our houses. We have no need to think about which point of the compass our residence shall face. With you upon earth, it is the desire of most folk to obtain as much of the sun's light and warmth as possible, hence the desire that the home shall face towards the sun, with the principal rooms situated on the sunny side of the house. But here, the sun shines perpetually, a great central sun, and it shines with equal intensity from all directions. Its light penetrates with the same constant luminosity into every room in the house, irrespective of the room's position. The front of the house will be as bright during every moment of its existence—I cannot say during every moment of the day, because we have no day, and therefore the phrase in its earthly sense becomes meaningless from our point of view—the front of the house will always be as bright as the back.

And in speaking of the back of the house, here again I can show you a notable difference between our houses and yours. Strictly speaking, our houses have no backs to them as do yours. With you, the chief entrance is usually situated in the front, and architectural features are more pronounced in front than they are at the rear of the house. With our dwellings we make no such distinction, chiefly because the interior disposition of our homes omits certain features that are superfluous in the domestic life of the spirit world. As you know, we have no need for food and drink, so that we do not require the indispensable earthly kitchen. The space, therefore, that would upon earth be occupied by this culinary necessity, is devoted to other purposes in the spirit world homes. We have no lack of uses to which we can put such rooms.

I am giving you this description of our homes in a somewhat detailed form. Although many of you may be cognizant of the fact that we have houses in the spirit world, yet many important considerations are apt to be overlooked touching these houses of ours. Such details may seem trivial to some minds, unworldly of a moment's thought, yet, to others the import of what I am telling you, and of what I am going to tell you, will present itself in all its fullness.

These very details help to make up our life in the spirit world because they concern our homes, and our homes concern our lives, *just as they do with you.* And that is my very point. You who are upon earth do not know what it is to live, really to *live.* And you will never know until you come here for all time. So that it is only by comparing some of the "trivial" details of our respective modes of living that you can gather any kind of idea of this perfect land in which I live. Merely to give a broad sketch of our life in the spirit world might be satisfactory as far as it goes, but it would leave a great deal unsaid. Much detail would be missing, and it would thus be left to your imagination and speculation to supply the missing information necessary to make a fuller and more comprehensive picture.

To wave aside such particulars as I am giving you because they seem trivial and very earthly and unworthy of consideration when "heaven" is under discussion, is to hold a totally wrong conception of spirit lands. We are live people living in a beautiful land, a land far more solid than the earth. We love the countryside and the city; we love our houses and gardens; we are blessed with delightful friends. But the country and the city; the houses and the gardens; and, lastly, our friends have more substance about them than can be found upon earth, and this substance is made up of such details as I am describing to you.

It is of no use assuming a lofty attitude—as do so many people of earth— and say, in effect, that if "heaven" is like that, why then, it is no better than the world in which we are living now. Or, at least, it is not much better, with its houses and churches, and rivers, and so forth. I would ask such people to be honest with themselves, to be truthful with themselves, and consider, if they do not like the things I am sketching to you, to formulate clearly and distinctly in their minds exactly what they *would* like. In other words, to specify, *exactly and in detail,* just what they want and just what they expect in their mode and form of life after they have "died."

At least I can give them this hint: from long experience I can positively assert that these particular people of whom I am speaking would be thoroughly miserable in the "heaven" fashioned from their ideas of what "heaven" ought to be. Many such people have told me that they were profoundly thankful to find things as they are and *not* as they stupidly thought things ought to be.

Once again, I am afraid, I have digressed. But I have been urged that it is necessary to stress the fact that the spirit world is more real and its inhabitants more alive than the earth and its inhabitants can ever be. And, moreover, I must stress the fact that the world and the life I am trying to describe to you are not the impossible imaginings of pure Utopianism. The spirit world is a *real* world, peopled with *real* individuals.

Life upon earth is composed of many items, and they are familiar to you as part of everyday life. So it is with us here. Now think for yourself just how many such items will constitute one day in your earthly life. Begin with the moment of your rising in the morning, and continue until you return to your bed at night. You will be surprised at the sum total of details consisting of various actions and experiences. It is the same with us here, but with us all those harassing and troublous minutiae of daily life are absent.

And now let us return to the house which I was describing for you.

As you have seen, by the omission of certain features necessary in your earthly houses, we are enabled to have greater space in our houses and to devote it to much pleasanter occupations and purposes.

It might be queried: what do you actually do with the extra rooms now that you have them? The answer is a simple one: we use them! They are not merely "spare" rooms, useful when a visitor comes to stay with us, or convenient to use as a lumber room. We have no lumber!

Let us examine the matter more closely. From whichever quarter of the house one may look, there is a magnificent view to be seen. Here, then upon the ground floor are the possibilities of a number of distinct and separate viewpoints from which to see the beautiful countryside. The number of rooms upon the ground floor is amply justified by the different views that are to be obtained from them, apart altogether from the variety in the planning and arrangement in the rooms themselves and the several uses to which they may be put.

Now let us mount the stairs and investigate the upper regions. The first thing we shall want to do is to gaze out of the window from our new and higher point of vantage at the same glorious countryside that surrounds us. Apartments which, on earth, would be bedrooms are, in the spirit world houses, used as sitting-rooms or living rooms, or utilized for whatever purpose takes your fancy—a study, perhaps, or for some form of recreation and amusement. Our friends will like to come and see us in these or in any other of our rooms, and we often find that our friends have a strong predilection for one or other of the apartments, which affords them pleasure in some way. And that alone is sufficient justification for our having that particular room. They may like our individual style of decoration in any or all of the rooms, and that, too, will add to their joy.

As far as the rooms themselves are concerned, they will vary just as much as do those in earthly houses, both in their size and their appointments. The beauty of the building materials is not confined merely to externals. Every fitting, every fixture (to use familiar terms), every thread of upholstery, the carpets on the floors, all are alike beautiful. The chairs in which we sit, in fact, the furniture in general, are in keeping.

You who have only seen earth world furniture can have no possible conception of the richness of spirit world furniture.

We have no mass-production methods; each piece of furniture, from the simplest article to the most elaborate, is the work of a master craftsman whose pride in his work is only exceeded by our pride in the great dispensation that can provide such treasures for our greater joy and happiness. Much of the furniture which I have since added to my home contains some of the most exquisite carving it is possible to imagine; such carving, indeed, one could never have believed to exist. Even the simplest piece of furniture can be so treated as to make it fit for a king—to use the old expression.

There is absolute freedom of choice as to what type of house one shall inhabit. Once you have earned the right to own a house which is to be your home, you are at liberty to choose just the style of domicile that pleases you most. It may be one that you have longed for all your life upon earth, but thus far you have been unable to gratify your long-cherished desire. Here in the spirit world your wishes are at length fulfilled. Or you may wish to have your spirit home in the same style as your earthly home, if by chance the latter suited you and brought you contentment and satisfaction. That is what I did, not because my old earthly home was particularly beautiful. It was quaint—it still is—and it suited my temperament and desires, and I grew attached to it. When I came to the spirit world I found my new home to be the exact counterpart of my ancient earthly home, but with all the various alterations made to it which I had been unable to carry out upon earth, and which I had been desirous of doing, and no doubt would have done eventually had I not left the earth.

Houses, again, vary in size, from the small but picturesque cottage to the larger mansion-houses that I have already touched upon. One must not be misled by appearances in regard to the size of dwellings here. That is a rule I learnt very early in my life in the spirit world. Frequently, what on earth would be termed a "humble" cottage, is here the home of a celebrity in some particular branch of human endeavor, a name that perhaps was a household word on earth. In the spirit world it is most unsafe to judge of the inmate by the size or shape or style of his dwelling. It is not that the owner of the cottage or small house is glad to live thus after living on earth in some rather palatial residence. It is rather that the charm of the cottage type of dwelling appeals to him, and no one will dispute his right to do as he pleases, and he will exercise that right still further when it comes to the matter of internal arrangements of whatever nature.

For example, we have no use for fireplaces in our houses as a means of warming the room. We have no winter or autumn or spring in these realms. We have only the glories of perpetual summer. Wintertime on earth can have its beauties and grandeur in the countryside, with its leafless trees and dark earth, with the mist upon the landscape and the feeling of quietness while all nature seems to sleep. But winter can also have its miseries and unpleasantness. The bitter cold, the storms of wind and rain, the fog that descends and narrows the earth till distance is lost. Certain it is that you have the spring and summer to help to compensate for these trials, but who is there who would not wish to prolong the earthly summer far and beyond its allotted period, if it were possible? Now, if you were to take the most perfect summer's day upon earth that you can recall to your mind, in so far as the weather itself were concerned, you would still be far, far below the splendor of the heavenly summer of these realms. And with us every day is summertime.

Incidentally, we never become tired of it. I have not found one single, solitary individual in these regions who has at any time expressed the wish for a change of weather. When you come here and sample it for yourself, you will feel the same about it, I am certain. If not, then you will be the one interesting exception that will prove the rule!

You can see how this will affect not only our lives but our homes as well. Our windows and doors can always remain wide open; there is a genial warmth penetrating into every nook and corner of our houses, just as the light diffuses its rays throughout. There is therefore no need to consider what means of heating we shall employ when ordering the disposition of our home. But a fireplace can itself be ornamental and pleasing to the eye, and for this reason you will find them in many a house. But other people prefer to dispense with them altogether. Their absence in no way spoils the general appearance of the apartment.

In their early days in the spirit world people will often have fireplaces in their homes, but as time goes on and they realize the permanence of the glorious summer, they abolish them. It is purely a matter of choice, and we can all suit ourselves in the matter. But whatever we do, we shall not be considered eccentric if we wish to indulge some fancy. Our friends will recall *their* early days in the spirit world when they were similarly situated, and, accordingly, we shall have their sympathetic support and co-operation in the fulfillment of our desires, whatever they may be.

And now an important matter arises. How do we arrange for the maintenance of our houses? By which I mean: who does the cleaning for us, and generally looks after things?—that is, those of us who need such help.

This is another point which irritates some minds. The incarnate person, upon the mention of spirit world houses, immediately thinks of them in terms of cleaning and upkeep, and the idea of houses in the spirit world then becomes distasteful.

Here again arises a confusion between your world and ours. Recollect what I have said about our world being incorruptible, and you will see at once that the two words *dust* and *dirt*, which are such a nightmare to those of my friends on earth who have the care of their own homes in their hands, simply cannot have any meaning in the spirit world. Dust and dirt are merely disintegration in progress, and so, where you have no disintegration, as in the spirit world, so you will have no dust and dirt.

Every house, here in these realms, is of a cleanliness where immaculate is the only term with which to describe it. Without the means to cause the dirt, you cannot have the dirt. With you on earth the gradual but persistent process of decay will always show itself in dust and dirt. You cannot avoid it. The most you can do is to invent and provide mechanical means with which to clear it away. But it will return and continue to return. I am, I know, stating what is a painfully obvious fact to so many good people, but I must do so to emphasize one of the outstanding qualities of our homes in this spirit world, namely, their superlative and everlasting cleanliness. In this respect, therefore, our homes will require no attention throughout the whole period of their existence, and that may be hundreds of years of your time. A house wholly unoccupied for such a protracted period would be, at the end of that time, as immaculate as on the first day of its erection. And that entirely without the least attention having been paid to it.

The fabric of the house comes under the same conditions, and these conditions are a law. We have no winds in the spirit world that will wear away the stones or bricks of which a house is built, nor do we have a smoke-laden atmosphere which win eat into the surface of our buildings or cause them to crumble away into dust. We have no rains to cause rot and rust to set in, and so to require various replacements. All our possessions within doors, our furniture and our hangings, our personal belongings, such as our books, all alike are subject to the same splendid law. They cannot deteriorate, receive damage, become soiled; the colors in our hangings and upholsteries cannot fade or become shabby. Things cannot get broken or cracked with age. We cannot lose our small possessions by mislaying them. The floor-coverings on which we walk can never become worn out with constant tread of feet.

And there are people who will say: why, the spirit world has houses with furniture, and so on. It is scarcely better than life on earth! Scarcely better than life on earth, indeed! Very well. Such people are at liberty to spend their spirit life in a field, if they so wish, but for me, and for millions like me, I find immense contentment and pleasure in owning a house to be occupied under perfect conditions, some of which I have recounted to you.

We have spent some little time considering the house itself. Let us now wander out and inspect the gardens or grounds round about our homes. But before doing so I would like to revert to a subject which is not unconnected with the gardens themselves.

I have already remarked that we are never hungry, from which it might be inferred that our social gatherings are entirely without refreshment. Such is not the case. We have the most delicious fruit in abundance. Our host or hostess, whoever it may be, will always see to that. But it is fruit that is very unlike yours on earth, we eat it for a very different reason, and it produces a totally different effect upon us. To take the fruit itself first. We have a much greater variety than do you, even taking into account the diversity to be found in the different parts of the world. All the fruits that you have we also have here, but with the quality there is no comparison. And the size, too, is remarkable. That you must see to believe! The fruit contains a great quantity of nectar-like juice, at the same time leaving the flesh of the fruit firm to the hold. It is perfectly formed, without blemish, a picture to behold, and its appearance does not belie it, for it tastes even more lovely than it looks. In eating the fruit we are not conscious of an internal satisfaction such as are you on earth with your fruit. We feel at once a powerful force running through our whole system, a feeling of exhilaration both mental and physical. We have no physical hunger that calls for satisfaction; whatever fruit we eat acts as a life force, and, as it were, stirs us up mentally and charges us with vigor.

It is difficult for you on earth to imagine yourself without hunger and the need for food. To be hungry and thirsty is instinct with human nature on earth. When you come to reside permanently in these realms of the spirit world, you leave your hunger and thirst forever behind you. You will never, therefore, miss the food and drink for which you no longer have any need. And that state in turn becomes instinct with human nature in the spirit world. You would even find that you could manage very nicely if you were never to partake of any fruit here, but once you have tried it and sampled its rich benefits, you have discovered a pleasure that you will never want to deny yourself. And there is no need to deny yourself upon any grounds whatsoever. There is plenty of it to be had simply for the gathering of it, and you may "tuck in" without fear of being dubbed a glutton!

Where does the fruit grow? Most people have a garden attached to their houses, and they are bound to have a favorite fruit tree tucked away in some corner that will amply supply them both for the requirements of hospitality and for their own personal needs. But there are large tracts of land here that are entirely applied to the growing of fruit of various sorts and for various purposes.

One of my earliest experiences after I had arrived in the spirit world was the discovery of a splendid orchard of fruit trees. The owner of it was quick to perceive that the illness that had caused my transition to these realms had been a short one, and he presented me with some fruit of a particular kind which, he said, would supply me with just that reinvigoration that I needed. Edwin was with me at the time (indeed, it was he who disclosed this orchard to me in the first instance), and although he had been many years here, he also partook of some fruit, greatly to his benefit likewise.

The whole of this orchard is a plantation of special fruit trees for the use of people who are newcomers to the spirit world. The owner of these trees— though I think he would prefer the appellation of "custodian"—is highly skilled in selecting just the right kind of fruit for newcomers. Once you have called upon him, he expects you to call again as often as you please. If he should be away from home at the moment of your visit, he explains, you are to walk in and help yourself, and the fruit trees will themselves act the part of host—and a much better one, he would say, than himself—and do what is necessary. The fruit is always there because it is always in season, and it is always in capital condition for consumption.

The genial soul who conducts this fruit farm, if one can so term it, is performing a very great service to all of us here, and you can readily imagine that he possesses a great knowledge of the technicalities of his work. He is, in fact, an institution in these realms, and is known far and wide not only for the services he performs but for himself, for one could not find a more amiable companion. He is the owner of the orchard and the dwelling house that is close by. He, himself, will tell you that he holds the orchard in trust for the whole of this realm, and by virtue of his services thereto, he enjoys the privilege and pleasure of "owning" it until such time as he will pass on to a higher state. And there is no one in these realms who would dispute not only his fitness for the services he renders, but his right to call the land, the orchard, and his dwelling house strictly his own for just so long as he wishes to extend his tenure of them. We shall be very sorry for ourselves when he transfers his noble activities to a higher realm, while we shall be happy on his account that he has reaped a rich and well earned reward.

I have spoken to you of food in the limited extent of fruit, but what of drink? Do we never feel the need for liquid of some sort? Never. But you must know that there is an enormous quantity of juice to be found in the fruit which would be sufficient to quench any thirst of reasonable dimensions!

However, the spirit world is not an arid waste, as you will by this time have gathered. There is water in abundance in the rivers and streams and brooks, and every drop of it not only fit to drink, but, indeed, like no water to be found upon earth. It glistens and sparkles; it is crystal clear; it is buoyant; one can slip beneath its surface and enjoy its warm embrace as it folds its living arms about you. It soothes, it invigorates, it inspires. It will produce the most beautiful sounds when it is disturbed on its surface. The ripples of the wavelets will reflect back a multitude of rainbow tints and will emit the purest of musical tones. Have you any water like that upon earth? I cannot remember ever seeing any such when I was there.

There is no such thing as stagnant water here; every drop of it is everlastingly living water of jewel-like purity. We can bathe within it, we can ride upon its surface in many a splendid vessel, or we can descend beneath it without harm to ourselves, because it is our nature that no harm can come to us.

And now, after this slight digression, let us return to our consideration of the gardens.

Our gardens are as much like the earth gardens as our spirit world houses are like yours. The first difference that you will notice is the absence of fences, or hedges, or walls, or any other means of indicating the boundaries of our "property." So that, when you look out of the windows of your home in these realms, the whole wonderful prospect will seem like a gigantic park, beautifully wooded, with streams and rivers to be seen sparkling in the light of the central sun, and flashing back countless rays like veritable diamonds. Apart altogether from their beauty, our gardens have an eternal freshness and orderliness about them that would be impossible of attainment in any earthly garden. My use of the word orderliness must not be misconstrued into anything approaching the somewhat rigid regularity to be observed in the public gardens of the earth. Beautiful as the latter may be, there is something of a cold orderliness about them; a lack of the sense of friendliness; a severe ordering of the flowers in their precise arrangement. They seem to be so very much on view, and one may have the feeling of being warned off. Even the simplest of our spirit gardens is immensely superior to the most assiduously preserved garden to be found upon earth.

The differences between our gardens and yours are numerous, so numerous and wide, in fact, that the only real point of resemblance is in the name. I am inclined to think, though this is only my personal opinion, that the absence of fences and hedges to which I have just alluded; indeed, the absence of all marks of our own "territorial frontiers" is one of the chief contributing factors to the great divergence between our gardens and yours.

In spirit world gardens one feels at once the sense and the reality of spaciousness which abounds everywhere. It is another instance of the freedom which we all know, feel, and enjoy. Freedom, you see, manifests itself in so many ways here, even in what might be deemed the comparatively unimportant matter of our gardens. It may seem unimportant to you who are still on earth, but to us here it is vital.

All our gardens, then, merge the one into the other, forming an unrestricted whole which constitutes the great countryside of these realms. The land is not entirely flat, of course. There are gentle hills and slopes, delightful valleys with streams and rivers running through them. There are pathways winding their pleasant course beneath verdant trees of every kind. And every inch of ground is under cultivation of one sort or another. There is no barren land here, no neglected land. We each of us keep our gardens alive, in every sense of the term, by the affection which we shower upon them. There is no constant battle with weeds and wild growths; nor are we at the mercy of the elements whether of wind or rain—or lack of rain; of cold or frost; or of too great heat.

In the perfectly tempered warmth of these realms every form of spirit nature has its full chance to grow, to flourish to its fullest extent, unhampered by such conditions as your earthly nature has to endure. If that is the case, it may be remarked, then there is no wonder that spirit world gardens are a perfect picture of heavenly delight. That is so, but it is a point that is so frequently overlooked, because people are apt to think too much in terms of the earth when considering life in the spirit world.

There is another feature marking the difference between our gardens and yours, and which will be of some interest to those of my friends on earth who are fond of gardening. With you in the earth world, once given the requisite ground, it will not be long before you will produce some sort of result by virtue of your possessing some general, though perhaps limited, knowledge of horticultural practice, and for the rest trusting to the plants to look after themselves, with occasional assistance from a more knowing friend. But a garden of the spirit world demands expert knowledge in its creation, not to prevent us from going wrong, but to produce any results at all. Without our knowing exactly how to produce flowers or other growing things, we should fail to create any garden whatever.

Most of us here have consulted the expert gardeners at one time and another, either in the first formation of our gardens or afterwards to make alterations and improvements. If we should lack ideas in the matter, these important functionaries will soon provide us with something of their own fashioning that will be sure to please us far more than we ever anticipated.

From time to time I have consulted with these good folk upon my own gardening arrangements, and it is astonishing how they have the faculty of knowing just what we most desire without our having expressed it openly. In any case, a hint is all that they require to evolve a dream of a garden, from the tiniest rustic nook to the great swelling banks of flowers with their innumerable color schemes which are to be found in the neighborhood of all the "public" buildings in these realms. But more recently a sprightly young lad named Roger has taken up his residence with us, who is himself an expert horticulturist.

Shortly after his arrival here, and at whose transition Ruth and I assisted, he became greatly attracted to horticultural work, and he has since become highly proficient in the art. So that now the gardens of our small domain are under his constant supervision and we have no need to venture farther afield than our own home in all matters appertaining to their arrangement or re-arrangement with such an expert living on the premises. Roger here carries out all manner of experiments in floral disposition and display which is as great an interest to the rest of us as to himself. We are never quite sure what new form our "grounds" are likely to take at any given moment, and our numerous friends are oftentimes treated, as we are ourselves, to many and varied horticultural surprises!

A great many of these expert horticulturists were either gardeners or lovers of gardens when they were upon earth. Being at liberty—as we all are here—to choose their occupation when they came here to live, it is but natural that they should put their previously gained knowledge to some further use, or that they should become fully occupied in what was on earth a diversion to be indulged in when time and opportunity permitted. It is true that a great deal of their earthly knowledge would be of little use to them as gardeners in the spirit world in any practical application, but it does not take them long to discard their old knowledge for the new, to exchange the earthly methods for the spirit world methods.

Not all of our gardening experts are practical gardeners. Some of them are designers of gardens only, leaving the actual creation of the garden to others. And others are creators of gardens only, leaving the designing to others. And again, some combine the two, designing and creating.

The horticultural architects are never at a loss for an idea, and you must know that designing a garden does not only mean arranging for the disposition of some small plot of ground such as one finds adjoining so many of the dwellings on earth. In the spirit world a whole countryside can be altered and rearranged down to the smallest detail, and the plans have to be made from which the actual creators are to work.

In the spirit world, planning and building a garden involves certain considerations which would not be heeded on earth. For example, the types of flowers and trees, with especial attention to their coloring, will largely be ordered or influenced by the kind of dwelling or other edifice which stands or is to stand in the particular ground. You will recall how the stones and so on in these realms are all glowing with beautiful shades of color. The flowers in the gardens, therefore, will all accord with the colors of the masonry of the nearest building, broadly speaking, so that the two shall form together a blend of perfect harmony. Color, you see, produces sound, and sound produces color, so that it is essential that consonance and not dissonance should be the resulting effect of all horticultural efforts in these realms. Discord of an unpleasant nature would not be permitted. So here is one point, at least, where our gardening methods differ from yours.

Again, we are not restricted, as you are, to seasons of a year. Our flowers and shrubs and trees are always in bloom and in leaf. We have combinations of flowers in our gardens that would normally be impossible upon earth through the passage of time, or because of the order of nature upon earth that causes flowers to come to maturity, flourish for a brief period, and then fade and die.

You, who love the flowers and the gardens that grow them, can you not imagine our joy, here in these realms, where we have our favorite flowers always with us in our gardens, never at the mercy of the elements or the seasons, never withering with age, but ever presenting themselves to the world in all their beauty, in all their simplicity or their grandeur, in all their wide range of colorings, from the most delicate tint to the most vigorous and compelling of bright colors and, lastly, always shedding their delicate perfumes upon the sweet pure air to delight us not only in the exquisiteness of their aroma, but to charge us with spiritual force—can you not imagine our joy at all this?

This is all very well, I can hear you say; but do you never become tired of all this perfection? With all this absolute perfection about you, how can you have any contrast, any light and shade? You surely need something that is not so perfect if one may so express it—to show off, to emphasize, what is perfect.

Certainly that is a point which might worry some people. The latter are dreadfully afraid that there may be a flaw somewhere in these details of spirit life which I am giving you; some important matter, some qualification which I have overlooked, that would tend to show that these realms are really, after all, not quite so perfect as one would be led to imagine. Or, in other words, there is bound to be something, somewhere, that we should dislike, or upon which we might frown in displeasure.

Well, now, the details I am giving you are drawn from my own experiences, firsthand experiences. I give you facts as I and millions of others see them in these realms; facts which we *know* to be the truth. There is no disputing the colors of the flowers, for example, just as there is no disputing thousands of other facts patent for all to see and observe and realize their truth.

Or, again, you feel, shall we say, that what I am telling you seems too good to be true. Perfection, you would rightly say, is unattainable on earth, but that is not to say that perfection does not exist somewhere else. Perfection, it will be objected, admits of no qualification. Either a thing is perfect, or it is not perfect. There can be no half measures about it. One thing cannot be more perfect or less perfect than another. That is the truth in its strictest sense. But perfection can be largely a matter of personal experience. We may imagine that a thing is perfect because we have never experienced or encountered anything better. We are therefore entitled to regard this particular thing as perfect, and we shall do no harm to ourselves or to any other person by so thinking.

These realms wherein I live are, to all of us who inhabit them, a state of perfection so far as our present experience takes us. The great majority of us can scarcely contemplate a state of greater beauty and happiness; that is, a state of greater perfection than this sphere where we have our homes and our life. We love every inch of these realms, we love every moment of our lives; we are supremely happy—we could not be more so; that is to say, we do not *think* we could be more so. But when we come to regard the strict truth we know that when we pass into a higher realm we shall be happier still. We have not yet enjoyed that experience, but those of our friends who have already mounted to a more exalted realm are continually returning to visit us and to tell us of the greater happiness which they are now enjoying, happiness which they did not think possible, and to speak of the *greater perfection* in their new realms of things which already seemed perfect to them. So that, perfection, after all, is a matter of degree, of comparison, of experience, and it is not possible to set any limitation upon perfection, because we do not know as yet how far it is possible for perfection to extend. So that when I say that everything here in these realms is perfect, I mean, of course, everything is perfect in so far as our present experience takes us.

And that applies to us all here. Even when we have visited higher realms for a period, however long or short, we have only *glimpsed* the *greater* perfection of those realms. We can see that things are immensely purer in all ways, the colors, the musical sounds, the flowers and forests and woods; the rivers and streams; and, lastly, the people themselves, all are more rarified. But those of us who have been so fortunate as to have visited a higher state never on any account feel dissatisfied with our own estate upon returning to our own realms. Dissatisfaction does not come by visual comparison of our present realms with higher realms. There are other causes for that which, for the time being, we will not consider. As far as my description of these realms is concerned, you need not be afraid that it is all too good to be true. To you who are still incarnate it may seem that it is impossible of attainment. To us, it is our everyday life.

Why should I depreciate the true condition of things here? Why should I pretend that the conditions are less wonderful and less beautiful than they are simply because some folk, still living on earth, cannot imagine anything being better than the state of existence upon earth? What is there against the particular beauty and grandeur of these realms to which such exception is taken? Because the same people have not experienced either or both, it does not follow that they do not exist in these realms. And if, by a deliberate perversion of the truth, I were to describe this state as being but a fourth-rate imitation of the earth, people would still be displeased. What! they would say in effect—is the next world no better than this world?

There are many parts in the spirit world that are a thousand times worse than anything that can be found in the earth world. There are many regions in the spirit world that are immeasurably more beautiful and more glorious than could ever be found upon earth. Yet there are minds who are thoroughly dissatisfied to learn of either! They need not perturb themselves unduly. When they pass into the spirit world they will go to that place for which, by their earthly lives, they have fitted themselves, and to no other. And in addition, they will go only to that place, or that description of place, which they think "heaven" ought to be. How long they will remain in their homemade "heaven" rests with themselves, but my observations tell me that it is usually not very long before such people emerge from their restricted "paradise" and join their fellows in the real "heaven" that has been waiting for them all the while. It so happens that their ideas of what perfection is, or ought to be, do not coincide with what perfection really is, even in the qualified sense we have just discussed. In the end they are bound to admit their error of judgment!

It is strange—is it not?—this strong disinclination upon the part of some minds to accept the fact that some sections of the spirit world, at least, should bear any resemblance to the earth, albeit a resemblance that involves considerable modifications. After spending their lives in an earth world where such objects as houses and buildings of every kind are to be found, where the countryside with its fields and meadows, its rivers and lakes, its trees and flowers are but commonplace facts of earthly existence, some people feel resentful that they should be asked to live on in a future state where so many of the familiar landmarks of the earth are again in evidence.

Of course, they are not asked, strictly speaking, to live amid these surroundings, but we have already considered that point. It is more the fact that a spirit world civilization exists at all that so annoys some of our friends on earth. Again I would ask, what would they have in place of these natural surroundings?

The aversion, I am persuaded, arises from the notion that these realms of which I am speaking bear some limited or modified resemblance to the earth. Now that in itself is wrong. It is to imply that certain regions of the spirit world have been constructed upon earthly lines; that the earth has been taken as a model and the spirit realms built upon that model, and that they therefore constitute something of a replica of the earth. Exactly the opposite is the truth. The earth bears a limited or modified resemblance to these realms, which is a different matter altogether. Spirit lands, in the realms of light, are a thousand times more beautiful than any part of the earth it is possible to mention.

It will doubtless be pointed out to me that in spirit lands there are houses that are a counterpart of earthly houses, and my own dwelling will be adduced as an example. That is true. My own house came into existence in the spirit world after I had earned the right to have it there as my home, to be set apart for me until I should arrive in spirit lands to live. But domiciles in incalculable numbers, having no counterpart on earth, had been in existence hundreds and hundreds of years before ever I was born upon earth. The inspiration that came to man to cover himself and his family with a roof of however rude a description came from the spirit world. You may say: nothing of the sort; it is no more than a natural instinct exerting itself, an instinct of self-preservation, to protect one's self from the rigors of wind and storm, of cold and heat. If you feel that you must adhere to your contention, then, so be it. I cannot provide proof of my assertion yet. You must wait until you come to spirit lands yourself, and I shall be pleased to show you where you can ascertain the truth for yourself. In the meantime, I will adhere to *my* contention, and I will venture further to assert that the whole range of earthly architectural design throughout the ages has been inspired and influenced, promoted and encouraged by great minds resident in the spirit world.

Inspiration is not a matter of physical brain cells self-functioning in such a manner as to produce a clever or brilliant idea in the mind of a person. Inspiration can come from any quarter of the spirit world, from the highest realms, from the lowest realms and from the gray lands as well. It remains with the incarnate as to which quarter of the spirit world he will lend an ear. If to the highest, there will come only that which is good; if to the lowest, only that which is evil and bad. In the former, among many other good things, you will have all the beauties of art and music, but they will be beauties and not hideous distortions masquerading under the cloak of pure art; you will have scientific discoveries for the benefit of mankind, as well as schemes for his well-being. You will have great works of dramatic and literary genius that will live through the years and never show signs of wear. From the dark realms you will have wars and strife, unrest and discontent; you will have literature that is a disgrace to so-called civilization, and music, even, that is an abomination of impure sounds, such sounds as would never exist for an instant of time in these realms.

No, the spirit world is not a copy of the earth. The spirit world was in being eons of time before the earth came into existence. Does man think that he has formed and fashioned all that is man-made upon earth entirely of his own mind and genius, then man is woefully mistaken.

Without the spirit world, the earth and mankind, who is barely living as judged by the greater life of the spirit world, would soon get into inconceivable difficulties. The beauties of the earth are but a foretaste of the beauties of the spirit world and the life that lies before all mankind. We do not copy you who are on earth—we have no need to do so. We give you glimpses of the spirit world so that you may have some slight acquaintance with the spirit world before you come to take up your life and residence here.

We seem to have marched a long step from our discussion of spirit world houses and their gardens, do we not? But these other matters that we have looked into are all relative to our one subject, which is the consideration of the spirit world and the life we lead here.

And now, how are the residents of the houses composed? Are they family groups or single occupants?

Doubtless, you will call to mind such concentrations as you have on earth, but you must also remember that even on earth family groups are continually altering their composition. The children in an earthly family grow up, and for various reasons they leave their parental homestead—upon marriage, for example, or for reasons connected with their business or occupation. People on earth live alone for equally varied reasons. And so the changing of family groups is constantly going on. In normal times on earth, families live their lives with these changes taking place in their family ties, and eventually they come into the spirit world.

Upon earth the number of generations of a family is fairly limited, but in the spirit world all previous generations of a family are co-existing. So that it might reasonably be asked: who will live with whom? That, as you can see, will raise a very considerable problem if viewed from the strictly limited viewpoint of the earth. But it presents no problem to the organization of the spirit world. Family ties, *as such*, have little significance in the spirit world. Here the one deciding factor in this matter of human relationships and family ties, is the bond of affection and mutual interest that prevails between any two or more people. The rule applies in all circumstances. It applies to husband and wife, to brother and sister, to father and mother, and to all the remaining degrees of family relationship. And it applies to ordinary friendships between individuals of different families and between both sexes.

In the spirit world we are at liberty to live as we wish. If we desire to join forces with one or more companions, we shall soon be able to find others, similarly inclined, to unite with us and share the one domicile. Many of us here do that. Apart from mutual regard and respect and interest, we may all be occupied in the same type of work, and so, sharing our knowledge and experience, we live our lives together under the one roof, and in complete accord. If at any time we should wish to occupy a separate establishment we can do so without fear of hurting the feelings of our companions.

When I first came to the spirit world I found myself the possessor of a replica of my old home on earth. There it stood, fully equipped and ready for my instant habitation. Edwin, my old friend and colleague, undertook to show me a little of the new world I had just entered, and during our tour of inspection I met a very charming young person whose name is Ruth. She joined our small expedition, since there were many things that she, too, had not yet seen, and finally, after spending so much time together in our peregrinations, the three of us felt that we should like to work together if that were possible. It was possible, and we have so worked ever since. Ruth and Edwin are each the possessors of very charming houses, of which they are "sole occupants," but we are so much together, the three of us, that Edwin and Ruth spend far more time in my house than they do in their own. Their homes are filled with their possessions and the things they value, but the prolonged absence of the owners makes no difference. They will always find their houses to be in the same state of good order whenever they wish to retire to them, as they do occasionally.

The same situation also applies to an old friend who has also taken up his residence with us. Gordon by name, he has but recently arrived in these lands. He had been in active communion and communication with us for a great many years of his earth life, and he was himself a powerful psychic instrument. It was a great pleasure to Ruth and me to assist at his passing, and to bring him to our home. He awoke to his new life to find himself reclining comfortably upon the couch in our main room, through the windows of which he had the first glimpse, as a permanent resident, of the land of his new life. Ourselves apart, there were other friends to welcome and greet him, friends of his earthly days: two small sparrows, his dog, and two handsome pumas. So that altogether our household is an animated and lively one. We are living a happy life working together, taking our amusements together, receiving our friends together, and visiting together.

It is no uncommon sight to see such arrangements; indeed, I think they preponderate in these realms. The bonds that unite us are firm and undeniable, otherwise the joint establishment would soon collapse. The plan fits in with our particular temperaments and tastes and desires, whether the latter be of work or of play. It is the wish of all five of us that our present system and arrangement of living shall always continue. And it will so continue, until the time comes for one or all of us to proceed to another realm in the natural course of our spiritual progression.

There are many couples to be found living in charming houses here; for example, a husband and wife who were happily married when upon the

earth, admirably suited to each other, and with a real bond of affection between them. Or there may be other family groupings such as I outlined to
you a moment ago. If you remember that all these small communities are
formed not because of blood-relationship, but because of mutual esteem and
affection, you will always find the answer to the question: who will live with
whom?—in the residential relationships of the spirit world.

Other reasons apart, if spiritual progression brings about the departure
of some member of a household in the spirit world, it might be thought that
it would cause some measure of unhappiness or sadness to the remainder of
the household. In such a case we should greatly miss the customary presence
of our former companion upon his proceeding to a higher realm, but we
should not feel the same rather blank despair as do you upon earth in other
circumstances of departure. We have a keen appreciation of the greater happiness which will be the good fortune of our departed friend, and that will
spur us on to attain our own progression, and so join him who has preceded
us. But it is not by any means certain that we shall take our next step in progression when it comes, if I may so express it.

There are many people to be found in these and other realms, both higher and lower, who have earned for themselves their undoubted removal into
a higher sphere of spiritual life, but who prefer to remain where they are for
a variety of sufficiently good reasons. For example, some of the great teachers in these realms are fully entitled to live in a higher realm, and actually
possess houses in those higher states, but they have chosen to remain where
they are and carry on their present form of work. This act of self-denial is
itself a means of still further progression, though it is to be doubted if any
such thought ever enters the head of the individual who elects to adopt this
course of action.

When I say teachers, I do not mean only teachers of spiritual truths and
so forth, but instructors of all kinds in the various arts and crafts of these
particular realms. There are thousands of people here who are learning some
form of work that is new to them, details of which I have already recounted
to you. In this case it is the work itself and the joy it brings in the service to
their fellow-beings that prompts such folk to postpone their advancement
of spiritual estate. One day, however, the time will come when they will be
obliged to betake themselves into their rightful sphere since to remain longer
in a lower realm might cause them some discomfort. But they can return
whenever they wish and make prolonged visits to their old friends, and even
resume for a limited period their former tutorial occupation, needless to say,
to the extreme delight of their colleagues and pupils.

It is not only teachers who postpone their permanent elevation and remain where they are, although entitled to reside in a higher realm. It is open to anyone, without exception, to do the same whenever the circumstances arise. The circumstances, in fact, are many in which this can happen. To instance one case: two people are mutually attracted while upon earth, a husband and wife, shall we say? The wife passes into the spirit world and attains to a certain sphere. Later on the husband in turn passes into spirit life, but goes to occupy a realm lower than that of his wife. But the mutual attraction still exists, and so the wife takes up her life in the lower sphere in order to be with her husband and to help him in his progression. Thus they will be enabled to advance together and remain together for all time, or until such other circumstances arise as will cause a natural severance of their present ties.

There are many selfless souls here who have done and are doing the very same thing. They are perfectly free to make their own choice in the matter. The greater happiness, generally speaking, that would be theirs in the higher state, receives some measure of compensation in their being reunited with some much-loved relation or friend.

So you will see, there are no sad partings, no dispersals of pleasantly situated little communities of relations or friends by the natural procedure of spiritual progression. We do not experience that crushing, almost overwhelming depression that you can experience upon the earth at the departure of one who is greatly loved.

Even if a cherished friend has departed into higher regions, and we should feel ourselves becoming saddened by the event, it must be remembered that we are in instantaneous touch with each other here. A thought sent out will bring back the absent one in a twinkling to our side, if that should be the only remedy for our desolation. But that would be an extreme case, a highly improbable eventuality, and scarcely ever to be encountered. Then again, we are unerringly in touch with each other here by thought in ways that I will explain to you later.

As I have had occasion to remark previously, the spirit world is not a static world. There is always movement, especially among its people. How, otherwise, could we eventually pass to the higher states if it were not so? At some time or another certain small communities of a few friends or kindred souls, who are occupying the same domicile together and working in concert, must come under the influence of the universal law of change that is one of the great elements of spirit life. But these re-groupings, with their consequent severance of earlier ties, are not terrible tragedies. They are the natural outcome of the march of progression. We must move onwards as the will to move exerts itself within us. None would hold us back, although we might elect to stay until other circumstances prevail. But you can be sure of this: we are all completely satisfied under this scheme of things, we know that no other plan would be feasible, and, what is most important from the point of view of our feelings in the matter, we are supremely happy under it.

In my references to the countryside, I have mentioned rivers. How do they flow? They flow in exactly the same manner as do earthly rivers. They begin their life as a small stream, perhaps as a little trickling brook, and they flow on and on becoming deeper and broader in their passage, and finally they flow into the sea. There is nothing very remarkable in that, but the rivers themselves are very remarkable when they are compared with earthly rivers.

The rivers of the spirit world are never fast-flowing streams, muddy looking, or heavy in appearance. Nor are unsightly buildings to be found upon their banks, with merchant vessels of all shapes and sizes and degrees of disrepair alongside dingy wharves. However picturesque the ships may be, we have no need for them here, and so they do not exist. Boats of all sorts we do have, but not of the description that I have just mentioned. And we do not have unpleasant factory buildings spoiling the beautiful riverside scenery. Instead, we have magnificent edifices built of spirit-world materials such as you are already familiar with, reposing along the waterside, with spacious embankments and splendidly laid-out gardens through which the river threads its placid way, slowly, very slowly, and calmly. When I first saw one of the spirit world rivers, so slowly was it moving that to my unaccustomed eyes I felt sure that it was not moving at all! But it is possible to see the movement and to feel it.

You can have no conception how glorious it is to glide along such a river in some graceful boat, passing through the rolling banks of flowers upon either hand, or through some peaceful meadow where the trees reflect their shapely forms in the tranquil waters; or again, to draw alongside some beautiful broad marble steps, to go ashore, mount to a greater height and view the ribbon of scintillating color that the river reveals itself to be from this higher elevation; or, yet again, to proceed up some sequestered backwater to find one's self in the midst of a friend's garden.

Nothing can possibly convey to you the brilliance of the color, always the color, that seems to abound in such full measure in the neighborhood of the rivers. Perhaps it is that the streams themselves reflect back so much colorful light from the flowers that this effect of seeming preponderance of color is produced. Whatever it may be, we all feel the same about it, and for that reason the rivers always have a very great attraction to the folk in their leisure moments.

The water is of the purest, as you know, but its most remarkable feature, in the opinion of so many of us here, is the ability it has of changing its colors and shades of colors. At times, I have seen the river which runs near my home to be nothing less in appearance than a ribbon of molten gold. All the different hues that are usually reflected in a thousand different ways, appeared to have vanished and in their place was liquid gold. At other times I have seen it shining as though of burnished silver. This rather unusual phenomenon puzzled me considerably in my early days here, but my invaluable friend, Edwin, soon instructed me in such matters as these. The explanation was simple enough. It was just that some visitant from higher realms was, or had been, in the neighborhood, and the influence which he brought with him was being reflected in the mirror surface of the water. As the influence became absorbed into the immediate surroundings, the river gradually resumed its customary appearance.

I only mention this small incident to show you how these realms of the spirit world are ever affording us some delight or another, unasked—which makes the enjoyment of it still more precious to us.

Akin to the rivers of the spirit world are, of course, the seas. They are like the seas of the earth merely as a body of water, but in no other respect. The waters of the rivers here, and the seas into which they flow, are of the same elements; that is to say, the water is what is known on earth as fresh water. As far as I was able to observe I could not trace the presence of any salt in the sea.

In general appearance there is not a great deal of difference between the rivers and the ocean. Each has the same brilliance of color, but the rivers by virtue of the fairly close proximity of their banks, with the large masses of flowers and the elegant buildings which adorn them, will have more colors to reflect in their surfaces, and so they will appear to be more colorful. But it must not be presumed that the sea lacks a full measure of color. Very far from it. No water, wherever situated here, lacks color. And the sea is never empty of the signs of life. There are always vessels of one sort or another to be seen sailing upon it or riding at anchor. In addition, however far one may travel one is scarcely ever out of sight of an enchantingly lovely island, upon which one is at liberty to wander to one's heart's content, and enjoy the special features which all these islands possess.

One of the islands, of which I have spoken to you before, contains a veritable paradise of bird-life, where some of the most beautiful specimens of birds in all the glory of their gorgeous plumage are to be seen at close hand. They are not segregated and confined in cages, of course, but they are free to pursue their life in their natural element, the air, or to remain upon the ground in the absolute certainty of their complete security from harm. Consequently, they are the friends of any of us who may visit their special domain.

This particular island is another favorite pleasure spot with us, and often do we go there to sit on the soft grass while birds of every description of vivid plumage and of every size come gathering round us, not for food, as one would imagine on earth, but just to demonstrate their knowledge that no harm can come to them, and to express their friendliness with all mankind in these realms. We are such regular visitors there that we know a great many of the birds by sight and by name, for some one is bound to give them names!

Of course bird-life is not confined solely to this one island; indeed, the birds are flying about throughout these and other realms, just as with you on earth, so are they here with us "abroad and everywhere."

I have not visited all the seas of the spirit world, but there is plenty of time yet. My visitations to the seaside have been chiefly to that ocean which is nearest to our particular quarter of these realms.

When viewed from an elevation that is fairly high above sea level, the water presents a scintillating expanse of color. There are no storms to agitate the surface violently, at the same time the sea is not always of a glassy smoothness. The gentlest of breezes will play lightly upon the waters, rippling the surface and forming little waves which take on a hundred tints in the smallest space, so that these rays of reflected light are for all the world like the flashes of color that are to be seen issuing from the purest of diamonds.

It is a thrilling experience to behold for the first time this glittering effect that is natural to all water in the spirit world. When I first beheld it I could hardly believe my eyes so unbelievably inspiring was the spectacle. And even now, although I have become to some extent a seasoned resident of these realms, I can still be thrilled by the interplay of color whenever I come within sight of river or lake or sea. And that applies to all of us here. Familiarity has not made us indifferent. There would be something radically wrong with ourselves if it did.

There are many fine vessels to be seen upon all the waters of these regions, many of them the homes of residents. Ownership of such boats—in fact, of any boat—is governed by the same law that applies to all ownership in spirit lands, the law that makes it a *sine qua non* that all our possessions must be earned before we can own them. As far as the smaller craft are concerned, the type which would be known as private river-craft on earth, many people have such boats and spend their leisure moments upon the water, just as do you on earth, but without any of the restrictions or dangers, even, that are to be encountered on earth. It is perfectly safe here for a small child to sail out in a boat entirely alone.

What is the difference, you might wish to ask, between country life and town life in the spirit world? In the form in which that question is framed there is doubtless the impression that life in the spirit world consists of a regularly recurring series of episodes, or functions, dividing life into a number of compartments, as it were, though the compartments themselves might be contiguous. That is how life is composed, more or less, upon earth. So to answer that question, I must place one or two considerations before you.

Your life upon earth is dominated by two factors at least, both of which are unavoidable. They are the need for rest through sleep, and the need for food. To maintain your life at all upon earth, you must provide for these two requirements. As you know, in the spirit world we need neither physical rest nor food. Your life is therefore punctuated by recurring periods of sleeping and eating. A certain part of your life is spent with darkness upon earth, and although you may illuminate the darkness with artificial light, the darkness still remains elsewhere.

In these realms, as you know, too, we have no darkness at all, *at any time.* Our life, then, is one of absolute continuity in perpetual natural light. We have no blank period in our physical life such as you have during your sleep. We are for ever awake. We carry on with our work until such time as we wish to stop, and then we stop. We can follow on with other work of a different nature, or we can betake ourselves to some form of amusement or entertainment, or we can indulge in our own particular pastime. At the conclusion of the latter, or at such time as we see fit, we will resume our work. Further, we live in a state of perpetual summer; we have no long summer or long winter evenings alternating.

You have no possible means of experiencing these various factors upon earth because they do not and cannot exist there. You must therefore call your imagination into play and try to picture to yourself the particular conditions which I have just outlined to you. You should then be able to see that there is really no difference between town and country life in the spirit world.

The cities of the earth are mere concentrations for reasons of commercial convenience. There being no commerce in the spirit world we have no need for such concentrations. But what has been done is to place all the great halls of learning of these particular realms in one locality. There is no pressing need that they should be so disposed; with equal facility they could have been distributed throughout a wide area of these regions. But it was felt that a number of magnificent buildings, such as are the halls of learning, would present a much more imposing appearance if they were arranged in an orderly plan, each within a moderately close distance of the other. We can think of no better arrangement. And so the buildings were erected many eons ago. They occupy an immense area of ground, and each is standing in gardens and grounds of peerless beauty. Exactly in the center of this group of buildings is a temple of unsurpassed grandeur. It forms the hub of the city, and from it radiate all other buildings of whatever nature.

We have no streets as you know them, for we do not require them, but we have broad, spacious thoroughfares of the softest grass upon which to walk. There is no traffic of vehicles here so that there is no necessity for special pavements upon each side of the roadway, as you have for your own security. Sometimes these broad walks are paved with some of the wonderful stone creations of these realms, but more often they are covered with grass.

When you come to view the countryside here you find that without hedges and walls and other boundary marks, the whole landscape becomes one vast expanse of parklands interspersed with rivers and streams and wooded land. Standing amid all these beauties are the dwellings of the inhabitants of these regions of the spirit world, and in a part of the countryside there stands what we call the city. Where one ends and the other begins, it would be difficult to say. There are no municipal or civic rights to be considered, no parochial boundaries to be thought of, no suburban or rural privileges to intervene in any way. The city is part of the countryside; the countryside is part of the city. The life of one is the life of the other, simply because of the continuity of existence in the spirit world, and because of the perpetual daytime and perpetual summertime. There is no hot and stuffy city to make a visit into the country air so pressing. There is no great commercial attraction of the city to draw folk towards that center. So that, in effect, the country and the city are one.

I promised, a little while since, that I would speak to you upon the subject of thought. Now, I think, would be a favorable opportunity to do so, leaving for the time such other matters of spirit life that are worthy of discussion.

CHAPTER THREE

SPIRIT PERSONALITY

WHEN THE spirit world is described as being a world of thought, where thought is the great creative power, and where thought is concrete and perceivable by all men, the conclusion is very often erroneously drawn that the spirit world is an unsubstantial place, and that we, its inhabitants, are vague shadowy people, lacking any real substance, and answering for all purposes to that very earthly designation of "ghosts"! Pursuing this mistaken deduction, the life of the spirit world people must inevitably be somewhat dream-like and illusive.

The incarnate think along these lines because to them thought is something that can be practiced unseen and unheard. On earth thought is secret to the thinker until such time as he wishes to give verbal or other expression to his thoughts. It is customary to say on earth: our thoughts are our own; we can think what we like; thoughts can never harm anyone, and so on. So that when we of the spirit world assert that our world is a world of thought, the incarnate immediately revert to their own thoughts and their unsubstantial nature, and thereupon place the spirit world in the same category of tenuous things.

Generally speaking, upon earth thought must have some form of concrete expression for it to be effective. The architect must first think of his cathedral, or whatever it may be, commit his thoughts to paper in regular order and with exactitude before the builder can make any commencement upon the outward and visible expression of his original thoughts. And so it is with a multitude of other things, from the simplest article to the most complicated instrument or ornate building. On earth thought must have a medium of some sort before it can find the slightest trace of outward expression. For this reason, among others, the incarnate are prone to regard the earth as being the one certain and substantial world in which it is possible to exist. The spirit world becomes the very opposite.

The incarnate do not realize the force and power of thought or else they would never think along such lines as I have indicated. Every thought that passes with force and purpose through the mind of an earth dweller is projected from his mind as a thought-form. To speak unscientifically, it is registered, at least for a time, upon the surrounding ether. It depends, of course, upon the thought itself, and of what it consists. If it is merely one of those passing thoughts that all folk upon earth have in their minds at various moments during the day, then such thoughts will be registered in the manner I have just indicated. If the thought is directed towards some friend who is now resident in the spirit world, that thought, if it is properly directed with purpose and intent, will inevitably reach that friend. It will reach him or her just as it is sent, no more and no less good or bad or indifferent. Thought may be invisible to the majority of earth dwellers but it is very much visible to spirit folk. People who are still on earth, and whose psychic powers have been developed, are often capable of seeing these thought-forms. That ability raises problems which sometimes lead to mistakes and misunderstandings.

Thought is upon a different plane, a higher plane of existence from that organ of the earthly body, the brain, through which thought functions on earth. Thought is upon the same plane of existence as the mind, and the mind belongs truly to the spirit world. And by higher plane I do not mean a higher spiritual plane, but one that cannot be observed by the ordinary physical organs of perception. In the spirit world thought has direct and instantaneous action upon whatsoever it is directed, whether it be upon a human being or upon what on earth is called "an inanimate object." (I cannot use the latter term appositely in connection with spirit world objects, because all objects, all things, have life, certain and unmistakable. There is no such state as that of being lifeless in the spirit world.) It is not until you come into the spirit world that you really know just what thought can do. And I do assure you, my good friend, that some of us are positively horrified when we find out for the first time!

In the spirit world thoughts do not become visible immediately upon their passing through a person's mind. They are not flying about in a loose fashion. The idle thoughts of which I spoke travel no further than your immediate earthly surroundings. Thoughts directed to some friend in the spirit world will reach that friend, and they cannot be classed as loose thoughts.

Imagine to yourself the state of confusion, of congestion almost, and of embarrassment if all our thoughts in the spirit world were visible. But because they are not immediately visible, that is not to say that they are not potent, for assuredly they are very potent. No, they are not visible as you regard it, but they will unfailingly reach their destination wherever it may be. If directed towards some friend upon earth, in many cases it is problematical whether the friend will perceive them; or, perceiving them, whether he will know whence they have come. But if our thoughts be directed towards some friend in the spirit world, there will be no such doubt or uncertainty.

How do we receive thoughts in the spirit world? One of the first and most interesting experiments that Ruth and I carried out under the friendly eye of Edwin during our early explorations of these realms, was that of hearing Edwin speak to us from a distance. Without recounting the full circumstances, it is sufficient to say that although Edwin was in sight of us both, yet he was too far away for us to hear his voice even if he had used it above his normal tones. But we both distinctly heard his voice sounding close to our ears. At first, of course, we could not believe our ears, and we were rather inclined to regard the whole thing as some trick or other that Edwin was performing for amusement and general merriment. But he repeated his message to us—it was merely bidding us rejoin him—and it was so unmistakable that we forthwith did as directed. As a prelude to hearing Edwin's voice, we had both perceived a bright flash to appear before the eyes. It was in no sense blinding or startling; indeed, the flash was too beautiful for that.

And that, I think, describes briefly but precisely what happens to all of us when a thought is passed between one and another of us. The thought is invisible in transit, it arrives at its destination instantaneously, when it manifests itself before us as a pleasant but compelling flash of clear light, and we can then hear the voice of our communicator speaking close to the ear, as it seems. I say *as it seems*, because here I am not attempting to give a scientific explanation of *how* it happens, but confining myself solely to what *does* happen. The voice always sounds to me to be close to the ear, and most people here say that the same thing occurs in their own case. It may be some sort of inner perception of the voice, though to me it always sounds far too like the owner's actual voice for that. My own view is that the sound of the voice actually travels through the air, and that we receive it upon the natural apparatus of our minds.

I confess that I have not looked into the matter in that deep manner that some people, perhaps, will think that I ought to have done, if only for the purpose of supplying them with a long and deep, accurate and scientific explanation of the whole process. But I am persuaded that the majority of my good friends will much rather have this frankly and obviously unscientific description of what takes place here during every second of time, just as a matter of course, than that I should lead them into some deep morass of scientific disquisition from which we should all have some difficulty in extricating ourselves! I do not profess to a knowledge of science, and I always feel that while we are peering deeply into causes and detailed explanations we are missing all the beauties of the very thing we are examining.

There is so much here that we take for granted, that is to say, we take things as they present themselves, without demanding learned explications of them. And it is the same with you who are still upon earth. Suppose, for example, I were to ask you (supposing, also, that I did not already know) how you managed to move yourself upon your two legs in the common feat of walking. I think it would much more suit your taste for you to tell me briefly just what you did with your legs and how tired they can become after prolonged activity, than to treat me to an erudite essay upon the various muscles of the leg, their names, their shape and size, their exact mode of action, their particular function, and so on. In the meantime, while the legs were being thus dilated upon, the friend, whom the two legs were supporting, was passing through some charming country, a description of which would be so much more entertaining!

And so it is with a great many other matters here—here in my world and in your world too. While science has its important place in both our worlds, yet we do not ponder every minute of our lives upon the inner working of the numberless functions of men and things that constitute life in either world. Science must have its proper position, but life would be rather dull and dreary, and certainly rather complicated, if we paused to inquire into the various modes of operation of so many common actions. We must just take things as they are. That is your general attitude upon earth; that is our general attitude here in the spirit world.

My chief purpose is to give you as many details as possible or practicable of our life in spirit lands. To state a fact as plainly as possible, to provide explanations only where necessary to an intelligent understanding of my account, and to leave it to others to probe more deeply into causes, must be my aim.

When thought is directed to us from the earth it takes the same form of a flash before the eyes. There is no difference whatever in the actual process. It matters not whence the thought has been directed, whether from your world of the earth or as an intercommunication in the spirit world. The process is universal, and there are no variations in it.

When I spoke to you, a moment ago, of the thought-forms you create in the ether immediately surrounding you on earth by your having idle thoughts in your mind, that must not be taken as also applying to us in the spirit world. If it did the spirit world would be a strange place, and the people in it would appear stranger still, for they would continually seem to be enveloped either in a kind of haze of thought-forms or something even more substantial.

The case is different with people on earth. That part of the spirit world which is immediately interpenetrating your world, that is to say, the invisible world in the immediate vicinity of the particular spot, for example, where you are reading these words, this spot is not part of the realms of light. It is dark. It may have its minute patches of light in certain well-defined places, but the greater part of it is dark. Thought, of the kind that contains no evil within it, will be bright, and therefore it will show up in the surrounding gloom, just as the light of a tiny flame will illumine the gloom of a chamber from which all other light is excluded. Even a limited diffusion of light will be the case. But take the tiny flame into the bright light of the sun and the diffusion seems to end, the feeble light having become absorbed by the greater light of the sun. The flame will still be visible, but its light will be strictly limited to its source.

This somewhat elementary analogy will serve, I hope, to illustrate the difference between thought in the invisible regions closely adjacent to your world, and thought as it is in these bright realms where I live. Even this simple analogy must be qualified by saying that however wandering may be our thoughts they are not visible like the flame of light in the sunshine. Things are far better ordered than that in the spirit world! We do have mental privacy here. Without it social intercourse would be trying, to say the least. We are living in a land of truth, that is certain; but we do not carry things to such an extreme that we must voice the truth openly upon all occasions. As with you, so with us; there are moments and occasions when silence is golden!

But it is essential that one should learn to think properly as an inhabitant of the spirit world. One of the first things one has to do here, as a new arrival, is to think properly. It is not a difficult achievement, and not nearly so formidable a task as it may sound. It concerns one's thought about people rather than thoughts of a general nature upon things. When thought is concerned with a person, the thought, if it has sufficient force behind it, will travel to that person. If it happens to be of a pleasant or complimentary description, or of a jovial and genial nature, then the percipient will be happy to receive it. But all thoughts are not of this innocuous sort, and our mental secrets may have passed out of our minds only to have found their destination in the very last place we wanted them to be, namely, in the mind of the person of whom we were so freely thinking.

The thought, however, must have a sufficient measure of directive power behind it to send it upon its journey, and this factor is the saving of many of us, because so many thoughts are mere birds of passage in our minds, and while they are there they have little really deep concentration upon the individual concerned. But the very prospect of what can happen is enough to make us keep a strict watch upon our minds, and in a brief period it becomes as second nature to us.

There are many things that we have to unlearn and re-learn when we first come to dwell in spirit lands, but our minds, being then free of a heavy physical brain, are at liberty to exercise their powers to the full. We are enabled, therefore, to acquire rapidly the methods of living under different conditions of existence. Our memories behave as memories should; that is to say, they are not erratic in their retentive performance, but can be relied upon to act perfectly. You can see how invaluable such an attribute will be when it becomes necessary to learn afresh how to do things according to spirit laws. It is in this rapid way that so many common actions quickly become as second nature.

Although, in the spirit world, thought has such direct action and is generally so powerful, that does not mean that thought makes physical effort practically unnecessary, or even undesirable. There are a great many things for our hands to do in the spirit world, and I would add that our feet also are constantly in use! We like to walk, just as we used to upon earth. What could be more natural? We are human beings after all, though some folk would deny us this characteristic. We are human, and we behave in a manner that is human. Our feet were given to us to use, and we walk upon them.

Because we can create so much with our minds, because we can fabricate things by the close application of thought, then, it might be imagined, there is precious little left for our hands to do, except to make up our full complement of limbs, and so obviate our presenting ourselves as something of monstrosities. The truth is that we use our hands in a thousand different actions during what you would call the day's work, or during a day in our life.

Think for a moment. Recall the scores of instances in which one may use the hands. For example, in our spirit homes we pick up a book, we open or close a door, we shake hands with some friend who calls; we arrange some flowers upon the table; we paint a picture, or play upon a musical instrument; or we may operate scientific apparatus of some sort. Such instances could be multiplied a thousandfold, and would become too tedious for words in their enumeration. We like to employ our hands in conjunction with our minds as well as exercising our minds alone, just as do you on earth. People take a natural delight in fashioning objects by hand, and so allowing the mind to work through their hands. There are plenty of things that could be created in these realms purely by thought and without the least interposition of the hand, but we like to go the long way round sometimes and find some employment for our hands, and we relish the enjoyment that comes from it.

But occasions do arise when we act quickly, in fact, instantaneously. We wish to go to a particular place in the realms which is, say, hundreds of miles distant, as distances are reckoned on earth. We could walk the entire distance without a trace of fatigue, but in such cases we prefer a speedier form of transportation. We therefore abandon the slow walking method of locomotion, and we bring our minds to bear upon the matter. By direct action of the mind we find ourselves instantaneously in the very place in which we wished to be.

As to how we think ourselves in a certain place, here again I would not offer you a scientific explanation for reasons which I have given you, so I will confine myself to this: in the spirit world our bodies are under complete control by our minds. The former do just that which the latter wishes or commands. A wish becomes a command in this case. Now with you, your mind may wish to be in a certain place, and no matter how hard you may wish it, you are entirely at the mercy of your physical body. You may even sit in your chair and imagine yourself, in every detail of circumstances, in the precise place. You can "see" yourself there, but the physical body must go too if you desire to be there physically. And that may raise all sorts of problems which will come readily enough to your mind—opportunity, for example; or the requisite time and means for getting to the desired destination. These are all considerations affecting the physical body, because you must take that with you, for in the physical body is the brain, and it is through the brain that the mind works. This is the natural and normal order of things on earth.

In the spirit world it is very different. We have no heavy physical body. The body which we possess is in every respect equal to our minds. Our minds have no heavy vehicle by or through which they have to function. Thinking is at once translated into action, but without the intermedium of a physical brain such as you know it. The brain which is resident within our heads is not as your physical brain; our bodies are not as your physical bodies. With us our whole being, our limbs, our muscles and so forth, are completely subservient to the mind in so far as their acting according to our will is concerned. For the rest, our bodies are subservient to the natural laws of the spirit world.

We also perform certain actions subconsciously in exactly the same way as do you. For example, we breathe in precisely the same way as you breathe.

Our hearts beat in a fashion exactly similar to yours, and they are subject to the same subconscious maintenance in their beating. But we have that which you do not have, namely, complete and absolute mastery of the muscles of our limbs. When we come to learn some new art, or endeavor to become proficient in some task that requires the mastery by the brain over the muscles, then you can see just how perfect is the attunement of our minds with our muscles. It is not really a mastery of the one over the other, although I have expressed it in that way. To be more accurate, it is an absolute attunement, the one with the other.

Now with you on earth, the effort of walking makes imperative the use of various muscles. First, you have a heavy body to move along the ground on which you are standing, and you have certain laws of gravity which are pulling you towards that ground. The gravity is so adjusted that your feet will fall to the ground easily without requiring any effort to push them down. The matter is nicely balanced. When your legs are tired after prolonged use they will fall the more readily to the ground than when you are fresh. Who upon earth has not experienced at some time or another that great heaviness of the limbs consequent upon fatigue? It is one of our constant joys that we never suffer from such disabilities. There is a law of gravity here in the spirit world, but we are not subservient to it. All else is, but we human beings are not so. Or to put it another way, our minds can and do at all times rise above it. That again is second nature to us. If we should tumble down, we cannot hurt ourselves because our spirit bodies are impervious to all injury in whatever shape or form.

Incidentally, we do not often fall because we have not the heavy and rather clumsy bodies that are essential upon earth. It is mostly newly-arrived folk who do the tumbling! When we have become fully acquainted with the power and force of our minds we never do such awkward things!

I am afraid this must seem rather a long way towards answering the question as to how we move ourselves instantaneously from one place to another, but you know how simple questions demand the consideration of other factors not unconnected with the original question in order to make the answer to the latter intelligible. Hence, therefore, my seeming deviation and protractedness.

The laws of gravity will keep all the "inanimate objects" of the spirit world in the place where they properly belong—the buildings, the rivers, the sea, and the rest. It will keep us there, too, but only in the qualified sense that I have just mentioned to you. Remember that on earth your mind is limited in certain directions by the abilities—or disabilities—of the physical body. If, say, you wish to write something down, your hand and your arm *must* be in a fit condition to do so. The same rule applies to the rest of your body. To walk, your legs and feet, and indeed, many other parts of the body, must be in a moderately sound state to do so. The speed at which your limbs can move is not limited by the wishes of the mind, but by the ability of the limbs to move. The performer upon a musical instrument knows how true this is from the unremitting practice which he has perforce to do before his hands can travel at the speed which the music makes necessary.

In the spirit world our bodies are always in a state of absolute perfection of condition. The muscles and the various parts of our bodies will respond as instantly and as rapidly as we wish the moment we set the thought in motion. We set the thought in motion, the thought sets the limbs and its parts in motion. There is no lagging, no perceptible fraction of a moment between our thought and its action. It will recall to your mind the familiar phrase: to think is to act. That is literally what takes place in the spirit world. Some of our actions are subconscious, as I have indicated to you; breathing, for example. We do not have to learn how to do that.

My mention of breathing has brought me to a point in our discussion where I think it would be acceptable if I were to speak to you upon the subject of what we both know as the spirit body. There are particular aspects about it upon which one of my friends upon earth has expressed the wish for further information. I am happy to give it to the best of my ability, but I would limit myself, as I have done throughout the whole of these writings, to knowledge which has been gained by my own experience. My reason for the latter is simply that it could be reasonably inferred that I might have recourse to the many books of learning upon all subjects that are to be found within the library of the great hall of learning. In effect, I should merely have to "look things up" in any work devoted to the subject under consideration. I have recounted to you how we have the truth here reposing between the covers of thousands of volumes. One has only to consult these, it might be said, to become possessed of an immensity of knowledge upon all subjects under the sun. Thus one could soon ascertain the literal truth upon so many of the questions that have puzzled generations of students and inquirers. The truth is there in those books, certainly, but information of a highly technical nature is not to be gleaned merely for the reading. We must understand something—in many cases a good deal—of our subject before we can plunge into technicalities which a full exposition of the truth will disclose. I must, therefore, know and understand my subject before I can pass on the information and knowledge with any hope of *your* understanding it. How, otherwise, am I to know that I have given you the correct answer to a question? It is the only satisfactory course to you, who have followed me so patiently thus far, and to me, that I should know what I am talking about, and so give you only those things of which I have specific knowledge or experience.

I have hitherto always tried to make it clear when I am only expressing a personal opinion, and when I am quoting from the knowledge and experience of my friends in the spirit world.

And now let us proceed with our friend's question.

My friend of the earth recalls my account of the orchestral concert which I attended here, and he says that "if people play wind instruments in the spirit world, they must have lungs that are capable of breathing air." And so he asks: "Do people breathe in the spirit world? If so, are the lungs used for oxygenating the blood?"

Such reasoning is perfectly accurate. The spirit world has air just as you have on earth, and we have lungs in our bodies with which to breathe it. And it does "oxygenate" the blood in what would be the spirit world equivalent of that process. Upon earth the air you breathe will help to purify the blood. In the spirit world we have good rich blood running through our veins, and we breathe the beautiful clean fresh fragrant air, but while your blood undergoes the process of oxygenating, our blood is *reinvigorated* by the spiritual force and energy that is one of the principal constituents of the air we breathe here.

Could one exist without it? Hardly. It gives us a measure of life-force just as it does you on earth. But you could not exist upon air alone. You must have food and drink. We do not need these two latter commodities, as you know, but we derive another part of our sustenance from the light of these realms, from the abundance of color, from the water, from the fruit when we wish to eat of it, from the flowers, and from all that is beautiful itself. As these realms positively abound in beauty you will see why we enjoy such perfect health.

But we also take in strength from the great spiritual force that is being constantly poured down upon us all from the Father of Heaven Himself. It is, as it were, an eternal magnetic current that is forever charging us with force and power, and giving us life.

It really comes to this, that we derive our life-force from a score of different sources; sources, moreover, that we do not have to seek as do you with your food and drink, but which literally envelop us wherever we go, whatever we do. We cannot shut ourselves off from the means of life, nor can the means of life be denied us or ever fail us here. The air we breathe cannot become polluted, nor can the water become in a similar state of impurity.

The earthly body is so constituted that through various processes and natural functions a firm resistance is made to the onslaught of germs that cause disease. When it is behaving normally and properly such disease will be successfully repelled. But even though the earthly body should successfully resist disease, the potential causes of it—the germs—still remain in the earth world. In the spirit world there are no such things as germs of any description, therefore there can be no disease of any sort whatever. Moreover, the spirit body is completely impervious to any kind of injury. It cannot be damaged by accident, and it is imperishable and incorruptible. So that whatever organs we possess they can never become disordered in the slightest degree. We are constantly enjoying a state of *perfect* health, upon which there are no two opinions among all of us here in these realms. The slightest trace of ache or pain is something not only unheard of, but from our point of view, *fantastically impossible.*

It is obvious from what I have told you that one or two organs of the earthly body would be manifestly superfluous in the spirit body. We do not eat food because we are never hungry. There is therefore no waste that has to be eliminated from our bodies as is essential with your physical bodies. The food that you eat goes through its processes, after you have consumed it, to provide what is necessary for the physical body, until it finally becomes waste matter. And to perform this series of actions various organs are vital.

We possess an interior mechanism which follows much upon the same lines as does yours, but there is this supreme difference, namely, that we have no waste matter that must be eliminated from the body. There is no such thing as waste matter in these realms. That which is not wanted either ceases to exist altogether, or is returned to the source whence it came. By ceasing to exist, I do not mean that which is not wanted is annihilated, but that it ceases to exist in the form it held *before* it became unwanted. Perhaps you will recall an amusing experience which I had shortly after my arrival here. I told you how astonished I was to find that the juice which had poured from some fruit that I was eating, and had, so I thought, run down my clothing, had, in fact, done nothing of the sort. *It had completely disappeared.* All that had happened in this case was simply that the juice of the fruit had returned to the tree whence the fruit had come. That is the explanation I was given, and that is what we all know to occur in any other circumstances of a similar nature. If you ask me *how* it happens, then, perforce, I will say honestly that I do not know. Lest my ignorance should appear too great that I should ever set myself to inform others, let me hasten to add that there is no one in these realms who could provide an explanation upon this point. There is no esoteric secret about it that such information should be withheld from us. It is just that our spiritual evolution has not proceeded sufficiently far for us to understand if we were told. What we cannot yet understand ourselves, it is impossible for us to expound for your understanding.

The organs that we possess, therefore, have their very definite purpose for their existence. We do not carry about with us organs that are redundant. Their purpose is to act as a channel for the life-force, the etheric power, if you wish to call it so, that emanates from a multiplicity of sources. There is no fear that some organs, or all of them, will become atrophied because they do not seem to be employed in the same manner as their counterparts in the earthly body. The organs of assimilation of the earthly body will become seriously affected if a sufficient quantity of food is not passed through them. No such situation could arise in our spirit bodies, because the life-force here amply sustains them and keeps them in proper working order, and thus they fulfill their objects.

The spirit body, then, possesses only such organs as are vital to it, and they can be regarded as a modification of their earthly counterparts. The further significance of this will be plainer to you when I tell you that, with the exception of the higher and highest realms, the spirit world, in which millions upon millions of us are living, is populated entirely from the earth, and from no other source. Procreation belongs to the earth, and has no place in the spirit world.

It has become a habit to begin the counting of time by some supposed date of the creation of the world. Time, in its measured sense, can be said to have commenced with the formation of the earth, but human life was already in existence long before then. The spirit world was long in existence before the earth, but the spirit world was not empty. It was inhabited by great souls whose knowledge and wisdom and spiritual progression and evolution have been proceeding steadily throughout the whole of this colossal period of time. All these beings possess a body which in its parts and its functions are exactly similar to the body of any one of us here, regardless of our position upon the ladder of spiritual progression, though, under certain conditions, that body would appear outwardly to us infinitely lesser beings as a blaze of light.

The spirit body which we all possess is the normal body. The earthly body, which temporarily covers the spirit body during its earthly passage, is a modification of the spirit body, an accommodation to earthly laws and conditions and modes of life. The life of the individual begins upon earth, it spends a limited period in that sphere, and then comes to us in the spirit world. The personality and individuality and attributes of the person are in their initial stages of formation upon earth, and the process is continued after his arrival in the spirit world. The physical distinctions of race will be preserved, borne upon his face, in the very color of his skin, and in other ways that will readily occur to you, and these he will retain in the spirit world.

The true sphere of life is the spirit world because it is permanent. The spirit world is therefore the standard of life as it is ultimately to be for us all, and so the spirit body, not the earthly body, is the standard of the human form.

In company with many others I have seen and spoken to at least one illustrious being whose period of life, in years, reaches astronomical figures. He possesses, just as do you or I, the ordinary normal complement of limbs; he has hair upon his head. His hands, anatomically like yours and mine, have their full number of fingernails. And so we might go on, through the complete catalogue of the parts of the human anatomy as it exists in the spirit world. The exalted nature of his being and the elevated realm in which he resides make him no different, anatomically, from the rest of us. His spirituality and wisdom and knowledge are, of course, in their high degree incomparable with us here. But we are not considering that for the moment. What we are considering is that when man, who has lived upon earth, comes to the spirit world to continue his life here, he sheds with his earthly body all such organs of that body as will be superfluous in his new mode of living. The organs with which he now finds himself are forever beyond harm of every description. No germ can attack the body; no destructive force can exert the slightest influence upon it. It is incorruptible. Its various organs, such as the heart and lungs, act *perfectly*. For example, the beating of the heart remains constant and normal under all conditions. We cannot *literally* become breathless. (I have sometimes said that some particular experience has left me breathless almost, but this is a figure of speech only.) Our respiration, like the action of the heart, remains always at its normal rate. And so it is throughout the rest of our bodies.

I do not pretend to the knowledge of a physician or a surgeon, but I do know that my body functions perfectly; that I enjoy, as we all enjoy, a state of perfect health such as I never for one moment enjoyed during my life on earth. Indeed, it is impossible to know what absolute, perfect health can be until one comes to live here in the spirit world. The body I possess is not a hollow drum, a mere empty vessel in the ownership of which I am able, in some mysterious fashion, to carry on my life. There is good rich blood flowing through my veins. There is no doubt about that, for I can observe the flesh-pink tinge it gives to my skin, as it does to us all. We have the complexions of healthy individuals, though the former may vary in the depth of their color by virtue of the various racial characteristics which you can easily call to mind. Whatever may be the precise shade of our complexions or of our skin in general, we none of us have the pallor that is usually associated either with a poor state of health or with some particular form of earthly occupation.

The circulation of the blood within our bodies is the means of diffusing the vital force that keeps us alive. If you should ask me why it should be necessary to have these organs to do this work, then I can only say that it is impossible for me to explain the fact of human creation itself. We might ask in turn, why does the incarnate person have his organs to do such work as is required of them? We should have to go to the very beginning and ask why has man come to be in the form that is familiar to us, and not in some other form. We must take things as they are in this instance at least. To do otherwise is rather to suggest that we could make several improvements upon the anatomy of our bodies were we given the opportunity. As far as we, in the spirit world, are concerned *no* improvement could possibly be made upon the structure and operation of our spirit bodies,

And I think that in these very bodies we have at least one assured example of perfection in our midst, and which we enjoy now. The greater perfection—I use this phrase in accordance with the terms of our previous discussion upon perfection—the greater perfection that awaits us when we proceed to a higher realm is a spiritual perfection, and will not apply to the state of health of our bodies. We may feel so much lighter, more etherealized, more rarified, but as far as I have been able to ascertain, we shall feel in a precisely similar state of buoyant, brilliant health as we do now in these realms.

It is manifestly impossible for me to take every organ of the body and deal with its particular functions in due order. What we can do, to sum up the matter briefly, is to reflect upon this: the spirit body is possessed of organs that are proper to it and to the world in which it carries out its functions. The earthly body will answer to the same description in its own sphere of action. The spirit body, coming first in the order of "creation," is the standard of human form and figure. The earthly body resembles it, but it has certain other organs added by which it carries out certain processes that are essential to its continued survival upon earth. The two principals of these processes are the means of assimilating food and the means of perpetuating human life upon earth. Food we do not need in the spirit world, and the population of spirit lands is derived, with the exception of those beings in the higher and highest realms to which I have referred, entirely from the earth insofar as this spirit universe is concerned. In discarding my earthly body at my physical dissolution, I found that my spirit body was without certain organs, the possession of which would be entirely redundant. Such organs have no counterpart in or upon the spirit body.

A question may naturally be asked as to how we can live with some of our organs missing. The answer is that they are not missing; they were never there! The spirit body performs perfectly because it is perfectly constructed, complete in all its parts, and only possesses such organs as it requires—in number slightly less than those required by the earthly body.

Now we come to another question from our same good friend, which is away altogether from the contemplation of our bodies, and concerns the intellectual side of life here. He asks in effect: "How is it that a person who was a clergyman during his earthly life and who was a firm upholder of his church's teachings and of what is orthodox in religious matters, how is it that such a person can, in communicating with the earth, give every sign imaginable of having quickly thrown off his religious beliefs and his orthodoxy?"

The same question could apply to a large number of people in a greater or less degree according to the views which they held upon earth. Orthodoxy is not the only thing that can mentally and intellectually shackle a being on earth.

Religious beliefs, both orthodox and unorthodox, can exert a most powerful hold upon the minds of human beings. The former, in general, are too widely known to need amplification, but of the latter, the unorthodox, there are many forms. A great many people hold that a firm belief in a book of ancient chronicles, without even remotely understanding a tithe of its contents, is fully sufficient to assure them of a safe journey to "the next world," and the certainty of a residence is some salubrious spot among the "elect."

Some people hold that a staunch belief in the merits of another will achieve the same results. Whatever form these beliefs take, they are most of them of the crudest description, and upon arrival in the spirit world, the ardent upholders of the childish creeds discover their true worth—which is precisely *nothing*. Now it is exactly according to the mental and intellectual make-up of an individual when he arrives in the spirit world as to how long it will take him to shake off the erroneous beliefs and mistaken ideas which he has accumulated during his life on earth. The person with an "open mind," provided that mind is not too "open" and therefore too easily swayed in one direction after another without perceiving the truth, such a person will the more quickly see what his new life involves in the matter of altered outlook. If he is ready to throw off the old life at once and take up the new life with equal celerity, then so much the better and happier will that person be.

It is possible of achievement. Many, many times have Edwin, Ruth, and I witnessed this very thing happening. You can appreciate how we rejoice— and our new friend with us—at this quick awakening to the truth. It is good for us all, and especially it reduces hard work to a minimum. But some people are very stubborn. They will scarcely credit the evidence of their own senses, and are therefore not very disposed to place much reliance upon our assurances and asseverations when we try to explain just what the new life means to them. Time will work its usual wonders, and so we are not in any great hurry when we find that an individual appears likely to require some convincing.

To come more specifically to the terms of our friend's question, it depends upon what is meant by *quickly* as regards the time taken by an inhabitant of the spirit world to abandon orthodox religious views. Here we are measuring time in earthly terms. A few hours taken to achieve this end would doubtless seem the extreme of rapidity in which to relinquish beliefs that have been held for a lifetime. But with the right type of mind it could be done; indeed, it has been done on many occasions to which I can bear witness of personal experience.

The age of the new arrival must also be taken into consideration, whether he or she be young, middle-aged, or elderly. So you see, there are a number of factors to be taken into account, either singly or in conjunction with each other. There is, for instance, another element which will weigh in the matter: how firmly were the beliefs held? Were they deep-rooted, or merely superficial? People will sometimes make a demonstration of holding certain religious beliefs because they have been brought up in those beliefs from childhood. They may not have bothered to think very much for themselves, and so they have proceeded through their earthly life in an easy fashion religiously, not really caring, but content to follow the rest of the family in their practices. So much for general terms. I can, however, speak from my own personal experience.

During my earthly life I was a clergyman of the orthodox church, but I was not entirely ignorant of the presence around me of an invisible world over which, so it appeared to me, my church had no jurisdiction whatever. My own psychic faculties were not very powerful, but at least they were strong enough for me to disbelieve what my church most emphatically taught in this connection, namely, that such manifestations as I was permitted to see were all the work of "the devil." Now here I could perceive no evidence at all of diabolic intervention. What I did see was decidedly harmless in every way. I therefore frankly disbelieved what the church taught me and told me to teach others upon the subject. But I did not voice this disbelief. That was a secret which I carried with me into the spirit world. I should have done no good had I expressed what I thought openly.

And so I kept these discoveries to myself. Naturally, I believed in a future state of life, and what I saw for myself, psychically, confirmed that belief. Secretly, I differed from the church in its attitude towards such experiences as I had had, but at the same time I chose to consider my own position in the world. The church's hold upon me was a powerful one, and this hold was made the stronger by the absence of greater and wider experiences of a psychic nature such as so many of my friends upon earth are enjoying at this present moment.

I was prepared in my own mind for surprises of considerable magnitude; ready, more or less, to reconstruct my whole outlook; ready, if need be, to jettison my orthodox views in the light of the truth whatever it might be. While I was still upon earth I tried to steer an even course between the little knowledge I had managed to glean of psychic matters concerning the "afterlife" and the church's teachings. In my mind the church's teachings weighed more heavily in the scales than did my scanty knowledge of psychic things, but I was fully prepared to find conditions totally different from the "hereafter" as sketchily touched upon by the church.

I had the great authority—at least, I *thought* it to be great—of the church behind me in whatever religious matters I spoke upon publicly in my preaching; I had no authority behind me in my psychic experiences. Indeed, those to whom I related these experiences at once pronounced me as being tempted by "the devil"!

Some there are, I dare say, who will say that I should have braved all, pursued my investigations farther and deeper, and abided by the result. The result, they would say, would have been inevitable. I should have discovered that the church's teachings were fundamentally wrong, and then it would have been the right and proper thing for me to renounce the church in favor of the truth as revealed to me through communication with the great spirit world. I wish that I had done so. However, as events have transpired, I have nothing to regret now. Through the kind offices of devoted friends and companions I have been enabled to attain to a state of happiness such as I never believed could be possible.

When I had reached the end of my journey upon earth and I found myself at last in the great world upon which I had contemplated so often and

so deeply, there to find myself in the very presence of an old friend and colleague who had "predeceased" me by some years, I think it is true to say that
I was prepared for anything, although I had no notion just what it might be.
What happened after this meeting I have already set down. It required but
"half an eye" to see that the church was wrong in so much that it had taught
me, and which in turn I had taught others. So overwhelmed was I by the
beauty of these realms, by the immensity of the splendid prospect that was
opening out before me under the able guidance of my friend, Edwin, that I
had no difficulty at all in forgetting what the church taught.

An earnest conversation with Edwin was ultimately sufficient to sweep
away from my mind all the cobwebs of dogma and creed which had hung
about me, and by a simple exposition of the truth to show me that I had not
a care in the world if I should so choose to regard the conditions of my new
life. The one regret which I felt has since led me back to the earth thus to
communicate, and in so doing I have achieved a hundredfold more than I
ever dreamed would be possible.

There are many cases parallel to mine. That I know from experience in
our work. It is nothing really remarkable, then, that I should so quickly throw
off my orthodoxy and become as one with the inhabitants of these sunny
realms.

It has been remarked, also, that some of us who come to the earth to
speak to our friends, seem to have altered, some of us only slightly, others
almost beyond recognition except by such certain evidence as we give of our
identity. How is it that we have so changed—for the better, it might be observed?

This apparent transformation of character is explainable by the fact that
upon earth there are few people who really show themselves to the world as
they truly are.

In ancient days upon earth, folk were in general much simpler in their
tastes and their habits and behavior than they are now. Then they were not
afraid to speak their inmost thoughts more openly to one another, provided
those thoughts were not of too violent a religious or political nature. People
were in many respects more neighborly in those days when life was simpler.
But in these times of greater "civilization," when the world has become more
sophisticated, when people seem less reliant upon each other, dwellers upon
earth have withdrawn within themselves until it is difficult to form any very
reliable opinion upon the true character of anyone. People are more shy of
expressing themselves openly.

The earth, too, has advanced in many directions, making life vastly
more complicated. Life is more harassing, it proceeds at a much swifter pace,

and a great concentration of energy is crammed into a few hours that would scarcely be spread over the same number of days in olden times.

Now all these conditions bring with them a consequent infirmity of temper. Under stress of such a life we do not always appear at our best. We can become irritable, or cynical; we think we are possessed of all truth, and inclined to regard as fools others who do not think as we do. We become thoroughly intolerant. We may sneer just to give vent to our feelings, and those same feelings may have been induced by something which has gone wrong or not pleased us. We may suffer from poor health of the physical body. We may be overworked or under-worked. We may have too much pleasure or not enough. And so one could go on multiplying causes for our giving exhibitions of character and temperament which are not really our own, which do not come from our "better selves," to use the old term.

That, broadly speaking, is life on earth as it affects a large number of people. Now let us contemplate the altered state of life upon our coming to the spirit world.

You know by now some few facts concerning life in these lands. As we step into these realms we leave all the worrying cares of the earth behind us. Gone is the poor health we may have had there. Gone, too, are the rush and bustle of earthly life in every department of its complex activities. We do not even need to worry about the state of the weather in these perpetually sunny lands, and that alone, almost, is enough to cheer the heart immeasurably!

Here in the spirit world we stand revealed as we truly are. There is no longer any question as to what description of person we are. We can give voice to our thoughts without the fear of being considered foolish, simple, eccentric or childish. We cease to be intolerant here because we find that others are tolerant to us, and there is precious little—indeed, nothing at all—to be intolerant about in these realms. We are a happy community of numberless millions of people, with each one of whom we can be upon the most friendly, genial, and affable of terms, giving and receiving respect to and from every one of our fellows. No single person has ever to endure that which is distasteful to him because there is no one here to cause that which is distasteful to others. The beauties and charms of these realms act like an intellectual tonic; they bring out only that which is and always was the very best in one. Whatever was not the very best in one upon earth will be swamped by the good nature and kindness which the very air here will bring out, like some choice bloom beneath the warm summer sun.

There is no room for the unpleasant phases of human character that are so often exhibited upon earth. They cannot enter these realms. And in so far as such elements of character and temperament as we show upon earth are not the true reflection of our real selves, we shall at once cast them aside forever as we enter the spirit world upon the moment of our transition.

I have previously said that a human being is exactly the same one minute after his dissolution as he was one minute before it. That is borne out by what I have just said. It is the great difference between our real selves and the personality which we present for outward view. We are just the same in our true selves, but we may not be *recognizably* so. It is not so much that we have altered but that we are no longer subject to the stresses that produce the unpleasant qualities that were observable in us when we were on the earth. Remove the causes of the distempers and the latter will disappear also.

Here in spirit lands we have nothing to disturb us. On the contrary, we have everything that will bring us contentment. Our true natures thrive and expand upon such glories and splendors as the spirit world alone has to offer. We work, not for an earthly subsistence, but for the joy that comes with doing work that is both useful and congenial, and above all things, work that is of service to our fellow beings. The reward which the work brings with it is not a transient reward as is the case with so much mundane labor, but a reward that will bring us eventually to a higher state of living.

To us here in the spirit world, life is pleasure, always pleasure. We work hard, and sometimes long, but that work is pleasure to us. We have not the tiresome wearying toil that you have upon earth. We are not solitary beings fighting for our existence amid a world that can be, and so often is, somewhat indifferent to our struggles. Here in these realms wherein I live, there is not one solitary individual of whatever nationality under the sun who would not come immediately to the assistance of any one of us upon the merest glimmering of our needing help. And such help it is! There is no false pride that precludes our accepting help from a fellow creature anxious to give it.

Millions of us though there be, yet there is not one sign, not one atom of discord to be seen throughout the immense extent of these realms. Unity and concord are two of the plainest characteristics to be observed and understood and appreciated to the full.

And so you see, my good friend, there are firm grounds for not returning to visit you upon earth with exactly those characteristics by which we were so well known to you when we lived on earth. Our tempers were very often sorely tried in those days upon earth. Those times are gone now, and you know us as we really are. You did not know us for our true selves when we were with you in the flesh. That was no one's fault but ours. Certainly it was not yours. We are sometimes sorry we were not outwardly of a more genial nature, but we were—and still are—but human after all, and it is upon this factor that we will all base our defense, if defense be needed. Had conditions been different with us, perhaps we should have been different, too.

When we come to the spirit world and look back upon that part of our life that we have spent on earth, we are ofttimes rather shocked by the quite ridiculous importance which we placed upon some trivial incident in our daily life, an incident which caused us to appear intolerant, shall we say?—or hasty or quick tempered.

When we return to you, who are still upon earth, we do our utmost to present ourselves as we now truly are, shorn of those earthly disfigurations in our characters and temperaments by which we were perhaps too easily recognized. Such apparent change in our personality should not be so mysterious to you now, after this brief exposition. The change may seem amazing upon first acquaintance; it may even lead some of our friends to doubt our identity! It is rather pleasant to be doubted upon such a basis. At least it demonstrates to us that we have cleared ourselves of the trammels of earthly inhibitions in the full expression of our real natures.

It must not be thought, however, that we lose our individuality in this process. We retain that always. It is something which we have built up during our lives on earth, something that will characterize us and distinguish us, each from the other. We are not all reduced to an insipid uniformity. We retain our tastes and predilections; but our virtues never become as vices in their outward expression. We are healthy in body and mind, but our outlook has in so many things undergone a fundamental change.

The joy of living is a phrase of which you cannot have even the barest understanding while you are yet upon the earth-plane. It is not surprising, therefore, that we should exhibit a little of that joy when we visit you on earth. Some of us, even, dare not show ourselves to you as we really are, because some folk might be shocked! There are so many people on earth who regard us from a restricted self-conscious point of view. There would seem to be a feeling of piety in the air sometimes which we are not pleased to see when we visit you. To receive us with bated breath is not a reception according to our liking. It savors too much of the suggestion that as we have now become celestial beings (to use a favorite term), therefore we must be treated as such, that is, with gravity, with decorum, and in a manner redolent of the church sanctuary. That is not a natural environment to us. It is, in fact, thoroughly artificial, both to us and to you. We like to be just ourselves as we are, and we like you to be yourselves just as we really know you.

It is strange to us that people should look upon us as a different race of beings merely because we have gone through the process known as dying. We have simply discarded our physical body for ever, left it upon the earth, and taken up our life in another and vastly superior world. The whole process of transition which is so much feared by the folk on earth, is a natural, normal, and painless process. It is as natural and painless as removing your outer garment when you have no further use for it. The world into which we have made our entrance is a real world, solid and perpetually enduring. The people who inhabit this spirit world are real people of flesh and blood, people who once walked upon earth as you do now.

All that is great in man survives and is taken with him into this very spirit world where new avenues, far greater, finer, and broader, are for ever opening before him. There is no limit to what immense heights he can reach, whether he be scientist, or artist, or musician, or a follower of any other of the myriad worthy occupations that are to be found upon earth.

Some of us here, in these and other realms, have made many brief visits to the earth to tell our friends there something of what transpires in this great spirit world. And in doing so we have seen the shadow that hangs over so many people's lives, the shadow of "death" and the "grave," those two ogres that frighten so many good souls, filling them with a dread that is utterly and completely unwarranted. Man was never intended to go through his earthly life with this monstrous dark shadow forever hanging over him. It is unnatural and thoroughly bad. It has been raised by men upon earth in remote periods of the earth's history, and it has so continued for the generality of earth's dwellers for generation after generation of the incarnate. It is but natural that, with the opportunity presenting itself, we should visit the earth, and by bringing with us a little of the light of knowledge, we should be able to dispel the fears of death of the physical body that haunts so many people, and in place of those fears to give some knowledge and information of the superb lands of the spirit world wherein we now live, and wherein you yourself will one day come to join us.

In place of fears of a speculative "hereafter" we try to show you something of the brilliant prospect that lies before you when that happy moment arrives for you to take up your true and undoubted heritage in the spirit world.

It has been my very pleasant occupation to give you some details of this land, and I am very conscious of the many thoughts and feelings of kindness and goodwill that are constantly coming to me from my friends upon earth. Your thoughts always unfailingly reach me, and each is answered, though, alas, you may be unaware of it. It is because of this inability to hear my personal and direct reciprocation of your good thoughts that I here thank you for them with all my heart. We have traveled some distance together in our discussions of life in the spirit world, although we have touched but briefly upon so vast a theme.

And so, in taking a brief leave of our subject, I will take also a brief leave of you, and in doing so I would say to you:

Benedicat te omnipotens Deus.

The LIFE ON OTHER WORLDS SERIES is a selection of classic accounts of the afterlife and otherworldly life, told by those who are already there or who have been shown glimpses of what awaits us when our lives on earth are over. Descriptions vary, yet a thread of similarity runs through them all. May this collection serve as a travel guide as we embark on the greatest adventure of all—the journey into the mysterious realms beyond this world.

VOLUMES IN THE SERIES INCLUDE

Earths in the Universe (1758) Emanuel Swedenborg
Death and the Afterlife (1865) Andrew Jackson Davis
The Realms Beyond (1878) Paschal Beverly Randolph
A Wanderer in the Spirit Lands (1896) Franchezzo
Intra Muros (1898) Rebecca Ruter Springer
The Angels' Diary (1903) Effie M. Shirey
Two Years in Heaven (1911) Rose the Sunlight
The Life Beyond the Veil (4 Vols.) (1920-21) G. Vale Owen
Spiritual Life on Mars (1920) Eros Urides
The Blue Island & Other Spiritualist Writings (1922) William T. Stead
The World Unseen (3 Vols.) (1954-59) Anthony Borgia

Profits from the sale of these works are donated to
FREESCHOOLS WORLD LITERACY
www.freeschools.org
www.servicetohumanity.org